International Bohemia

INTERNATIONAL BOHEMIA

———————— ❧ ————————

Scenes of Nineteenth-Century Life

DANIEL COTTOM

PENN

UNIVERSITY OF PENNSYLVANIA PRESS

PHILADELPHIA

A volume in the Haney Foundation Series, established
in 1961 with the generous support of Dr. John Louis Haney.

Published by
University of Pennsylvania Press
Philadelphia, Pennsylvania 19104-4112
www.upenn.edu/pennpress

Printed in the United States of America on acid-free paper
10 9 8 7 6 5 4 3 2 1

Library of Congress Cataloging-in-Publication Data

Cottom, Daniel.
    International bohemia: scenes of nineteenth-century life / Daniel Cottom.
      p. cm.—(Haney Foundation series.)
    Includes bibliographical references and index.
    ISBN 978-0-8122-4488-5 (hardcover : alk. paper)
    1. Bohemianism in literature.   2. Bohemianism—History—19th century.
3. Bohemianism—History—20th century.   4. Alternative lifestyles—History—19th
century.   5. Alternative lifestyles—History—20th century.   I. Title. II. Series: Haney
Foundation series.
PN56.B63 C68 2013
809'.933552—dc23   2012041245

For Sharon Leslie, *bohémienne*

CONTENTS

Preface

In this book I am concerned with how the vagabond word *bohemia* migrated across various national borderlines over the course of the nineteenth century and, in doing so, was developed, transformed, contested, or rejected. I focus on how individuals and groups sought to take possession of this word and make it serve as the basis for the elaboration of identities, passions, cultural forms, politics, and histories that they wanted to bring to life. With a nod to Henry Murger, whose *Scenes of Bohemian Life* was the closest thing the century had to a Bible of bohemian types and tropes, one might think of my work here as looking in on scenes from the life of a word. I begin with the invention of the modern sense of this word in Paris during the 1830s and 1840s and then trace some of its most important twists and turns, through the rest of this era and into the early years of the twentieth century, in the United States, England, Italy, and, to a lesser extent, Spain and Germany.

This is not a survey or general history, and I do not make any claims to comprehensiveness. I have chosen the individuals, works, scenes, and episodes to which I turn my attention here simply because I found them especially rewarding for thinking through the bohemian phenomenon. These do, however, cumulatively serve to represent what I take to be the most important aspects of the career that this much-debated word eventually came to have. The topics I address include the figure of the Jew in bohemia, the cultural politics of masquerade, capitalism, the political economy of art, the gospel of work, the nature of community, the question of the parasite, the intersections of race and class, the representation of women, the designs of modern desire, and the value of nostalgia.

Even when they traveled under the banner of *l'art pour l'art*, the bohemians of this era generally saw little reason to observe borderlines between their life and their art. On the contrary, they were eager to mix up the one with the other, and their critics often reproached them on this account, as when they claimed that bohemians were all talk—do-nothings frittering away their lives in cafés and taverns. To help draw out the implications of this feature of bohemianism, I have woven into my arguments in this book discussions of the lives of several notable figures: Thomas Chatterton, George Sand, George Eliot, Murger, Alexandre Privat d'Anglemont, Walt Whitman, Ada Clare, Iginio Ugo Tarchetti, and Arthur Conan Doyle.

A note on orthography: except when quoting others, I have reserved *Bohemia*, with a capital letter, for the Eastern European country of that name, and have used *bohemia* for the modern cultural formation. Translations not otherwise noted are my own.

CHAPTER I

Bohemian Poseur Jew

Much later, Madame Aurore Dudevant would say that her transvestism was nothing more than a practical expedient, a matter of common sense. As an adolescent, she had been permitted to dress in masculine attire to go riding. When she began to appear in public dressed as a man, in 1831, she did so because she had moved to Paris and quickly found the city to be hell on a lady's wardrobe, soiling and spoiling it at a terrifying rate. She might have avoided the problem by spending more of her time at home, but she had come to this city to get out into the world, not to shut herself away from it. Now that she was separated from her husband and living on her own, she needed to keep a close eye on her expenses; and wearing men's clothing, she realized, would be much cheaper than trying to maintain her finery. She claimed to have gotten the idea from her mother, who remembered how she and her sister had adopted this expedient when they were thrifty young wives who wished to go out with their husbands.

As she remembered it, the plan worked like magic. "I flew from one end of Paris to the other. It seemed to me that I might have gone round the world."[1] Looking like a student in her new clothes, she had the freedom of the city. Her disguise protected her from the dirt of the streets and made her feel safe among the passersby, lending her a welcome anonymity. In her boyish liberty she used to think of herself as enjoying the life of that familiar type of Parisian street urchin, the gamin.[2] As she worked at learning how to become a writer, this outfit allowed her to move undisturbed through crowds everywhere in the metropolis. No one even turned to look at her. She traveled "from the club to the studio, from the café to the garret," while exploring "the intermediary world between the artisan and the artist."[3] In doing so, she became George Sand, one of the most famous authors of the nineteenth century and, at the same time, one of the century's most notorious figures, as well known for her sexual affairs as for her romantic fiction. "The illustrious hermaphrodite" one writer called her.[4]

More than a decade after Sand's sartorial transformation, Rosa Bonheur pleaded the exigencies of her artistic labors when she sought and was granted legal permission to wear men's clothing. (Her *Permission de Travestissement* was officially issued by the police "for reasons of health.")[5] Although Sand did not mention Bonheur when she was looking back on her own transvestism some years later, she did seem to be writing as if she had this famous artist's more conservative example in the back of her mind. The middle-aged Sand preferred that the public should think of her mode of dress as merely a utilitarian choice, one so uncontroversial that it was not only blessed but even recommended by her mother.[6]

If this story was plausible, it is also true that Sand had considerable experience in the invention of plausible stories by the time that she came to tell it.[7] In any case, even if her motivations had been as simple as she claimed, her cross-dressing still would not have appeared to the world at large as nothing more than a sign of economic prudence in an earnest young person seeking to learn how to succeed in her chosen profession. Instead, with good reason, it became an iconic image of bohemian provocation.

Looking back on the image of her youthful transvestism, Sand wanted her public to see an ingenuous provincial, newly arrived in the city, seeking to support herself and her children as well as she could. Today, however, as in her own era, the image is more likely to evoke a sense of the artistic freedom that Sand celebrated in her life and words. No doubt the young Sand had found it necessary to keep her accounts, as would any good grocer—to use the scornful term, *épicier*, that she and other bohemians employed when they wished to mock a member of the bourgeoisie. Nonetheless, she had also found opportunities for revels. She would later remember, for instance, a "fantastic moonlit promenade" across the Latin Quarter with one of her lovers, Jules Sandeau, her editor at *Le Figaro*, Henri Delatouche, and a friend, Félix Pyat, during which Pyat stopped at every store they passed to serenade the proprietors with his full-throated rendition of "A grocer is a rose."[8] In the passage about this adventure in her *History of My Life* (1854–55) Sand does not record what clothes she was wearing on this particular evening, but anyone can see how her habit of masquerade might have graced this occasion, as it did so many others.

But it was not only through irregular dress or habits, such as smoking in public, that Sand made herself a bohemian. Along with Pyat, who wrote of

Figure 1. A[lcide Joseph] Lorentz, "Miroir drolatique" (c. 1848) [caricature of George Sand]
("If this portrait of George Sand / Should your mind somewhat perplex—/ Genius is hard to understand/ And as we know has no sex") (Print Collection, Miriam and Ira D. Wallach Division of Art, Prints and Photographs, The New York Public Library, Astor, Lenox and Tilden Foundations).

bohemians in a notable essay, she was one of those who played a crucial role in redefining this term during the 1830s, preparing it for the lasting fame it would acquire through the stories of Henry Murger in the following decade. In contrast to Pyat's caustic account of bohemian artifice, Sand portrayed the bohemian as an artistic wonder. Between them, they framed a future for a signifier of marginality that would be central to the articulation of modernity not only in France but internationally.[9]

In Pyat's characterization, the bohemian was artificial in the sense of being ridiculously affected. This accusation would enjoy a long afterlife, as in John Reed's use of the term "neo-Bohemian" for those denizens of Washington Square whom he sent up in his poetic romp *The Day in Bohemia, or Life Among the Artists* (1913).[10] In recent years a similar impetus has produced the neologism *fauxhemian*. For Sand, however, the bohemian was artificial in a quite different sense, which would also prove influential in the years to come. As she presents it, the bohemian's entire way of life is an artistic creation and as such represents all that is best in the human spirit. Whereas Pyat's bohemian is a poseur, pure and simple, Sand declares him to be a figure who transcends the false posturing demanded by "this code of hypocrisy called society" in which one's life is spent "running from deceptions to deceptions."[11]

These divergent characterizations helped launch the figure of the bohemian into cultural prominence as a subject of ongoing debate. Conflicting views like these gave vitality to this figure throughout the nineteenth century, in which the question of the poseur was inseparable from the fate of the bohemian. They would continue to influence oppositional cultural movements in the twentieth century and on into our own day.

This question of the poseur proved so crucial because bohemia, under any definition, was supposed to exist outside society. As Gypsies, foreigners, vagabonds, and persons popularly judged to be morally and legally suspect, the bohemians of old were categorical outsiders, and it is this condition of eccentricity in relation to society that motivated the modern transformation of the word *bohemian* and the vexed question of who truly deserved to bear it. Although, as Robert Darnton has noted, something approaching its new meaning had already appeared by the end of the eighteenth century, it was not until the 1830s and 1840s that the modern usage of *bohemian* was firmly established.[12] Without dislodging its traditional meanings, which persisted alongside it, this usage announced the posing of a difference, a social borderline, where none had previously been given formal recognition. It asserted a new individual identity, social organization, historical understanding, and cultural will. It converted the established connotations of this word, which were generally understood pejoratively, into a positive metaphor of community. In doing so, the new usage conveyed the oppositional stance of those who identified themselves with the word. In the marvelously envenomed words of Jules Barbey d'Aurevilly, this change may be summed up by saying that modern bohemians put themselves forward as "the cream of the scum of the earth."[13] Keeping the same characteristics in mind but writing somewhat less polemically, Julius Bab described bohemia in the conception brought to us by the nineteenth century as "a peaceful experiment in *practical anarchism*."[14]

Once the modern usage was established, it was gradually naturalized, as frequently happens in such cases, until over time few people had any sense of its former meanings when they uttered the word *bohemian*. In the first half of the nineteenth century, however, this new usage made sense only because people recognized the semantic transfer within it. The bohemian, in the modern sense, initially appeared as a second-order figure, an imitator defined through the appropriation of an exotic image. In this respect, the change in this term was akin to Parisians' use of *apache* to designate the ruffians native to their town. Granted due consideration of historical differences, the issues at play in this nineteenth-century revision of the word *bohemian* are broadly comparable to those raised more recently by Norman Mailer's notorious role-playing in "The White Negro" (1957), by the phenomenon of outsiders masquerading as Native Americans (so-called Wannabe Indians), and by similar borrowings, thefts, and mockeries of identities.

As the accounts of Pyat and Sand indicate, the question of the poseur directs us to the cultural politics of self-representation. Their accounts also give us a glimpse of the other grounds on which this question of the poseur would play out during the rest of the century. In terms of social organization, the question would concern the policing of group boundaries. In terms of historical understanding, it would focus attention on the processes by which emergent ways of life arise from the revision or suppression of preexisting traditions. The issue of cultural will, meanwhile, would be determined by the workings of bohemian fantasy and desire as these met with, struggled against, or were even created by the demands of the social world to which they were ostensibly opposed.

Most famously, this question of the poseur played itself out in the relation of the bohemian to the bourgeois. For all its importance, though, the attention paid to this relation has obscured how the bohemian only really met his match in the figure of another outsider, the Jew.[15] As the implications of Pyat's and Sand's disagreement unfolded themselves over the course of the century, it was around this figure that they would finally drape themselves. What Jeffrey Mehlman has described as "a sustaining anti-Semitism" in French cultural achievements played an especially perverse role in the historical development of bohemianism, and to understand this role we need to follow the debates over this new cultural formation from their beginnings.[16]

Focusing on the fad for Romantic medievalism that influenced the jargon, dress, and manners of artistic young people early in the 1830s, Pyat helped to establish the modern understanding of bohemia by describing dirty, bearded, long-haired youths who gloried in their poverty and took joy in mocking the bourgeoisie. The "Bohemians of today" make themselves such, in his telling, by deliberately estranging themselves from society.[17] They suffer "the usual mania of young artists," which is the desire to be different, "to live outside of their own times with other ideas and other manners."[18] Despite her friendship with Pyat, who came from the same region of France as she and who was one of the first literary men she met when she settled in Paris in 1831, Sand could not have disagreed with him more.[19] As might be expected of one who had made such a striking change in her own dress, as well as in her previous way of life as the convent-schooled wife of Baron Dudevant, Sand held to a different concept of art and artists. She explained this programmatically in *The Last Aldini* (1838) through its narrator-protagonist, an Italian opera star known as Lélio.

The name by which his public knows him is not that with which this artist was born. His story returns his listeners to a past of which his present appearance, or masquerade, gives no indications. He explains that his original name was Daniele Gemello and that he was raised as the son of a fisherman. Having become a gondolier, he fell in love with a young widow with distinguished aristocratic connections, Bianca Aldini, and she with him. Despite the immense difference in their social positions, she wished to marry him, but he felt compelled to decline her offer. Sharing the fierce sense of pride of his working-class family and friends, he did not wish to be thought a mere greedy adventurer; and he also realized, as the rather naive Bianca did not, that her late husband's relatives would have the power to take away her beloved daughter if she were to contract such a scandalous marriage. Some years later, after his singing as a gondolier has led him to an opportunity for professional training and an illustrious career in opera, he happens to meet a fifteen-year-old girl, Alezia, with whom he falls in love—only to make the discovery that she is Bianca's daughter. This discovery compels him to a second renunciation, at the height of his career, of the same sort of desire that he had felt ethically compelled to renounce at its outset.

So we are given to understand that the liberty of the bohemian artist is not to be mistaken for libertinism. The calumnies of the world, which "makes a crime of our best actions," would have one believe otherwise, says La Checchina, a former street singer who is Lélio's friend and assistant. Nonetheless, the truth of the matter is that bohemian freedom is a "gentle and honest liberty."[20] Masquerades of the sort involved in artistic performance actually demand a heightened sense of personal integrity and responsibility. The fact that this famous singer was once a poor fisherman does not make him a poseur, in the negative sense; rather, it makes him a finished artist, one who has created his identity out of his own abilities, opportunities, and sacrifices. Bohemians do disdain all local prejudices, such as the familial concern with rank that made it impossible for Lélio to marry Bianca. "The artist," announces Lélio at the outset of his story, "has the entire world for his native land, the great *Bohemia*, as we say."[21] As the story makes clear, however, "the superiority of the artist," which saves bohemians from being imposed upon "by the customs of the world and by the laws of propriety," also makes them more generous in their sense of honor.[22] Thence arises the credo of the novel, as voiced by La Checchina: "Scorn the pride of the great, laugh at their stupidities, spend riches gaily when we have them, accept poverty without worrying about it if it comes, preserve our liberty above all else, enjoy life no matter what, and long live Bohemia!"[23]

In his characterization of the new sense being given to this word, Pyat retained its low associations with poor wanderers, especially Gypsies, and, by extension, with all those acting or living in a vagrant, disorderly, disreputable, or criminal manner. These so-called artists, in his portrayal, were another such community of people living by their own codes and deserving to be held in contempt by everyone else. Despite their medievalist affectations, they were not a fit subject for romance. The new meaning of *bohémien*, for him, was continuous with its established definitions, whereas Sand made this new meaning serve also as a revaluation of the social history written in this word. By making her exemplary artist the son of a poor fisherman, she dramatized the word's low associations so as to propose their Romantic reversal.

Lélio's story gives dramatic form to the semantic change that was urged upon this word in this era in which young people appropriated it so as to claim for themselves an outlaw mystique. Instead of being denigrated, socially marginal figures would be given a redemptive role. In fact, the marginal would now be revealed as the universal through "the vagabond vocation of the bohemian artist."[24] In this fantasy, art takes on the clothes of otherness—of the poor, the déclassé, the *homme sans aveu* or masterless man—and, through this act of transvestism, achieves its ideal. Sand would go on to represent this in other novels as well, such as *Consuelo* (1842) and *The Countess of Rudolstadt* (1844), in which she backdated the new meaning of *bohémien* to the mid-eighteenth century. She also saw this ideal incarnated in the socialist philosopher whom she called her "master," Pierre Leroux, that "sublime Bohemian."[25]

Something like the generosity of spirit that defined Sand's conception of bohemian camaraderie appeared in this same era in the writings of Alexandre Privat d'Anglemont. In his description of the various fads that swept through the Latin Quarter during the first half of the nineteenth century, such as the affected medievalism described by Pyat, Privat portrayed the Left Bank's successive generations of style-conscious young people as being extraordinarily sensitive to the influence that art, especially plays and novels, exerted on fashion. The youths he portrayed are passionate in adopting the popular styles of their day, but they are not simply slaves of fashion. The overwhelming popularity of certain styles at any given time is at once a measure of and means toward the community that the young people of each period make for themselves. When their reading of Victor Hugo and Sir Walter Scott inspires students to wear a bastardized version of medieval dress and to adopt a new sort of slang, they are not simply being frivolous. Their concern with issues of image and identity is serious, even though they are also capable of playing around with their masquerades, as when one group decides, for a goof, to dress up as Bedouins and smoke long pipes while walking around in front of the church of Saint-Germain-des-Prés.

Privat's portrayal is in keeping with his conception of a bohemian community that includes not only artists and students but also all the travelers, vagrants, and suspect sorts marked out by the older definition of this term. In addition, his conception includes all the eccentric workers, poor, and street people struggling to survive in the modern city. If a young working girl, for instance, should name herself after one of Sand's heroines, such as Indiana or Lélia, or after a grisette in Eugène Sue's *Mysteries of Paris* (1842–43), doing so does not make her a poseur, as far as Privat is concerned.[26] Like students, grisettes are free to redefine themselves by appropriating aspects of their identity from the culture around them. At some times this might mean that one desires to wear an article of fashion that rich middle-class ladies wear, such as a cashmere shawl, at others that one feels like taking a new name for oneself from a popular novel. In such copying Privat saw nothing unnatural. On the contrary, he regarded it as one of the crucial ways that culture was enlivened.

For observers such as Pyat, however, this sort of behavior was an unhealthy sign of social disorder, even a kind of sickness, which encouraged people to become parasites on the few original spirits around them. Even Pyat was willing to admit that among the bohemians he described were some exceptional individuals, certain "privileged natures"; but the rest, he complained, were the victims of "a fashion—what am I saying!—a rage, a furor, a contagious, epidemic, endemic malady, a scourge worse than cholera, a veritable plague from the Orient," which he called "artistism."[27] Where Privat saw a vital, vibrant, ever-changing, and highly amusing youth culture, as rich in its own way as the subterranean culture of Parisian workers, bums, tramps, street performers, refugees, and vagrants of all sorts, Pyat saw a travesty of culture, a masquerade that would be pointless if it were not so destructive.

Throughout the nineteenth century the figure of the bohemian would suffer further struggles over its definition, such as the ones that arose from the extension of this term to include the floating population of the urban lumpenproletariat, which appears, for instance, in Karl Marx's *Eighteenth Brumaire of Louis Bonaparte* (1852). In the midst of all such complications, however, as in the writings of Pyat and Sand, the discourse of bohemia would always take on definition in relation to the masquerader known as the poseur.

Occasionally the poseurs were actual imposters. Although he followed Pyat's lead, heaping disdain on the modern conception of bohemia, even Gabriel Guillemot would feel some sympathy for the last days of Henry Murger, which were darkened, Guillemot said, by the news that someone was not only pretending to be him "in diverse locations, notably in Aix-les-Bains," but was carrying the imposture so far as to be displaying in his buttonhole the red ribbon of the Legion of Honor recently awarded to Murger.[28] More generally, though, the poseurs in question here were not outright identity thieves. A much bigger problem turned upon those associated with the community of bohemia whom others felt did not properly belong there.

This is not to say that bohemia in its modern conception always bristled with antagonism. Most uses of this term in the nineteenth century, for all their differences, evoke something of the spirit we see in Sand's and Privat's images of bohemian camaraderie.[29] Even in the most joyful depictions of this camaraderie, though, the problem of the parasite always hovered around it and existed in tension with it. In fact, this tension was epitomized in the life of Privat, who was celebrated in the 1840s and 1850s as the arch-bohemian, "the most complete type of the bohemian, as people in general think of it."[30] Early on he was seemingly known to and beloved by all, a figure so universally embraced that he might be jokingly lauded as "the bond of modern society."[31] Yet he eventually came to be seen as one whose bohemian trust in chance had gone so far and lasted so long as to make him less a man than a child. In other words, some came to view him as a parasite on the social order of modernity, which, therefore, might understandably grow sick of him, "wearied of hearing Privat talked about."[32]

Anyone familiar with later versions of bohemia, such as the twentieth-century Beat and hippie scenes, will not be surprised to learn that in the nineteenth century *parasite* was the epithet always waiting to be flung back at those who insulted representatives of the bourgeoisie by hurling the word *philistine* at them. This response was established long before the *Almanac of the Grisettes and Balls of Paris* (1848), for instance, reserved the term *bohemian* for long-time inhabitants of the Latin Quarter who would take new arrivals under their wings, the better to mooch off of them.[33] Aside from exceptional figures such as Privat, who dared to set himself in uncompromising opposition to the calculating common sense of political economy, modern bohemians from the beginning were acutely sensitive to this tendency to view them as lazy good-for-nothings whose supposed dedication to artistic ideals was but a cheap disguise for their slack characters. Privat did refuse to participate in the kind of thinking that would legitimize *parasite* as an insult, as did a few others, such as Paul Lafargue, the socialist author of *The Right to Idleness* (1880). These, however, were exceptions. Most prominent nineteenth-century bohemians were more like Sand, who found it important to insist on how hard she worked.

As a result, bohemians' supposedly oppositional stance toward social convention was always liable to flip over into a fiercely conservative policing of the borders of their own community. In a sense, this tendency simply means that bohemians were not immune to a commonplace sociological phenomenon, historically exemplified in communities as diverse as those formed by early Christians, twentieth-century surrealists, and twenty-first-century professors of literature, in which the pressure for unity against outsiders breeds schisms among the insiders of a group. The example of bohemia is of distinctive interest, however, because in the aftermath of Murger's success the metaphor of bohemian community gained great discursive power in the absence of any founding scripture or organization. In contrast to contemporary artistic brotherhoods such as the Nazarenes, the Pre-Raphaelites, and Murger's own tiny proto-bohemian club of "Water Drinkers," which struggled on for a couple of years in the early 1840s, bohemia in the second half of the nineteenth century never mapped itself over a restricted set of persons. It differed also from earlier groups of rebellious youth, such as the rowdy republican *bousingots* who tore up the Latin Quarter in the 1830s; from other organizations with which it was often associated, such as those of the St. Simonians and the Fourierists and other sorts of socialists; and even from loosely defined cultural movements of this era, such as the table-rapping "Modern Spiritualism" that arose at the same time as his *Scenes of Bohemian Life* was bringing Murger international fame. Unlike these social and cultural formations, bohemia never had a clearly established ground from which it might venture out to seek converts and extend its dominion. It did not even have a dress code, as common parlance came to stick the bohemian label on artists, writers, and intellectuals dressed almost in rags, such as the characters who figure in Murger's *Scenes*; on dandies flaunting their exquisite taste, such as Charles Baudelaire; and on others, such as Privat and Nadar, who dressed like dandies when they could afford to do so, like bums when they could not. The rigidly organized group of impoverished Water Drinkers to which Murger had belonged did become part of the mythology of bohemia, as a result of his stories; but the popularized notion of the bohemian, as Pyat, Sand, Murger, and others established it, was organized only through certain images, tropes, and themes, not in terms of one specific body of people who might constitute an orthodoxy.

Consequently, since no one was born with this identity and since no institution existed to regulate it, to be a bohemian, in the modern sense of the word, was perforce to be a poseur: someone pretending to an identity to which he or she could have no preexisting claim. By reproducing at another remove the distinction between the traditional and the modern bohemian— between the Gypsies of old and the gypsy youth of the modern metropolis— the distinction between the bohemian and the poseur actually created and sustained the bohemian.[34] The very word *bohème* existed as testimony to that flagrant copying of others' identity which defined the originality of this new type of individual. In his contention that "the manufactured Bohemian is an impossibility," the popular American writer and actor James Clarence Harvey could not have been more wrong.[35] The bohemian was artificial through and through.

Harvey was not alone in his error. As a result of this situation, wonderful ironies would arise when American writers such as William Dean Howells doubted that a true bohemia, "the genuine thing," could take root in their country.[36] In American novels from the last quarter of the century, such as

Charles De Kay's *The Bohemian: A Tragedy of Modern Life* (1878) and Robert Appleton's *Violet: The American Sappho* (1894), bohemian groups are portrayed as being largely composed of dilettantes, imitation bohemians. The insults can be funny, despite the broad satire frequent in such works; a latter-day reader might compare them to the mockery of the phony beatniks, the Empathical-ists, who attract Audrey Hepburn in *Funny Face* (1957). De Kay, for instance, depicts a group of individuals called "Expressionists" who affect bohemian fashions made famous in Paris—"velvet jackets, loose cravats, and shovel hats"—but then revert to conventional dress and behavior when, like all their neighbors, they dutifully make their way to church on Sunday mornings.[37] The most obvious irony here, though, is that the supposed sophistication of these authors, as marked by their ability to spot faux bohemians for what they are, actually demonstrates their naïveté, since they fail to realize that bohemia has never been anything but artificial.

Far from invalidating the concept of bohemia, the presence of poseurs in and around it was always crucial to its definition. Walt Whitman's theat-rical pose as an unaffected man of the people, which led to his adoption as the mascot of the bohemians at Pfaff's tavern in antebellum New York City, may serve to exemplify the blatant artifice of the genuine bohemian.[38] In this regard, we would do well to recall that the words *pose* and *poser*, as they de-veloped in France after 1840, did not always carry a negative connotation. On the contrary, although they could be used for purposes of mockery, they could also be used to suggest that someone possessed a modern spirit.[39] This ambiva-lence out of which the term *poseur* developed was perpetuated in the definitive indefiniteness of the divide between the bohemian and the poseur. Modern bohemia was less a genuine thing than an occasion contrived for posing the question of the poseur.

This condition of bohemia was often explicitly recognized, as when a group of the Italian bohemians known as the *scapigliatura* objected to being characterized as "a caste or a class."[40] For them as for others in this period, the liberty of bohemia lay precisely in a loosely defined, self-willed, spontaneously manufactured sense of community for which there was no founding figure, text, or historical origin as such. In the beginning was the poseur, the *so-called* bohemian. To follow what Sand referred to as the vocation of the bohemian was recklessly to call oneself into being in the absence of any established authority for one's claims upon the attention of the public. The world of bohemia, as the *scapigliato* Roberto Sacchetti would write, was "an equivocal world."[41]

The metaphorical vagueness that granted bohemia its liberty, however, also determined the fact that bohemians would require more than the opposition of bourgeois philistines to maintain their self-definition. In the mocking form of the poseur, they would have to oppose their very selves. In order to exist, bohemians would actually *need* poseurs, persons whom they might call out of their so-called community so as to affirm their own calling. This modern invention, the bohemian, could never have come to life and could not have continued to exist without its systematic misrecognition of itself in and through this other figure. The poseur was the sacrifice made to pay off the immeasurable debt—in personal identity, group definition, historical understanding, and cultural will—that was contracted in modern bohemia's appropriation of its name.

The most wrenching irony of bohemia's conception of liberty, then, lay in the predictably bitter destiny of its utopian attempt to treat the improvisatory bonds of friendship as if they might replace the formal structures of political, economic, and social order. The question of the poseur, in this respect, marks the inescapability of political structure within the utopian freedom claimed for the realm of culture. The bohemian turn away from the established order could be sustained only through the unceasing production of false friends, poseurs, among one's comrades.

So wherever one finds the bohemian, one finds the poseur. In 1864, one of the characters in Enrique Perez Escrich's novel *The Blue Dress Coat* inveighs against the false bohemians in Madrid who deliberately rip their shirts, dirty their coats, and muddy their boots in their attempt to fit in among those truly suffering for their ideals.[42] By 1921 it seems little has changed, for we find Emilio Carrere making scathing remarks about "a great mob of so-called bohemians" in this city.[43] In 1869 Junius Henri Browne warns of the "pseudo-Bohemian class" of reporters in New York, from whom those writers "who are Bohemians in the best sense" take care to distinguish themselves; and in 1884 a journalist writing in the *Brooklyn Daily Eagle* still feels the need to warn against "false Bohemians" because "there have been many interlopers in the land of Bohemia."[44] In 1877, remembering the *scapigliato* poet Emilio Praga, Raffaello Barbiera laments "those who confound the true *bohême* with the false"; Bab tells of the "superficial poseurs" of turn-of-the-century Berlin; Julio Cambio has to fight against the "avalanche of vile imitators" in the Latin Quarter of the early twentieth century.[45] The examples are endless.

Having already been suggested by Pyat's and Sand's contrasting visions of bohemia, this history of the poseur was dramatically foretold by Murger's novelized version of *Scenes of Bohemian Life*, which collected and supplemented a series of stories its author had published in *Le Corsaire-Satan* between 1845 and 1849, when their adaptation into a play, which he cowrote with Théodore Barrière, made him famous. It was but a short step from the literary and theatrical entertainment that Murger made out of his life to the manufacture of bohemians as a tourist attraction for the "would-be Bohemian" whom the journalist H. C. Bunner observed in the environs of Bleecker and Houston streets in New York City.[46] With Murger, the ironies were already in place that would have Miriam Hopkins's bohemian chums in the movie *Wise Girl* (1937) picking up a few bucks from the owner of a café by hanging around his place so as to draw in customers looking for an authentic downtown experience. From the moment of Murger's success one might already look forward to Anton Kuh's joke, in *Simplicissimus*, a journal associated with Germany's bohemians at the turn of the century, that "the false bohemians are those who won't let their lifestyle be sold!"[47] Writing of the opening night of Murger's play, in fact, Alexandre Schanne would remember how the actor playing the role of Schaunard came to him the night before to borrow his pipe, made famous in the *Scenes*, and thereafter displayed it, practically glowing still from Schanne's puffing on it, before the audience in the theater who had eagerly paid to see *la vie de bohème*.[48]

In the preface to the *Scenes,* Murger hastened to distinguish "the true Bohemia," which he went so far as to term "the official Bohemia," from all manifestations of "amateur bohemians" and other sorts of poseurs.[49] Anticipating critics such as Guillemot, who would condemn the entire bohemian phenomenon as consisting of nothing but parasites, Murger added a final chapter to his original series of articles in which one of his main characters repents of his bohemian adventure. Marcel, an artist, tells Rodolphe, the character modeled on Murger himself, that he regrets their recourse "to the shameful contrivances of parasitism."[50] Murger also began "Francine's Muff" (1851), a story included as a chapter of the *Scenes*, with an invocation—"Among the true bohemians of the true bohemia . . ."—designed immediately to put poseurs on notice.[51] A few years later, in his introduction to a narrative based on the group he had formed with his friends a decade and a half earlier, *The Water Drinkers* (1855), he was still elaborating on this point. "In thus studying the life of the artist in a particular milieu, our design is not to undertake the glorification of a certain class of parasites who, by grabbing onto it, some to conceal their lack of occupation, others their incapacity, have rendered the title of artist so banal and so little respected."[52] Through these measures, as through the generally ironic style of his narratives about bohemia, Murger established the true bohemian, whom the reader is invited to identify with his artistically successful self, as one who must struggle to escape from a preexisting environment of woeful fakery. He did so even as he noted that all the Water Drinkers were themselves unapologetic "imitators" of the famous cenacle in Honoré de Balzac's *A Great Man of the Provinces in Paris* (1839)—and despite the fact that this inspiration might appear rather startlingly self-indicting, given Balzac's portrayal of Lucien de Rubempré as a fundamentally unscrupulous character, a poseur if there ever was one.[53] Ignoring such ironies, Pierre Larousse's seventeen-volume *Great Universal Dictionary of the Nineteenth Century* (1866–67) bowed to Murger's claims, adapting its primary definition of the modern sense of bohemia from the *Scenes* and including "the false bohemian" among the types associated with this community.[54]

Even those who were angered by Murger's condescending attitude toward his former bohemian comrades did not actually disagree with him about this question of the poseur. Adrien Lélioux, for example, while outraged by Murger's air of superiority, still suggested that there was a distinction to be drawn between "those who, in good faith, believe in their vocation, and the intruders who make a pretence of believing in it."[55] Asserting that he had never found anything less than genuine camaraderie among their old crowd, Nadar also criticized Murger's portrayal and yet, while doing so, observed that matters were different in the other bohemian circle he frequented, the one centered on Charles Baudelaire. There he certainly did find "banal simulators" of the style that was "inborn" in the poet. "The familiar word *pose*, whence we get *poseurs*, must come from that," he wrote.[56] Always excepting Privat, that uniquely excessive character, one seemingly could not be a bohemian without marking oneself off against the parasite.

The relation between the bohemian and the poseur was such a commonplace that even those who tended to think all bohemians were phonies would still meditate on this relation. This was the case with Edmond and Jules de Goncourt, for example, when they described the aspiring painter Anatole Bazoche, in *Manette Salomon* (1867), as being "less called by art than attracted by the life of the artist."[57] From a friendlier perspective, but to a similar effect, Alfred Delvau would characterize Murger's portrayal of bohemia as "joyous lies" and caution those who, "trusting in the word of Henry Murger, have believed that all bohemians in reality resemble the bohemians of the book."[58] In other words, he would continue the mission of policing the boundaries of bohemia by calling out even Murger's true and official bohemian as something of a poseur. Others also jumped into this game of impeaching the patent on bohemia that his success seemed to have given Murger, as when Jules Vallès, in *The Insurrectionist* (1886), contrasted his predecessor's portrayal of things, which had given rise to a "bohemia of cowards," to "the truth" represented in his own novel.[59] Following his lead, Pío Baroja, in 1906, also contrasted the praiseworthy bohemia of this writer and Communard to "the false and ridiculous bohemia" of Murger's tales.[60] In that same year, writing in Karl Kraus's *Die Fackel*, Erich Mühsam began his definition of the bohemian by distinguishing this figure from the poseur—and then promptly proceeded to place Murger's characters in the latter category.[61]

Camille Mauclair, however, had already taken this question of the poseur to what might be called its logical conclusion. In 1899 he had denounced the entirety of Murger's most famous work, together with *La Bohème* (1896), the opera Giacomo Puccini had developed from it. The so-called bohemian, he angrily proclaimed, is "the parasite of the poor artist," a "false spirit" from the very beginning.[62] In other words, in Mauclair's telling there could be no such thing as a true or false bohemian because the bohemian was a damnable lie, a mistaken image, through and through.

In the cumulative history of such responses during the second half of the nineteenth century, we hear a number of common refrains. To the distress of all concerned, real bohemians are forever finding themselves mixed up with fakes. It also seems that bohemians must ever and again be shown to be no different from the members of the bourgeoisie for whom they flaunt their scorn. (So Guy de Maupassant shows us that Madame de Marelle, the "true bohemian" of *Bel-Ami* [1885], is actually just a bourgeoise who likes to go slumming.)[63] We also learn that the fondly remembered bohemians of yesteryear may be used as sticks with which to beat the youth of today over the head. ("And they think with a word they can bring to life what they lack," said Oreste Cenacchi, witheringly, of the Italian realists of the late 1870s and early 1880s who had dared to adopt the word *bohème* for themselves.)[64] We must find, too, that bohemians are always selling out, becoming a commodified form of themselves so as to entertain tourists, as in the Chat Noir of late nineteenth-century Montmartre, for example, or as in the smoky, raucous *Tingeltangels*, music halls, of early twentieth-century Munich.[65] Ultimately, then, as these sorts of confusions plague us, making us feel nostalgic for a better time that must surely have existed before this whole mess showed up around us, we forever rediscover that the very notion of the modern bohemian was dubious from its beginnings—and thus find ourselves returning to the question of the poseur as it arose in the discourse of Pyat, Sand, Murger, and their contemporaries.

The nostalgia, as it happens, was also there from the beginning. Because the conditions of the bohemian metaphor virtually compelled its adherents jealously to police its boundaries, rooting out the poseurs who were supposed to have ruined it, or at least to have threatened its ruin, this community was committed to nostalgia from the time of its birth. As François Villon was among the first to suggest, yesteryear is always bohemia's best year; or, as Arthur Bartlett Maurice put it in 1916, "Whatever else Bohemia may be it is almost always yesterday."[66] Although there is no single moment at which the modern sense of this word came into being, it always came trailing clouds of the imaginary glories of a poseur-free past. The medievalist nostalgia of Pyat's bohemians did not last, but in all its iterations nineteenth-century bohemia was haunted by the fantasy of an earlier age, a purer age, prior to the reign of modern commerce, industry, and finance, when the arts might be supposed to have been honored by society and untainted by capital.

At times, for those of Murger's generation, this nostalgia might be little more than an envious glance back at the successes of the previous generation of Romantics, but it was also a more general fantasy of an art for art's sake, to use the contemporary catchphrase, for which one sought support in the past because the utilitarian middle-class present was so clearly inimical to it. This fantasy is displayed in the genealogy Murger invented for his kind in the preface to his *Scenes of Bohemian Life*, which traced a line of descent that included Homer, Villon, Michelangelo, Raphael, Torquato Tasso, Molière, Shakespeare, and Jean Le Rond d'Alembert. Murger designed this roll call of the greats not only for the purposes of self-glorification but also to assert a conception of art preexisting and towering over the pressing realities of its situation in the contemporary marketplace with which he and his struggling bohemian comrades were all too well acquainted. The accompanying nostalgia was built into the very name of the modern bohemian, which drew on the older sense of the word to evoke, as in Murger's preface and Sand's *The Last Aldini*, a conception of the modern artist as being spiritually allied to romanticized images of the strolling Gypsy singers, troubadours, and bards of earlier times.

This nostalgia lent support to the irony, dramatized in Murger's life and endlessly reiterated ever since, that bohemia must cease to be whenever it is rewarded with popular recognition. (One thinks of the late twentieth-century rock-and-roll cliché, "Remember when it used to be about the *music*, man?")

Emilio Carrere called this irony "the sadness of 'arriving' "—that is, of encoun-
tering the success that requires one to leave behind the beloved privations of
one's bohemian struggles.[67] In truth, however, this phenomenon of bohemia
being killed by its own success is not really an irony at all. It was predictable
from the very beginnings of this phenomenon, inscribed in those aspects of its
founding mythology that identified it with transient youth and with an oppositional stance at once rebellious and reactionary. The result was an attitude
of personal nostalgia with heavy investments in collective cultural fantasies
about the past.

This nostalgic preoccupation is on display in *The Last Aldini*, in Lélio's
focus on the thwarted desires of his younger days, just as it is in Murger's
work, which was epitomized for his nineteenth-century audience by his famous refrain, "Youth only comes around once."[68] Murger knew very well that
the nostalgia they would feel in the future reaches deep into bohemians from
the earliest days of their adventure. It dramatically manifests itself in their
desperately cheerful reliance on chance, or on a Providence in which they
have no faith, even as their revelries are shadowed by portents of sickness,
loss, early death, and the worse death of betrayal. The comic irony with which
Murger composed his *Scenes*, a kind of stylistic middle ground between Sand's
unbuttoned Romanticism and Pyat's cynical debunking of youthful idealism,
effectively embodies this sense of nostalgia, which arises when one mourns in
imagination what has never existed in reality. A style of marked artifice, it con-
tinuously reiterates the question of the poseur even as this is simultaneously
elaborated by the drama and themes of his stories.

At the same time as it destined bohemia to nostalgia, this question of the
poseur also associated it with imitative behavior in general. Like Pyat, who
portrayed it as a sickness, Théodore Pelloquet, one of Murger's friends and biographers, described this copying as a scandalous masquerade, a travesty. Bohemians, he wrote, "have taken on the costume—or, rather, the disguise—of
poets, of artists, and of thinkers, so as not to have to make an honest living."[69]
Some, no doubt, simply shrugged off this criticism as possibly having some
application to others but obviously not to themselves. For others, though, it
was completely obtuse.

When Gustave Courbet, in 1850, announced his intention to make his
debut "in the grand vagabond and independent life of the bohemian," he was
clearly assuming a theatrical pose in his words much like that into which he
cast himself in the painting popularly known as *Bonjour Monsieur Courbet*
(1854), in which he showed himself in his informal artist's garb being formally

greeted by his patron, Alfred Bruyas, and Bruyas's servant. "Yes, dear friend, in your ever so civilized society, it is necessary for me to live the life of a savage," he wrote.[70] Like Lélio or Sand herself, he did not see his copying of others' ways as any kind of fault, although he was concerned to be understood as a specific kind of bohemian, one who was serious about his art and who drew that art out of his rebellious socialist sympathies. Just as the writer Alejandro Sawa, in Madrid, did not feel that he had compromised the bohemian nature of his favorite dog by naming it Bel Ami, after Maupassant's character, so did Courbet feel that trying on others' looks, copying others' images, in no way contradicted the realism and authenticity of his art.[71] In writing to Bruyas about a series of self-portraits, for instance, he saw nothing wrong with describing each as representing a known type. One was "the portrait of a fanatic, of an ascetic"; another "the portrait of a man in the ideal and absolute love in the manner of Goethe, George Sand, etc."[72] Similarly, when James McNeill Whistler, Courbet's admirer and soon-to-be friend, identified himself as a bohemian while writing to Mario Proth in 1859—"I always belong my dear to the Bohemian life"—he was gladly assuming a persona as stereotyped, and yet as freeing, as Sand's suit of men's clothes.[73] According to his friends, Whistler in his early days in Paris "was always quoting Murger," having studied his works carefully before he left the United States; and he had learned very well what Murger had to teach about how to present oneself as a modern artist.[74] A similar pleasure in copying is evident in a narrative by the Spanish writer Rafael Altamira, "A Bohemian" (1886), in which the protagonist's eager identification with the characters in Murger's *Scenes* makes him a true and pure bohemian, not some kind of fake.

As these examples indicate, the modern metaphor of the bohemian was designed to be played: performed, toyed with, tried out, or entertained. The bohemian had no original, or only such an original as was itself a copy of indeterminate origin, as in Murger's genealogy or Alphonse Duchesne's characterization of Privat as a "younger brother of Villon."[75] Therefore, the same conditions of being that made the poseur a threatening figure for which one had to be on the watch would also lend an impression of innocence to all the affectations, disguises, and gestures that defined the bohemian. In declassing their identities, bohemia freed people for experimentation and drew them into an imaginary community in which this might be encouraged.

Some, to be sure—even some bohemians—would criticize this experimentation. Introducing Léon Cladel's *The Ridiculous Martyrs* (1862), Baudelaire complained that many of Murger's admirers among the young of the next generation had overlooked the "bitter mockery" with which *Scenes of Bohemian Life* had portrayed bohemia. "Behold Murger (poor shade!), transformed into an interpreter, a dictionary, of the language of bohemia, into a *Complete Handbook for Lovers* of the year of our lord 1861."[76] Like Cladel's, however, his tone of superiority was that of one who wishes to rise above, to the point of completely forgetting, all the fits, starts, and flounderings in his own youthful exercises in self-dramatization.

Ironically mirroring the abhorrence of the poseur, this joyous parasitism of copying explains why the dandy could be comprehended within the metaphor of bohemia. Writers did sometimes draw distinctions among various groups of bohemians, as Nadar did in distinguishing Baudelaire's circle from Murger's. Similarly, Théophile Gautier carefully differentiated Murger's bohemia from that of Balzac's "Prince of Bohemia" (1844) even as he retrospectively identified it with the life established some years earlier in the rue de Doyenné by himself, Camille Rogier, Arsène Houssaye, Gérard de Nerval, and Édouard Ourliac: a bohemia of youths possessed by "love of art and horror of the bourgeois . . . bravely pursuing the ideal in the midst of poverty and ever-renewed obstacles."[77] The metaphor of bohemia, however, proved sufficiently capacious to encompass many such differences and, along with them, the figure of the dandy, who might show up in almost any of them—as the dandified Baudelaire, for instance, was known around mid-century in Murger's circle as well as in those of Courbet and Gautier.

With his cultivation of an elegance in appearance and a sophistication in manner marked by disdain for all sorts of vulgarity, the dandy might seem the antithesis of the high-spirited, ragged, love-struck struggler of *Scenes of Bohemian Life*. Contemporary discourse, however, managed to assimilate them under the same category, just as it would later gather in various latter-day groups, such as the Impressionists.[78] Like Philibert Audebrand's light-hearted conception of "high Bohemia," in which he placed "Madame the Baroness Aurore Dudevant, known as George Sand," Charles Hugo's novel *Gilded Bohemia* (1859) was premised on the notion that the rich dandy and the poor bohemian are brothers under their skin; and common usage recognized as much, as with Baudelaire, the dandy's greatest interpreter.[79] In his 1868 biography of Baudelaire, Charles Asselineau noted that in the 1840s persons like this poet were known as bohemians. This was a word difficult to define, he allowed, but one that in any case did not carry the "vulgar" meaning of vagabonds, parasites, and *gens sans aveu*.[80]

As Asselineau's defensiveness indicates, some tensions did always linger around the representation of the bohemian. Telling differences announce themselves, for instance, in any comparison of the working-class image that Paul Cézanne cultivated to the studied pose of a gentleman adopted by Édouard Manet and Whistler. G. L. M. Strauss, to give another example, would note the distinction made in English circles between the bohemian and the dandy-like "swell."[81] In general, though, the category of bohemia could easily incorporate the artifice of the dandy because the bohemian had never been anything other than a creature of artifice. After all, the fact that necessity sometimes forced bohemians such as Murger to dress in unconventional ways, wearing bizarre secondhand clothes, did not mean that this clothing was any less affected than the exquisite fashions that Beau Brummell had commanded from his tailors. Once promoted and recognized as "bohemian," it was a style, a masquerade, even when it was sported by those who had little in the way of alternatives. Similarly, Courbet holding court at the Brasserie Andler, playing at being the rough provincial parvenu—loud, arrogant, vulgar—was just as surely putting on a performance as was Baudelaire, with all the calculated eccentricities of style, manner, and language with which he sought to shock new acquaintances, or as was Sand in her disguise as a student.

The cool elegance of the dandy signified his independence—his refusal, like that of the hero of Alfred de Vigny's *Chatterton* (1834), to assume a servant's livery—and so, too, did the rags of the Water Drinkers in Murger's stories. Like Sand, the dandy was a kind of transvestite, an "Androgyne," as Barbey said, in his stereotypically feminine care for his appearance and exquisite behavior. This unmasculine style of dress fitted in perfectly with the more general consciousness among bohemians, arising from their broadly oppositional stance toward social conventions, of their dress as a kind of costume.[82] It was with good reason that onlookers associated bohemians with masquerades at popular dance halls and, as commentators such as the Goncourts or the critic Paul de Saint-Victor observed, with Carnival.[83] Continually recruiting all the poseurs it so anxiously sought to exclude from its ranks, bohemia could incorporate the pose of the dandy even as it proclaimed its intolerance for the kind of artifice represented by this social type.

Just as the seeming irony in the bohemian betrayal of its ideal of friendship was not really an irony at all, so, too, was the question of the poseur never a real question. The only possible solution to that irony lay in its reiteration, as bohemia was enlivened by its commitment to disappointment, to desire in the mode of nostalgia; and much the same was true of the question of the poseur. Its only answer lay in its reiteration, which served to assert the legitimacy of a cultural community and, within that community, of the privilege of any given individual's talent or judgment. As Asselineau's discussion of bohemia indicates, it was not new claimants to it that actually troubled this word but rather the claims that "vulgar" history made upon it. The real problem lay in bohemians' founding act of imposture: their initial appropriation of their name from its traditional use.

The year 1849 solidified the modern meaning of *bohemia*, making Murger famous in the process, as a result of the fantastic success of the dramatized version of his stories that he cowrote with Barrière. As T. J. Clark has pointed out, this was also when the French government ended universal male suffrage and instituted a residence qualification of three years. "At one blow the electorate shrank by three million, and the men who lost the vote were precisely those who took the dangerous ideas into the countryside: the landless labourers who followed the harvest, the village artisans, the nomads who moved from town to country seeking work."[84] The modern sense of bohemia had been in existence for more than a decade by that time, and there is no direct relation between the two events; but the coincidence is suggestive. As the historian Carl Ploetz observed in 1862, the bohemia that Murger identified with the strolling musicians of yore was emerging at a time when vagabonds of this kind, if they lacked the proper papers, were likely to end up in jail. "Principled homelessness and homelandlessness," Ploetz drily observed, "comes into unpleasant conflict with the codes of criminal law of all civilized modern nations in general, and with the French *Code pénal* in particular."[85] Alexandre Dumas emphasized this fact in the first volume of his *Mohicans of Paris* (1854), in which an early scene finds a lost orphan being cautioned by those who find her that she must accept their help or else risk being arrested as a vagabond.[86] Writing in 1865, Proth made explicit the relation between the rise of modern bohemia and the suppression of the bohemians of old when he declared that the vagabonds whom he was praising had "nothing to do with the police or with Béranger"—the latter, of course, being the "national poet" of gypsydom.[87]

As an imaginary community of urban gypsies, bohemia was not invented *tout court* out of the repression of a real society of traditional bohémiens: matters were not so simple. Traditional types of vagabonds would continue to roam through France and other countries, in the nineteenth century and on into our own day. It is the case, however, that *bohemian* was becoming a popularly recognized term for a modern sense of dispossession among students, artists, intellectuals, and other rebellious youth at the very time when the authorities were greatly concerned to control the sorts of persons who fell under the traditional sense of this term. In his study *Of the Dangerous Classes of the Population in the Large Cities, and Of the Means to Improve Them* (1840), for instance, Honoré-Antoine Frégier at this time was characterizing the vagabond as the arch-criminal: "the original type of all the forces of evil" and "the personification of all the classes of evil-doers."[88]

The appropriation of the term *bohemian* in this particular era was a sign of modernization.[89] Through the metaphorical appropriation, idealization, and dismissal of those formerly referred to as bohemians, a new cultural formation effectively consigned the traditional populace of vagabonds to the past, whose exotic and nostalgic allure would thenceforth enliven the new metaphor of bohemia.[90] In 1851, the year that Murger's novelized *Scenes* appeared, a writer for the *Magasin pittoresque* wrote of these pre-Murgerian bohemians as the "laggards of civilization, the rear-guard of that multitude of adventurers come in confusion from all the corners of the globe and now changed into nations. . . . Like so many other things, the Bohemians have had their day, and before long their existence will be no more than a memory."[91]

On the one hand, when *grocer* becomes an insulting term for *bourgeois*, we witness a synecdoche motivated by snobbery: the petit-bourgeois *épicier* is made to stand for every bourgeois, no matter how grand. On the other hand, when *bohemian* becomes a complimentary term for would-be artists, writers, and intellectuals, along with all those who move in their orbit, we witness a metaphor charged with idealization. The figure being idealized, however, is also being dismissed from reality, converted to a figure of imagination. This dismissal at times could be quite dramatic, as in Proth's writing or, a decade earlier, in the first issue of Charles Pradier's short-lived journal *Le Bohême*, which hastened to declare that it bore no relation to "the gypsies, those brigands that Egypt has vomited over Europe."[92] More generally, the creation of the modern sense of bohemia simply implied a modernization of society that had made the existence of people without a fixed occupation or home seem outdated, out of character with the present time, and hence a suitable subject for romance. Sports teams are not named after Indians until Indians are viewed, by the culture at large, as no longer having a meaningful living presence and fate; similarly, only when the bohemian no longer seems real can bohemia become the land of art.

Measures against vagabonds were by no means unique to the era when George Sand rose to fame. Ever since the fourteenth century governing authorities in France had made efforts to restrict or eliminate the population of vagabonds, whether these be Gypsies, simple beggars, travelling performers, itinerant gamblers, or others among those who were *sans feu ni lieu*, without hearth or home. From the sixteenth century on, various attempts were made to confine or imprison these types of people, and bohemians had long been viewed as persons masquerading under a suspect identity—as *so-called* bohemians.[93] In the seventeenth century, officials skeptically referred to them as "those who claim to be" bohemians or as "those who live the life of bohemians," and in the nineteenth century administrative documents still spoke with suspicion of those "known under the name of Bohemians."[94] In that century the public's acceptance of a new conception of the bohemian did not put an end to efforts such as Frégier's to bring bohémiens, in the old sense of the word, under control, but it did indicate their increasing irrelevance. The conditions of modern economic, social, and cultural life were proving much more efficient at doing what laws targeting vagabonds had sought to do, which was to neutralize their perceived threat to the order of things. When the artist and playwright Henri Monnier addressed letters to Murger's old buddy "Schaunard" by writing, "To Monsieur Alexandre Schanne, painter and musician, *member of the dangerous classes of society*," he was making a joke about bourgeois fears; but this joke is also revealing about how the bohemian could serve as a kind of domesticated savage, more a cultural pet than a social threat.[95] For all the controversy aroused by this figure, as in Pyat's fulminations, the modern bohemian's arrival on the social scene might seem to be that of a tamed vagabond; of a so-called wanderer who, as Walter Benjamin suggested, was in reality a counterpart to the gentlemanly *flâneur*; and thus of a supposed opponent of the bourgeoisie who was actually the very model of the modern bourgeois *gentilhomme*.[96]

To remember the definition of *bohemian* displaced by the newer sense of the word is, then, to recognize that bohemia was not only an effect but also an agency of modernization. Through this new sense of bohemia art accommodated itself to the conditions of modern life by idealizing its own marginalization—and, in doing so, rejecting cultural possibilities represented by ways of life that these conditions refused to accommodate. Unsurprisingly, as the nineteenth century went on and the modern sense of the word *bohemian* became increasingly naturalized, it also tended to become neutralized. Despite contrary impulses, by the turn of the century it had become commonplace to maintain, in France, Germany, England, and the United States, among other places, that to be bohemian no longer necessarily meant that one was lacking in respectability, gentility, manners, or wealth. As in Hans

R. Fischer's study of Berlin's bohemia, one could then speak of a "bohemian *comme il faut*"—of a *proper* bohemian.[97]

Still, no matter how innocuous it became, this modern sense of the word continued to be haunted by its symbolic dispossession of the vagabond of old. Behind the bohemian's enemy twin, the masquerading *poseur*, lurked the traditional bohémien, the vagabond foreigner. This figure shadowed bohemia's utopian will to transcend conventional determinations of time and space. It was a disturbing reminder of differences of race, nationality, economics, culture, and history that could not be wished away even among the best of friends at the most carnivalesque of moments.

This legacy of bohemia's founding act of imposture may have revealed itself most clearly in early twentieth-century Munich, where *Schlawiner* became another word for *bohemian*. History, with haunting differences, replayed itself in this term. Originally people used it to refer loosely to foreigners, indiscriminately lumping them together as Slovenians, Slovakians, or Slavs but treating them all as stemming from a distinct, and lesser, nationality or race. *Schlawiner* then took on an extended definition in the second and third decades of the century as a name for the metaphorically foreign artistic types (as viewed by middle-class natives) who had come to populate Munich's Schwabing district, or "Schwabylon," as it was jokingly called. Thus, in Georg Queri's 1912 dictionary of Bavarian idioms, *Schlawiner* is still closely attached to persons presumed to be literally foreign, although it does also suggest, in particular, an impoverished individual from that foreign background.[98] Within two years, however, Fritz von Ostini, who, like Queri, was a prominent figure in Munich literary and journalistic circles, would describe it as a word used by natives of Munich to refer disparagingly to all artistic types, both male and female.[99] Thereafter it came to be recognized as a synonym for *bohemian* that bohemians themselves might use without any deprecatory intent, though others might still wish to employ it as an insult.[100] By 1921, René Prévot could refer to Schwabing as "a hospitable free state for all Schlawinerdom."[101]

In contrast to the word *bohemian*, which originally arose from the popular belief that Gypsies came from the foreign land of Bohemia, *Schlawiner* reflected a popular desire to treat modern bohemians as if they were akin to foreigners looked down upon by *Münchener*. Rather than being seen as dwelling in an avowedly ideal country, a Bohemia of the imagination, the modern bohemian is imaged as an alien interloper. Through the term *Schlawiner*, in other words, modern bohemians were sent back to their disavowed origins among the historical outcasts of society. Whereas the terms *bohème* and *bohémien*, in post-1840s Paris, suggested a self-willed exile, a metaphysical emigration, *Schlawiner* in early twentieth-century Munich suggested an invasion. Instead of a perceived difference in social identity being aestheticized, as happened when modern youths assumed the mantle of the outcasts of old, we witness a perceived cultural difference being nationalized and racialized, as the bohemian is lumped in with the *Schlawiner*.

This development, then, was a xenophobic reversal of bohemia's founding act of imposture, in which young people had playfully made a romance out of the stigmatized image of all the vagabonds associated with Gypsies. The resulting identification was only figurative, of course, but figures of speech do have consequences. The *Schlawiner* shows us the ominous implications for politics that could arise out of the question of the poseur. Soon enough, the pacifist Carl von Ossietzky would be describing Adolf Hitler as "a half-crazy *Schlawiner*"; a few years later, the journalist Konrad Heiden would argue that Hitler was "disguised as a normal man," having deliberately designed an appearance for himself that would make him seem "as far away as possible from the bohemian and '*Schlawiner*.'"[102] The gruesome irony here is that the courageous antifascism that led both men to portray Hitler as a poseur reiterated the kind of tropology that would help to legitimate the driving of other perceived aliens, including Gypsies as well as Jews, into concentration camps. At this very time, for instance, Julius Petersen was writing of "restless Jewish literati, like Gustav Landauer and Erich Mühsam," as bohemians who had been associated with Heinrich and Julius Hart's mystical socialist community and "whom one later rediscovers in the Soviet Republic of Schwabing's *Schlawiner* in Munich."[103] Amid these historical complexities, as in the question of the poseur among bohemians, the representation of identity turns out to entail a haunting, unfathomably consequential, ineradicable dispossession of the self.

The question of the poseur in bohemia has still further ramifications, which extend all the way back to its modern beginnings. As the nature of Sand's streetwise disguise indicates, one of the most obvious of these ramifications concerned the status of women in bohemia. Given the customary and institutional barriers that impeded women's participation in civic life in general, and in the arts and intellectual life in particular, it is not surprising that nineteenth-century bohemia was a predominantly male enterprise. Considering that even men were discouraged from entering the fine arts and, once having sought an artistic career, often met with terrible difficulties, it was no wonder, Privat said, that a woman whom he had known as a copyist in the museums, an accomplished painter named Charlotte, should have ended up as a dancer, a *femme galante*, at the Prado.[104] Sand was an exceptional figure; most of the women who figure in bohemian annals were grisettes, models, or other demimondaines who, like Charlotte, were the associates or mistresses of the men in this world.

Henry James distilled the popular image of this situation into his portrayal of Noémi Nioche in *The American* (1877). Unwilling to earn her living as a grisette, she becomes a copyist, despite her lack of any talent for painting, and ends up as the mistress of a man wealthy enough to maintain her in the comfort to which she had yearned to become accustomed. It is notable that James did not make Mademoiselle Nioche an aspiring, frustrated, or failed artist, though it would have been possible for him to observe, as Privat had, the legal, institutional, and customary impediments that stood in the way of such a woman. Instead he left his readers with the impression bohemia itself generally conveyed: that creativity was to be expected of men, such as the protagonist of James's own *Roderick Hudson* (1875), to whom women would be expected to play a secondary and subservient role. Decades earlier Champfleury had detailed this expectation, with crude candor, in his "Confessions of Sylvius" (1852). Reflecting on a woman who is painting in the Louvre, his narrative tells us that such an occupation unsexes a woman, making her (as in Émile de La Bédollière's characterization of Sand) "almost hermaphroditic."[105]

Pierre-Joseph Proudhon castigated bohemia as the source of contemporary movements for the emancipation of women, but the reality fell far short of his paranoid fantasy.[106] Noémi, James is careful to point out, deliberately chooses to be a *femme galante* in preference to a humble marriage of the sort that is the only other fate, besides the tedious labor of the grisette, that appears to be open to her. ("Grocers and butchers and little *maîtres de cafés* I won't marry at all if I can't marry more *proprement* than that.")[107] As in Sand's case, bohemia in some instances did offer women a sexual freedom and a liberation from other social conventions that allowed them to be treated by men as "comrades," to use the bohemian word for informal friendships of all kinds, including extramarital relationships between men and women. Beyond this limited freedom, however—which could itself become a new source of oppression—women in bohemia were generally regarded as being qualified, at best, for copying, as opposed to being capable of important original contributions to culture. For all the scandal associated with the social and sexual liberty of the bohémienne, one need only read memoirs and contemporary accounts of this era to see the extent to which women appeared in it primarily in their service to men's desires. In this regard, their fate corresponded to that of the bohemian vagabonds of old who were now admired as a source of metaphor but, with few exceptions—as in Sand's heroic socialist portrayal of the traveling journeymen whom she called "the bohemian artists of industry"—disregarded as fellow adventurers.[108]

Despite the socialism of Sand and some other bohemians, the exclusion of members of the working classes from bohemia was also an issue in the relation between bohemians and poseurs.[109] In fact, a defining moment in many narratives of bohemia, dramatically prefigured in Vigny's *Chatterton*, involves their protagonists' refusal to countenance the idea of supporting themselves by accepting a working-class job and, with it, a working-class identity. The exhilaration in Ludwig Meidner's 1919 socialist manifesto for artists—"None of us is a worker, no!"—had many precedents.[110] In novels as diverse as Sand's *Horace* (1842), Cladel's *Ridiculous Martyrs*, Alejandro Sawa's *Declaration of a Loser* (1887), and Willy Pastor's *The Other* (1896), this deliberate bohemian rejection of a working-class identity is marked.[111] It is also marked in the common trope, which one finds, for example, in the writings of Baudelaire, in which bohemians are equated with prostitutes. On the one hand, this stands as a protest against the commodification of identity or, in other words, the demand that all must take themselves to market, putting themselves up for sale. On the other, this equation of bohemians with prostitutes conveys the conviction that ordinary labor is a degrading affair and ordinary workers, therefore, alien to the bohemian, who paradoxically exults in his economic marginalization and degradation. To call oneself a prostitute, in this context, is to assert that one ought to be treated as if one were an aristocrat.

Murger himself had helped to establish this ritualistic separation of the bohemian from the working classes in an 1851 story, "The Funeral Supper," in which an aristocratic bohemian desperately tries and grotesquely fails to overcome it. Works such as these communicated the insight that bohemians could be popularly represented as déclassé types only because, in rejecting genteel middle-class respectability, they yet seemed to hold themselves apart from the working-class population among whom they might live and with whom they might mingle—not excepting the working-class grisettes whom they might love and who might work to support them, as in Murger's tale. Terms such as *proletarians of the intellect*, which came to be synonyms for bohemians in the closing decades of the nineteenth century, served only to emphasize this point all the more. Like bohemia's tendency to slight women, it is a point so obvious that it risks being overlooked. Exceptions did exist; but to be bohemian, generally speaking, was to separate oneself from the life of the working classes just as Murger separated himself from his father, who had wanted him to follow his own example and become a tailor.

Less obvious, but no less consequential, was the attitude toward Jews that played a part in the making of nineteenth-century bohemia and thus prepared the way for the anti-Semitism of modernists such as Ezra Pound, that swaggering bohemian of the next century. As the vagabond foreigner lurked behind the adventitious poseur, the enemy twin of the bohemian, so did the Jew lurk behind that foreigner, as when Proudhon wrote of the Jewish race as being analogous to "the Bohemians or Gypsies, and the Polish émigrés, the Greeks, Armenians, and all who wander."[112] In fact, modern bohemians who assumed the pose of the traditional vagabond also identified with the Wandering Jew, as in Proth's assertion that this figure was now to be found everywhere ("c'est tout le monde").[113] This name was always being applied to someone or other in the formative years of bohemia in the 1830s and 1840s. Sand applied it to herself, for instance, and Murger's friends used to joke that he was "The Wandering Christian."[114] One could hardly avoid running into this character condemned endlessly to wander the earth, as punishment for his insult to Christ on the road to Calvary. Sue, for instance, wrote a novel in which the Wandering Jew becomes an evangelist for socialism, and Champfleury wrote a scholarly work on the variants of this figure's legend.[115] Often he was portrayed as a sympathetic figure, repentant of his sin; frequently he was absorbed into the Romantic fascination with a cursed, vagabond, defiant subjectivity. Courbet, for instance, used a popular image of the Wandering Jew as the model for a portrait of Jean Journet, the Fourierist enthusiast admired among the bohemians of his time, and, in addition, for his own portrait in *The Meeting*.[116]

As the modern bohemians' embrace of traditional vagabonds served metaphorically to eclipse these others, so, too, did this bohemian identification with the Wandering Jew carry with it a very different attitude toward Jews who were not legendary, those who were living contemporaries of modern bohemians. When Courbet included an image of a money-loving Jew as one of the figures in *The Painter's Studio* (1855), there could be no doubt of the tendency of this representation, which was of a piece with the anti-Semitism that figured in Proudhon's thinking and in much of nineteenth-century bohemia, just as it did in the broader culture from which bohemia was supposed to stand apart.[117] In regard to the figure of the Jew, at least, bohemians did have traditional homes and homelands, despite their pose as outsiders; and there the Jew was generally perceived as an alien intruder.

As the dandy was generally opposed to vulgarity, but with particular disdain for women, so was bohemia as a whole generally opposed to bourgeois philistinism, but with particular disdain for Jews. Even as bohemians stereotyped themselves as vagabonds who were impoverished parasites on the body of society at large, they deliberately distinguished themselves from the traditional stereotype of Jews as rootless cosmopolitans who were rich parasites on the body of Christian nations. In the nineteenth century the bohemian became the popular, visible, marketable symbol of all those who did not accept, or were not acceptable to, the logic of the capitalist marketplace; but in their imaginary independence they also figured as a symbolic antithesis to the popular association of Jews with the vagabond amorality of money. This association pervaded all parts of society. It was the royalist Catholic Charles de Ricault d'Héricault who was pleased to describe the era of his friendship with Murger by saying, "The reign of the Jews and the Freemasons had not yet ulcerated the French spirit and infused into our pure Gallic-Frankish blood an acrid Semitic purulence that a bunch of low newspapermen renew each morning," but the socialist Lafargue was no less pleased to write of a bankrupted factory owner prostrating himself before "the Jew," offering "his blood, his honor" to "the Rothschild," all in vain, in his desperate attempt to keep his works going and his laborers employed.[118]

This is the milieu in which it made sense to Nathaniel Hawthorne that he should frame his portrait of a beautiful and successful woman artist in *The Marble Faun* (1860), Miriam, between a reference to ghetto Jews who "lead a close, unclean, and multitudinous life, resembling that of maggots when they overpopulate a decaying cheese," and a reference to her rumored origin as "the daughter and heiress of a great Jewish banker."[119] He contrasts the deadly sexual perversity incarnate in this figure of the woman artist to the "white wisdom" of Hilda, who is only a copyist, whereas Miriam paints works that are strikingly passionate and colorful—albeit faulted on technical grounds by other artists.[120] As Hawthorne portrays her, Miriam is so egregious a bohemian poseur that she must collapse into her supposed antitype, the Jew; and, in fact, she does turn out to have "a vein . . . of Jewish blood."[121] In his writing and character Hawthorne was about as distant as one could be from the bohemian camaraderie centered on Pfaff's tavern in New York City, but this portrayal was perfectly in keeping with the representation of Jews in the *New-York Saturday Press*, the house organ of these bohemians, in the year in which *The Marble Faun* was published. The Jew, the paper said, "is not large-hearted enough or human enough to be a Bohemian." One finds instead that "the Jewish characteristics of worshipping wealth, of following the letter and disregarding the spirit, of loving forms, and neglecting essences, their pride, cruelty, and lust of power, [are] all opposed to the spirit of Bohemianism." Even the famous actress Rachel, though "a Bohemienne as far as her genius carried her, . . . could never eradicate her Jewish nature."[122]

William Makepeace Thackeray had pictured the male counterpart to Hawthorne's Miriam in *The Newcomes* (1855), in which one of the students in the atelier where Clive Newcome studies is "a young Hebrew . . . upon whom his brother students used playfully to press ham sandwiches, pork sausages, and the like."[123] Nothing daunted, and with the backing of his father, a usurer to whom the head of the studio is indebted, this lad is able to grow wealthy through a career that begins with him peddling supplies to his fellow students. As, for Hawthorne, a woman who is a bohemian artist must be some sort of Jew, so, for Thackeray, a Jew in a studio must be an imposter, not really a student at all. (Fitz-James O'Brien, a member of the crowd at Pfaff's, singled out Thackeray's portrayal of this character for special praise, quoting one of his money-grubbing lines and commenting, "The history of Israel is written in the sentence.")[124] One might further note, as Champfleury and others did, that the same antithesis between bohemians and Jews must hold for artists' models. Whereas the famed bohemian whom Champfleury celebrates, Cadamour, "was too much of an artist to worry about tomorrow," the Jewish models who "invaded" French studios in the 1820s and thereafter possessed "a rare avarice, a Jewish avarice."[125]

Well deserving of the praise it earned from Édouard Drumont in his bestselling popular compendium of anti-Semitic invective, *Jewish France* (1886), the repulsive portrayal of the Jewish model who is the title character of the Goncourts' *Manette Salomon* is no aberration.[126] Sand wrote at least one work, her play *The Mississippians* (1840), in which her anti-Semitism is on full display as she portrays a vulgar, brutal, social-climbing Jewish financier devoted to the manipulation of currency and gold. Although one can glimpse it in her letters and novels, this anti-Semitism is not prominent in her early works about bohemia, and it does not by any means appear in all of the contemporary writings related to this community; but neither is it merely incidental to them.[127] Murger's *Scenes of Bohemian Life*, for example, features a Jewish dealer in secondhand goods of all sorts who is also an art dealer. Solomon—or, to call him by his nickname, Father Medicis—is described as "possessing a genius for making deals to a degree to which the greatest adepts of his religion hitherto had not arrived."[128] Parasitic upon "the whole of literary and artistic bohemia, with whom he was in constant contact," Solomon makes a commodity of everything.[129] "All the products of nature, all the creations of art, everything that emerges from the bowels of the earth and from the genius of humanity, Medicis made an object of trade. His commerce touched on everything, on absolutely everything that exists; he did business even in the *ideal*."[130] When he sought to update Murger's work a decade later, Cladel did not forget this aspect of it. At one of his lowest moments in Paris, his protagonist, an aspiring writer, thinks of turning to Jews, to "those filthy brokers" in their "pandemoniums of fraud," those "social lepers" in their "receptacles of cupidity," who, when he does request their aid, add personal insult to racial injury by refusing to consider his signature a sufficient basis for a loan.[131]

Even though it was not universally copied—among the *scapigliatura*, for instance, it did not play an important role—this portrayal found writers eager to further it almost everywhere that bohemia took up lodgings. In this matter Vigny's *Chatterton* had helped to set the pattern, with the venerable Quaker in the play prophesying that if things go on as they are at present a Jewish usurer will rule over the capitalist society represented by the businessman, John Bell, who figures in the play as Chatterton's romantic and ideological opposite.[132] As it did with so many other contemporary tropes, *Scenes of Bohemian Life* picked up this bit of cultural business, enriched as it was by anti-Semitic legacies stretching back through the ages, and then really made it pay off as the concept of bohemia proliferated throughout the nineteenth century and into the next. Mr. Jacobs in George Moore's *A Modern Lover* (1883) is directly descended from Murger's Father Medicis, as are the characters Padre Israel and Pas-joli in Pío Baroja's *The Last Romantics* (1906).[133] In his novel about bohemia, *Stilpe* (1897), Otto Julius Bierbaum allows his title character to demonstrate his comical opportunism by taking up anti-Semitic journalism at one point in his career, but Bab was entirely serious when he noted that one cannot expect to find the same qualities in bohemians such as Heinrich Heine as in "the full-blooded Aryan bohemian."[134] In using a Jewish businessman who is also a self-professed bohemian to spur on its plot, occasioning strife within the families of two impoverished brothers who share earnest literary ambitions, Ernst von Wolzogen's *The Rabble* (1891) is another work that contributed to this picture of the Jew as a would-be interloper, an *echt*-poseur, out to corrupt the principles of the true bohemian idealists.[135] The "hideous Jew" who manages a theater in Oscar Wilde's *The Picture of Dorian Gray* (1891) serves a similar end, as does the "loathsome little Jew" who figures in a novel of bohemia by the American writer Robert W. Chambers, *In the Quarter* (1894).[136]

In *The Tragic Muse* (1890) it was Henry James's genius to recognize this crucial association between bohemians and Jews, as it was his baseness to exploit it in his portrayal of the relationship between Peter Sherringham, a British diplomat, and Miriam Rooth, an aspiring actress who is disturbingly attractive, Jewish, and bohemian. Her late father is another relative of Murger's Father Medicis—"a Jewish stockbroker, a dealer in curosities" (7: 62)—and it is surmised that he bequeathed to her "the aesthetic element in her character" (7: 220), as this element is considered to be common among people of her kind.[137] Desiring her, Sherringham nonetheless is appalled to find that she is a thoroughgoing poseur engaged in a continual masquerade: "It came over him suddenly that so far from there being any question of her having the histrionic nature she simply had it in such perfection that she was always acting; that her existence was a series of parts assumed for the moment, each changed for the next, before the perpetual mirror of some curiosity or admiration or wonder— some spectatorship that she perceived or imagined in the people about her" (7: 188–89). Reprising a theme from James's earlier *Watch and Ward* (1871/78), Sherringham has a vision of himself spiriting her away from her vulgar mother and louche background to an imaginary theater that would be dedicated to art for its own sake, art in its purity. She, however, proves herself resistant to his charms and instead marries just such a man as he had feared would take charge of her. "I don't know," she says, mockingly, "how he ever came to stray at all into our bold bad downright Bohemia: it was a cruel trick for fortune to play him" (8: 313). We are not far away, at this point, from Philarète Chasles's description of Rachel as a "little bohemian tiger, a lascivious Jew," vampire-like in her "carnivorous" soul—a "sublime hyena" who manifests "the barbarity of the Pariahs, of the Jews, of the Bohemians, summed-up, concentrated, and refined by the barbarity of the streets of Paris."[138]

Thus does James reinforce, even as he satirizes, the nineteenth-century obsession with distinguishing bohemians from Jewish poseurs. He does not even hesitate to urge the word "ham" into the name of the repulsed lover of this Jew, just as Thackeray's art students had jokingly thrust pork products toward the son of Mr. Moss, the usurer. A woebegone would-be Pygmalion, Sherringham must undergo the tragic lesson that the poseur cannot be eliminated from the ranks of bohemians; and paralleled to this realization is the experience of his cousin Nicholas Dormer, who, when working on a portrait of Miriam, finds himself "troubled about his sitter's nose, which was somehow Jewish without the convex arch" (8: 49). Given his supersensitive eye for an intrusive Jewish nose, Dormer's decision to give up a political career in favor of one as a painter does suggest, however, that at least one bohemian will continue to struggle against the poseur in this world, and thus will maintain the bohemian ideal, even in the face of his relative's tragedy.

The lessons writers such as James distilled out of the history of modern bohemia were carried to their metaphysical end, one might say, in what Viktor Mann called the "house-trained bohemia" of Ludwig Klages and his associates in turn-of-the-century Munich.[139] Klages extended the defining bohemian romance with gypsy types to a more general exaltation of paganism, of which gypsydom was, in his telling, a mere remnant, and in contrast to which *Jewish* was the appropriate term for all that was most loathsome in modernity.[140] Klages also scorned Christianity and used *Jewish* as an all-purpose insult, not exclusively applicable to those with names such as Solomon and Rothschild; for him and his associates, "cosmic" was the highest conceivable term of approbation. Despite these refinements, however, his thought perfectly reproduced the dominant tendencies in the nineteenth-century discourse on bohemia. Capitalism, utilitarianism, bourgeois individualism, philistinism, the ideal of progress: all these features of the modern world Klages found to be essentially "a contrivance of Judaism."[141] His anti-Semitism, a kind of bastardized Nietzscheanism, all-too-humanly carried to "cosmic" lengths the traditional bohemian identification of the Jew as the quintessentially reprehensible poseur.

In the context of this tradition, it makes sense to view James's masterly *Tragic Muse* as the bohemian—or poseur—comrade of *Trilby* (1894), the best-selling potboiler that George du Maurier published four years after James's novel appeared. It also makes perfect sense that a novel representing all the romance of bohemia at the end of the century should feature as its villain a man who is at once an artist and a Jew: the insidious mesmerist Svengali. As Du Maurier was canny enough to recognize, the attributes that mark the Jew out for persecution, as in the analysis Max Horkheimer and Theodor Adorno would later present in *The Dialectic of Enlightenment* (1944), could just as easily be taken to describe the bohemian: "happiness without power, reward without work, a homeland without frontiers, religion without myth."[142] In 1885 Guy de Charnacé had based his novel *The Vampire Baron* on precisely this confluence of identities, tracing the rise of a vagabond youth from the country of Bohemia into the fabulously rich Baron Rakonitz, the representative of all the Jews who, in Charnacé's telling, had come to dominate Christian Europe, sucking the blood out of it. Whereas Charnacé's forthrightly anti-Semitic polemic promptly dropped into obscurity, however, Du Maurier's more insidious tale left a permanent mark on popular culture.

Du Maurier's Trilby, an innocent model who loves the life of bohemia, falls under Svengali's spell and consequently finds success, riches, dehumanization, and death at his hands. Summarizing the tradition he inherited, through the character of Svengali Du Maurier suggested that the antagonist of the bohemian was not so much the bourgeois as the Jew—and that this was because the bohemian himself was so close to the Jew, or so much of a Jew. If it incorporated the demonization of the Jew, Du Maurier saw, the nineteenth-century mythology of bohemia could yet hope to live on—for the very good reason that this kind of treatment, through which bohemia disavowed its origins in the political economy of modernity, had been there virtually from the beginning.

This demonization played a crucial part in the invention of the artifact that is the modern bohemian: the poseur who is also a scapegoat for the disavowed utopian desires of an entire civilization. Yet to observe this demonization and scapegoating is not to wrap up all there is to say about the ideal of bohemian liberty. Just as the vagabond ideal of bohemia cannot simply be dismissed as an irresponsible metaphor or its ideal of romantic freedom as nothing more than another device by which men may continue business as usual in their subordination of women, so is there more to bohemia than anti-Semitism. If Munich's bohemia nurtured Klages, for instance, with the hatred of Jews that he sought to dignify as philosophy, it also nurtured Mühsam, the Jewish writer, anarchist, and antifascist. Before he was slaughtered in the Oranienburg concentration camp in 1934, Mühsam defined the bohemian as "a man who, out of deep despair over not being able to achieve an inward connection with the masses of his fellow men . . . , heads straight out into life, experiments with chance, plays at seizing the moment, and unites himself with ever-present eternity."[143]

Precisely because it did not wholly constitute bohemia, however, the anti-Semitism that went into its making may have been all the more dangerous, since it could hide itself in the question of the poseur, where it has lingered to this day while generally being treated reluctantly, when it is observed at all, as a personal matter having nothing to do with the concept of bohemia in and of itself. The reluctance is understandable enough. One of the friends of whom Mühsam wrote most admiringly was Munich's famed bohemian queen, Franziska zu Reventlow, one of whose lovers was Klages: it is difficult even to begin to conceptualize the posing that must have gone into these relationships.

Haunted by gypsies, because of the founding act of imposture that gave it its name, bohemia was also haunted by Jews. Trilby had to be mesmerized by a bohemian so that she could represent the ideals of bohemia; she had to be mesmerized by a Jew so that bohemia could continue to maintain its pose of being utterly unconscious of any defining relation to the capitalism the Jew was popularly taken to represent. In its modern conception, whether we look high or low, to masterpieces or to would-be masterpieces or to works just made for trade, the bohemian must resentfully acknowledge his dependence on the Jew so that he may deny his enthrallment to the political and economic forces summed up in the vagabond character of money, that ultimate poseur, *son semblable, son frère.*

CHAPTER 2

Maggie, Not a Girl of the Streets

The grisette leaves home, and she goes to work: so her story begins. Before it ends, this carefree girl will divide nations and novels, antagonize even some of those most attracted to her, and, in her provocative simplicity, raise questions so complex that they might seem to draw one inexorably to tragic conclusions. From the way she is represented by the writers of her time, we might easily be led to believe that historical developments such as the industrial uses of steam power and the onset of the Napoleonic Wars were of no more significance to nineteenth-century Europe than was she. Her story was written by authors as diverse as Eugène Sue, Paul de Kock, Alfred de Musset, George Sand, Charlotte Brontë, Edgar Allan Poe, George Moore, and, perhaps most notably, George Eliot, whose Maggie Tulliver provides this chapter with its title. If we trace this story, the grisette leads us on a journey through the nineteenth century in which we can see that she is many Maggies, some of which may present a far sadder sacrifice than that of the Maggie whose story we know. The legendary grisette shows the culture of this age leaving its home in tradition so as to venture forth in search of its desire. The course of her career, as a social type, figure of fantasy, aesthetic examplar, and historical representative of bohemianism, richly illustrates the politics of art in the nineteenth century and their implication in the political economy of sex, gender, and class. The grisette serves as a measure of modernity not only for France, her country of origin, but also for England, which is repulsed by her celebrity, and the United States, whose writers revise both French and English literary traditions in their portrayals of her. In all these countries it seems that any mastery of modernity must find its truth in the working-class girl.

Oblivious to her portentous cultural destiny, wearing her little bonnet and her calico dress, the grisette leaves home. A pot of flowers in a mansard window will mark her habitation, for economy dictates that she will usually be lodged among the rooftops of the city. "Like artists and writers," Auguste Ricard observed, grisettes "have a decided penchant for the upper stories."[1] Though she, too, will be an object of desire, she is in a world totally different from that of Théophile Gautier's notorious *Mademoiselle de Maupin* (1835), whose young narrator, in his search for a mistress, rules out the choice of a grisette as being insufficiently refined.[2] It is as a needleworker or shopgirl that she will be best known, but the grisette may work in any sort of humble occupation. As a contemporary pamphlet helpfully pointed out, she may be an embroiderer, a laundress, an ornamenter, a seamstress, a burnisher, a dancer, a milliner, a florist, a lacemaker, a haberdasher, a breeches maker, a cook, a linen draper, a couturier, a market woman, or an extra at the Opera.[3] In any case, since she has little education and no family resources, her financial position will be precarious at best. She will be well acquainted with her "aunt," as she and her friends refer to the local pawnshop. "You ask about my new dress?"

Figure 2. Paul Gavarni, "La grisette," from *Les français peints par eux-mêmes* (1840–42).

Figure 3. Gustave Courbet, *Young Ladies on the Banks of the Seine River* (1856) (Erich Lessing/Art Resource, NY).

she might laugh, explaining, "Oh, I left it at my aunt's!" In her most desperate straits, she might even think of the expedient pursued by a dancer from the Moulin Rouge mentioned in Frank Wedekind's journal: "Kaduja says, she has pawned all her jewelry and pawned the pawn tickets."[4] The grisette laughs, though, for she takes pride in her independence, despite the scrapes into which it leads her.

Besides, if the grisette's dress is at her aunt's, perhaps an "uncle from America" will come along, a moneyed man willing to help her out of her distress. One never knows what tomorrow may bring. It may even deliver a cashmere shawl, which is the grisette's symbol of luxury, as Gustave Courbet memorably recorded in the depiction of two reprehensibly well-attired daughters of the people in his *Young Ladies on the Banks of the Seine* (1856). If the gentleman she is currently seeing does not think to give her one, she may be able to save enough money to rent one, from among those displayed at shops that cater to girls like her, before she goes out to dance at the Bullier Gardens or La Chaumière.[5] Meanwhile, carefree and careless, the grisette does not worry about tomorrow so long as she is happily living today. She is the antithesis to the seamstress in Thomas Hood's dolorous poem "The Song of the Shirt" (1843), and her life could not be more unlike that of the "underground of toilers" that Edith Wharton's Lily Bart joins when she is reduced to working as a milliner.[6] It is for this reason that Karl Marx expressed his stern revolutionary disdain for the utopian socialist Charles Fourier by accusing him of "*grisette*-like naiveté."[7]

Yet the grisette's existence is not always a bed of roses, much less the sea of lemonade that Fourier deliriously imagined—far from it. Her life is hard, wrote the most famous bóhemian in mid-nineteenth-century Paris, Alexandre Privat d'Anglemont, who adored the grisette and mocked her and identified with her, all at once. "I cannot keep myself from trembling in thinking that the unfortunate child is now forever repudiated by society because she has desired knowledge, because she has given herself to someone, or simply because she has been led on by the hope that she might dance, do nothing, be free. Because for poor girls, as for negroes," wrote Privat, whose ancestors included slaves in Guadeloupe, "liberty is quite simply the liberty to stroll around and do nothing." You cannot conceive, he lamented, how these poor pretty girls must strain their imaginations simply in order to feed themselves.[8]

By Privat's time the grisette had been around for at least two centuries, and she was always poor, always pretty, always scorned by respectable society, and always independent—so much so that she was famous for her inconstancy in matters of love. (Privat called her "the living image of caprice.")[9] Officially admitted into the sixth edition of the dictionary of the French Academy in 1835, her name had already passed into English literature by the eighteenth century, and by the 1840s she had acquired a reputation in America, Germany, Spain, and Italy, too. She was said to have taken her name from the cheap gray cloth that her ancestors had worn, but those who spoke of her never pictured her as a gray figure. On the contrary, as a young worker living away from home, on her own, a female who evidently had cut herself loose from family ties, and so seemingly from other restraints as well, the grisette was seen as a loose woman. She was "a young woman of mediocre station and suspect virtue," as one French dictionary put it in the mid-1840s.[10]

We might compare the grisette to the girls at a public dance whom Thomas Hardy describes in *Jude the Obscure* (1895) as "light women of the more respectable and amateur class" or, in other words, as "frolicsome girls who made advances—wistful to gain a little joy."[11] Sociologically, the grisette was a recognized type, the sexually available working-class girl; but her name as it was popularly understood would be better translated into contemporary English by idiomatic terms, such as "good-time girl" and "party girl," which suggest one who is notoriously "easy." Parisian argot of the early 1830s included the expression *faire une grisette*, "to make a grisette," as one might speak now in English of "trying to make some girl" or of wanting to "do" some girl; and the writer who recorded this new bit of slang generously provided his readers with simple how-to instructions toward this end.[12] This image of easy sexual availability had already been fixed by the seventeenth century, as in Jean de La Fontaine's "Joconde" (1665):

> A grisette is a treasure
> Because, with no real exertion
> Or even a ballroom excursion,
> You easily reach your goal.
> You tell her whatever you want, or often nothing at all.[13]

It is important to keep in mind, though, that in nineteenth-century France fallen women did not all fall under one name. True, close distinctions were not always made; in *The Splendors and Miseries of Courtesans* (1845), for instance, Honoré de Balzac referred to his prostitute heroine, Esther Gobseck, as a grisette. Nonetheless, the grisette was customarily distinguished from the lorette, or kept woman, who in turn was distinguished from the ordinary prostitute who plied her trade in a brothel or on the streets. In *The Latin Country* (1855) Henry Murger built his plot around precisely these distinctions, carefully tracing how a country girl becomes a grisette in the Left Bank of the 1840s, turns herself into a lorette when her romance with a medical student falls apart, but then finally reclaims herself by returning to her identity as a grisette. As the writer and journalist G. L. M. Strauss said, there was a "narrow boundary between grisettism and lorettedom," but still the boundary was observed.[14] Balzac himself had earlier written of the grisette as a distinct figure belonging in "a category apart from the other classes."[15] "Take note," wrote Louis Huart, in an opinion echoed in almost all discussions of this figure, "that in her loves the young grisette never lets herself follow some base calculation of self-interest; she always gives and never sells herself."[16] With her, Huart enthused, love is an absolutely pure gift.

In Louis-Sébastien Mercier's classic definition, set down on the eve of the

French Revolution, a grisette is a young girl "who, having neither rank nor wealth, is obliged to work in order to live, and who has no other means of support than the labor of her hands." These girls, Mercier continued, "separate themselves from their poor parents when they are eighteen years old, rent their private room, and live there just as they like—a privilege that the daughter of the comfortable bourgeois does not have."[17] Later writers, such as Hans Wachenhusen, generally followed Mercier's account, but the grisette's character acquired further definition as time went on.[18] Most notably, in the early decades of the nineteenth century she came to be closely associated with students, as in Murger's work, especially those students who were called bohemians, and at times she herself was simply referred to as the student's companion, an *étudiante*, or as a *bohémienne*, the female of this species.[19] The authors of the *Physiology of La Chaumière* (1841) exalted this pair as sharing "the same tastes, the same passions, the same insouciance toward the future," adding that "the student would not be fit for anything without the grisette."[20]

It was during the July Monarchy that the grisette really came into her own.[21] The grisette of this era reveled in her fame, at times even borrowing a name for herself from her counterpart in a popular novel, such as the adorable Rigolette in Sue's *Mysteries of Paris* (1842–43).[22] Pierre-Jean Béranger was her bard, complaining of her infidelities even as he drank to his unceasing love for her, exclaiming, "Mais vive la grisette!"[23] The apostrophized "Lisette" of his rhymed lines set the pattern for the stereotypical grisette name, as in Sue's narrative and also in Murger's *Latin Country*, in which the medical student follows the prevailing fashion by giving the newly arrived country girl the nickname "Mariette." During the 1830s and the 1840s Paul de Kock was one of the grisette's most enthusiastic chroniclers and, not incidentally, was supposed to be her favorite author.[24] Even more influential was her portrayal in the series of sketches that Murger published between 1845 and 1849 in *Le Corsaire-Satan*, which then became the basis for a wildly successful play that he cowrote with Théodore Barrière (1849), a compilation of the stories into the form of a novel (1851), and eventually, in 1896, Giacomo Puccini's beloved opera *La Bohème*. Eugène Scribe, with his one-act comedy *The Grisettes* (1822), Émile Souvestre, with *The Ladder of Women* (1835), Musset, with *Mademoiselle Mimi Pinson: Profile of a Grisette* (1845), and Champfleury, with *The Adventures of Mademoiselle Mariette* (1853), were among the other notable writers who joined with a host of forgettable scribblers to transform the grisette into a legendary figure. Popular illustrators such as Henri Monnier, Paul Gavarni, and Tony Johannot further contributed to her celebrity, as did writers abroad, such as Poe, who portrayed her in "The Mystery of Marie Roget" (1842–43). By the middle of the century it was possible to maintain that her disreputable relations with the bohemian student of the Left Bank might actually bear comparison to the immortal loves of Hero and Leander or Abelard and Heloise.[25] She might even represent a new kind of love entirely, one in which men will treat the one they desire "more as a good comrade than as a woman," as the Mariette in Champfleury's narrative says. Gérard, a young man keeping house with her, in what was jokingly called a "marriage of the thirteenth arrondissement"—there being at the time only twelve such districts in Paris—explains to his shocked mother that they live outside ordinary laws. They dwell amid a group of like-minded friends, without disturbing anyone, he insists, and freed of the concerns with money that enter into bourgeois marriage. "We take our women with us to all the public places where we go," he says, "and we respect them as if we had married them."[26]

Of course, as a recognizable social type, the grisette had always been a figure of fantasy as well. As Musset wrote, she was a "dreamy" and "romantic" kind of being.[27] As if to safeguard the fantasy, Wachenhusen took pains to assure his readers that when the aging and impoverished grisette sees her former lover now prospering in distinguished positions, "she makes no claims upon him."[28] When Mark Twain set out to debunk the legendary attractiveness of grisettes in *Innocents Abroad* (1869), then—"They were like nearly all the French women I ever saw—homely"—he was actually acting more like an ignorant lout than an innocent tourist.[29] A European humorist might as well have complained that the frogs of Calaveras County did not live up to their reputation for athleticism. Paul Lindau, a German commentator on Musset's work, showed more astuteness when he described the grisette as a "poetic image."[30] As Lindau noted, her historians typically portrayed the grisette as belonging to the good old days before the present time—that is, before whatever time it was when a given author happened to be writing about her. Even in these sorts of nostalgic accounts, though, the grisette's nature as a figure of literary fantasy was more or less openly acknowledged, as when Murger apostrophized Musette, in his *Scenes of Bohemian Life*, through an identification with the stories of Musset: "O charming girl! . . . O Mademoiselle Musette! you who are the sister of Bernerette and of Mimi Pinson!"[31]

Authors pointed readers toward this same recognition that the grisette was a literary invention when they portrayed her not only as borrowing her name from the works of popular authors such as Béranger, Sue, and De Kock but also as being self-conscious about her fictional status. In the last act of

Murger's and Barrière's play, for instance, Mimi describes a desperate state of mind in which she was ready to kill herself by saying, "I went straight out onto the bridge, like a grisette in a novel."[32] Grisettes, in other words, were made to speak of their own artifice; and others, too, when they admired the grisette, recognized that she was a kind of living doll, or sex toy, with which men liked to play. In fact, Champfleury claimed that in the late 1840s he and Courbet came across an old wax museum whose proprietor had made for himself "a wax figure representing a young girl dressed as a grisette"; this man, he said, later ran away with this figure after his wife found him sleeping with it.[33]

We see the grisette as a fantasy figure even in the pioneering journalistic account left to us by Mercier. When Mercier argues that the grisette is happier than the daughter of the bourgeois, as a result of the "complete liberty" she enjoys, today's readers may be led to remember Depression-era films such as the *Our Gang* comedy in which some poor kids decide to play hooky while the envious rich kid, prodded by his chauffeur, must reluctantly leave them to be driven back to school in his dad's fancy car.[34] Throughout the nineteenth century the figure of the grisette was made to enjoy this sentimental idealization, which we need not strain ourselves to recognize as the kind of love that gives ideology a bad name.

The flip side of this love, in which sentimentality makes the grisette a tragic figure, also proved to be entertaining. Murger showed how one could wittily turn from one side to the other in the space of a single sentence when he wrote of grisettes "asking nothing of God but a little sunshine on Sundays, vulgarly making heartfelt love, and sometimes throwing themselves out of windows."[35] In a more serious mode, the conclusion to the section on the grisette in the melodramatic *Ladder of Women* is a speech that a disgusted young medical student pronounces at the autopsy of the girl whom one of his former friends has trifled with and then abandoned. "This is justice," he says, with lugubrious irony. "You have worked, you have suffered, daughter of the people! Now you have achieved your destiny: your body has served for the *amusement* and *instruction* of the fortunate. In recognition, society will give you, in return, your place in a pit in the cemetery!"[36]

These forms of sentimentality might seem to run counter to portrayals of the grisette in which appreciation for her pleasure-loving attitude, careless of conventionalities, continued to show traces of La Fontaine's smutty lubricity. (A notable example would be Jules Janin's characterization of her as "a fine game bird that is caught by the most commonplace bird-lime.")[37] In reality, however, there was no contradiction. We can see as much in Balzac's

The Duchess of Langeais (1834) when Armand de Montriveau literally and figuratively brings the duchess to her knees, compelling her to love him and thus moving her to say, "I would be a grisette for you and a queen for the others."[38] This dramatic moment simultaneously reveals the romantic image of the grisette and the brutal social infrastructure of that fantasy.

In art as in life, the grisette was subject to exploitation, liable to be treated as nothing more than a prop in a masculine drama. Whether that drama at any given moment happened to involve admiration, tears, or leers, it was still subordinating the grisette to its ends. As university towns now often experience an increase in the numbers of abandoned dogs at the end of each semester, so did grisettes find the long vacation at the end of the university year a trying time.[39] The love that joined students and grisettes, Émile de La Bédollièrre wrote, is not really the sweet passion represented in theaters; often the student treats the grisette "scarcely better than a servant."[40] The anonymous authors of the *Physiologie of La Chaumière* had proclaimed that "the grisettes are the houris" of the students, but in everyday life these were houris whom men found "as easy to leave as to take," as Auguste Luchet observed.[41] In "A Prince of Bohemia" (1844) Balzac took the measure of this situation when he reported that bohemians had created a "burlesque maxim" about love: "Toutes les femmes sont égales devant l'homme."[42] Women in bohemia, in other words, are not equal *to* men, but equal *before* them, or for all intents and purposes interchangeable with one another. Even De Kock, the enthusiastic panegyrist of these good-time girls, said that "if you have known two or three grisettes, you know them all."[43] According to Wedekind, who was the notorious author of the sexually frank *Spring Awakening* (1891), among other works, this situation remained much the same in his era. When he observed students living with "the world-renowned grisettes" of the Latin Quarter, his disillusioned comment was that the way his artist friends in Munich played around with their models was more romantic.[44]

This fundamentally negligent attitude toward grisettes was so prevalent that no one would have dreamed of contesting it. Murger, for instance, boasted that bohemians would never let their devotion to a woman get in the way, even for a second, of their bonds with male friends.[45] So much for the comradeship to which Champfleury made his Mariette testify, knowing full well that such equality is not so easily gained.[46] A careful reader might remember, too, passages such as the one in *The Water Drinkers* (1855) in which Murger drew an implicit parallel between paying off one's creditors and dismissing one's grisette lovers: "One has creditors when young, just as one has mistresses, because it's necessary to live, and it's necessary to love, but the creditors do not prevent one from becoming a respectable man, just as the mistresses do not prevent one from being an excellent husband."[47] Despite his reputation as a great sentimentalist, Murger did not hesitate to let his grisettes show their awareness of how they were being toyed with, as when Mariette in *The Latin Country* speaks of the student who was her first love: "On the arm of Edward I was nothing but the living flag of his vanity."[48] The fantasy of the grisette was indeed one directed toward pure pleasure, but everyone—except, perhaps, writers from Hannibal, Missouri—understood that one could not take this fantasy too seriously.

It was an exceptional moment, then, when Murger's close friend Nadar, who was neither a sentimentalist nor a Fourierist advocate of women's rights, felt that Murger had gone too far even for him. At the dress rehearsal of the semi-autobiographical play that would make Murger famous, Nadar was shocked when he heard its protagonist, Rodolphe, cry out at the death of his beloved Mimi, "Oh, my youth! It is you that we bury!"[49] Afterward, he bitterly complained about this "abominable" phrase—all the more egregious in its egotism, surely, given Nadar's acquaintance with the real-life counterpart to the character nicknamed Mimi, a young woman who bore this character's original name of Lucile. Murger, however, calmly shrugged off his criticism, saying, "It's true to life."[50] Nadar comes off as the more likable figure in this exchange, but Murger was the realist, as any grisette who had chanced to overhear the two men speaking would surely have recognized.

While it is crucial to note how the grisette was made to amuse and instruct men, however, this recognition only begins to provide what we need to know about her. As a cultural figure, the grisette in this era is remarkable precisely because she herself rejects the idealization and objectification that entered into the social reality of her legend. As Théodore Muret said, describing her relation to the predictable tears, farewells, promises of faithfulness, and realities of abandonment when the students of the Quarter came to the end of their studies, "The grisette knows all that."[51] She knows perfectly well that she must contend with exploitation, just as she knows that hers is not a position of much power. "Boys are much happier in this world," says Anna, Souvestre's exemplary grisette. "When they are born poor, they can become rich through their work; if they love somebody, they are not dishonored as a result. Oh, I would really have liked to be a boy!"[52] In the culture of this era the grisette's awareness of her social condition explains why the happiness she promises, in all its attractive simplicity, is irreducibly complex: a promise of inconstant love, reckless generosity, freedom more asserted than real, and pleasure that senses its bad end from its very beginning. The grisette leaves home, she goes to work, she takes pride in her independence—and she knows as well as everyone else what pride goeth before, not only in Christian homiletics but also, and even more compellingly, in the world of modern work.

As a cultural figure of uncompromising promise, the grisette exceeds both her grim social history and the oppressive cultural attitudes that enter into her representation. Although she stands outside traditional morality, she does not accept the alternative ethics enjoined by the modern marketplace. As commerce strips the world of pride, replacing that quaint human affectation with the occult powers of capital, she dares not to be for sale. She is no more the glum barmaid of Édouard Manet's *A Bar at the Folies-Bergère* (1881–82) than she is the sweated seamstress of Hood's poem. What is more, she refuses to act on the basis of self-interest, and she refuses to be accountable for how she does act. At the same time that she takes pride in the independence she gains from her work, she insists on desiring in utter defiance of economic reality. She is a consumer, yes; in thinking of his inconstant Mimi, Rodolphe considers that her infidelities were usually with "a shawl, with a hat, with things and not with men."[53] As this comment illustrates, though, her attraction to such things does not detract from her integrity. Like the shabbiness of her surroundings, the grisette's consumer desires contribute to her allure and allow her to stand, in propria persona, as a powerful rebuke to the glamour of commodities. She is not one of them; and, though she likes and desires them, she is not their devotee. As Janin wrote, hers is "a separate world within the world."[54] She is economic unreason personified and made so radiantly attractive that the very inconstancy in her relations with men becomes an essential part of her charm. Possessing practically nothing, "she is much more than rich."[55] With a heart full of joy, "gay in her work, wild in her pleasure," she never stops singing, even in her suffering: "her life is a dream."[56]

We see her in a characteristic moment, for example, in a comedy by Paul de Kock and Charles Labie, *The Clerk and the Grisette* (1834). When her bourgeois suitor complains of her expensive tastes, she responds by declaring, "Nothing is too good for me!"[57] As Charles Coligny wrote in 1861, "What the grisette wants, or rather what the grisette wanted once upon a time in the Latin Quarter, was equivalent to the divine law."[58] This attitude was nicely captured in the libretto Giuseppe Giacosa and Luigi Illica wrote for *La Bohème*, in which Musette is brought to exclaim, quite simply, "I want to do as I please."[59]

Her symbol of luxury may be "a cashmere," but in her desire for such things the grisette rejects any boundary between necessity and luxury. Consequently, in her own person she serves her culture as a figure who transcends this opposition. If in the figure of the grisette we see an exploitation of social, economic, and cultural differences, as we assuredly do, we also see a search for the courage to live up to the desires that literature assigns to her, as when it suggests that she "simply follows the laws of nature, the naive and sincere movements of pleasure and of voluptuousness."[60] While it serves as an occasion for the exercise of imagination, then, the poetic image of the grisette also registers deep social dissatisfactions, which erupt in her divinely impatient insistence on diversion.

In their most obvious aspect, the energizing dissatisfactions at work in the popular legend of the grisette form a critique of the institution of marriage and the family. Murger said that the grisette's thirteenth arrondissement is ruled over by "the minister of caprice" because spontaneous alliances, temporary sexual relationships, and improvised moralities within this imaginary district seem effectively to displace the established social order.[61] Viewed from this perspective, the grisette may call to mind Fourier's criticism of the "incoherent" nature of domesticity in modern civilization, which is "incompatible with the nature of the passions"; and certainly some argument at least distantly akin to this courses through her legend, in which housework and procreation never appear except when situations turn tragic, putting an end to the poetry of her life.[62] Going beyond this argument, though, the legendary figure of the grisette plays an even more provocative role. She calls into question not only domesticity but also political economy. It is not only the order of the household but also the order of the modern nation that she transcends.

It seems inevitable, then, that her transcendence should be short-lived. Utterly spontaneous and happy in her disreputable life, taking pride in both her labor and her love, the grisette refuses to be useful or calculating, abject or cynical, in either of these activities. Powerful as it is, however, her pride cannot withstand the economic logic of modernity. This is the lesson her career in nineteenth-century literature, art, drama, and popular culture teaches us. In an increasingly utilitarian world, her inconsequentiality is an intolerable affront. In the end, she must be defeated.

This defeat takes a special form quite unlike the punishment dealt out to her sadly erring bourgeois sisters. Because the grisette cannot be made to pay in commercial terms, because she refuses to be merely useful or merely calculating, she must be broken. This event may take place by way of immiseration, self-betrayal, a tell-tale cough, or advancing years, but take place it must. From the very beginning the prospect of this end is essential to her beauty. Theodor Adorno would no doubt have wished to demur, given his devotion to high culture, but the grisette perfectly illustrates his claim that art does not represent the promise of happiness (as in Stendahl's well-known formulation) but rather reminds us of "the ever broken promise of happiness."[63] It is because she was always to be broken that the grisette could be such an enchanting figure in nineteenth-century culture. If such had not been the case, she would have appeared as something else entirely: an angel or demon unbearable to look upon, a figure destructive of all humanity, like the loose woman as she appeared to Pierre-Joseph Proudhon's panicked vision in his notorious tirade, published posthumously, *Pornocracy, or Women in Modern Times* (1875).

In other words, the grisette was a fantasy figure that came complete with built-in disillusionment. She was a compromise formation, and her contradictions constituted her appeal. In the grisette one could entertain revolutionary aspirations and postrevolutionary aimlessness, all at once, while still persisting in desire; and writers of the time were fully aware of the role assigned her.[64] Accordingly, in Auguste Ricard's 1827 novel about this figure, the happiest state to which one can aspire is that of a grisette "who, fresh, pretty, and still youthful, has just abandoned a lover with whom she did not get along and, free of all ties, happy in the hope, the gaiety, and the independence that is her lot, disengaged in the present, unconcerned about the past, smiles at the future with all the abandon of her light heart and easy morals."[65] Complete with epigraphs from Béranger and narrative interjections that express liberal sympathies for the working classes, Ricard's novel presents the grisette as a figure who most truly exists only in the vanishing instants of her life. The rest of her time is spent in passing from one unsatisfactory lover to another, abandoning her child, finding that her sexual history narrows her opportunities, trying out a marriage that ends in failure, and, finally, returning to her life as a girl of the working classes, which by that point no longer appears as an ideal of independence but instead seems an inescapable condition.

Privat, too, saw the grisette as a figure whose idealization encompassed disillusionment. In his booklets on the Prado and the Closerie des Lilas, dance halls that were the native habitats of grisettes at play, Privat blazoned their charms and proclaimed their cultural significance, going so far as to attribute to Saint Theresa the contemporary bohemian cliché about the Latin Quarter of one's youth: "How happy I was when I was so unhappy!"[66] Nonetheless, in the midst of such praise he was perfectly capable of delivering a withering analysis of married men who delude themselves into seeing flirtations with grisettes as restoring the freedom of their youth, showing these guys as being stupidly trapped in yet another version of the commercial competition that structured their daily lives. We are so enslaved by civilized prejudices, Privat said, that we love to get the better of one another; and so, if a grisette chances to distinguish us for a moment, "we feel certain that we have beat out at least twenty-five of our fellow citizens, and we are happy."[67] In describing the grisettes' own stories, Privat was just as unsparing. "All tell you the same romantic and unbelievable tale of being kidnapped by handsome and charming young men. . . . All have been betrayed. . . . He was a count, never a marquis, or sometimes a baron, and most often a viscount." With all their tales taking the form of variations on commonplace themes, such as the one in which the grisette loses her innocence in a painter's studio, we are led to conclude that "nothing is as sad and tedious as a woman of pleasure."[68] In pitching his proposal that he ghostwrite a novel for Sue about girls of this sort, Privat depicted them as laboring in workshops from the time they were six years old, frequenting the Latin Quarter as grisettes between the ages of sixteen and eighteen, and then entering a bordello, the theater, a marriage with a rich foreigner, or a hospital.[69]

The fluffiest pieces of grisette literature, such as De Kock's story "The Grisettes' Ball" (1842), might not bother to display this sort of disillusionment in any explicit way, but still it always environed this cultural figure. After all, even aside from any of their other distresses, grisettes could have but a brief career. It was always assumed that they were washed up by the age of thirty, which was also the age when the typical bohemian was expected to bow to the yoke and become a responsible adult. (In putting a stop to the grisette's career at the age of eighteen, as in putting her to work at the age of six, Privat was exaggerating in his strenuous attempt to sell Sue on his project.) Everyone knew that there was a fatality to the grisette's carelessness and that this was a crucial aspect of her charm, just as everyone knew that there was something exploitative in the cult of the grisette, for all her vaunted independence. After all, she was, as the saying goes, generous to a fault. Had she not been so, she could not have held out so much meaning to the culture of her time; for this fault, her predetermined doom, was what enabled her to stand as a reproof to the endless progress supposedly represented by the modern marketplace. Edmond and Jules de Goncourt showed her in precisely this role when they complained of a depressing evening at a masked ball in 1857, which led them to feel that "pleasure is dead": "The lorette is no longer that lorette of Gavarni, still retaining a little of the grisette and idling away her time in amusing herself—it's a woman-man of affairs who submits to the marketplace without flourishes."[70] Here we have the antithesis to the bohemian "hermaphroditism," as it was termed, of George Sand. Similarly, when Friedrich Nietzsche offered his sour observation in 1886 that " 'the woman as office boy' is written on the entrance to the developing modern society," he was picturing a marketplace that had no memory of, much less any feeling for, all that went into the legends around the grisettes at work in the shops, factories, and businesses of Paris in the second quarter of the century.[71]

Predictably, the high point of this figure's ascendancy was also the time when a generation of writers began to complain that the grisette of their youth, like the snows of yesteryear, had disappeared. In a story set in the aftermath of the July Revolution, Nadar described her as already having disappeared at that time.[72] Antonio Watripon, a contemporary chronicler of the Latin Quarter, agreed with him, saying that she died in 1836; and both he and Nadar preserved the lyrics of a popular song from around 1840, "My Old Latin Quarter," which declared that "today the *étudiante* is a lorette."[73] She now wants nothing more to do with students, Privat complained in 1846; Murger echoed this lament in 1851. In an 1860 *roman à clef* about Sand, Musset, and Gustave Flaubert, Louise Colet had Musset, too, regretting the transformation of grisettes into lorettes around the middle of the century; and in 1864 De Kock nostalgically looked back to the 1840s, lamenting that grisettes were no more to be found.[74] The dating may be very approximate, and other writers, such as Wedekind, would still be observing grisettes throughout the rest of the century; but it is true that the heyday of the grisette was coming to an end around this time, in which the specific issues of class, gender, and economic rationality played out through her legendary character were increasingly overshadowed by broader questions about women's nature, role, and place in society. Although the grisette is still completely recognizable, for instance, in Diego Vicente Tejera's poem "Celia," written in the late 1870s, and in George du Maurier's *Trilby*, which was published in 1894 and set in the 1850s and 1860s, by the second half of the century she was being absorbed into a more generalized figure of the female bohemian, losing her distinctively working-class genealogy.[75]

Even with this transformation, however, the disturbing force of the grisette's modernity lived on, as Proudhon recognized when he identified bohemians as prime culprits in the creation of independent women who were threatening to drive society into utter chaos. In his portrayal of bohemia in this era, Proudhon set out the reactionary position in a form that could not have been much more extreme. Woman was not the only object of Proudhon's fury; he liked to indulge in racism and anti-Semitism as well as misogyny. His outrage over women was especially robust, though, and is tellingly related to the reconsideration of the grisette after the mid-nineteenth century, when she was being absorbed into the more generalized figure of the female bohemian.

In his memoirs, Champfleury noted that Proudhon, in the middle of Paris, still remained bound to his origins in Franche-Comté, "a region where, in the villages, women serve at the table and sit down only after the men have left"; but the philosopher's opinions were not merely provincial or idiosyncratic.[76] The conservative Elme-Marie Caro, for instance, who denounced the revolutionary Paris Commune of 1871 as the logical outcome of bohemianism, was happy to identify himself with this socialist's ideas about women.[77] For Proudhon, any woman who is out in public in any way, whether literally in the streets, figuratively putting herself forward through her writing, or simply thinking of emancipation, can be accounted a prostitute, a *fille publique*. Proudhon wrote specifically in opposition to the French feminists Juliette Lambert and Jenny d'Héricourt and also against contending socialist camps, like the Saint-Simonians and the Fourierists, who had supported the idea of equality for women, but bohemia was his catch-all category for such misguided persons.[78] Bohemia is, he said, the party of pornocracy, whose ethos he scathingly summarized as "Work little, drink a lot, and make love."[79]

Through his apocalyptic criticism the venerable socialist demanded, in so many words, that the grisette must be subjected to the political economy she seemed to flout. In this respect his work closely resembles the Goncourts' contemporaneous *Manette Salomon* (1867). In this novel the protagonist is transformed from a model possessing the lyrical spirit of the typical grisette— "Life without independence, the right to do whatever she pleased, was incomprehensible to her"—into a vulgar, domineering, completely mercenary figure for whom, "as a woman and a Jew," the only meaning art has lies in the price it may fetch.[80] For Proudhon as for the Goncourts, it was no longer sufficient that the grisette be broken after her evanescent youth. She must instead be considered a prostitute from the moment she leaves the sanctity of the home, which is the only place she is allowed to escape reduction to a marketplace commodity. Their attitudes echo that of the former police commissioner of Paris, F.-F.-A. Béraud, who gave over the last two chapters of his two-volume work on prostitution, *The Prostitutes of Paris, and the Police Who Oversee Them* (1839), to the grisette. Even though his portrayal of this figure was generally faithful to the popular stereotype, showing her as a light-hearted girl who "lives happily in her garret," he could not countenance her desire to escape economic strictures. To make the grisette a proper subject of political economy, in keeping with his responsibilities as an administrative official, while at the same time recognizing her popular image, he was forced to resort to an oxymoron, "disinterested prostitution," to describe her activities.[81] The public had to be taught that the grisette's freedom, like everything else, had a price.

Just as Johann Wolfgang von Goethe's *Wilhelm Meister's Apprenticeship* (1795–96) prefigured the invention of nineteenth-century bohemia, so did his *Elective Affinities* (1809) anticipate the social disorder that figures such as Proudhon would attribute to this invention. In fact, references to this work often crop up in conjunction with representations of bohemia throughout this century, as when an aspiring writer describes his work-in-progress in a novel by the English writer J. Fitzgerald Molloy, *It Is No Wonder: A Story of Bohemian Life* (1882): "All the characters fall in love with those they should not *à la* elective affinities."[82] Bohemians, naturally, made light of their reputation for disreputability, sexual and otherwise. Alexandre Schanne, for instance, who had been one of Murger's intimates when both were young men, tells in his memoirs of how he used to receive letters from Henri Monnier that were addressed "To Monsieur Alexandre Schanne, painter and musician, *member of the dangerous classes of society.*"[83] Then as now, young men would spoof their elders and have their fun. In the second half of the century, though, Proudhon was far from being alone in seeing bohemia as a world that perverted women and through these women threatened society in general with catastrophic consequences.

By the last two decades of the century, in fact, this sense of threat had even traveled overseas, appearing in American works such as Charles De Kay's *The Bohemian: A Tragedy of Modern Life* (1878), Lily Curry's *A Bohemian Tragedy* (1886), and Henry S. Brooks's "A Catastrophe in Bohemia" (1893). In all these narratives bohemia takes advantage of female vulnerability and so leads to female destructiveness. In De Kay's semisatirical and thoroughly ridiculous melodrama, a young woman who associates herself with some would-be bohemians drives one of them to throw himself under a train by light-heartedly repulsing an advance from another man with amusement, rather than with the outrage he considers appropriate to the occasion. Like De Kay's novel, Curry's *A Bohemian Tragedy* also describes a group of imitation bohemians as the backdrop to a deadly romantic tragedy, which in this case involves a young woman betrayed by a man who had promised to leave his wife for her; in revenge, she shoots herself in front of the tenaciously married couple. Confronted by one of the young woman's friends, who has read her diary— "I did not know how you had labored not only to blast her life through love for you, but also to destroy her faith in all others—even her faith in God Himself"—the guilt-stricken seducer, with no oncoming train at hand, must resort to the *pis aller* of throwing himself to his death down a convenient elevator shaft.[84] Brooks's "A Catastrophe in Bohemia" takes the same sort of plot even further by making its protagonist a girl raised in a bohemian household from her infancy. Due to the effects on her character from "the unsuitableness of her surroundings," she must end up bearing responsibility for the deaths of both her lover and her father.[85]

Other American works further agreed with Proudhon in explicitly identifying bohemia as the *fons et origo* of agitation over the emancipation of women. These include Marie Le Baron's *The Villa Bohemia* (1882), William Dean Howells's *The Coast of Bohemia* (1893), and Margaret Sherwood's *A Puritan Bohemia* (1896), which virtually cover the spectrum of possible attitudes toward the Woman Question in this era. *The Villa Bohemia* is a satire in which four girls rent a house so they can live independently and free of social conventions; the title page's engraving of the sign in front of their house, "No Man Permitted on these Premises under Penalty of Law," invites the reader to smile in anticipation of the novel's conclusion, in which all four girls will discard their silly feminist impulses in favor of suitable marriages.[86] This work might be contrasted to the satire by the English socialist Robert Blatchford, *A Bohemian Girl and McGinnis* (1899), in which a gentleman's romance with a music-hall singer stands in contrast to spokespersons for the "New Woman," women's rights activists, and women with literary pretensions; but in both cases bohemia is the vehicle through which the question of woman is defined and denigrated, in keeping with reactionary attitudes toward the legacy of the grisette. Howells's novel nearly reaches an equivalent level of silliness, telling as it does of a young woman whose affair with an established male painter is almost ruined because once, years before, she had let another man kiss her. Howells does manage, however, not to bring railroad trains or elevator shafts into his plot, and he gives some voice to the tensions within female ambition—"If I can't succeed as men succeed, and be a great painter, and not just a great *woman* painter, I'd rather be excused altogether"—even as he mocks the notion that the life of bohemia could find any real purchase in American soil.[87] A quite different tack is taken by Sherwood in *A Puritan Bohemia*. Her protagonist, Anne Bradford, is an aspiring New England artist embroiled in a romance with one Howard Stanton, a painter of modernist sensibility and socialist politics. Refusing to subordinate her artistic ambitions to a marriage with him, she finds herself in a community, "a new Bohemia, woman's Bohemia in a Puritan City," among other "earnest women" like herself.[88] There she again refuses Stanton, choosing instead to end the novel in a Boston marriage, sharing a house with a female friend. The novel then ends wickedly, perfectly, with Stanton, the suitor Bradford has spurned, pledging his love to one of her friends by using exactly the same words with which he had earlier proposed to her.

Whatever she may have been in La Fontaine's time, then, by the nineteenth century the grisette was no longer a plaything for any passing rogue. She was still a public figure, but she was not just any girl of the streets. What made her attractive as a cultural subject was also what made her disturbing. Mercier had made this point early on when he said that the grisette's life might justifiably inspire envy in the daughter of the bourgeois, and the fact that he had done so in the mode of sentimental idealization does not detract from the importance of his observation. One can readily understand why the grisette's example might seem dangerous to bourgeois parents with daughters of their own at home even when they were prepared to wink at their sons' affairs with this sort of working-class girl. Though he admired their freedom and proposed compassionate social policies to ameliorate their lives, Mercier himself could not refrain from expressing his "astonishment" at "this immense mob of nubile girls who, because of their position, have become strangers alike to marriage and to celibacy." In his astonishment we can see all the enchantment that the figure of the grisette would hold over the nineteenth century, and in it we can also see the fearfulness of that enchantment. Ultimately, Mercier concluded, there is no middle ground: "Either we must grant women the same liberty enjoyed by the men with whom they are continually mixing, or, following Asiatic customs, they must be sequestered and have no communication with the outside world."[89] He recommended the former plan, but he understood the latter urge. Thus, presciently, he described the divisive force that the grisette's legend would exert right to the end of the nineteenth century.

In a quick caricature, such as a long-haired artist might sketch on a studio wall, early nineteenth-century bohemia might appear to consist of the rebellious sons of the middle classes pursuing the arts and, with them, the loose daughters of the working classes. This depiction would hold some truth, and yet it gives us little help in understanding the power of the humble grisette, which was so great that it even alarmed observers in Victorian England who could know nothing of the hysteria that the aged Proudhon was setting to paper. Before America learned to associate bohemia with the Woman Question, England taught it how to make the grisette pay for her pleasures. To name only a few examples, her story is at the heart of important novels by Charlotte Brontë, Thackeray, and Eliot. One might be tempted to say that these anti-grisette novels reflect the fact that France had the syphilitic Charles Baudelaire as its most brilliant critic of art whereas England had the moralizing and, it was rumored, impotent John Ruskin, but they cannot really be explained by clichés about national character or mores. What we see in these novels is that English tradition must defend itself against the grisette precisely because this figure is viewed as bearing the truth of modern desire. She has to be treated as a foreign invader only because she appears all too native to England.

The heroine of *Jane Eyre* (1847), for example, is plain but otherwise almost perfectly grisette-qualified: poor, independent, and careless of conventions. Having been incompletely inoculated against his bohemian ways through an affair with a willful French actress, Brontë's hero tries to persuade this heroine to move abroad with him, where they can be strangers alike to marriage and to celibacy. Reader, she does not go with him, though she is so powerfully tempted that she ends up literally crawling on the ground and eating pig slop as she struggles to contend against her desires. Crawling on one's belly like a reptile makes for a powerful image; but still Brontë felt the need to rework this plot and clarify its intent in a posthumously published novel, *The Professor* (1857), in which the narrator, William Crimsworth, explicitly refers to his beloved as his "poor little grisette sweetheart."[90] Crimsworth has turned to his lacemaker sweetheart because he fears that his involvement with a woman affianced to another man might otherwise lead him to become embroiled in a "modern French novel." His grisette fulfills the expectations he has had of her by proving herself to be studious, dutiful, and quite emphatically not sexually free, in marked contrast to her counterparts in those French texts he so despises.[91] Even as she nominally included a grisette in her decidedly English novel, then, Brontë effectively rejected this figure, since she stripped her of everything signified by the French word *grisette*. She simply emptied out this word and filled it with her notion of a respectable English girl.

A comparable rejection of the grisette is achieved in *Vanity Fair* (1848), but in this case by tracing the consequences of just such a relationship as Jane Eyre rejects. In Thackeray's novel a poor, pretty, independent love child of bohemian parents ends up posing a Napoleonic threat to England's men and maidens until she finally reverts to type at the end of the narrative, where we find that she has resumed a louche existence abroad. She does not do so, however, before Thackeray candidly presents Becky Sharpe as the truth of the desires that drive modern English society. His "novel without a hero" does have a heroine, and the resourceful, brave, and mercenary Becky, as he takes pains to point out, is it.[92] Eliot's *Daniel Deronda* (1876) provides yet another version of this anti-grisette plot through the character of Mirah Lapidoth, who is both literally and figuratively a Bohemian. Born in Prague and raised in various countries within a poor, theatrical, immoral household, Mirah finds true love and authentic art only after she breaks away from her father, who wants to pander her to a count who would then transform her from a grisette into a lorette. Once again, as we see Mirah properly domesticated, the desire represented by the grisette is repulsed even as its disturbing reality is acknowledged. In this case the acknowledgment is reinforced through the figure of Daniel Deronda's mother, the antitype to Mirah: a once-celebrated performer who is proud of the bohemian independence that led her to abandon Daniel as an infant. Through her the attractiveness of the grisette's modernity is recognized—for Daniel is duly impressed by his mother's fierce sense of pride and determination to be an independent woman—and yet finally, in the overall scheme of the novel, the grisette is made out to be alien to English art, aesthetics, and social life.

In *Jude the Obscure* (1895) Hardy reflected on the consequences of this anti-grisette tradition in the past half-century of English literature. In the happiest episode of the novel he allowed Jude to live a wandering gypsy life with Sue Bridehead, the classical grisette: a poor, pretty girl who works in a shop, values her independence, has lived with a student, and can be made amenable, after an interval of suitable English *froideur*, to extramarital sex.[93] Like George du Maurier's *Trilby* (1894), another fin-de-siècle reflection upon the grisette, *Jude the Obscure* seeks to counter her condemnation in the mid-Victorian novel. *Trilby* works to create sympathy for its protagonist by showing that her rejection by proper English society pushes her into the arms of the musician, promoter, and mesmerist Svengali, the ultimate in demonic and perfidiously Jewish bohemians, whereas Hardy creates sympathy for Sue by showing that her eventual capitulation to proper English society must entail her submission to the disgusting touch, the godawful marital demands, of the petit-bourgeois Richard Phillotson. Taken together, these two novels—one a sensational popular success, the other an occasion of popular scandal before it was canonized as a masterpiece—mark the bitter end of Victorian literature's determination that the would-be grisette must learn never to leave home and never to wish to do so.

The problem was not that the grisette was immoral. As a loose woman, a social and cultural figure subject to exploitation, the grisette posed no problem to the English novel, which could easily have embraced her with its own idealizing, tragic, and lubricious measures, such as those applied to fallen women in Frances Trollope's *Jessie Phillips* (1843), Charles Dickens's *David Copperfield* (1850), Elizabeth Gaskell's *Ruth* (1853), and Eliot's *Adam Bede* (1859). The problem was that the grisette refused to be a proper subject of political economy. In France her recklessness might look like a compromise formation between revolutionary aspirations and postrevolutionary aimlessness, but in England, with its very different social, political, economic, and cultural history, this recklessness looked like an absolute perversion not only of women's nature but of human nature in general. Through her history the grisette suggested that political economy did not have a foundation in the home, through her character that it had no foundation in desire, and through her attractiveness that it was rationally unfounded; and all these suggestions were as intolerable to the logic of the nineteenth-century English novel as they were to the popular image of the English nation. Therefore, in works such as *Jane Eyre*, *Vanity Fair*, and *Daniel Deronda* the life of the grisette is imaginable only in terms of abjection, as with Jane and Mirah, or cynicism, as with Becky. These are precisely the terms on which the popularized figure of the grisette in France refused to live, but they reflect the fact that she could be translated into English only if she were first subjected to the premises of political economy and thus, as a cultural figure, made to pay. Brontë, therefore, had Crimsworth's sweetheart in *The Professor* work her way up from lacemaker to schoolteacher and then to schoolmistress in the course of the novel, thus exemplifying her identification with a notion of middle-class economic progress that her doom-laden antecedents in French literature and art were designed to mock.

This rewriting of the terms that define the grisette was not entirely a mistranslation. Even in the heyday of the grisette a few French commentators, such as the aforementioned Béraud, insisted on subjecting her to the demands of political economy, thus presaging the scornful revisionary works of the Goncourts and Proudhon.[94] As I have been concerned to emphasize, in her native land it was always clear, too, that the popular image of the grisette was a fantasy allowed to dance free of its ostensible origin in the social reality of working girls' lives: the reality of poverty, powerlessness, constraint, and victimization that environs the mythology of the grisette and explains the fatality of her carelessness. In his melancholy story "The Last Rendezvous" (1851), in which former lovers look back on their bohemian youth, Murger himself suggested that "all joy must be paid for."[95] In the long run, the grisette's life was as untenable in France as it was in England.

The difference is that the Victorian novel, in effect, takes the grisette's ultimate doom as her utter negation. Defining the terms of its realism in contradistinction to the pride and independence of the grisette, insisting as well on a formal, thematic, and ideological faith in individual development and social progress antithetical to the grisette's spectacular recklessness, the Victorian novel refused to be entertained by her. A figure of modernity—and so distinctively urban but not exclusively French—the grisette was not really foreign to England, as Victorian writers recognized. The commonplace identification of France with sexual license and political radicalism, however, invited English novelists to misrecognize desires venturing forth from their own homes as threats coming from abroad. As a result, the anti-grisette tradition grew to be constitutive, in large part, of English literature of this era. The truths of womanhood, desire, domesticity, and sociality in the Victorian novel could never have emerged as they did without the inspiration of this misrecognition.

Jane Eyre, *Vanity Fair*, and *Daniel Deronda* are all noteworthy contributions to the nineteenth-century English novel's record of near-perfect success in repulsing the grisette. The greatest work of this kind, however, in part because it is the most generous in appreciating the enchantment of the pleasure-loving grisette, is Eliot's *Mill on the Floss* (1860). If we see her in relation to the grisette, we find why Eliot's Maggie Tulliver briefly runs away from home, always feels at odds with it, works away from it, dreams of escaping it, eventually is driven out of it, fears that she will have to wander far away from it for the rest of her life, but, in the end, returns to it and, in her heart, has never really left it. We learn why Maggie, stuck where she is, cannot have a life like that of Mary Ann Evans, the woman who came to be known as George Eliot, the internationally famous author of renowned literary works. We discover that the home Maggie never really leaves is not her place of birth by the river Floss but the birthplace of bohemia by the Seine. Maggie is circumscribed by the modern city of Paris, not the provincial environs of St. Oggs. She cannot leave her home because she has never been there.

The bohemia of the grisette borrowed its name from the people known to the English-speakers of this era as Gypsies, and Maggie from her birth is associated with Gypsies and once even tries to run away to join them and be their queen. The consummate grisette "never reflects until after she has acted," and this is also the case with Maggie throughout her life.[96] Eliot descants on her recklessness in relatively minor actions, as when she impetuously chops off her tormentingly nonblond hair, and in those of greater consequence, as when she permits herself the ecstasy of being rowed down a river by a handsome young man while putting out of her head any thoughts of the consequences certain to follow from the fact that he happens to be engaged to her cousin, who is a pattern of propriety. The grisette's working-class background is paralleled by that of Maggie, whose family loses its borderline middle-class status when her bankrupted father is reduced from master to employee and her brother from would-be gentleman to common clerk. As the grisette is aware of how much better men have it in the world around her, so, most emphatically, is Maggie. Like the grisette, Maggie is a needleworker, doing plain stitching, when she is not laboring as a teacher under miserable conditions—for she, like the grisette, has not had the benefits of much formal schooling. Like the grisette, too, Maggie takes pride in her work, insisting on living independently despite earnest entreaties from her brother and one of her aunts that she come to live with them. The typical grisette must, of course, have an affair with an artist, and so must Maggie, with Philip Wakem, an aspiring painter. Although their relationship is entirely intellectual and emotional, the hatred between Mr. Tulliver and Philip's father lends this affair all the charge of a scandalous sexual relationship—illicitness, danger, intense pleasure, and shame—while withholding only the epidermal friction. Living just as she likes, the grisette is inconstant in her affairs and often considers trading up from a bohemian lover to a bourgeois who might buy her a cashmere and perhaps even marry her, as the illustrious poet Heinrich Heine, for instance, married Augustine Mirat, whom he met when she was working as a shopgirl selling shoes; and Maggie abandons Philip Wakem for Stephen Guest, the dreamboat scion of Guest and Company, a thriving trading concern. Stephen's attraction to her, in fact, is spurred on by the pride that Maggie shows in openly admitting, within the genteel environment of her cousin Lucy's house, that her sewing is so accomplished because she has been obliged to earn her living by it. "If Maggie had been the queen of coquettes," Eliot comments, "she could hardly have invented a means of giving greater piquancy to her beauty in Stephen's eyes" (332).[97] Knowing this much, one need scarcely be told the rest: the grisette must be broken, and so must Eliot's heroine.

Although she is never named as such, Maggie is obviously a grisette, but Eliot's brilliant version of the anti-grisette story subtly tweaks certain of its elements. Philip, for instance, is a bohemian who never wanders away from home and who receives his father's support even when he confesses his inappropriate love for the daughter of the abhorred Mr. Tulliver. Whereas the stereotypical bohemian might be described as a disinherited prince who bears a grievance against the father, society, and history that refuse to honor his vocation, Philip is simply disabled as a result of a childhood accident. In no way is he an unrecognized genius; he is merely ineffectual and, therefore, thoroughly unromantic. It only makes sense, then, that Stephen should be similarly at odds with what one would expect of his bourgeois brethren in France. Although he is wealthy and self-satisfied, he does not represent bourgeois philistinism. Instead, he possesses all of the intoxicating sexuality of which Philip's character has been stripped. It is Stephen who suggests that he and Maggie should go abroad, in good bohemian style, once they have recognized their love for each other. Just as Maggie is the anti-grisette and Philip the antibohemian, Stephen is the antibourgeois. Thus did Eliot, step by systematic step, transform the modern urban world of independent desire represented by the grisette into the traditional provincial world of duty, obligation, and resignation that is *The Mill on the Floss*. She demanded that the grisette surrender her happiness, swallow her pride, forget about the very notion of fun, bow to economic rationality, and return to her home. No reader of this novel can be surprised to learn that when Eliot read Béranger, a little more than a year before she set to work on *The Mill on the Floss*, she professed herself "thoroughly disappointed" with his verse.[98] Nor will the reader be surprised to learn that Eliot, while willing to credit Murger's *Vie de bohème* with some wittiness, thought this author's heroines would be much better off if they learned how to keep accounts.[99]

A comparison of *The Mill on the Floss* to Franziska zu Reventlow's *Ellen Olestjerne* (1903) can help to clarify just how close Eliot came to writing a bohemian novel. Like Eliot, Reventlow had left her family and made herself a figure of public notoriety by deciding to become an artist and, in the course of doing so, flouting the social and sexual conventions of her society. As a child, her heroine, like Maggie, is interested in stories of the devil, is disappointed she cannot be like a boy, and wants to run away with Gypsies. Like Maggie, too, Ellen is ostracized by her family, has an artist lover, divides her affections between him and another man, and has to work to support herself; and her story, too, ends with her falling into poverty and despair, feeling that she has been totally cut off from society. The similarities are limited but striking enough to make one wonder whether Reventlow had read Eliot's novel and had set out to rewrite it, either deliberately or unconsciously. Reventlow's novel is also very different from Eliot's, however, because she lets her protagonist read Murger, as well as Henrik Ibsen and Nietzsche, and then introduces her to the "adventurous dreamland" of Munich's fin-de-siècle bohemian community, where she lives with her artist lover, works to become an artist, gets pregnant, marries that other man in her life, has a miscarriage, and then separates from her husband before falling seriously ill and, as previously noted, into despair.[100] In the end, Reventlow's novel does not unfold a happier story than *The Mill on the Floss*, but it does at least give its heroine a fighting chance at a world outside the family into which she was born. Ellen Olestjerne's story could actually be Maggie Tulliver's if we could imagine an Eliot who had not been so determined, in the character of Maggie, to repudiate the grisette and all that she stood for.

True, throughout her brief life Maggie never has sex, despite the reputation she gains for being a loose woman. Yet in this respect, too, she belongs to the world of the grisette. A recurrent character in the literature on this figure is the chaste grisette: the working-class girl who is careless, free, and happy-go-lucky while remaining virginal, against all odds and despite all expectations for her kind. Even De Kock and Huart, who were among those who did most to popularize the image of the grisette as a loose woman, employed this sort of character as a device in their works. "Say what you like and laugh as you will," wrote Huart, "one finds innocence and virtue in dress shops"—not very often, he immediately added, but one does find them.[101] *The Mill on the Floss*, in this respect, belongs to a line of literary works that includes *The Married Grisette* (1829), a light comedy by F. V. A. d'Artois de Bournonville, L. E. Vanderburch, and C. F. J. B. Moreau de Commagny; Sand's *André* (1835); Sue's *Mysteries of Paris*; *The Journal of a Grisette* (1847), by Eugène Cormon and Eugène Grangé; Herbert Vaughan's *Cambridge Grisette* (1862); De Kock's "Grisettes' Ball"; and Morley Roberts's *In Low Relief* (1890).

Eliot's portrayal of the grisette is much more compelling than anything to be found in these other works, however, and one reason for its superiority is that Eliot provides, through the character of Maggie, the most wondrous portrayal of sexual passion in the nineteenth-century English novel. Eliot takes quite seriously the grisette she is determined to repulse, and as a result her Maggie is like Milton's Satan, a character who might lead a Romantic reader to infer that its author was secretly of the devil's party. In Maggie the grisette's pleasure-seeking nature is allowed to be powerful, complex, and aesthetically significant. Its promise of happiness will be decisively broken, but it is not to be derided or dismissed.

Writing of Maggie's attraction to music, for example, Eliot says that her enjoyment was not "of the kind that indicates a great specific talent; it was rather that her sensibility to the supreme excitement of music was only one form of that passionate sensibility which belonged to her whole nature, and made her faults and virtues all merge in each other—made her affections sometimes an impatient demand, but also prevented her vanity from taking the form of mere feminine coquetry and device, and gave it the poetry of ambition" (352). In her sensibility Maggie *is* art, and like all grisettes she develops her sense of love out of the commonplace stories of her culture, following this theme through its many variations. Therefore, in describing her first meeting with Stephen, Eliot says that Maggie was not really thinking of him or of his evident attraction to her but rather feeling "the half-remote presence of a world of love and beauty and delight, made up of vague, mingled images from all the poetry and romance she had ever read, or had ever woven in her dreamy reveries" (338). Yet Maggie's passion, like the grisette's, is not simply a dreamy abstraction but also an urgent pleasure-seeking drive whose symptoms Eliot lovingly details, as when she describes Maggie's almost orgasmic response to Stephen's singing: "When the strain passed into the minor, she half-started from her seat with the sudden thrill of that change." In this scene Maggie's eyes become "dilated and brightened," there is "the slightest perceptible quivering through her whole frame," and her overwhelming pleasure is so evident that her darling cousin Lucy impulsively hurries forward to kiss her (366). A bit later, when Maggie surrenders to Stephen's offer to take her for a ride, Eliot describes "her heart beating violently," her "helpless trembling," her intoxicated sense of a "stronger presence that seemed to bear her along without any act of her own will," and her subsequent "overflowing of brim-full gladness" in the "enchanted haze" of her half-unconscious consciousness (406–7).

Comparable passages occur throughout *The Mill on the Floss*, from the time when Maggie is a small child to her death as a girl barely out of her teens, as Eliot shows her sympathy for the pleasure-loving girl whom she yet will not allow to be the grisette she was born to be. Her original title for *The Mill on the Floss* was *Sister Maggie*, and for a good reason: Maggie is not permitted to have an identity independent of her family.[102] Maggie must decline to go abroad with Stephen, must reject her passion for him, and must strive to stay at home at all costs, finding happiness only in an embrace with her estranged brother at the moment of their death in a calamitous flood. Whereas the grisette thinks that nothing is too good for her, Maggie thinks nothing is too bad. She could not be more different from the bohemian woman whom Edward M. Whitty wryly described in *The Bohemians of London* (1857) as "not being surrounded by that public opinion of friends, connections, [and] family, which restrains the moral world in that misery which is so useful to the best interests of society."[103]

With her utter disdain for political economy, the grisette does not care whether her happiness is earned, but Eliot does; and so Maggie must be mortified, systematically and comprehensively, until nature itself joins in to overwhelm the last pitiful remnants of her pride. Tom dies at the same time, and he is the male principle incarnate, so perfectly subject to political economy that even the uncle who employs him does not like to hear how miserably devoted he is to his work (350). Even though he and his sister are undivided in death, however, his demise is far from being equivalent to hers. He chose his burden and found pride and honor in it, whereas Maggie was driven by her desire and encountered nothing but shame. Tom's death is an accident laden with irony, Maggie's a symbol of the hopeless impasse to which her life had come. Tom dies, but Maggie is crushed.

Reading this brilliant intervention into the mythology of bohemia, those familiar with Eliot's biography can scarcely avoid the temptation of seeing this novel also as Eliot's tortuous attempt to rewrite her own history. This was the author, after all, who did leave home and go abroad with George Henry Lewes, a man who was not merely engaged but actually married to another woman, with whom he had four children. At the time when Eliot went abroad with Lewes, his wife Agnes was in the process of producing four more offspring with Lewes's friend and editor Thornton Leigh Hunt, who, meanwhile, had been making himself responsible for the bringing of ten other children into the world with his own lawfully wedded wife. This fact, however, only highlights how comparatively trivial is the moral quandary that Eliot assigns to Maggie and Stephen when they recognize that they have attached themselves to the wrong persons. Eliot was willing to brave rejection from her own family members, including a brother who brutally broke off relations with her despite the fact that they had been especially close as children; but she would not allow Maggie ever to feel free of her cruel, overbearing, quintessentially masculine brother Tom. When she was twenty-five, Eliot had considered a proposal from an artist, a "picture-restorer," before quickly rejecting it; in her early thirties, after an abortive romance with Herbert Spencer, she appears to have been romantically involved with the publisher John Chapman while living in the same house with him, his wife, and his mistress; but Maggie must consider the throbbings she feels around Stephen Guest to be potentially destructive of all civilization.[104] Eliot, having enjoyed a provincial girlhood in a family belonging to the upper ranks of the working classes—her father, Robert Evans, was an estate manager with little formal schooling—was able to move away from home after her father's death, eventually to live in London and abroad with Lewes, considering herself to be his wife and demanding that others address her as such even though they could not legally marry; but Maggie can imagine only that if she were with Stephen, who is willing and able to marry her, "she must for ever sink and wander vaguely, driven by uncertain impulse" (413). Eliot could laud that prototypical novel of bohemia, *Wilhelm Meister's Apprenticeship*, despite its depiction of "irregular relations in all the charms they really have for human nature" and its association of "lovely qualities with vices which society makes a brand of outlawry"; but Maggie is allowed no such perception when she sees herself as "an outlawed soul" (413).[105] Eliot's international public image was such that characterizations in the last two decades of the nineteenth century would place her in the company of George Sand as a type of bohemian license in sexual behavior, and yet Maggie is made to shrink within herself because one insipid young man on the streets of St. Oggs bows to her "with that air of nonchalance which he might have bestowed on a friendly bar-maid" (434).[106] From the literature she esteemed and from her own life, Eliot knew of a freedom she forbade Maggie to recognize. She demanded that Maggie feel as an inescapable moral and social reality what she herself had chosen to regard as an imperfect and dismissable social convention. Confronting the image of her own desire in another—the image of a grisette's desires within herself—Eliot could see only such disaster as she envisioned when she declined an offer publicly to address the Woman Question, which was the Victorian term for the issue of how one should conceive of women's nature, role, and place in the modern world. "It seems to me to overhang abysses," wrote Eliot, as if Proudhon were whispering in her ear, "of which even prostitution is not the worst."[107]

Eliot's caution on this score is certainly understandable in relation to her own exceedingly delicate social status as the wife of a man legally married to another. Considering her unequivocal support for women's education and her general sympathy for measures such as John Stuart Mill's advocacy of the franchise for women, it is easy to attribute to the same cause her hesitation publicly to support initiatives for women's rights. After all, even once her identity as George Eliot became widely known, Marian Lewes, as she named herself in later years, could not help but be aware every day of how anomalous her position was. Behind her respectable exterior she was her own private bohemia, and she was aware of the consequences that came with this state

of being. She made it a rule, for instance, that she was at home to visitors
on Sunday afternoons but that she herself did not make visits. She claimed
that she had adopted this rule as a necessary strategy to avoid wasting time
by accepting the many invitations she received, among which few actually
interested her, and there may have been some truth in this explanation; but
this was also clearly an expedient for avoiding social embarrassment. Marian
Lewes did not have to ask what her friend Barbara Bodichon meant when she
immediately guessed her to be the author of *Adam Bede* (1859) and gloried in
her success: "That you *that you* whom they spit at should do it!"[108] One visitor wrote in 1869, "She is not received in general society, and the women who
visit her are either so émancipée as not to mind what the world says about
them, or have no social position to maintain. Lewes dines out a good deal,
and some of the men with whom he dines go without their wives to his house
on Sundays."[109] This characterization makes her situation appear rather more
exiguous than it was, especially as the years went on and her celebrity grew,
and Eliot was always received in distinguished company abroad; but still it
provides a broadly accurate image of the attitudes she had to anticipate. Even
when Eliot delighted in a fan letter from Elizabeth Gaskell, for instance, since
this was just the sort of writer whom she admired and to whom she wished to
be compared, she had to overlook Gaskell's closing comment, "I should not
be quite true in my ending if I did not say before I concluded that I wish you
were Mrs. Lewes. However that can't be helped, as far as I can see, and one
must not judge others."[110]

Such are the circumstances that at one point led Eliot to defend the "sacred bond" of her own exceptional relationship by throwing to the wolves the
common sort of relationship for which grisettes were known.[111] In this case she
was writing of the clandestine affairs of well-bred society, but in doing so she
was also implicitly condemning the open and unashamed manners of Musset's
Mariette and others of her ilk. "Light and easily broken ties," she wrote, "are
what I neither desire theoretically nor could live for practically. Women who
are satisfied with such ties do *not* act as I have done—they obtain what they
desire and are still invited to dinner."[112] Whereas the term *realism* was often
used in mid-nineteenth-century France as a near synonym for *immorality*, as
in critical attacks on Baudelaire and Flaubert, Eliot was determined that her
realism should bear no trace of bohemian license.

As is demonstrated by the anti-grisette tradition in nineteenth-century
English literature, Eliot's biography bears no necessary relation to our understanding of *The Mill on the Floss*. Eliot's distinctive genius as a writer aside, one

can readily imagine this novel having been written by someone with a quite different background, so well does it fit in with the literature of its time. Still, it can be heartbreaking to see Eliot portraying what she knew to be damaging social conventions as if they were moral and emotional necessities. Writing to her good friend Bodichon, a pioneering advocate of women's rights, in 1860, the year that she published *The Mill on the Floss*, Eliot could boldly embrace her disreputable marital situation by declaring, firmly and uncompromisingly, "I prefer excommunication."[113] So why couldn't she have written *The Mill on the Floss* so that it was something more like, for instance, Christian Reid's *A Daughter of Bohemia* (1874)?

Christian Reid was the pseudonym employed by the American novelist Frances Christine Fisher. In *A Daughter of Bohemia* Reid appropriated the figure of the female bohemian, as it had been revised in the English anti-grisette tradition, and revised it once again. Her heroine, Norah Desmond, has a half sister, Leslie Grahame, who has been raised in the American South, in a culture of wealth and gentility, while Norah and another half sister, children of their mother's second marriage, have been raised on the Continent in "wild Bohemia" (14).[114] At the outset of the novel Leslie has just become engaged, as in "the ending of a novel or a fairy-tale" (19), to an extremely eligible young man named Arthur Tyndale. This ending, however, is only the beginning of the story, for Leslie takes it into her head, in this time of her happiness, that she should invite her half sister Norah to visit her. The aunt and uncle who serve as her guardians try to dissuade her from this plan, since they think that Norah's bohemian upbringing unfits her for Leslie's company. It is precisely this background, however, that determines Leslie's interest in her half sister, as she wishes to rescue Norah from it. So she proceeds with her plan, despite her guardians' warnings and even despite the vigorous opposition of her fiancé. What Leslie fails to realize is that Arthur's opposition does not stem from a general suspicion of bohemians but instead arises from from the specifically discomfiting fact that while he was abroad he had known Norah and asked her to marry him. When he left Europe, he was supposed to return; but he encountered Leslie, affianced himself to her, and never bothered to communicate further with Norah, even to break off their engagement.

From the outset, then, it is respectable society that is put into question in this novel, with the bohemian girl as the innocent figure that this society, in the person of Arthur, not only betrays but also slanders so as to disguise its own hypocrisies. Knowing the same literary tradition that led other American authors in the last decades of the nineteenth century to portray bohemia as a moral cesspool, Reid took this tradition in a radically different direction, much as Sherwood later would in *A Puritan Bohemia*. Arthur does not tell Leslie the truth. Instead, when Leslie shows him a picture of her half sister, he says that he recognizes her as a "fast flirt" (59) who, as such, was "somewhat of a celebrity" in Baden-Baden and Hamburg, where he had chanced to see her (12). As one would expect, complications then ensue. Given this opening glimpse of a murky family history and romantic secrets, we realize that we are in the realm of the "sensation novel" of this era, with the likelihood of further secrets, betrayals, and even madness or violence to come. Such proves to be the case, and before the novel ends we encounter a sudden storm; a letter whose leaves are dispersed in the winds of said storm; further sexual intrigue, including Arthur's attempt to reengage himself to Norah without bothering to inform Leslie of this latest shift in his affections; various persons spying on various others; an apparent murder; scandal; an innocent individual put on trial for his life; and a final revelation of the truth. This melodramatic plot owes something to novelists such as Wilkie Collins, to whom Reid pays obeisance at one point (109), but, interestingly enough, Reid's writing actually seems to be modeled at least to some degree on Eliot's novels. It includes poetic epigraphs as chapter headings, in a lumbering style of poetry that resembles Eliot's own; an emphasis on "sympathy" as the key word for human relations; narrative intermixed with sententious commentary; and, as in *The Mill on the Floss*, marked attention to the injustices faced by women. Of Arthur's cousin, for instance, Reid comments, after he gets a bad opinion of Norah from his first meeting with her, "Like a great many other people, Captain Tyndale forgot to ask himself by what authentic standard he had measured his ideal 'true woman;' or whether, after all, his abstract idea of what the sex should be, in general, was quite a fair rule for judging Miss Desmond in particular" (54).

Despite the slanders against her, Norah is as chaste as Eliot's Maggie. Reid even includes a scene that might have been lifted from *The Mill on the Floss*, in which Norah is outraged when a man who is in love with her treats her as "flirting material" (159) by daring to kiss her hand, much as Maggie is enraged when Stephen, momentarily alone with her at a party, suddenly begins to shower kisses on the "unspeakable suggestions of tenderness" in her arm (388). Reid, however, writes of her heroine in terms that Eliot refused to entertain. Unlike Maggie, Norah feels nothing but anger and disdain toward those who are unjust to her. She is proud, invincibly proud, not only of her honor but also of the bohemian upbringing from which her half sister thinks she needs to be rescued when, in fact, the situation is quite the reverse. With her "bohemian defiance and recklessness" (79) Norah is able to see through Arthur in a way that Leslie cannot, and it is she who ends up instructing Leslie in morality, as when she explains why she will not marry a wealthy man who has just proposed to her. "I would rather share a garret and a crust of bread with a thoroughly sympathetic person," she says, "than live in a palace with one whose ideas, tastes, and opinions jarred upon, wearied, and yet controlled me" (126). A repressed image of bohemia thus breaks through the anti-grisette tradition that Arthur had trusted to shield his past. What was said of the sensation novel by Ada Clare, the "Queen of Bohemia" in mid-century New York City, is à propos here: that it appears as a reaction to "the excessive inanity which custom entails upon every day life."[115]

In this return of its romance, bohemia now explicitly links the grisette's economic irrationality to her triumph over male insolence. "You look surprised?" Norah says to her suitor when she refuses him. "I believe a woman in your world is not supposed to suffer any loss of self-respect when she barters herself away for a good establishment—but we think differently in Bohemia"—where, she adds, if she did love him, she would have no hesitation in marrying him, "let the whole world say what it would" (49). Although she is an "outlaw and Bohemian" (122), like Maggie, Norah is able to boast, "I could not endure the bondage and stagnation of ordinary respectable existence—of your ideal woman's existence, for example—for an hour!" (80). Bohemia is made to appear as the realm where truth lives and in which women can live and love in truth. Norah, in the end, will return to it, accompanied by a fiancé (the chastened hand kisser) who has had to win her love on her own terms. Reid's novel thus approaches bohemia through the tradition of English literature, reinterprets it as a romantic, principled, feminist alternative to the world of genteel respectability, and out of this reinterpretation constructs a model for American womanhood that rehabilitates Continental fantasy while effectively rejecting British-style realism as being naive at best and for the most part simply cynical and corrupt. Poor Maggie, on the other hand, in freedom must see license and destruction; in love, divisiveness and betrayal; in a life abroad, homelessness.

Reid's work is almost as exceptional in nineteenth-century American literature as it would have been if it had been produced by an English author. Still, it gives us a sense of how an Eliotian writer might rise to the challenge of the grisette instead of recoiling from it as if by an ingrained ideological reflex, and so it can extend our understanding of the agonizing sacrifices at work in

Eliot's fiction. In every desire that drives Maggie throughout *The Mill on the Floss*, as in its every criticism of the provincial mores of St. Oggs, *A Daughter of Bohemia* is another novel Eliot almost wrote; and yet, like *Ellen Olestjerne*, it is a novel whose appeal to disruptive sensation represents precisely such truth as Eliot ultimately refused to entertain.

Even though she showed more intelligence in her conception of bohemia than did the internationally renowned novelist who, in *The Mill on the Floss*, cannot even be brought to mention its name, Reid, like the forgotten Sherwood, was a mediocre American writer with whom Eliot might justifiably have dismissed all aesthetic comparisons. If we wish to dismiss Reid on aesthetic grounds, though—for instance, by overlooking the challenge to programmatic realism in *A Daughter of Bohemia* and condemning it as precisely such romance as Eliot was dedicated to expunging from art—other exceptions will still remain to show us the departure from home out onto the public streets that Eliot was determined to withhold from Maggie. The most remarkable of these may be "Married Abroad" (1880), a forgotten masterpiece by the nineteenth-century American journalist and writer George Alfred Townsend.

This is a startlingly modern story, closer in tone to Ernest Hemingway than to Eliot or, for that matter, Henry James, in the works in which he described Americans venturing abroad, such as *Roderick Hudson* (1875), *The American* (1877), and *The Ambassadors* (1903). As fully realist a work as Eliot could have desired, it represents the carelessness of bohemian life not only in the usual happy-go-lucky sense but also, much more pervasively, in the sense of cruel, thoughtless, embittering recklessness. Its artist protagonist, Ralph Flare, meets Suzette, his grisette, when she is seventeen, a dressmaker currently working as a grocer's clerk. We are told that she lost her virginity at fifteen and has a child resting in Père-Lachaise, the cemetery on the east side of Paris. At the casual suggestion of an acquaintance, the two move in together. What follows is an intimate portrait of their relationship, written in a cool, detailed, clear-eyed style, in which we see them quarreling over money, over her thriftlessness and jealousy, and over his demand that she go back to work. Ralph cruelly teases Suzette, too, with talk of bringing her to America and making her his wife, only to slap her in the face with reality as he sees it: "My people would never speak to me if I behaved so absurdly" (119).[116] They break up, and at the Closerie des Lilas he deliberately torments her by taking up with another grisette; he rejects her when she begs him to take her back; he then ends up pleading with her to return. After his mother catches wind of their relationship and intervenes by offering him a chance to leave France for Italy, he deserts Suzette, sensing that in doing so he is "passing from sinfulness to a baser selfishness—the stamp and seal upon his bargain with ambition, whereby for the long future he was sold to the sorrow of avarice and the deceitfulness of fame" (141). Nonetheless, he persuades himself that Suzette was "a tolerably bad person, who had bewitched him" (142), until one day he dreams of meeting her when they are both aged, "and the moments of grief he had wrung from the little girl of the Quartier Latin revived like one's mean acts seen through others' eyes" (145). He seeks her pardon in his dream and then returns to Paris and tries to find her, finally writing to her home village and receiving in reply a note that says only "*Ralph, Merci! Pardonne!*" (146). At this moment, just when one might think the tale had taken a sentimental turn, Townsend ends it by writing, "He felt no loss. He felt softened toward her only; and he turned his back on the Quartier Latin with a man's easy satisfaction that he could forget" (146). In this story we vividly see the homelessness of home, the modern truth borne by the grisette, which Eliot had determined could not be granted cultural legitimacy no matter how real it might be.[117]

To be sure, Eliot's portrayal of bohemia may seem less conflicted in *Middlemarch* (1871–72), where it is represented by Will Ladislaw, that shining youth; but her greater complacency in this novel is to be expected, since the only grisette or bohémienne it mentions, Will's mother, has long been dead by the time the novel begins. Will himself can find a home only through the endlessly earnest Dorothea, in a symbolic wedding of the Bohemian and the Puritan that submits the former to a public career while offering the latter some wifely pleasure in return. This is a rather amusing reversal of the pattern in which the grisette marries the gentleman, and there is bravery in this novel, as in *The Mill on the Floss*, in Eliot's depiction of a woman's sexual desire; but still it is dispiriting to see that in *Middlemarch*, as throughout her works, Eliot cannot accept the realm of bohemia as anything other than a neighborhood that is ripe for gentrification. Despite all their differences, she resembles Murger in being a realist representing what seems only natural to her, but in her case this wisdom pays for its sympathy toward women out of the profit gained by turning desire into the model colony of a progressively advancing commercial nation. So Eliot signals the propriety of her heroine's decision to remarry by having Dorothea tell Will that they can economize; she will learn what everything costs (801). Early in the novel she struggled to understand political economy, and she will continue the struggle. Eliot's fiction thus conveys a sense of progress that would trouble the movement for women's rights throughout the remainder of the nineteenth century and that would continue to have consequences for feminist movements right up to our own day. Woman can step forward only if the grisette is made to step aside.

CHAPTER 3

The Indignity of Labor

Before he became known as the most famous chronicler of nineteenth-century bohemia, Henry Murger was a young man rebelling against his father. His friends all knew the story, and after Murger's death they bequeathed it to posterity.[1] A tailor and apartment-house concierge, Claude-Gabriel Murger had assumed his son would also become a tradesman. Accordingly, when Henry turned fourteen, a traditional age for apprenticeship, his schooling came to an end. His mother, however, managed to dissuade the elder Murger from binding their child to a future of manual labor in a trade like his own. Her wish to give the boy a more genteel career may have been assisted by a neighbor who helped him obtain a position as a messenger boy in the office of a lawyer. Once there, Murger seemed less interested in the profession of law than in the irregular lives led by some artists to whom he was introduced by his fellow clerks, Émile and Pierre Bisson, who had artistic ambitions of their own. His horizons broadening, he briefly tried his hand at painting before deciding his talents lay in the direction of literature. From that time on all his passion went into the writing of poems.

What happened next was predictable. Claude-Gabriel caught his son in the act of committing poetry, and he responded as if he had witnessed a crime against nature. Any man in his position might have done the same. Henry himself would later explain this response in a story, "The Biography of an Unknown" (1849), in which a working-class father simply cannot see his son's artistic vocation as anything but "idleness" (6: 252). For a boy of his class, what could poetry be but a distraction from his lot in life? Such a boy's future would lie in mastering his craft or, with a start in life like Murger's, possibly even in climbing into a bourgeois profession. For such a boy poetry could be of no concern, just as cultural pursuits in general ought to have been none of his business. To be sure, poetry was not unknown among the working classes; but even if Claude-Gabriel had known of the worker poets of his era, such as Charles Poncy, who was championed by George Sand, or Eugène Pottier, his son's mentor and friend, it is doubtful that he would have responded any differently.[2] It was only by work, after all, that one could make one's way in the world. Poetry was something else entirely.

Understandably, then, Murger's father came down hard on him. The tailor commanded his son to desist from any further activity of this sort "if he did not wish the pen to be snatched from his hand so that a needle might take its place."[3]

After that day Murger did his best to placate his father, hiding his literary aspirations while he was at home. When he was about sixteen he obtained a new post, at a slightly higher salary, as secretary to a correspondent for Russia's Ministry for Public Instruction, Count Jacques Tolstoy. Evidently pleased, his father rented Murger an attic room in the apartment house he served and continued to provide his evening meal at his own table. Murger was pleased, too, since his duties with the count usually left him ample time in which to pursue his own affairs, literary and otherwise.

Under these conditions the family conflict twisted into a somewhat different form. It had been one thing for Murger's father to warn him off his ambitions as a poet, but now the old man was threatening to hobble his romantic pursuits. The precipitating event this time was Murger's absence during a night spent with his girlfriend or, perhaps—stories differ—in grieving over his breakup with her.[4] Told by his father that he would have to return to the family table each and every evening, and with his mother no longer alive to intercede between them, Murger angrily rushed away from the apartment house in which he had spent his boyhood.

He found refuge with a companion, Adrien Lélioux, one of several acquaintances with whom he would share garrets over the course of the following years. The others included the writer Jules Fleury-Husson, later to be known as Champfleury, who would urge Murger to give up poetry in favor of fiction, prodding him toward what would turn out to be his signature work, *Scenes of Bohemian Life* (1845–49).[5] Those who know this work in the form of the later play (1849), novel (1851), or Giacomo Puccini opera (1896) will remember that its drama stems from the meeting of a handful of young men in flight toward culture and away from commerce, toward love and away from domestic respectability, toward a liberating friendship above all else.

So this move away from home proved momentous in Murger's life, but still the old quarrels trailed after him. An 1842 letter recounts yet another example of the obdurate paternal behavior he found so insufferable. This latest drama had erupted as the result of a new opportunity, one that would have been a wondrous stroke of fortune to many a striving son of the laboring classes. A merchant who wanted a secretary to help with his business affairs had offered Murger the job, which included the provision of lodging, the prospect of advancement, and a starting salary much higher than the forty francs a month he had been receiving from the count during the previous four years. This was an opening to a career, a pathway to security, possibly even a broad and smooth highway that one day would lead to wealth—and Murger wanted none of it. His father was outraged when he learned his son had turned down such an eligible position, and Murger in turn was infuriated by his outrage. He announced to his friends that the elder Murger's behavior had compelled him to break off all relations with him in a "definitive rupture."[6] Yet the drama between them continued, as evidenced by a passage about his father in a letter Murger wrote almost two years later. At this time the future author was still living a hand-to-mouth existence that was made even more miserable by the skin disease, purpura, that would harass him for the rest of his life. In the letter he confided to a friend, "He told me, the other day, that in my position I ought not to have any pride and that rather than live as I do I ought to become a servant. Now isn't that horrible, and isn't it enough to make you crazy?"[7]

Although Murger was nothing but an obscure clerk at the time, in retrospect we can see his struggles with his father guiding him toward his destiny as bohemia's chronicler. He was a child not only of his father but also of the 1830s, the decade that gave rise to the modern meaning of *bohemia* as the imaginary land occupied by those whose cultural ideals shine through the poverty-stricken conditions in which they must often pursue their unconventional lives.[8] He could scarcely have had a better apprenticeship for his role as its chronicler, so perfectly did his struggles fit into the mythology beginning to develop in this decade around Parisian students, artists, vagabonds, layabouts, street people, and assorted hangers-on. When Murger *père* and *fils* were storming away at each other, the image of sons rebelling against fathers was already taking form in the mythology of bohemia.

Even before he turned it into fiction, then, Murger's life had the quality of art. In the popular imagination of this time, as ever since, bohemia arises when youths rebel against father figures who seem to incarnate all the coarse, materialistic, utilitarian values of a society dominated by business and industry. We might almost conclude that Murger, if he had not been given the life he had, would have had to invent it. Although he himself suggested other contexts for the bohemian existence he went on to describe, such as the lives of great artists throughout history and, more recently, Honoré de Balzac's novel *A Great Man of the Provinces in Paris* (1839), all his friends regarded his fiction as thinly veiled autobiography.[9] Armand de Pontmartin was typical in saying that "it is evident Murger used himself as his subject" and typical as well in seeing in this fact a characteristic of bohemianism in general. "It was reserved to our modern bohemians to look into their social condition, into their selves, into the incidents of their lives and of their entourage, for the subject, the mise en scène, the *ultima ratio*, the permanent inspiration of their spirit and of their art."[10] In this respect, at least, Murger's familial torment was a blessing.

As a modern cultural invention, bohemia included both men and women, including quite exceptional women such as Sand.[11] As Murger's fiction would help to establish, however, in the 1830s and 1840s most women came to bohemia in a way very different from that of men. Their story took form in large part through the legend of the grisette, the fun-loving young woman who joins the men in their bohemian adventure. The story of the young man was quite different. Whereas grisettes were supposed to be typical working-class girls, the young men called bohemians were definitively unlike the generality of their kind. Whether born of the working classes or the bourgeoisie, they found themselves in a relation to society at large, and thus, often enough, to their fathers in particular, that was undergoing a dramatic transformation.

One crucial factor was their education—Murger being atypical in this regard, as he was sorely aware. It was nothing new for fathers and sons to be at odds with one another, but the modern situation of educated young men with cultural aspirations was significantly different from what it had ever been before. In 1843 Alexandre Privat d'Anglemont wrote of bohemians as young men "disabled by education," and others would follow him in discerning bohemia's origins in a disproportion between the numbers of degreed young men and the positions available under Louis Philippe, the Second Republic, and Napoleon III; but bohemians confronted something more than an employment problem.[12] Literati, members of the intelligent classes, proletarians of the intellect: whatever they were called, they faced a new historical reality. Looming over them all was a change in the fundamental nature of work; and, as Murger's life and writings illustrate, this changed almost everything.

It goes without saying that work had always been a hard fact of life. In the nineteenth century, however, it became something more than the burdensome toil it had been from time immemorial. In this era work became spirit.

SENTIMENT.—(*Artistic-minded Youth* (*in midst of a fierce harangue from his father, who is growing hotter and redder*). " By Jove, that's a fine bit of colour, if you like ! "

Figure 4. "Sentiment," from *Mr. Punch in Bohemia* (1898).

As in the dialectic of the master and slave in Georg Wilhelm Friedrich Hegel's *Phenomenology of Mind* (1807), work came to be seen as the driving force of culture. Like nineteenth-century socialism and communism, bohemia was born as a repercussion of this event.

The connection of bohemia to these other movements may not be obvious. After all, it was just an odd historical coincidence that Murger's childhood friend, Pottier, would go on to write the "Internationale" (1871), the famous communist anthem, and it was a coincidence still that Murger was writing his *Scenes of Bohemian Life* in the revolutionary year of 1848 while the socialist-anarchist philosopher Pierre-Joseph Proudhon was his downstairs neighbor. In these times and in days more ordinary, Murger was not at all radical in his politics. From his treatment of the 1848 revolution in the first edition of his *Scenes*, one would never guess that Elme-Marie Caro would find cause to trace responsibility for the 1871 Commune straight back to him, thus portraying him as a firebrand, albeit an unwitting one.[13] Reportedly, Murger's conservatism at times angered his republican friends, as when Lélioux was upset by the episode in the *Scenes* that mocked the political events of 1848, leading Murger to remove this chapter from the book after its second edition.[14] This conservatism, too, was symptomatic of the broader issue that Jerrold Seigel has termed

"Bohemia's political indeterminacy."[15] Even if Gustave Flaubert was not literally thinking of Murger when he portrayed Hussonet, the bohemian in his *Sentimental Education* (1869), as mocking the 1848 revolution, it was with some historical reason that he contrasted the stern Sénécal, a fiercely committed republican, to Hussonet, a rambunctious joker with the conventional anti–Louis Philippe sympathies of the young. It even appears that Murger's employment by Jacques Tolstoy may have led to a weird moment in 1848 when the tailor's son acted as an intelligence agent for the czar, attending some workers' meetings and dutifully reporting back to Tolstoy that the question most upsetting the provisional government was "the organization of work, for which the people stubbornly continue to demand a solution."[16]

Nonetheless, Murger's bohemia was affiliated with nineteenth-century socialist and communist movements through their shared relation to the changing nature of work in this era. At the same time, on a more intimate scale, the conflicts between Murger and his father were also shaped by this change. Unremarkable if seen in isolation, in their historical context these familial conflicts exemplify this era's fundamental questions about vocation, class and professional identifications, and the determining relations among economic structures, cultural values, and individual desire.

Of course, just as work had always been a hard fact of life, it was nothing new for a young person such as Murger, or for people in general, for that matter, to chafe at its demands. When William Hogarth, in a series of etchings entitled *Industry and Idleness* (1747), presented the gruesome end of Tom Idle as a warning to any boy who might feel tempted to give his master something less than his all, he was drawing on traditions about disobedient apprentices that went back centuries and, for good measure, referring to moral adages as old as the Bible. (In the serialized version of *Trilby* published in *Harper's* in 1894, George du Maurier would remember this tradition in his caricature of his old buddy James McNeill Whistler as "Joe Sibley, the idle apprentice, the king of bohemia.")[17] Dreams of escape from labor—visions of Eden, Arcadia, Lubberland, the Land of Cockaigne, *Schlaraffenland*, and the Big Rock Candy Mountain "where they hung the jerk that invented work"—have an equally long history.[18] The difference in the nineteenth century, which Hegel so influentially characterized, was that work in this era was being internalized in and as culture.

Nineteenth-century writers and artists would try to trace out a distinguished genealogy for their attitude to work, digging up precedents such as the ancient motto *laborare est orare*, "to work is to pray." Thomas Carlyle often liked to recall this bit of inspiration; John Rogers Herbert made it the subject of an 1862 painting; in a novel left unfinished at his death in 1869, Iginio Ugo Tarchetti portrayed a bohemian who remembered, nostalgically and ironically, how he had written this motto in his schoolbooks when he was a kid.[19] The modern conditions of life in the nineteenth century, however, made it serve ends quite different from those of St. Benedict, the sixth-century founder of monasticism to whom it is attributed. As far as the organization of work was concerned, in this century the master had changed. Think only of how marginal a role the dramatization of work plays in the entire corpus of William Shakespeare's drama, and then think of how central its description is to nineteenth-century novels by writers such as Balzac, Sand, Charles Dickens, Elizabeth Gaskell, George Eliot, Émile Zola, and Thomas Hardy, and one cannot help but see the difference.

Culture had formerly been seen as a monopoly of the leisured ranks of society. Prior to the nineteenth century, speaking of "folk culture" would have been nonsense, "primitive culture" an oxymoron, and "popular culture" an ironic jibe. Yet these formulations and others like them were created and taken quite seriously in the nineteenth century, in which the social, economic, and political developments of recent times culminated in the newfound power of the middle classes to define matters of the spirit in terms of their own cherished self-image, as the triumph of dignified labor. "A small Poet every Worker is," declared Thomas Carlyle.[20] Where work had once been seen as punishment, the sweat-beaded brow a legacy of original sin, its redemptive promise was now emphasized. Formerly viewed as the antithesis to culture, which might be symbolized by the pale, sensitive, gloved hand of a lady or gentleman of leisure, work now appeared as a moral virtue, a spiritual discipline, the surest mechanism of social control, and, if not the ultimate origin of all values—here most would still nod to the Deity—at least their proximate source. In the words of Léon Faucher, "Work is the providence of modern peoples; it takes the place of morality, refills the emptiness of faith, and appears as the principle of all good."[21] Author of the treatise *Of the Dangerous Classes of the Population in the Great Cities, and of the Ways to Improve Them* (1840), Honoré Antoine Frégier agreed. "The role of work in the destiny of man," he intoned, "is not that of a purely material agent; the creator has elevated it to the rank of a virtue . . . it includes in itself all the force and the efficacy of prayer."[22] The modern epic, Carlyle concluded, must sing of "Tools and the Man."[23]

The study of political economy was exemplary in its startlingly modern postulation, by Adam Smith and David Ricardo, of labor as the foundation of all value. Work was such an all-absorbing reality in this age, however, that even many of those who vociferously criticized the premises of political economy, such as Carlyle and John Ruskin, still preached the gospel of work as the salvation of humankind. Throughout his career Carlyle declared that work was the answer to the intellectual confusions, spiritual doubts, and political restiveness of modern times. "Work while it is called Today; for the Night cometh, wherein no man can work": thus spake Diogenes Teufelsdröckh, Carlyle's mouthpiece in *Sartor Resartus* (1831), paraphrasing the gospel of John.[24] Devoutly following in Carlyle's footsteps and, like him, becoming an internationally recognized sage in matters of public concern, Ruskin lectured on work as a sacred and humanizing duty, contending that "no man can retain either health of mind or body without it."[25] Any persons trying to avoid work, he said, "should be set, under compulsion of the strictest nature, to the more painful and degrading forms of necessary toil, especially to that in mines and other places of danger," where they might "come to sounder mind respecting the laws of employment."[26] Meanwhile, more radical critics of political economy, such as Charles Fourier and Karl Marx, were so conscious of the new nature of work that for them it defined, in reverse, their predictions of the future. Fourier anticipated a new day in which work would resemble festive play, as in the "delectable visions of the spiritualization of labor" that Nathaniel Hawthorne described in *The Blithedale Romance* (1852), which was based in part on the Fourierist experiment in communal living that he and others had tried at Brook Farm.[27] Marx called for a society that would do away with labor as hitherto understood, transforming it into a pleasurable and freely willed activity.[28]

Such was the era in which the word *bohemia*, together with the word *culture*, was taking on new meaning. Although Hegel's philosophy yields no direct references to nineteenth-century bohemia, the image Hegel chose to epitomize that philosophy—the spiritualization of work—describes this context of its development. At the beginning of the nineteenth century Hegel made the fate of work the defining question for the modern spirit of philosophy. Whether or not they were as influenced by his thought as Marx was, and even if they were unaware of it, innumerable bohemians would trail behind him as they struggled to come to terms with what work had wrought in the world that was learning to call itself modern.

The *Phenomenology* allegorically describes the development of mind in terms of a gradual but inevitable transformation in the consciousness of a master and a slave. As Hegel tells the story, the master initially establishes himself as such by commanding the labor of another, who bows to his command because, unlike the master, he quails before the fear of death. The master, in his own mind, is then able to believe that he exists independently of all degrading activity, since this is delegated to his slave. Eventually, however, he faces a problem. In order that he should truly be the master he wants to think himself to be, it is not enough that he should have a slave labor for him. Not only must the slave labor for him, he must do so knowingly and submissively. In other words, the master desires the slave's unconditional recognition of his mastery. To come to this realization of what he desires from the slave, however, the master must admit to himself that he is not, has never really been, and in fact cannot truly be a master, in the absolute sense in which he had understood that identity. (This is the point in Hegel's reasoning that Carlyle and Ruskin, with their nostalgic politics, never reached.) Ironically, then, in desiring the slave's recognition, Hegel's master must find that he is dependent on his dependent. He had been mistaken when he thought his consciousness could transcend his relation to the slave, to the slave's labor, and to mortality. In effect, he has learned that his consciousness exists outside himself, in a world of labor, even as that world also exists within him, working away at his identity. In ways he is only beginning to appreciate, he moves in and is moved by the course of history.

Along with the slave in whom he has now found his truth, the master has changed, and he will never be the same again. Out of this existential condition, according to Hegel's allegory, all of history unfolds as a progressive dialectical interchange between interiority and exteriority, mind and body, individuality and sociality, and every other pair of the seemingly opposed concepts through which the human spirit grasps, and is grasped by, the world. From the first stirrings of human identity to its end, this argument traces out the implications of the union of culture and work that history made visible, made distinctively modern, in the nineteenth century. "Spirit" does all the work in Hegel's philosophy because its author came to philosophical maturity in a century in which, he recognized, work was becoming the spirit of culture.

Because it seeks to summarize, critique, and move beyond it, an 1880 manifesto by Paul Lafargue helps further to clarify the world thus described by Hegel. This manifesto, *The Right to Idleness*, stands in stark contrast not only to the socialist demand for a right to work associated with Louis Blanc and the Second Republic but also to Hogarth's moralistic nineteenth-century heirs and all the centuries of tradition they claimed to represent. Whereas Carlyle had claimed that by a "Law of Nature" men who do not work have no right to

exist on earth, Lafargue pugnaciously insisted that they have a positive right
to lounge around at their ease.[29] His position approximated that of a communist whom George Orwell would later describe, who "could prove to you by
figures that it was wrong to work."[30]

Lafargue knew that the title of his manifesto, which could also be translated as *The Right to Laziness*, would look like some kind of joke. As he was at
pains to point out, though, it would look funny only to those who were dupes
of "the god of Progress, the eldest son of Work" (126).[31] It was a peculiarity of
the modern world that a right to idleness should need to be declared, much
less defended. Whereas it was taken for granted in earlier times that work was
a calamity, "our epoch, they say, is the century of work" (126). Human nature
cries out against this situation, Lafargue argued, drawing support for his position from anthropological accounts of noble savages, who were supposed to
be blissfully unproductive. What has happened in this modern age, he asked,
to the likes of François Rabelais, with his celebration of untrammeled festivity,
or to Denis Diderot, the philosopher who was so struck by the playful bodies
and spirits of the Tahitians encountered by the explorers of the South Seas?
Does not our joy in holidays and feasts show where our desires would lead us
if they could? Jesus Christ himself praised the lilies of the valley, who neither
toil nor spin, and throughout history our greatest thinkers have declared work
to be an outrage on the human spirit, an activity suitable only to slaves. Plato,
Aristotle, Virgil, Cicero: all testify to the virtue of idleness, which engenders
"sentiments of pride and independence" (124). Only recently, Lafargue maintained, have events so conspired as to enforce upon humanity the perverse
demand that they should find virtue in work.

Whereas *The Communist Manifesto* (1848) had dismissed out of hand accusations that the abolition of private property would result in "universal laziness," Lafargue seemed more attentive to a moment in the first volume of
Capital (1867) in which Marx, his father-in-law, noted that "to be a productive
labourer is . . . not a piece of luck, but a misfortune."[32] Assailing proletarians
for their submission to the gospel of work, mocking deluded notions about
the nobility of labor, flailing away at anyone tempted to buy into mere piece-
meal reforms (such as a pitiful "right to work"), Lafargue called for a society
in which no one would be employed for more than three hours a day. This
change, he said, would fix everything. Once it was universally accepted and
accompanied by ongoing innovations in machinery, that great "redeemer of
humanity" (153), this restriction on the hours of work would eliminate the
problems of unemployment, overproduction, overconsumption, and waste.

His manifesto concluded that everyone might then have a life as ideal as that of the American farmer, whose use of agricultural machinery has transformed his labor into "an agreeable pastime that he performs while seated in the open air, nonchalantly smoking his pipe" (144).

As a cultural phenomenon of the era stretching from Hegel to Lafargue and beyond, bohemia was itself a kind of manifesto on the nineteenth-century culture of work. In this case the manifesto was proclaimed through the lives of all those who struggled, as Murger did, to get out from underneath this culture. "And to think about regeneration through work, I knew through experience that was impossible," says the bohemian protagonist of Alejandro Sawa's *Declaration of a Loser* (1887).[33] It is not really so surprising, then, to find that the title of Lafargue's treatise repeated the very words with which Murger's *Scenes of Bohemian Life* had described the 1848 revolution: "Then, since the right to idleness had just been proclaimed in favor of arts and letters, the bohemians crossed their arms, admiring themselves at their window and regarding the comedy with complete disinterest" (399).

Continuing to evoke popular images of Gypsies, whose life other people of this era considered to be premodern—primitive, lawless, unsettled, and licentious—Murger's bohemia expressed a nostalgic desire for a progressive alternative to modern culture. As George William Curtis said in 1859 from his "Editor's Easy Chair" at *Harper's*, "In the history of literature there are famous names which illustrate the Bohemian spirit. But it was not until literature became a profession that Bohemians were a guild."[34] Like the socialist and communist movements that gave rise to Lafargue's call for a reorganization of labor, this modernized metaphor of bohemia was a by-product of nineteenth-century industry. When Murger, using Fourierist terminology, referred to the community in the *Scenes* as a "bohemian phalanstery" (186), he showed his awareness of its implicit affiliation with these sorts of social movements, which took on living form in Jean Journet, the addlepated Fourierist apostle whose eccentricity was enjoyed by Nadar, Champfleury, and others among Murger's convives. After he had gained renown as a caricaturist, journalist, balloonist, and photographer, Nadar would fondly remember these affiliations. The young people of the 1860s, he said, would be amazed if they could realize how his own youthful days had seen socialist fantasies—"phalansteries, familisteries, dreams of Saint-Simon, Fourier, and my dear deluded apostle Jean Journet"—come into reality.[35]

True, these affiliations were vague, but bohemia, as a form of cultural protest, owes a good deal of its lasting influence to the useful vagueness in its conception. In its later transformations, as in its early form, Murger's bohemia was not anything like a political party or movement. Edmond and Jules de Goncourt were capable of many and great stupidities, but one of their most egregious was the charge that Murger embodied a socialism that supposedly reigned over the literary world of their day and sought to damn as mere amateurs men of letters, such as the Goncourts themselves, who had the misfortune of being well born.[36] Far from having planned his work on bohemia as a publicity campaign designed to prepare the ground for him and his friends to take power in that world, as the Goncourts feverishly imagined before further acquaintance somewhat softened their feelings about him, Murger at this or any other point of his life could not have organized his way out of a wet paper bag. Aside from the short-lived club of "Water Drinkers" that he and a few of his friends formed in the early 1840s, his bohemia was scarcely even recognizable in terms of a defined group, and it never would produce a formally composed manifesto. Instead this bohemia remained a metaphor evoking an informal sense of community that drifted like a spirit of desire through the nineteenth century. This person or that might seek to lay claim to the metaphor, but it was always open to dispute and contradiction, always up for grabs, and over the course of time was subject to major reconceptualizations.

In 1859, for instance, Charles Hugo sought to popularize the term "gilded bohemia" to describe rich youths who, aside from their wealth, possessed the same qualities as the artists of "dirty bohemia": alienation from the world of work, a carefree nature, eccentricity in relation to respectable society, thriftlessness, sexual and political irresponsibility, reliance on credit, and a devil-may-care unconcern about the morrow.[37] Although Hugo concluded that mud, in the end, stains less than does gold, by the last two decades of the century it had become commonplace to note that bohemians no longer needed to have any connection with poverty, scandalous behavior, or improprieties of any sort. Just as one could be a gentleman and a scholar, one could now be a gentleman and a bohemian.[38] Even in this etiolated form, though, the metaphor still conveyed something of the profound dissatisfaction with the century of work that had motivated it when it was first used in the 1830s to describe students, poets, and other cultural workers, as we might now call them. For all its ridiculousness, the Goncourts' conspiracy theory did touch upon a truth of bohemia, that it did pose a real challenge to the reigning culture of work, even if it did not actually fire "red-hot shot" at prominent *littérateurs* in doing so.[39]

Murger and many other so-called bohemians did hold jobs, some of them working very hard indeed. Eugenio Torelli Viollier, the founding editor of

Milan's *Corriere della sera*, would comment that Murger himself "could be cited in a book by [Samuel] Smiles," the author of the best-selling *Self-Help: With Illustrations of Character and Conduct* (1859), "as an example of noble pertinacity and of literary dignity" in his work habits.[40] Still, a whisper of *non serviam* attached even such hard-working bohemians as Murger to their imaginary nation.

This is why Marx was just as disgusted by them as the Goncourts were. He saw them as a reactionary element in society and refused to distinguish the modern meaning given to their nickname from the older, more pejorative senses of this term. As Adolphe d'Ennery and Eugène Grangé had noted in their popular and oft-revived drama *The Bohemians of Paris* (1843), these senses had come to embrace shiftless and criminal urbanites of all sorts: "that class of individuals whose existence is a problem, whose condition is a myth, whose fortune is an enigma; who have no fixed dwelling, no known sanctuary; who are nowhere to be found, and whom one meets everywhere!"[41] Murger's intent was rather different, as his friend Auguste Vitu noted in his review of the theatrical version of his stories, jokingly contrasting Murger's drama to the interpretation of bohemia given by "the Magyars of the Boulevard du Temple, MM. Denneriski and Grangersky."[42] Seeking to draw a clear boundary around this intent, in the opening sentence of the preface to his *Scenes of Bohemian Life* Murger states that "the bohemians who are the subject of this book have no relation to the bohemians whom the playwrights in their light comedies have made synonymous with crooks and assassins" (29).[43] Marx, however, was having none of it, adopting a sense of the word far more in keeping with the sinister characters in *The Bohemians of Paris* or in Xavier de Montépin's *Confessions of a Bohemian* (1850). As far as he was concerned, in its new dispensation bohemia remained the same politically irresponsible pseudo-community that it had always been, its members as one with the lumpenproletariat of criminals, prostitutes, and indigents.[44]

Marx was not totally misguided in deciding upon this conclusion. Privat is one example of a bohemian who did, in fact, revel in his association with motley crowds of low people, the "irregular or hostile beings" who lived in the "unknown Paris" that he took for his native land: exiles, fugitives, ragpickers, beggars, whores, street performers, vagrants, and poor workers of all sorts.[45] Some other commentators, too, such as the English writer James Glass Bertram, portrayed bohemians sympathetically even while emphasizing their association with the lower depths of the criminal world that Eugène Sue had depicted in *The Mysteries of Paris* (1842–43).[46] In *The Eighteenth Brumaire of Louis Bonaparte* (1852), however, Marx showed no tolerance for this sort of sympathy. He excoriated all bohemians as Bonaparte's natural constituency and the supporters of his coup d'état: "vagabonds, discharged soldiers, discharged jailbirds, escaped galley slaves, rogues, mountebanks, *lazzaroni,* pickpockets, tricksters, gamblers, *maquereaus,* brothel keepers, porters, *literati,* organ-grinders, rag-pickers, knife grinders, tinkers, beggars—in short, the whole indefinite, disintegrated mass, thrown hither and thither, which the French term *la bohème.*" He even identified Bonaparte himself as a "princely lumpen bohemian."[47] Despite its very different political intentions, in this regard his work is comparable to the moralizing of Carlyle, who saw in "nomadism" an evil state of human affairs, who drew no distinction between idleness and criminality, and who opposed his prophetic words to the "strange new religion" that had "Balzac, Sue and Company for Evangelists, and Madame Sand for Virgin."[48] Predictably, Ruskin followed his master on this subject, as when he described the cancan, one of the dances that symbolized the freedom of bohemian desire, as a "rapture of blasphemy," its object being "to express in every gesture the wildest fury of insolence and vicious passions possible to human creatures."[49]

Bohemia experienced these kinds of ongoing disputes over its very definition, not to mention its possible implications and consequences, because no one could begin to address it without also addressing the spiritualization of labor that was redefining all of culture and society in this era. The present was changing and, with it, the past, as this cultural formation emphasized by repurposing a word that had generally signified a timeless tradition of vagabond life—*bohémien*—into a term expressive of disruptive modern transformations. However one might define it, argue over it, or evaluate it, the word *bohemian* now pointed to an appropriation of the past in the service of modernity. In such a situation, disputes that reach down to the very bottom of words and out toward all parts of society—popular dances, religion, coups d'état, crime, ragpickers, gentlemen, you name it—are to be expected. Not only on the grand scale of universal history, as with Hegel, but also in terms of the fashioning of modern memory, the movement of work into culture made for stunning changes in representation.

A case in point, one crucial to the contest over the modern definition of bohemia, arose from the life of a poet who was remembered very differently in the 1830s, 1840s, and 1850s from how he had been remembered in the immediate aftermath of his suicide, at the age of seventeen, in 1770. One cannot hope to understand much about Murger, in whose garret "a Chattertonian tendency reigned," if one does not know something about this poet, Thomas Chatterton.[50] Like the word *bohemian*, the word *Chatterton* would come to signify many of the conflicts that the spirit of work put into play in the nineteenth century and, more particularly, in Murger's life, work, and reputation.

Of humble origins, about which he was acutely self-conscious, Chatterton was respectably apprenticed at the age of fourteen to a lawyer, John Lambert, in Bristol, his native town. He found himself under an easy master, his work often requiring his attention no more than two hours a day. Nonetheless, although accounts portray him as having been reliable in the performance of his duties, he was dissatisfied. He had poetic ambitions, and he displayed what Lambert judged to be a "sullen and gloomy temper."[51] Chatterton's apprenticeship came to an abrupt end when Lambert discharged him after he was found to have threatened suicide in a "Last Will and Testament" that someone in his house discovered and brought to his master's attention. In this document Chatterton had complained, with biting irony, "The most perfect masters of human nature in Bristol distinguish me by the title of the Mad Genius."[52] At this same hectic time the Mad Genius was beginning to make a name for himself by advertising his possession of certain manuscript poems supposed to have been written by a fifteenth-century monk, Thomas Rowley. Although Chatterton was unable to obtain the patronage he sought from the eminent author Horace Walpole, whose friends advised him that the manuscripts were obvious forgeries, a number of people were impressed that a provincial youth should have made such a startling discovery. The controversy over these poems would continue after Chatterton's death, but even many of those who doubted their authenticity saw in them the work of a poetic talent quite remarkable for one so young. Meanwhile, Chatterton was undismayed by the loss of his position and emboldened by the attention he had received, on the strength of which he decided to seek his fortune in London, where he predicted a glorious future for himself. Once there he sought to earn his living by his pen, consorted with grisettes ("so many pretty milliners, &c."), and soon fell into dismal poverty.[53] Less than a year and a half after his arrival in the metropolis, he swallowed a fatal dose of arsenic. When his body was discovered, his room "was found covered with little scraps of paper"—poems torn to shreds. His corpse was placed in a shell, or cheap wooden coffin, "in the burying ground of Shoe-Lane work-house."[54] Thereafter his story became widely known as supporters published his poems, accompanied by biographical notices of his life, while various men and women of letters gossiped about his fate in conversations and in print.

Not realizing that Chatterton kept ochre and charcoal in his room to use in giving his manuscripts an antique appearance, his mother had once gotten a peculiar idea that these "were to colour himself, and that, perhaps, he would join some gipsies, one day or other, as he seemed so discontented with his station in life, and unhappy."[55] At the time of her boy's death, though, this reference to Gypsies did not have the metaphorical resonance it would later possess. No one then would have thought of presenting Chatterton, as writers such as Murger later did, as an archetypal figure of *la vie de bohème*, a concept that did not yet exist, or as anything even remotely like this. Contemporary commentators certainly saw his story as a sad one that illustrated the plight of unrecognized talent and the dire effects of poverty and despair, but Chatterton was not the idealized figure he was later to become.

In the years immediately following his death images of Chatterton were quite varied, as were judgments of his end. For instance, in evident reference to his boasts, while he was in London, that he wrote for any political party willing to pay him to do so, Thomas Warton called him "an adventurer, a professed hireling in the trade of literature, full of projects and inventions, artful, enterprising, unprincipled, indigent, and compelled to subsist by expedients."[56] The editor of his posthumously published *Miscellanies in Prose and Verse* (1778) bluntly opined that Chatterton "possessed all the vices and irregularities of youth, and his profligacy was, at least, as conspicuous as his abilities."[57] Sir Herbert Croft wrote sympathetically of him but saw no special lesson in his life or death: "But who can bear to dwell upon, or argue about, the self-destruction of such a being as Chatterton? The motives for every thing he did are past finding out."[58] George Gregory, on the other hand, did see a lesson, but not the one the nineteenth century would find. According to Gregory, "We are certainly to attribute his premature death" to Chatterton's "irreligious principles." Moreover, "the whole of Chatterton's life presents a fund of useful instruction to young persons of brilliant and lively talents, and affords a strong dissuasive against that impetuosity of expectation, and those delusive hopes of success, founded upon the consciousness of genius and merit, which lead them to neglect the ordinary means of acquiring competence and independence. The early disgust which Chatterton conceived for his profession, may be accounted one of the prime sources of his misfortunes."[59] Walpole, too, had advised Chatterton that his best course was to stick to his profession.[60]

The bad apprentice chastised in these reponses is far from the figure who would be seen one day, as in Henry Wallis's 1856 painting *Chatterton*, as a bohemian dedicated to his art, suffering for his ideals, starving in his garret, and dying tragically young as the victim of an uncomprehending society. That Chatterton would be limned almost four decades after his death by William Wordsworth, in "Resolution and Independence" (1807), as a "marvellous Boy" whose fate was admonitory in a way eighteenth-century commentators had not anticipated. "We Poets in our youth begin in gladness," wrote Wordsworth, "But thereof come in the end despondency and madness."[61] The others who helped to raise his reputation into its modern Romantic form included Samuel Taylor Coleridge, who repeatedly revised his schoolboy "Monody on the Death of Chatterton" (1790) over the next forty years, and John Keats, who dedicated *Endymion* (1818) to him not long before his own untimely death. In works such as these this obscure provincial lad who had hastened to his end in a pauper's grave was on his way to becoming a model for Murger and his friends, who all felt their only way up in the nineteenth century must somehow be a way out of it.

The author most responsible for transforming Chatterton into a legendary bohemian ancestor was Alfred de Vigny. Starring Marie Dorval, Sand's close friend, Vigny's *Chatterton* was a sensation when it was first performed on February 12, 1835 at the Comédie Française, where it was seen by its partisans as a well-deserved slap in the face of the theater's bourgeois patrons. Vigny had based it on familiar elements in the poet's life story, but he emphasized that he was making no pretense of being faithful to biographical detail. He was not concerned with Chatterton as a boy who had lived and died in a foreign land three generations earlier. Rather, he was interested in making him a symbol for his own time. To achieve this end, he realized, the aspiring poet's character had to be simplified, and his death had to be made to illustrate a single cause, a distinctively modern cause: the ignobility of labor.

What Vigny focused on in the extant accounts of Chatterton was his pride—the very attitude that Claude-Gabriel Murger would soon be complaining of in another boy who was self-conscious about his low origins and who briefly worked for a lawyer while nursing dreams of poetic fame. Chatterton himself had identified this predominant element in his character when he explained the contemplated suicide that had cost him his apprenticeship: "You must know that nineteen-twentieths of my composition is pride."[62] Writing to his mother in the wake of his dismissal, after he had decided to make his way as a freelance writer, he had struck the same note: "Though, as an apprentice, none had greater liberties, yet the thoughts of servitude killed me."[63]

CHATTERTON.

From a picture in the possession of George Weare Brackenridge, Esq.

Figure 5. Supposed portrait of Thomas Chatterton, engraved by R. Woodman after a portrait by Nathan Cooper Branwhite, from John Dix, *The Life of Thomas Chatterton* (1837).

Eighteenth-century commentators had certainly noted the indications of this character trait in Chatterton, but they did not make of it what Vigny did. Out of this sort of evidence Vigny fashioned a Chatterton whose pride was not personal but missionary. The preface to his play was a manifesto on the political economy of art in the modern world. Presenting through his death "the perpetual martyrdom and the perpetual immolation of the Poet," Vigny's Chatterton calls for "the right to live," to exist without servility, without being forced into ignoble labor, and, in fact, without being called upon to do any work at all outside the boundaries of his art (258).[64] The entire burden of this preface is the terrible wrong that is committed in expecting that a poet should need to work as any other man must. Unlike Hawthorne, who seems merely to smile when the utopian colonists of Blithedale find that their supposedly spiritualizing labor "symbolize[s] nothing" and leaves them "mentally sluggish in the dusk of the evening," Vigny cries out for a legislative solution to this social outrage.[65] To rationalize the culture of work, he demands the public provision of a dependable "garret and a loaf of bread" (270) for those who give signs of talent.

Like the provocation Lafargue would publish later in this century, Vigny's manifesto boldly challenges the world of work that the nineteenth century had become. Lafargue's pamphlet, however, enjoyed little influence in the world at large and even in socialist circles appeared as an eccentric intervention in contemporary debates. In contrast, Vigny's proved to be perfectly in tune with its historical moment. His *Chatterton* became a template for the invention of bohemians because it so perfectly captured the vexed position of art in an age in which work was becoming culture.

For centuries artists had sought greater social distinction for their occupations, as had writers and other laborers in the vineyards of culture. They desired to be recognized as gentlemen professionals, as opposed to mere craftsmen and employees. The pressure for this change in status had to become even more intense at a time when the arts were beginning to feel squeezed between a declining economic system of royal, aristocratic, and church patronage, on the one hand, and a growing cultural spirit that granted no transcendence to art over labor, on the other. In the same year that saw the first performance of *Chatterton*, Augustin Jal wrote, "To make art a question of industry is to degrade it, to kill it."[66] Franz Liszt, too, inspired by Vigny's play, wrote a treatise on the condition of artists that deplored the loss of "their noble prerogatives," lamenting "the shameful *subalternity* of their *discrowning*" and "the *infamous deconsecration* of art and artists."[67]

Having long wished to escape the category of workers, artists were left in a state of confusion when work became culturally central to modern society. Since the conception of culture to which they had dedicated their wish was being radically transformed right in front of their eyes, having it fulfilled at that point would have dropped the ground out from under their feet. What good would it do to be granted a higher rank at a time when industrialists and merchants were beginning to claim the title of gentleman for themselves— and when art itself was becoming a commodity sold on the open market? In these circumstances, when the ideal of art as it had been traditionally understood seemed threatened with a loss of any place in the world, so, too, did writers, artists, and intellectuals. The opening of the marketplace to them, it seemed, might also mean a degrading of their profession and a threat to their livelihood.[68]

Such is the background to Alfred Delvau's assertion in 1861, in a memorial essay on Privat, that "the working of the mind is just as sacred as the working of the hand, just as meritorious, just as heroic, just as laborious—when it is not more so."[69] This is also the occasion for Nadar's plea, in his contribution to the cowritten *History of Murger, to Serve as a History of the Real Bohemia* (1862), that the state should pay as much attention to artists as to artisans. "Now that Maecenas is dead and the Medicis as well," he writes, the modern equivalents of the great lords who once supported the arts are preoccupied with affairs such as the administration of railroads. Under these conditions, are poets and intellectual workers to find that patronage exists only in the hospital bed that will be provided for their dying bodies? "Bricklayers are very interesting, undoubtedly; but once they have been provided for, does there not remain at the bottom of the sack an obole for the poets?"[70] Similarly, the Goncourts' journal entry for January 28, 1861, bitterly remarks that France's government ministers "are always very generous in seeing to the burial of men of letters; it is too bad that men of letters cannot get hold of the money spent on their interment before their deaths."[71] Gustave Courbet, though, foresaw an end to this bitter irony when he argued in an 1863 letter to Proudhon that a properly organized socialist society would "easily abolish the literary and artistic bohemia," since it would provide for the support of people in these fields.[72] Bohemian scenes that arose in other countries during this era also provided a platform for similar complaints and proposed solutions. In preaching an anticlerical, peaceful, scientific, and feminist bohemian socialism in early twentieth-century Spain, for instance, Ernesto Bark would suggest the establishment of employment bureaus for artists, which might at least provide them with counsel on how to find a socially useful job "even if this should be a position inferior to their knowledge and justified aspirations."[73] In this regard the loose metaphorical association between bohemia and Fourierism comes into sharper focus, for Fourier had singled out artists, writers, and intellectuals as types of workers that would especially find their lot improved in his new order.[74]

The changes that drove figures such as Fourier, Liszt, Delvau, Nadar, and Courbet to their complaints did not arrive all at once. In France, for example, although art dealers had begun to appear in the 1820s, it was not until the second half of the century that their influence was decisive in the buying and selling of artworks.[75] Even thereafter official institutions such as the École des beaux arts and the annual or semiannual Salons, along with government grants, commissions, purchases, and pensions, continued to play a major role in the economy of art. At one point, for instance, when the dying Lucile Louvet showed up at his apartment, Murger himself received a grant of five hundred francs, which was conveyed to him by none other than Alfred de Vigny, who by that time was a member of the Académie française.[76] The timely grant enabled him to come to the assistance of this former lover, whom his friends knew as one of the women on whom the character of Mimi in *Scenes of Bohemian Life* was based. In the 1830s and 1840s, Victor Hugo, Heinrich Heine, Alexandre Dumas, and Alfred de Musset were among the writers supported by government pensions or sinecures.[77]

Not until the 1880s, in the judgment of the historian Gérard Monnier, was there a final passage in the economics of the visual arts in France from "a system of monarchical tradition" to the marketplace.[78] Meanwhile, literature, the rest of the arts, and other forms of intellectual work had their own histories, which varied from region to region and also, of course, from nation to nation, with many irregularities in the incursions of the modern marketplace. Despite all the complexities and uneven developments that were to come, however, by the end of the eighteenth century there had already been a growing perception that the economic basis of art was undergoing a change that would have tremendous consequences for all those in the future who might wish to contribute to cultural pursuits of any kind. Art was coming to realize the fix it was in as it found itself threatened with reimprisonment, in mobile capital, at the very moment its autonomy, from a fixed system of patronage, was becoming imaginable. Henceforth all declarations of art's transcendence, as in the nineteenth-century slogan of "art for art's sake," would be haunted by the sense that its autonomy might signify its irrelevance: its ruthless devaluation in a commercial, industrial, democratic age.

Vigny, then, was writing out of the same historical moment that saw Immanuel Kant attempting to preserve art by declaring its autonomy in relation to utilitarian crafts, Hegel rudely declaring that art's day was done and that it must make way for the more spiritual discipline of philosophy, and Percy Bysshe Shelley proclaiming with the utmost seriousness the patently absurd statement that poets were the unacknowledged legislators of the world.[79] Like these others, Vigny was addressing the crisis of art's position in the world when he presented his compelling picture of a poet unwilling to work as the exemplary figure of oppression in society. From *Chatterton* it is but a short step to the young Murger exclaiming, at his hard-working father's quite ordinary expectation that his son should labor for a living, "Now isn't that horrible, and isn't it enough to make you crazy?"

Undoubtedly Murger had many reasons for responding as he did to Claude-Gabriel's words. For one thing, his father may have been trying deliberately to upset him when he suggested that he might work as a servant. *Chatterton* aside, for many in the working classes domestic service represented the lowest form of labor because it did not involve a skilled apprenticeship and because it entailed living with one's master or mistress, thereby surrendering one's independence. Moreover, in the stories Murger told his friends about him, his father was always a narrow-minded, unimaginative, penny-pinching, and thoroughly unlikeable man. Even if his father's suggestion was maliciously intended and Murger's stories about him entirely true, however, Claude-Gabriel's character explains nothing about his son's evident assumption that work should be to him something radically different from what it had been to the man who passed his life as a tailor and concierge. "Now isn't that horrible, and isn't it enough to make you crazy?": to grasp why Murger did not think his exclamation ridiculous is to begin to understand how so many people could have taken Vigny's ludicrous Chatterton as representing an inspiring ideal.

From this perspective, bohemia appears as an attempted solution to a historical problem. It was a fantastic reimagining of class history in which the narcissism of the aristocracy, its ideological legitimation as the bearer of culture, was burlesqued. The slogan of the bohemian Floro-moro-godo in Enrique Perez Escrich's *The Blue Dress Coat* (1864) would be "*Nobody has a right to the necessities of life while I lack the superfluities.*"[80] Through devices like this, the writers, artists, and intellectuals who had historically been dependents of those in the upper ranks of society now appropriated their erstwhile patrons' air of superiority, independence, and invaluable uselessness—their distance from the hubbub of everyday labor. In bohemia, as Marilyn Brown has written, "déclassé and *arriviste* became merged."[81] With carnivalesque license, historical servitude simply asserted its mastery, bypassing any need to work for this change. "Work dishonors" is the pithy adage of Prince Casimir Kraminsky, the echt bohemian in Oscar A. H. Schmitz's *Bourgeois Bohème* (1913); and so had Liszt thought when he declared that it was an insult to offer Hector Berlioz a position heading the orchestra and rehearsing the choirs at the Porte-Saint-Martin.[82] So, too, had Charles Baudelaire believed, as his friend Charles Asselineau noted in 1868, commenting, "If he loved work as art, he abhorred the work-duty."[83] Coming at this issue from the opposite direction, when an Italian critic writing in 1883 wished to insist that "true artists work," he did so in express opposition to Murger's writings.[84] Provoking this kind of criticism, bohemia proposed that culture could escape both the dead hand of the past and the dirty hands of the present if it could be conceived of as a vocation, a calling, and thus as work that rose above work. This is the formula of *Chatterton*.

No matter what his class origins were, the male bohemian that emerged from this formula was the figure of the gentleman *in extremis*, split between the historical archetypes of the aristocratic patron, who believes himself dignified by ancient right, and the bourgeois paterfamilias, who thinks himself dignified by the spirit of progress. The bohemian could not accept gentility as an unmerited inheritance, which would make him the servile client of any fool with a coat of arms, but neither could he accept it as a reward of ignoble labor, which would make him what Privat called "a prostitute of the intellect" bound to serve anyone with jingling pockets.[85] In either case the prize would not be worth the winning. The prideful attitude that emerged between these extremes offered bohemians a democratized vision of the aristocratic privilege of birth, in the form of individual talent, while rejecting the demeaning submission of cultural values to social, economic, or historical necessities. In the dramatized version of *Scenes of Bohemian Life*, this is what Marcel refers to when he speaks of the "obstinate vocation" (12) that defines bohemians. In the preface to his novelized version, Murger claims this prideful attitude for the "official bohemia" of those who "truly have an artistic calling" (40).

In effect, bohemians opted out of the laborious dialectic of the master and the slave. As in a parody of persecution, they deliberately made themselves outcasts, *sans feu ni lieu*, "without hearth or home," and then dared history to ignore them. This exile was a plunge into the sense of dispossession that animated them, driving them on. Youthful, undomesticated, rubbing shoulders with the working poor, and bearing an imaginary identification with national and racial outsiders, male bohemians—the women associated with this meta-phor always remaining a very different case—willingly declassed themselves. Whether from middle-class backgrounds or—like Murger—from working-class families, they deliberately cast into question any genteel status to which they might have a claim. In doing so they could then strive to reconstitute the very nature of social distinction through their identification with cultural masters that they not only chose but also defined for themselves: figures such as Chatterton, Alfred de Musset, Eugène Delacroix, and Victor Hugo.

Walter Benjamin's analysis of this situation would have it that the bohe-mian was simply a figure of the intelligentsia looking "to find a buyer" in the marketplace, but this is far too reductive.[86] Like the life imagined in the for-eign adventure genres of this century, as in the writings of Jules Verne and H. Rider Haggard, the domestic adventure of *la vie de bohème* was a kind of test. As Curtis wrote, "It is the modern sphere of the spirit that formerly coursed the world for adventure—but now prefers to explore the universe in a micro-cosm, and finds a metropolis the best of all."[87] In the collection of tributes to Murger appended to his posthumously published poems, Paul de Saint-Victor also pointed out this analogy. "Like those voyagers who gain immortal-ity while wintering in a desolate region, Henry Murger owed his renown to that bohemia of the arts and letters where he passed such a long and difficult interval" (12: 279). This bohemia was an experiment in the revivification of cultural ideals from a ground imagined to exist outside them and thus con-ceived to be an effective standpoint for evaluating their pretensions. When a bohemian of a later day sang that "to live outside the law, you must be hon-est," he was brilliantly reproducing precisely this aspect of bohemian mythol-ogy.[88] We might compare his words to the reply Eugène de Mirecourt made to contemporary accusations that the stories Murger wrote were immoral: "One senses that there is honesty in his very demoralization."[89]

Like most everyone else, of course, bohemians usually did not feel at all heroic. In an 1889 entry in his diary, for instance, the playwright Frank Wede-kind wrote, "Not seldom I am tormented by the question of whether my work is indeed work."[90] Bohemians typically found the solution to such doubts, though, through their insistence on a redefinition of the prevailing concep-tion of work. Given the power generally attributed to the supposed dignity of labor, degradation would have to be their road to truth. As Johann Wolf-gang von Goethe had noted in *Wilhelm Meister's Apprenticeship* (1795–96), his proto-bohemian masterpiece, Shakespeare had created a precedent for this experiment in the young Prince Hal's roisterings with John Falstaff and other commoners in *Henry IV, Part I* (c. 1596–97).[91] Like a prince in disguise, the bohemian would make his immersion in an anarchic demimonde an ironic measure of his pride and, it was to be hoped, future glory. In contrast to the situation in Shakespeare's play, however, in which labor is not really an issue, the modern bohemian's rule would be "To live outside the law, you must be idle." Critics of bohemians typically referred to them as parasites, but from the bohemian perspective to call another a parasite is to proclaim one's own servitude. To live outside the dominant culture of the nineteenth century required that prideful individuals dramatically hold themselves above work.

Equally disgusting to Marx, the bourgeoisie, and workingmen such as the elder Murger, this rebellious attitude became the most fundamental element in the definition of the bohemian. It also turned into one of the most lasting popular stereotypes of this figure, in which the bohemian critique of the culture of work appears as nothing but ordinary laziness. Only a year after Murger had published his *Scenes* in book form, Alphonse de Calonne came out with his scathing *Voyage to the Land of Bohemia* (1852), in which he said of the bohemian, "The prospect of having something to do frightens him; a regular job horrifies him."[92] Many others hastened to join in the refrain.[93] Ruskin, for example, certainly knew his enemy when he described "one kind of mind, the meanest of all, which perpetually complains of the public, contemplates and proclaims itself as a 'genius,' refuses all wholesome discipline or humble office, or ends in miserable and revengeful ruin."[94] He might have been thinking vaguely of Lord Byron, or specifically of Chatterton, or of Romanticism in general, but in any case he was taking dead aim at bohemia. Dickens's portrayal of Harold Skimpole in *Bleak House* (1853) is another example of such condemnation of the bohemian idler, as is, in a rather more complex fashion, Eliot's portrayal in *Middlemarch* (1871–72) of Will Ladislaw, a modern gypsy who redeems himself in the end by finding work, a wife, and a settled home. In his wild 1862 novel of bohemia, *The Ridiculous Martyrs*, Léon Cladel made this issue of idleness central to his narrative through the strained relationship between his protagonist, the aspiring author Alpinien Maurthal, and Alpinien's father, an uneducated but successful provincial farmer and businessman. Wishing to reconcile the two, his mother appeals in vain to Alpinien: "Be reasonable; after all, my child, this poor man has earned what he has by the sweat of his brow, and it wouldn't be right to spend wastefully what he has been at great pains to earn."[95] This kind of reasoning made no sense to the bohemian, though, and so in 1883 the American sociologist William Graham Sumner saw this figure as "sacrificing most of the rights and turning his back on most of the duties of a civilized man, while filching as much as he can of the advantages of living in a civilized state."[96] On the other hand, when the Peruvian writer Ricardo Palmas wanted to praise Acisclo Villarán, he came up with a phrase that drew a parallel between being a great bohemian and being extraordinarily lazy: "Acisclo es mucha pereza y mucho bohemio!"[97] As Murger's life demonstrates, the familial tensions that resulted from these conflicting attitudes were not only the stuff of fiction; one might also think, for example, of Baudelaire's hatred for his stepfather and of the pestering and manipulative letters, patently lacking in candor, with which he was forever trying to wheedle money from his mother.

The prideful poverty of the bohemian was already a stereotype by the end of the 1830s, when Thackeray satirized the attitude of art students toward "the sober citizen" by describing how "from the height of their poverty they look down upon him with the greatest imaginable scorn."[98] As in this description, scorn was returned for scorn, as their critics accused bohemians of being poor only because they were unwilling to work. Gabriel Guillemot, for example, wrote of bohemia, "It is born from *idleness* combined with *vanity*."[99] Henri Monnier and Jules Renoult made light of these divergent opinions in *Painters and Bourgeois* (1856), a verse comedy in which an artist's wife complains to him, "You call your idleness love of painting."[100] Not making light of the situation at all, two years before Murger's death Champfleury adopted much the same attitude in irritably shrugging off the label of bohemian, arguing that it was forged "out of idleness, ignorance, and dubious morals."[101] By 1855 an American writer, Fitz-James O'Brien, could trust his readers to recognize with amusement the well-worn stereotype when he had a bohemian describe himself by saying, "I don't want a profession. I could make plenty of money if I chose to work, but I don't choose to work. I will never work. I have a contempt for labor." He could also trust his audience to know the primary source for this image. His self-assured idler asks another character, "Have you read Henri Murger's *Scènes de la Vie de Bohème*?" When the response is in the affirmative, he remarks, "Well, then, you can comprehend my life."[102] The stereotype would travel far and wide, and it would prove enduring. American readers of a certain age may remember the interrobang—"Work!?"—that inevitably followed whenever this subject was broached within earshot of the beatnik Maynard G. Krebs in the television series *The Many Loves of Dobie Gillis* (1959–63). To this day Maynard G. Krebs lives on, and not only in reruns; in 2009 the Chinese city of Lishui, home to an industry of mass-produced paintings, advertised itself with the quasi-bohemian slogan "A Village of Art, a Capital of Romance, a Place for Idleness."[103]

As if in anticipation of negative reactions, in the first act of Vigny's drama Chatterton is allowed to explain that it is not for lack of trying that he has no job. He has sought to harness himself to an occupation, but his best efforts have brought him no success. Meanwhile, society refuses to see any value in his poetry writing. As the play approaches its climax, he considers suicide, but he is dissuaded from it by a confidante who tells him that his married landlady, Kitty, of whom Chatterton is enamored, reciprocates his feeling. In killing himself, he is admonished, he would be killing her as well.

Thus thwarted in art and trapped by romance, Vigny's Chatterton decides that it is not poison but his pride that he must swallow. He writes to the Lord Mayor of London, a friend of his late father's, beseeching his assistance, and the Lord Mayor offers him a job. Soon, though, he learns he is being falsely accused of having plagiarized his poems, which someone claims are actually the work of a tenth-century monk. Then, still reeling from the shock of having his poetic reputation stolen from him, he finds that the position the Lord Mayor has planned for him is that of a mere servant, a valet. Driven beyond all bounds, he throws caution to the winds and his papers into the fire, and he now does poison himself, leaving Kitty to fulfill his friend's prediction when she expires at the unexpected sight of him in the act of ceasing to be. These climactic events have no basis in the historical Chatterton's biography, and the false accusation of plagiarism in particular is an odd distortion of the historical record, wherein Chatterton actively sought to hoodwink the public with his fake medieval poetry. Vigny manipulated his plot in this way, though, so as to dramatize how crushingly humiliating common work must be to a true poet.

This play might have been expressly designed to justify Murger's resentment of his father, that ogre who dared to make the crazy suggestion that his son ought not to have too much pride to take a position as a servant. Through the love Vigny's Chatterton shares with Kitty, who is saddled with an insensitive, mercenary husband, Vigny might even seem to have anticipated the trouble that arose between his father and Murger as a result of the romantic affair with a married woman, Marie Fonblanc, that Murger would soon be drawing upon as material for his stories. So it makes sense that Vigny's version of Chatterton should have become a model for Murger's bohemians, as when Rodolphe, Murger's persona in his *Scenes of Bohemian Life*, comes up with the idea, "renovated from Chatterton," to heat his freezing apartment by burning his old manuscripts (158). After all, only a year or so before he began to write the *Scenes* Murger seemed to be renovating Chatterton within his own self by the way that he described his devotion to art: "There is no longer in the world but one thing that is good and beautiful for me, and that is art." In his miserable poverty he was breathing air that was killing him, perhaps, but at least he was still breathing, while otherwise, he said, he would be suffocating. He knew perfectly well what others would say—"pride, pride!"—but he did not care.[104] Critics might feel free to interpret bohemians' attempts to evade landlords and creditors as revealing an amoral sleaziness of the sort that Thackeray dramatized when he had *Vanity Fair*'s Becky Sharpe teach Rawdon Crawley "How to Live on Nothing a Year," as one of his chapter titles put it. To his admirers, though, the comedy Murger made out of such maneuvers was a deeply moral rebellion against the inhuman demands built into the economic system of modern nations.

This distinction between bohemia's critics and advocates gets confused, however, when we read Murger's preface to his *Scenes*, which was composed approximately five years after he began writing this series of stories and less than a year after he completed them. Here we find Murger all but spitting on Chatterton's grave. Along with the names of other "unhappy artists and

Figure 6. Karl Arnold, "Bohème," from *Simplicissimus* 13 (16 November 1908) ("I have so many ideas that I don't know which I should follow up on first, and so it's already been three years now that I haven't gotten to work").

poets," such as Victor Escousse and Jacques Charles de Malfilâtre, he mentions Chatterton's as one that has been "too frequently, too imprudently, and above all too uselessly thrown into the air." Chatterton's tomb has been turned into a "throne from whose height the martyrdom of art and of poetry is preached." Murger strenuously condemns the "immoral lies" and the "murderous paradoxes" that lure young men out of paths that could have led them to success and into a life in which they will come to a miserable end. Those with "a real vocation," he allows, are justified in pursuing such a course in life; but he is clearly more concerned with susceptible youths who have been led astray (37–38). This complaint had already been current when Murger was young, as when Félix Pyat grumbled in 1834 about the "epidemic malady" of a sick devotion to art that was afflicting young men who might otherwise have made perfectly good notaries, lawyers, and heads of families.[105] In this preface, though, Murger seems almost to have leapt back in time to those eighteenth-century commentators who saw in Chatterton's life a moral about sticking to one's profession while shielding one's eyes from delusive dreams of glory.

This attitude appeared in some of Murger's other writings as well, as in a story, "A Poet of the Gutters" (1851), that he first published in *Le Corsaire-Satan* along with the original episodes of the *Scenes*.[106] In this tale the narrator praises Vigny's *Chatterton* as a "beautiful work" only so that he can immediately qualify that judgment in utterly devastating terms:

> But its success must often have weighed heavy with remorse on the conscience of its author, who nonetheless ought to have foreseen the dangerous influence that this drama might exert on those of weak mind and vain ambition. *Chatterton* is one of those creations that has all the attraction of an abyss; and this text, which is, after all, in a dramatic form, nothing but the apotheosis of pride and of mediocrity, with suicide for its conclusion, has, perhaps, opened many tombs. And certainly performances of *Chatterton* have created that lamentable school of whimpering and doleful poets that criticism has not treated with the severity it deserves. (9: 231)

A few years later, in *The Water Drinkers* (1855), Murger was still returning to this topic. One of the characters in this novel upbraids another for his pride by saying that he himself would not hesitate to don a servant's livery, "as Chatterton refused to do" (1: 292), if he had a master who would leave him enough time to pursue his art once his duties as a valet were performed.

What happened? Murger had never been a political radical, but neither was he like the insipid contributor to the *New-York Saturday Press* who
made bohemians sound like Boy Scouts ("honest and brave, generous and
just, . . . charitable and courteous") while gravely noting that a man "may do
a servant's work, and yet be none the less a Gentleman or a Bohemian."[107]
Had Murger then metamorphosed, as Verlaine would later tell his bohemian
friends, into a "pseudo-Murger"?[108] What had become of the aspiring poet
whose own pride had seemed to be anticipated, explored, and given dramatic
legitimation by Vigny's play, even down to such details as his outrage at the
thought of donning a servant's livery?

Certainly Murger's stories had always presented his bohemian subjects
with amusement, and from the beginning he had shown a sharp eye for the
follies and silly eccentricities of his characters. In Byronic terms, his approach
in *Scenes of Bohemian Life* was closer to *Don Juan* (1819–24) than to *Childe
Harold's Pilgrimage* (1812–18). Murger had shown notable restraint even in the
few scenes of pathos he included, such as the death of Mimi. For the most
part this work consists of light-hearted anecdotes that have almost nothing
in common with the frantic Romantic extremes of Vigny's drama. Balding,
dumpy, weepy-eyed, poorly dressed, with a funny-looking red beard and bad
skin, Murger himself had never cut a Romantic figure, and his stories portray
decidedly ordinary young men and women, not professed symbols or ideals.
Even though Murger gained a reputation among his friends for writing to
the moment, composing new episodes in his original series of articles on the
basis of the daily events in their lives, the overall impression one gets is of a
writer looking back on his Romantic youth from a distance that allows him to
leaven his fond memories with a good deal of irony. Even so, the characters in
this work are presented as amusing types who display an admirable generosity
of spirit throughout their stumbling adventures, despite all their foolery and
failures. At worst, they are harmless. So what are we to make of this change
in Murger from one who represented his fellow bohemians so affectionately
to one who prefaced his book with a nineteenth-century version of a parental advisory sticker warning his readers that its contents might be dangerous
to children?

The change in attitude was so marked that it could not be allowed to pass
without comment even in Lélioux's memorial remembrance of his old friend,
published a year after Murger uttered his last words, which were, according to
a popular but very dubious legend, "No more music! No more noise! No more
bohemia!"[109] Lélioux was quite critical of Murger's ungenerous and superior

attitude in the epilogue to *Scenes of Bohemian Life*, in which all the surviving principals are shown to have embarked upon conventional adult lives, and in its preface, with its discouraging picture of bohemia as a sanctuary for goof-offs, idiots, do-nothings, and poseurs. Having welcomed Murger into his rooms when he broke with his father, having been there at the creation of his coterie, Lélioux still was upset, more than ten years later, at how his friend had decided to frame his stories. "And why forbid himself from pitying those who die along the way?" he asks. "Why mock those who fall? Why this glorification of success?"[110] He suggests Murger may have been badly advised by some of those who were around at the time when he was completing his book, after his play had brought him fame and more money than he had ever seen before. However that may have been, he deplores Murger's seeming assumption that one must worry about the dangerous impression books might have on the children in a household, thus catering to those "who wish to understand virtue only in the form of a eunuch."[111] He imagines Murger's new acquaintances insidiously whispering in his ear, "Take care! You have arrived. Look carefully around yourself, and you will understand that your interests are no longer what they were!"[112]

Lélioux was not alone in finding something unseemly about the way Murger reacted to success. Delvau, for instance, in what is otherwise a flattering biographical account, thinks that Murger was cruel at times in the way he represented his less fortunate comrades. He offers us a picture of Murger, as he moved up into serious literary circles of distinguished authors, hastening to take leave of the scrappy satirical paper that had first welcomed his work: "Farewell, *Corsaire*! Greetings, *Revue des deux-mondes*!"[113] The model for Schaunard, one of the main characters in *Scenes of Bohemian Life*, also could not forbear remarking that after his success Murger did not waste any time in leaving the Left Bank behind, moving across the river from his little room on the rue Mazarine to "a very dignified bourgeois apartment at 48 rue Notre-Dame-de-Lorette."[114] Even Théodore Pelloquet, one of his contemporary biographers and a man who very much approved of Murger's emphasis on bourgeois values, considered that he may have "sometimes pushed his new opinions too far."[115]

Obviously, Murger's life had been transformed by the success of his play. To begin with, it had enlarged his audience from the handful of Parisian literary figures who had enjoyed the occasional appearance of his sketches to huge numbers of theatergoers and readers—an audience that included, among other notables, Louis Napoleon, who had been present on the opening night of the play. (One wonders if Marx, when he was grousing about bohemians, knew of this fact.) The change in his circumstances was still evident when Murger died of complications from an arterial blockage in his leg, at the age of thirty-eight. The thousands attending his funeral included not only crowds of students, old friends such as Lélioux and Nadar, and distinguished literary acquaintances such as Théophile Gautier and Baudelaire, but also Charles Augustin Sainte-Beuve, François Ponsard, and Jules Sandeau, representing the Académie, and Philippe de Saint-Albin, the personal librarian and representative of the empress, who was a fan of Murger's work.[116] The funeral was paid for by the state, and Murger died a chevalier of the Legion of Honor, having been given this award a year earlier. No more bohemia, indeed!

Nonetheless, judgments such as those of Lélioux and Delvau need to be regarded with a certain amount of caution. The image of the comrade who sells out, betraying his fellows by joining the bourgeoisie, was a bohemian trope from the very beginning. These critical judgments about how Murger handled success might even be taken to support his retrospective condemnation of many so-called bohemians as parasites with no real talent who get in the way of truly deserving artists. As is suggested in one of the more savage episodes in *The Water Drinkers*, which has many passages of this sort, sniping at others' success could be a predictable result of this situation. The bohemians Murger describes are eager to praise one another's talent only as long as they all remain equally obscure in relation to the public at large. Should the public actually grant one of their fellows any success, there follows "a brusque turnabout, and the comrades leave in solitude the one newly chosen by the crowd" (1: 6). Here, a few years after his success, it is as if one sees Murger seeking to justify those additions to his *Scenes of Bohemian Life* that had caused such hurt to some of his closest friends.

Despite their differences, Murger did maintain ties with almost all his old comrades, and it seems highly unlikely that he himself could have missed the irony of his changed social status. Publicizing his life as a bohemian, he had ceased to be one. His worries over money would never end—he received only five hundred francs for the successful book version of the *Scenes*—but everything else was different. As if he had never quarreled with his father, he had become the gentleman his parents had dreamed he might be. The vocation that had led him into exile from the possibility of *embourgeoisement* had, in the end, carried him to just that goal. The nineteenth-century culture of work, it seemed, was more complex than one might have imagined, since Murger's mockery of industriousness had turned out to be a remunerative form of labor.

Figure 7. Pierre Petit, photograph of Henry Murger, from Théodore Pelloquet, *Henry Murger* (1861).

Murger's fiction shows that he was, in fact, acutely aware of bohemia as a complicated response to the modern culture of work. On the one hand, when he was in his early twenties, he and his friends, all wretchedly poor, had banded together to share their scanty means and extravagant dreams. This earnest, generous, and sometimes silly group deemed water the official drink at its meetings so that those too poor to afford wine would not be embarrassed. They were dedicated to helping one another persist in their high artistic ambitions even as they all toiled away at various mundane jobs to support themselves.[117] On the other hand, in the "Francine's Muff" section of the *Scenes*, Murger represented his friends' fellowship in poverty as a rigidly organized group that anathematized the very idea of utilitarian labor. Whether consciously or not, he reworked a theme from Sand's *Horace* (1842), in which Sand's supremely egotistical, ambitious, Romantic protagonist is disgusted when one of his friends is willing to take menial jobs—willing even to become a servant if need be—because he needs the money to aid his sister and the woman he loves. Similarly, when a sculptor who has been a loyal member of the Water Drinkers falls for a poor, sick girl and determines that he must take any work he can in order to help her, the group immediately excommunicates him and tells him he is no longer an artist. As narrator, Murger takes his side and assures the reader that the group is wrong on this point.

In *Scenes of Bohemian Life* Murger still implicates himself in the prideful idleness of bohemia, as when Rodolphe gives mocking voice to the defining cliché of his time: "Work is the holiest of duties" (131). The frame imposed by the preface and the epilogue, however, along with episodes such as "Francine's Muff," give us a glimpse of the direction Murger would take in his later stories. Here the quarrels over work with his father get reproduced, but now with Murger assuming the paternal role while the bohemians under his narrative supervision are made out to be wayward youths.

Conflicted family relations of this sort always tend to come up in narratives of bohemia because bohemians' relation to the culture of work is so entangled in their image as "ridiculous martyrs," in Cladel's phrase, who have chosen to live in poverty.[118] One of the most popular legends of bohemian origins tells of selfish young men "deluding [their] self-denying parents."[119] Auguste Villemot sardonically commented, "Perhaps there are some depraved young men who can recognize their professors—but these deplorable exceptions cannot taint the good reputation of the student body."[120] As the legend would have it, they come from the provinces to study in Paris, spend more time in cafés than in classrooms, and plunge into poverty only after their families cut off their funds once they discover the kids' wastrel ways. This type of narrative was so popular that it appeared even in Cletto Arrighi's representation of bohemia's Milanese counterpart in *The* Scapigliatura: *A Novel of Contemporary Society* (1862).[121] A variant of this tale featured youths, such as two of Murger's comrades among the Water Drinkers, the brothers Joseph and Léopold Desbrosses, whose fathers refuse to support them because they insist on pursuing a career in the arts instead of going into business. When Cladel set out to satirize bohemia, it was this stereotypical history that he assigned to Alpinien Maurthal, his protagonist.

The fathers in question may belong to the bourgeoisie or, as with Claude-Gabriel Murger, to the working classes. In either case, these popular images of bohemia show how their offspring are placed in an ambiguous social position. The implication is always that bohemians could take up a trade or a professional career if they chose to do so, and so their poverty is really a kind of play-acting. Cultured young men who pretend to be modern gypsies might as well be costuming themselves for a ball. They may live among poor people, they may have to make do with very few coins in their pockets, but they are victims of laziness, not of want. In contrast, the grisettes with whom these bohemians share their beds, like the workers and the unemployed among whom they have established themselves, do not have a ready way out of their economic condition, if indeed they have any chance at all of escaping it. Cladel calls attention to this situation when he has his impoverished protagonist think, for just a moment, of becoming a workingman. Why not? thinks this aspiring writer. "Where is the dishonor? Where the infamy? Is it my fault if society rewards the sweat of the body but has no bread to give to those who want to serve it with their mind?"[122] Immediately, however, following the *Chatterton* tradition, he rejects the notion, even though he reminds himself that his mistress, Claire, is laboring as a humble hat trimmer. With such a story in mind, one might conclude that living among the poor, for the typical bohemian, is indeed a kind of slumming.

This is also the implication that might be drawn from the splendidly cynical portrayal of bohemian fantasy in Guy de Maupassant's *Bel-Ami* (1885). This novel features as its "real bohemian" a petit-bourgeois wife who gets her kicks by dressing down and then venturing out with her lover to working-class dives.[123] Similarly, in George Moore's contemporaneous account of the "excitement of climbing up and down the social ladder," we meet with an image of bohemians playing at the game of republican fellowship without ever really endangering their status, privileges, or values. In contrast to Maupassant, Moore writes with a show of passionate sincerity about his participation in bohemia, but this is, at best, akin to the sincerity of the white New Yorkers of the 1920s who would seek out an authentic experience of society's downtrodden by having dinner at Harlem's Cotton Club. "One evening we would spend at Constant's, Rue de la Gaieté, in the company of thieves and housebreakers; on the following evening we were dining with a duchess or a princess in the Champs Elysées. And we prided ourselves vastly on our versatility in using with equal facility the language of the 'fence's' parlour, and that of the literary salon; on being able to appear as much at home in one as in the other."[124] As Moore unwittingly reveals, so-called bohemians may feel at home everywhere only if they bring their privileged origins with them wherever they go. Idleness in these circumstances is in no way a rebellion against the spirit and organization of labor. Nor is it a reformulation of aristocratic mastery into a sense of pride capable of doing battle with the demeaning culture of the modern marketplace. In this case idleness is simply a self-involved dilettantism, a search for entertainment. Here bohemia's association with the history of outcast vagabonds exists only as a form of aesthetic exploitation of the sort one finds in picturesque Romantic descriptions of thatched country cottages that their actual inhabitants know to be noisome, damp, cramped, bug-ridden hovels.

Murger was sensitive to this image of dilettantism, identifying it with those he called "amateurs" in his preface to the *Scenes* (39). Like Champfleury, Murger also wrote of *soi-disant* bohemians whose manners were based on "laziness, debauchery, and parasitism" (39). In the dramatized version of his *Scenes* he even gave his protagonist, Rodolphe, a rich uncle who serves, in effect, as a safety net for him—one that poor Mimi does not have. Murger, then, was aware that the poverty of many bohemians was not the same as that of the other poor and unemployed people among whom they dwelt.

The fact that the bohemian association with poverty could sometimes appear as a kind of slumming, however, does not mean there is no more to say about it. Bohemian poverty could also be, and undoubtedly sometimes was, a matter of principle. It was then a matter of choice only in the sense that one may choose not to be slavish, corrupt, base, and cowardly. Here one might think of Friedrich Nietzsche's remark that "the 'blessing of work' is the self-glorification of slaves."[125] If this turning away from the fate common to most people might be a vain pretence, as in a fatuous boast by the twenty-two-year-old Murger that he was "virginal" as far as any work that smacks of trade is concerned, what principled commitment may not? In the same letter in which he made this foolish claim, Murger made another that gives us a sense of the risks he chose to take in those days when he could not know that they would eventually lead to bourgeois success or, for that matter, to anything else. (The fate of Nerval, found hanging in the rue de la Vieille-Lanterne in 1855, always shadowed the bohemians of this era as they struggled to carry on.) "I've gone too far to turn back," Murger wrote, "and, whatever may happen, I will not deny my gods."[126]

Well aware of the frequently risky choices that gave rise to it, Nadar suggested that bohemia was a utopian socialism put into practice immediately, without waiting for a systematic transformation of society as a whole.[127] It required commitment, and it exacted its price. This is what has not been properly recorded by anyone, even Murger, Nadar argued in 1862. The most important facts about "that little pleiad" to which he had belonged, "born of famine, cold, and vagabondage," are "the absolute, precise, and utterly unpoetic details of that poverty some suffered during such a long time." Therefore, while applauding Murger's success as well deserved, Nadar urged his readers also to remember the martyrology of those who had fallen by the wayside. He used the word *martyr* without irony, not finding these lost souls at all ridiculous. He did not call attention to them, he insisted, out of either pride or humility; he called attention to them because he owed it to the good faith of his youthful comrades, who, in their "fraternal community," never failed each other.[128] We may add to his account the martyrology published by Firmin Maillard a dozen years later in *The Last Bohemians: Henry Murger and His Times* (1874). Serving as a precedent for later masterpieces in the bohemian tradition such as Antonin Artaud's essay "Van Gogh, Suicided by Society" (1947), Allen Ginsberg's poem *Howl* (1956), and Jim Carroll's fiery song "People Who Died" (1980), Maillard's book tells of a certain Barthet, currently in the madhouse at Charenton; Mailfer, an aged engraver, who hanged himself; Léopold Flameng, who also hanged himself; Jean Duboys, who died mad—and so on.[129] Testimonies like those of Nadar and Maillard invite us to recall a bohemia that sought to live its desires without compromise. At a later date and from those who were not part of the original experience, the aging bohemians expected, as they defied, disbelief.

In contrast to Marx's dismissal of bohemia as a reactionary social formation, accounts such as these give us a basis for understanding why this metaphorical community could prove attractive not only to the young Italian patriots portrayed in Arrighi's novel and to the nonfictional *scapigliati*, such as Felici Cameroni, who identified with the politics of the Paris Communards, but also, for example, to the Irish patriot John Boyle O'Reilly. Transported to Australia for his political activity, O'Reilly made his way to the United States, where, as he became an influential journalist, a popular poet, and a good friend of Walt Whitman, he eventually saw bohemia as the most apt name for the utopian land he imagined in his republican struggle against the prejudices of race, class, and religion. "I'd rather live in Bohemia than in any other land," he wrote in an 1885 poem, "For only there are the values true"—there, where "the wise . . . are never shrewd," where there are no inherited titles, no honors "garnered for thrift or trade," only "a faith sublime" uniting pilgrims from "every class and clime and time."[130]

Examples such as O'Reilly's can and should serve to counter the recurrent stereotype of bohemia as nothing but an aesthetic flight from political engagement, a carnivalesque distraction from serious efforts toward social change. This point is reinforced by Flaubert's *Sentimental Education*, which, by the time it reaches its conclusion, does not support any simple distinctions between impulses toward carnival and toward revolution. The same can be said of all of bohemia's nineteenth-century manifestations. Admittedly, the image of carnival was encouraged by some bohemian voices, such as that of Murger, in the first edition of the *Scenes*, or that of the German journal *Simplicissimus* at the turn of the century.[131] Despite such voices, however, many people agreed with figures such as Cameroni and O'Reilly in finding bohemia to be a fitting homeland for anarchists, socialists, communists, and others seeking social transformation. Bark proclaimed "the sacred trinity of bohemia" to be "art, justice, action."[132] More straightforwardly still, in 1906 Erich Mühsam proudly declared his déclassé affinities: "Criminal, vagrant, prostitute, and artist—that is the bohême that knows the pathways of a new culture."[133]

The complex tendencies of the bohemian phenomenon were addressed, if not resolved, in "The Funeral Supper" (1851), perhaps Murger's most remarkable story and certainly the one that holds his most telling assessment of the modern culture of work. The story's protagonist is Count Ulric de Rouvres, a man so fabulously rich that at a young age he has exhausted all the world's attractions. Disillusioned, radically dissatisfied with his life, he decides to take on a pseudonym so he can masquerade as a worker of the lowliest sort, performing brute physical labor in a factory. Initially Ulric rejoices in his new position, believing that he has discovered in the depths of society a populace free of the corruption that he had met with at the end of all the pleasures open to a wealthy and titled playboy. Within six months, however, he is as disillusioned with the supposed goodness and fraternity of workers as he is with everything else. Moving on to a new amusement, an eighteen-year-old grisette named Rosette Durand, he ends up unemployed after a fire in his factory occurs simultaneously with a commercial crisis that has led to layoffs everywhere in the region. Rosette works extra hours to support them both, and Ulric enjoys the "peculiar voluptuousness" (9: 67) of watching her sacrifice herself for him as they grow ever more impoverished. He decides to reveal his real identity to her, to carry her with him back to his life of wealth and ease, only after her excessive labors and privations put Rosette in the hospital, where, as it turns out, she dies before he can tell her his secret. Devastated by her death, he then chances to meet another girl, Fanny, who looks exactly like Rosette but who is her opposite in character: a totally cynical lorette, or courtesan. In return for a salary of a hundred thousand francs a year Fanny agrees to his request that she impersonate Rosette, dressing and acting the part while pretending to live in poverty with him—thus becoming something like the wax-doll grisette of which Champfleury wrote.[134] After Ulric asks Fanny to put on the last dress

Rosette owned, the one she wore when all her other clothes had been pawned to help support him, the lorette shows him what she has found in one of its pockets: a letter from his accountant. Realizing then that Rosette had known the truth about his wealth even as she was literally working herself to death for him, Ulric immediately faints and then dies shortly thereafter.

Despite his riches, Ulric's assigned role as a caricatural bohemian is evident from the beginning in his prideful alienation from conventional society, his vaguely republican inclinations, his Rousseauean idealization of common people supposedly uncontaminated by civilization, his Byronic world-weariness, and his idealist aesthetics. As personified by the count, bohemia in this story is just that glorified slumming its critics supposed it to be. To the extent that he has serious reasons for his actions, these are shown to be not only delusive, in terms of what they expect of others, but also self-deluding, in terms of his inability to understand his own motivations. The utter inanity of his supposed social consciousness is driven home as we see the readiness with which he transfers his attention from his initial ideals to an exercise in completely selfish, not to say sadistic, pleasure.

Murger could not have found a way more thoroughly to distance himself from his origins than by this rewriting of the bohemian adventure as the idle fancy of a jaded aristocrat. So much for the hideous cold, hunger, and misery he and his friends had actually suffered: in this revisionary image, none of it meant anything. Nothing was risked, not really. It was all a masquerade, and even at that not a harmless entertainment but a vicious bit of playacting, one whose principals deserve to be as conscience stricken as Vigny, in Murger's mature opinion, ought to have been. Bohemian idleness is caricatured here not simply as being a consequence of foolishness or vanity but also as having its own evil consequences. Here the search for aesthetic effects that is supposed to justify idleness is, in fact, what makes it a killing business. We may remember the rather creepy passage in the dramatized *Scenes* when Rodolphe says to Mimi, "Poor girl! . . . you have loved me, and in my egoistic love I've linked you to my life of poverty . . . every day I've witnessed your patient martyrdom, and while you were trembling with your feverish shivers . . . I warmed myself with the heat of your love" (100–101). Instead of the martyrology of bohemia, in "The Funeral Supper" we meet with bohemian death as a well-deserved punishment for trifling with the world of work.

The story does not stop there. At the same time as he so thoroughly erases his own mythology, damning its idleness, Murger refuses to allow any mythology of labor to take its place. Rousseauean sentiment, the revolutionary principles of equality and fraternity, and socialist rhetoric about the dignity of labor are all travestied and trashed. So, too, are moralizing middle-class ideologies of work, as we see the factory owner lecturing his employees about justice, reason, and merit and then taking the first opportunity he has to screw his new overseer out of what justice, reason, and merit would declare to be rightfully his. The proletarians in this story are not only petty and grasping but also just plain stupid, and the superior intelligence of their boss serves only to make him more effectively hypocritical than his workers can manage to be, try as they might. So bohemia does appear as mere slumming, but it cannot be said to victimize the poor into whose realm it swans its way. There is no more romance to be found among the real workers than there is in the idler who comes to live in their neighborhood as if he were one of them.

Murger himself does not come off any better in this nightmare. From the time that the dramatization of his stories of bohemia made him a celebrity, Murger's identity had been inextricably linked with the death of Mimi, Rodolphe's great love. From this moment on he had also been seen, at least by some, as exploiting this doomed figure. Nadar had pleaded with him to change the cry that Rodolphe utters at her death—"Oh, my youth, it is you that we bury!"—and at that time Murger had claimed to find nothing wrong with the line.[135] In this very play, however, he had shown Rodolphe entertaining the notion that his love for Mimi was just an egoistic "caprice" or "fantasy" (81), and in "The Funeral Supper" he systematically reconsidered the propriety of making another's end a symbol that caters to one's own narcissism. What we see in this story is a pseudo-bohemian poseur treating the suffering and death of a grisette as a bit of stage business designed for his viewing pleasure. It is difficult to imagine a harsher indictment of the tearjerking by which Murger had made his name.

Even Rosette, the grisette, does not escape this story's vortex of revisionary cynicism. The selflessness of this modern Patient Griselda might seem to make her the one character in the story who is simply and inarguably good, but it is so extreme that it also makes her nothing but an atrocious symbol. Having helped to contribute to it, Murger knew the legend of the carefree grisette and was certainly aware, as well, of how it had transformed a historically recognizable social type, the working-class girl, into a figure of fantasy. In legend, the grisette was defined above all else by her carelessness about money, and in this story Murger demystified the fantasy by pushing it to its logical extreme. Here the grisette's defiance of political economy becomes Rosette's masochistic willingness to accept the count's pretence that he is poor even at the cost of her own life. In nineteenth-century French popular culture the grisette was always a prop in a masculine drama, among other things, but here she is portrayed as nothing more than that. She is a figure whose purity is entirely imaginary, as is she—a point made all the more unmistakable when the count is able to hire a lorette to replace her. The ease with which the count is able to pay someone to reproduce her image lets us see that Rosette was only a perverse image to begin with.

Murger's friends tended to see all the young women in his stories and, for that matter, in his life as variant exemplars of a single type. The critic Rafael Cansinos-Assens made the even more sweeping judgment that "next to bohemia there is always a sacrificed woman."[136] In any event, here Murger himself goes to elaborate lengths to dramatize the phenomenon of women as copies of men's fantasies. In addition, through this substitution Murger mocks another aspect of bohemian mythology, according to which the heyday of the grisette ended around the middle of the century when her kind was replaced by the mercenary lorette. In Murger's own *Scenes of Bohemian Life*, as in Paul de Kock's writings and those of many others who contributed to the legend of the grisette, her replacement by the lorette represented a general loss of innocence for the 1840s generation of bohemians, as the youthful idealism that had persisted in their hopes under the July Monarchy gave way to age, weariness, and a post-Romantic realism. In "The Funeral Supper," though, far from representing any loss of innocence, the substitution of the lorette for the grisette only emphasizes all the more what had been apparent from the start: that the sexual relation in this story is a fantasy wrought from conditions of domination and servitude, as are all the economic and social relations it portrays.

Thus did Murger put paid to the gods of bohemia. He nested this story within a gossipy, frivolous, antic frame tale involving a dinner party of rich young men accompanied by four beautiful young women, but "The Funeral Supper" is a savage work. In its strange, strained, melodramatic turnings, it is a thought experiment designed to search out the nightmare that bohemia would appear to be if the very worst that could be said of it were taken to heart. What results from the experiment is the discovery that work is neither dignified nor undignified. It does not fit under such terms because it has taken over the entire world, structuring fantasies, pervading relationships, hounding the very image of idleness to its death. As *Scenes of Bohemian Life* is the template for innumerable subsequent narratives of the joyful misery of bohemia, "The Funeral Supper" is ancestral to narratives such as Luise Westkirch's *A Student*

Marriage (1898), a socially and psychologically acute review, in the form of a romantic melodrama, of damaging bohemian tropes at work among young Germans toward the end of the nineteenth century. Luis Antón del Olmet's "Why I Am a Bohemian" (1909), an account of an unintended fall into a bohemian life of poverty, hunger, and misery unrelieved by either carnivalesque pleasure or revolutionary hope, is another story that descends from this one.

Yet there remains a crucial difference between "The Funeral Supper" and other writings about bohemia, both early and late. Count Ulric, after all, is a nightmarish vision of bohemian pride and self-absorption, a grotesque and exceptional character, not a figure who appears to be representative of any group. The result is a vision that all of Murger's writings suggest we must take seriously, but we also see that this character notably lacks the bonds of friendship that had historically defined bohemia as a communal rather than an individual adventure. Even at their most critical, Murger's other writings convey the sense that it ought to be possible, if only in youth, to create a realm outside work sufficient at least for passing manifestations of ecstatic friendship, love, and art, even if these will then soon be dragged toward the grave of nostalgia. This is what alarmed the Belgian critic Georges Rodenbach: that bohemia is above all else a "way of life," a "life in common," in which the bohemian lives "outside himself," without discipline or rules. "Instead of possessing himself in silence," as Rodenbach thought any productive writer or artist must do, bohemians only "talk their books, their paintings."[137]

What Rodenbach saw as a vice, though, others saw as bohemia's virtue: that it was not concerned with productivity.[138] Appalled by the indignity of labor, bohemians were concerned, first and foremost, with the possibilities of community. Their desires did indeed course through the emblems that Rodenbach chose to represent their idleness: through "an existence of cafés, of balls, of farces, of noctambulism, of expedients, of all sorts of objectionable actions."[139] These desires moved out of the house, out from under the father, and even, in a sense, out of the capitalist marketplace and modern nation, to try their luck in an intentional community structured not by families and work but by comradeship.

This community, always fragile and often ridiculous and self-deluded, was very small potatoes in comparison to the worlds limned in the revolutionary predictions of figures such as Saint-Simon, Fourier, and Marx. Making at best a modest claim on reality, it was a great comedown from the Romantic dreams of the generation of 1830. Its modesty is captured in Murger's famous refrain, "Youth only comes around once."[140] Yet this seeming modesty could cloak important ambitions. At the very least, in the nostalgic attitude around it, youth is not wasted on the young, and maturity is forced to recognize its inglorious prudence, the time-serving nature of its wisdom, its servile submission to its labors. Zola beautifully captured this aspect of Murger's legacy when he depicted the burial of the artist Claude Lantier, whose great aspirations lead to his terrible mad failure in *The Masterpiece* (1886). This funeral ceremony causes one of Lantier's old friends, a writer, to feel Murger's voice echoing within him—"now it seemed to him that they were going to bury his youth"—before he wraps up the whole dispiriting business by saying, in words whose irony lies too deep for words, "Let's go to work."[141]

Like the vagueness in the very conception of bohemia, the modesty of its adventure was also its virtue. Murger did not want to be a slave, but neither did he aspire to be a master of anything but art. Through hunger, cold, grief, and sickness he had to battle his father and his entire world, really, in seeking to sustain his desire for a sense of dignity that could not be reduced to a reason, product, or reward of toil. Ironically, as no one knew better than Murger—the irony is written in all his stories—idleness is hard work. One does not entirely leave bohemia, however, as long as one persists in seeking a community outside the bounds of this horrible irony, which is enough to make one crazy.

CHAPTER 4

Unknowing Privat

Almost nothing was known for certain about the deceased, but at least one fact was established by his funeral cortege as it made its way through the streets of the faubourg Saint-Denis in the summer of 1859. Alexandre Privat d'Anglemont's body in that coffin proved that mocking the Romantic desire for an attractive case of consumption, as he had, did not grant one immunity from this disease.[1]

The same might be said of other Romantic fads that had infected so many members of this procession when they were young and youth was all in all. The mourners may have left these influences behind, may even have made light of them, but that does not mean they were free of them. In some ways that past was still all around them. On July 21, 1859, for instance, in the same issue in which it noted that the funeral of Privat would take place the next day, *La presse* had announced the presentation, at the Vaudeville Theater, of "*La Vie de Bohême*, the masterpiece of MM. Barrière and Murger."[2] When Mimi dies in this play, her lover Rodolphe sees his youth die with her on the stage of the theater where they are playing their roles; and we may suppose that even the most disillusioned of Privat's mourners felt that they were burying something of themselves on this day, on the stage of history. In Victor Cochinat's words, they were on their way to inter someone who was more than a man, one who was "almost a *country*."[3]

Appropriately, given its bohemian features, this procession had begun by breaking with convention. It had not set out from a church. Before he died of the ailment that practically defined *la mort de bohème*, Privat had made clear his wishes on this point: "It goes without saying that more than ever I remain faithful to Voltaire and to the *Encyclopédie*."[4] So the body of this arch-bohemian was being conveyed directly from the Maison de Santé Dubois to a

Montmartre cemetery, where Édouard Fournier, man of letters and historian of Paris, would pronounce the obsequies. Among the notables following the hearse was Murger, whom Privat had found to be a "charming observer" and an author of notable originality.[5] Murger had won fame a decade earlier with his tales of Rodolphe and Mimi and the other denizens of bohemia, which would maintain their power through subsequent generations and on into our own times, as in the Broadway musical *Rent*. On this day, however, his own health was so precarious that he might have counted himself fortunate even to be able to attend the funeral of the old pal who used to hang out with him at La Rotonde and the Café Momus.[6] Those who were well acquainted with him would have no cause for surprise when they learned a scant two years later that Murger would never see his fortieth birthday. As if in keeping with the lives that had leapt from his pen during all those nights, fueled by astounding quantities of coffee, in which he kept ink flying across sheet after sheet of paper, he would die young. And Privat? He was famous enough for his death to be publicized in Germany and the United States, as well as in France.[7] Still, Privat seemed to have been receding into the fabulous past even before the funeral procession that was now taking place. When he was hospitalized for long periods in the years immediately preceding his death, visitors were scarce.

Recalling Plutarch's tale of the Athenian who could no longer bear to hear people refer to Aristides the Just, Alfred Delvau suggested that the situation was much the same with his friend Privat. By the time of his death, Parisians had become "wearied of hearing Privat talked about" and "wearied also of hearing him talk."[8] Fittingly, under the circumstances, it was Privat that Edmond and Jules de Goncourt would remember some years later when they were meditating on the pathos of the bohemian who has outlived his youth and, with it, all the fun-loving freedom of his kind. In *Manette Salomon* (1867) they borrowed from him a quotation summing up that idyllic sensation of time, "the long succession of todays," which suddenly disappears when the bills for one's recklessness come due.[9] An iconic figure of the mid-century bohemia in which the Goncourts' novel was set, by the end of the 1850s Privat appeared to some observers to be one of its last vestiges. In the year of Privat's death Champfleury was writing of bohemia as a stupidly overblown myth and describing his former companions in this community as but a dozen or so young men practiced in "laziness, ignorance, and doubtful morals" and held together by nothing more than a weak thread of romanticism.[10] A year after the publication of *Manette Salomon* Gabriel Guillemot would try to finish stitching up this era's shroud, arguing that bohemia was an anachronistic term and voicing his suspicion that it had never really existed in the first place. Such thoughts were already circulating, perhaps even among those following his coffin, when Privat, who had never abandoned his bohemian ways, was carried to his grave.[11]

If some thought it was all over and had never been much to begin with, though, others felt differently. On that sad day of Privat's funeral a man burst into the street, astonishing the crowd of mourners moving along it. Some of them recognized him as a waiter, Baptiste, from an establishment on the rue des Martyrs, a gathering place so well known that all referred to it simply as the Brasserie. What was the story here?

Baptiste, at least, was not ready to be done with Privat. He had come running from the Brasserie, determined to catch up with the train of mourners before it was too late. As he fell into step with the somberly attired crowd, panting, disheveled, still wearing the vest and apron of his occupation, he apologized for his appearance. His boss had refused to give him leave to attend the funeral, and so he had had no alternative but to sneak out of work. Not to accompany Privat to his grave was unthinkable. One had to go all the way, "jusqu'au bout," with a man like that. He would rather have lost his job, he explained, than not to have kept faith with him.[12]

Or so the story goes. For when it comes to the life, or even to the death, of Alexandre Privat d'Anglemont, distinguishing stories from matters of fact is all but impossible. His peculiar celebrity draws our attention to the manufacture of stereotyped images by modern media and their relation to the genre of the novel, the structuring of economic rationality in a developing industrial economy, the construction of national and racial identities, and the heritage of colonialism. In the end, Privat's own writings explain why his life had to take the form of fiction. His was a kind of renown virtually demanded by his time, in which his contemporaries saw him as exemplifying what we can now see to be a remarkably persistent Romantic trope of selfhood, the figure of tragically misunderstood celebrity. Living through this trope, Privat wrote his way out of it while he endured, and rebelled against, its consequences.

Even his closest friends were unable to separate Privat the man from the stories about him, many of which he himself had taken pleasure in elaborating. He was a famous talker and no less famous a fabulist. In the words of Nadar, who was to become a celebrated cartoonist, balloonist, and photographer, "This Privat who was acquainted with the entire universe" was also this "great liar Privat d'Anglemont." He was a master of *blague*, which was the contemporary term for the bullshit, the mockery of serious talk, that

Honoré de Balzac identified with the very spirit of bohemia.[13] "As for Privat
d'Anglemont," wrote *Le Figaro*, making sport of him in this regard, "it is a well
known fact that he has twice refused the throne of Spain and the Indies; at
least Privat has told me that, and I believe him incapable of a lie."[14] The chief
of the Sûreté in Paris during the Second Empire called him a "joyous mysti-
fier" and claimed that he was not above a bit of low-level con artistry when the
opportunity presented itself.[15] According to Nadar, he and his friend even used
to enjoy an ironic little ritual based on Privat's self-mythologizing reputation.
"From afar," Nadar said, "when I glimpsed him coming over the crest of the
Pont-Neuf and cried out, 'Privat, it can't be true!', invariably he responded, his
hand over his heart, 'Word of honor!'"[16]

The poet Théodore de Banville felt that Privat was closer to him than
to anyone else, but even so he knew next to nothing about his friend's past.
"Twenty times," Banville remembered, "in moments of effusiveness, he told
me he was satisfying an overpowering need in recounting his history to me,
and he did indeed recount it to me, down to the most precise details, with a
convincing air of reality—but each time a different reality!"[17] Storytelling was
so essential to Privat's being that it seemed whatever he did not invent for
himself would be invented for him anyway, and not only by gossipy strangers
but even by intimates such as Banville, with whom he had shared lodgings and
adventures. One thinks, for instance, of the story Banville tells of his friend's
disarming response— "But I am Privat!"—to some thugs who accosted him
and demanded his money. The thieves had a good laugh, according to the
story, once they realized that they had tried to rob a beloved figure known to
everyone in Paris for his bohemian poverty; and so they embraced him and
took him out to feast and to drink champagne under the stars, where all were
entertained by Privat's wonderful talk.[18] This narrative takes on a rather different character, however, if one compares it to the letter to Alexandre Dumas in
which Privat described the mugging that may have inspired Banville's account.
In this telling, it was a considerably more painful and upsetting experience.[19]

As in this instance, one can manage to find at least a few details that seem
to stand out as warrantable facts in a life otherwise belonging to the precincts
of story, fantasy, and myth. All accounts agree, for instance, in describing
Privat as a man of mixed race, a mulatto, from the Antilles. Even on this point
there was room for joking: Nadar scoffed that Privat was such a fabulist that
one could not know whether he was a mulatto, a Jew, or a Bulgarian.[20] In the
terminology of nineteenth-century France, though, Privat was indeed a mulatto. Everyone knew he had come to Paris to go to college, some had heard

Figure 8. A. Lecleu [?], caricature of Privat d'Anglemont, from *Rabelais* (8 June 1867).

him say that he had grown up in southern Brittany, and others were aware that he was born in the town of Sainte-Rose, in Guadeloupe, in 1815. He had come to France at the age of ten and had moved to Paris for his studies, attending the Collège Henry IV, where Privat passed what he would remember as the most beautiful years of his life.[21] A light-skinned, good-looking young man, he was crowned with a mass of tightly curling black hair that sometimes led people to mistake him for Dumas.[22]

Cochinat, who was himself a mulatto from Martinique, described Privat as the offspring of a "rich and respected family of color," orphaned young and raised by an older brother who ran the family's sugar plantation.[23] Delvau and Banville wrote a little more bluntly in describing him as the illegitimate offspring of a liaison between a rich creole and a native woman.[24] In all accounts he was more interested in the Parisian streets and nightlife than he was in his studies. After receiving his *baccalauréat* from the Collège Henry IV he briefly enrolled as a medical student but quickly dropped these studies in favor of devoting all of his time to the streets. Subsequently, and unsurprisingly, his brother Elie-Victor became concerned about money matters and is said to have pressed him to return home. Privat then supposedly sailed back to Guadeloupe, on a voyage that would have taken more than a month, officially signed his name to a legal document his brother had worked out, and promptly turned round and set sail for France, having stayed in his homeland less than a day. Whatever the truth of this story may be, there is no report of Privat returning home at any other time. It is clear, too, that during and after his college days he was utterly spendthrift with whatever moneys his brother may have remitted to him.[25]

Famously, Privat preferred to live by his wits, by his talk, by cadging meals—by whatever means or mercies came his way. According to his own account, which his friends would have considered characteristically extravagant, he held body and soul together at various times by playing the violin and cornet at dances; decorating bakeries and fashionable wine shops with paintings; ghostwriting novels, study guides, books of poems, historical researches, and parliamentary speeches; and doing translations from Latin, Greek, English, and German.[26] As his comrade Delvau put it, alluding to a line from the play by Murger and Barrière, often "he slept at the inn of Providence after having supped at the table of Chance."[27] A German observer early in the next century would write that bohemians do not really possess their life, which is only loaned to them; and such was Privat's life in his time.[28]

In his attitude toward money Privat might remind us of a story told by

AL. PRIVAT D'ANGLEMONT.

Imp. A. Clément _ Paris.

Figure 9. R. de Los Rios, "Al. Privat d'Anglemont," from *Paris anecdote* (1885).

another emigré widely admired in this era's bohemia, Heinrich Heine: that when he was a schoolboy he was punished for responding, when asked the French word for faith, that it was *le crédit*.[29] Privat seems to have followed this faith not because he ever desired money but because he despised it, could not be bothered to concern himself with it. "Money," he wrote, "nothing but money, nothing plucks at their heartstrings but that."[30] He would quote an old joke: "Ideas never die, and neither do creditors."[31] Despite his carelessness about finances, however, and in spite of the fact that he was better known as a man of the streets than as a man of letters, he did manage to publish in a wide variety of genres while also ghostwriting an indeterminate number of works that appeared under the names of others. According to the research of Pierre Citron, he published articles in *Le Corsaire* (where the episodes of Murger's *Scenes of Bohemian Life* [1851] first appeared), *Le silhouette*, *Le siècle*, *Le bon ton*, the *Gazette de Paris*, and the *Messager de Paris*; and another scholar, Jean Ziegler, has identified as Privat's some theater reviews as well as a series of articles about various sections of the Louvre, such as the rooms devoted to Egyptian sculpture and antiquities from the Americas.[32] His other works include a booklet about a dance hall with an associated garden, the Closerie des Lilas, and another about the Prado, which was the name given to the Closerie in the winter; an article about the encyclopedists of the Enlightenment, who "made nature fashionable"; other fugitive pieces, such as a pantomime, a few poems, and a contribution to a gossipy send-up of high society to which Charles Baudelaire also contributed; and, most famously, essays about the hidden lives, neighborhoods, and corners of Paris.[33] He published these in journals before some of them were gathered in 1854 in *Paris Anecdote* and others in a posthumous collection entitled *Unknown Paris* (1861).[34] At one point he had advertised a forthcoming book entitled *The Shady Life: The Story of Seven Bohemians Who Have No Castles*, but Auguste Vitu's contemporary comment remains true: "This difficult enterprise remained worthy of Bohemia, in the sense that the author has yet to write the first line of it."[35]

In the last years of his life Privat was repeatedly hospitalized and often in dire need of money. Throughout his life, and after his death, it was rare to find anyone who had a bad word to say about him.[36]

So much, more or less, is known. In the end, though, the fact of Privat's legend is probably more important than any details that can be recovered about the facts of his life. For Privat accepted and lived this legend as the great fact of his life, and before he died he did not fail to reflect upon the storied nature of his existence. He himself might almost have written the account of

Baptiste's appearance on the day of his burial. Baptiste belonged at this funeral because Privat, in all his storied being, shared his sympathies with unknown workers far more than he did with the notables and aspirants to fame who were his friends but who risked nothing in following him to his grave.[37] Joseph Barbaret said as much in the opening sentence of *The Bohemia of Work* (1889), which portrayed Privat as pioneering the study of "unknown trades"—that is, those usually ignored by the world at large.[38] Privat had become famous in the course of writing about the uncelebrated lives of people just like this waiter.

Baptiste's insistence on joining Privat's funeral procession, his willingness even to lose his job if need be, is such a touching anecdote because it is, quite appropriately, too good to be true, whether or not it was a matter of fact. As no one knew better than Privat, to be too good to be true goes with the romantic territory of the bohemian, the creature of stories whom Privat embodied to impossible perfection. After all, from the very beginning bohemia was defined by the eventual comedowns lying in wait for it: the tubercular coughs, the sellouts, the disillusionments, the despondency and madness, the sad funeral processions. It was not without reason that Murger had described it as "the preface to the Academy, the hospital, or the morgue."[39] In his death as in his life, Privat, as the epitome of bohemia, was too much for truth to handle. Despite his fame, he was not really understood, because "everything about him was unlikely."[40]

If Murger was universally recognized as the poet whose pen scribbled into being the myth of bohemia, Privat was recognized by his contemporaries as the one who most fully lived that myth. He seemed to unite the various meanings of *bohemian* that were current at the time: the vagabond, the artist, the foreign outcast, and the suspicious figure of the urban streets "whose existence is a problem."[41] He was the "threefold bohemian," the "pureblooded bohemian," "the most complete type of the bohemian, as people in general think of it."[42] "In accordance with the traditional reasoning that says one should lend only to the rich," wrote Firmin Maillard, "people lent to him the most unbelievable adventures, astonishing mystifications, and certain feats . . . that [François] Villon would not have disavowed."[43] The press, said Delvau, "contributed to the legend of Privat. Every time that a newsman in a bit of trouble needed a name to designate a bohemian, he unceremoniously took that of Privat d'Anglemont."[44] In the words of Alphonse Duchesne, "He was the scapegoat, he was the target, he was the plaything."[45] For instance, in describing an attack on Privat—perhaps the same mugging he wrote of in that letter to Dumas—*Le Figaro* turned it into a joke: "The mythological part of it is that Privat alleges that they stole seven and a half francs. An inquiry is underway into the causes that could have resulted in Privat possessing seven and a half francs. This last part of the affair is very mysterious and of great concern to the magistracy."[46]

Further adding to the legend through his own incessant and incredible storytelling, Privat did not trouble himself over the inventions made in his name. He seemed unconcerned with the facts of his life, never seeking to set the record straight until he finally became fed up a few days before he died.[47] He even agreeably acknowledged, without protest or correction, those fools who mistook him for Dumas.[48]

He was unlikely in every aspect of his being. Though he came from a country the French always thought of as sunny, night was the best time of day for this "king of noctambules."[49] Although he was an emigré, he made all of bohemia his native land even as he remained an outsider to society at large. From its boulevards, theaters, cafés, and dance halls to its most dodgy, dingy, louche, out-of-the-way, and simply unbelievable parts, Paris was his city. A vagabond, he could nonetheless make himself at home anywhere within it, whether in a slum or, in the last year of his life, at a dinner of the Society of Men of Letters also attended by Gustave Flaubert, Nadar, Murger, Alexandre Dumas *fils*, Jules Janin, and Théophile Gautier, among others.[50] Poor as he was, Privat owned this city; and yet he did belong to the poor, to what he called "the great family of the disinherited."[51] He was proud to number himself among the Left Bank's "exiles of Paris," all of them "inhabitants of an impossible land."[52] As Cochinat suggested, he virtually *was* this country of bohemia.

Alexandre Privat d'Anglemont could never have become this universally recognized and beloved Privat if he had not left Guadeloupe for the metropole of Paris at precisely the historical moment when the character of the bohemian was being defined and popularized, a shabby suit perfectly cut to his measurements. Individuals never make themselves living legends, or "the unconscious idol" of a "singular cult," solely by their own efforts, indispensable as these must be.[53] They need a social and cultural world in some way open to their aspirations; and, in addition, even if they are well suited to the world in which they find themselves, they need some sort of publicity machinery to make them known. As a gregarious man of letters, Privat found that machinery in the public sphere of metropolitan life.[54]

The nineteenth-century capital of France was permeated by multiple forms of information, printed and oral, authoritative and gossipy, coming from above and below and all around. In this modernizing city information could quickly circulate so as to create public figures in the promiscuous modern fashion institutionalized in the pages of the daily newspaper before its functions were overtaken by radio, cinema, television, and the Internet. In George Sand's words, "It takes only two people to tell a secret to all of Paris."[55] While the popular press could tear people down—Alphonse de Calonne portrayed bohemian journalists as little more than extortionists who played upon fears of character assassination—it could just as readily make them celebrities.[56] We can see how this process took place through the accounts of Privat left to us by his contemporaries. Privat still would never have become Privat, however, if he had not also fulfilled a specific exigency of his time: the demand that within modern life, with all its complexities, savage disaggregations, and hurtling confusions, one must find a redemptive unity.

This was the task undertaken by the most important literary form of the nineteenth century, the novel, in its most distinctive manifestations: to show society to itself, unified and whole and comprehensible, within the figure of the individual. Nineteenth-century novels became "large loose baggy monsters," in Henry James's impatient phrase, precisely because this demand for a comprehensive view of things was so insistent and yet so impossible to satisfy.[57] Balzac tried to respond to it in the series of works that eventually composed his *Human Comedy* (1829–47) even as Charles Dickens took it up in his later works, such as *Bleak House* (1853) and *Our Mutual Friend* (1865). We see this demand articulated in the very form of these sweeping, panoramic, quasi-sociological novels and in the many others akin to them. These range from Elizabeth Gaskell's 1855 *North and South* (whose very title bespeaks this anxiety over unity), William Makepeace Thackeray's *Vanity Fair* (1848), George Eliot's *Middlemarch* (1872), and Anthony Trollope's *The Way We Live Now* (1875) to the extraordinary documentary realism of Émile Zola and, at the end of the century, the even more extraordinary unreality of Arthur Conan Doyle's Sherlock Holmes.

Although rarely thought of in the company of authors such as Balzac, Dickens, and Eliot, Conan Doyle actually represents the culmination of their attempts to prove that a common ground must lie beneath the pullulating bewilderments of modern society. With his unique combination of artistic sensibilities and scientific knowledge, his ability to enter into any corner of society, his power to analyze signs, uncover secrets, reveal truths, and support the legal system of the English nation and empire, Holmes embodies the nineteenth-century demand that society must be made whole within the consciousness of the individual. In fact, he is this unifying figure at the end of its tether: depressive, misanthropic and misogynistic, drug addicted, and, in his superhuman character, redemptively unreal. After Holmes, who might be called the last of the great nineteenth-century bohemians, modernists such as Marcel Proust, Virginia Woolf, and James Joyce would feel the need to revolutionize the form of the novel, the concept of bohemia, and, along with these, the very nature of the self.

"Known to all of Paris," "acquainted with the entire universe," Privat was this Sherlockian figure in an earlier historical moment still touched with romance.[58] His "almost universal notoriety" was as much the cause as the consequence of his legend.[59] Since he was said to know everyone and go everywhere, no one acquainted with him would have been surprised, for example, by Charles Monselet's recollection that Privat had been strolling around with Gérard de Nerval on January 25, 1855, the night before the morning this poor soul was found hanging from a grille in the muddy, odious rue de la Vieille-Lanterne.[60] As the perfected form of the vagabond bohemian, in his peregrinations Privat seemed to draw together a social unity that otherwise seemed doubtful, if not in fact utterly lost. The crime he solved was the crime of modernity itself, and he solved it in his own person.

Some of those whom he linked together were socially prominent people, or people who eventually became prominent. For instance, it was he who separately introduced both Banville and Nadar to Baudelaire. Most of his multitude of acquaintances, however, were destined to remain as anonymous as the waiter from the Brasserie. The anonymity of this multitude was crucial to Privat's legend, since it made his connections seem ubiquitous and so made him seem a kind of all-knowing figure. Accordingly, Banville claimed that when he traveled with Privat and the two of them entered a theater, café, or dance hall in any town, "immediately twenty women's voices would cry out simultaneously, 'Good evening, Privat!'" Banville's dubious anecdote about the time Privat was mugged also represents this fantasy.[61]

Privat, Banville said, was even described by one wit as "the bond of modern society."[62] Further burnishing the legend, Banville compared the impoverished and ignobly born Privat to the hero of Eugène Sue's *Mysteries of Paris* (1842–43), Rodolphe, the fabulously rich Prince of Gerolstein.[63] A prototype of Sherlock Holmes (complete with his own version of Watson, the Englishman Walter Murph), Rodolphe disguises himself so that he can delve into the underside of society, solve crimes, and right wrongs, thus demonstrating that a unifying Providence actually rules over all the coincidences that structure

Sue's narrative. (Giuseppe Rovani, the novelist who was a leading figure in
Milan's bohemian circles later in the century, aptly referred to Rodolphe as
"the traveling salesman of Providence on earth.")[64] Privat, Banville suggests,
was a more credible figure, and, we might add, a more modern protagonist.
Whereas Rodolphe suggests that society is unified transcendentally, through
divine foresight and command, Privat's legend suggested that this unity must
be sought in the curious uncertainties, unknown labyrinths, and mortal delights of human life. Remembering the risky explorations of the underworlds
of Paris on which Privat based his writings, Fournier took note of this aspect
of his legend in his funeral oration, in which he spoke of Privat having died as
a result of his "mission of experimental literature."[65]

In relation to Privat, an emphatically anticlerical figure, one cannot speak
of Providence except ironically, for he did not presume to solve anything or to
take power over anyone. His Providence was improvidence; inutility was his
utility. "In order to be able, as he was, to recognize and study Paris through
all its ins and outs, to live in the most humble and terrible surroundings, to
travel across all the social worlds and to be accepted within them as a harmless
creature," wrote Banville, "he had to let everyone remain in ignorance of his
real personality; and to be even more convincing he took the radical step of
forgetting it, ignoring it, himself."[66] So the legend developed, with the inevitability of a classic nineteenth-century narrative, of a man known to all, binding all together, effectively "replacing Christianity" in doing so, but, in doing
so, losing himself.[67] "We barely knew Privat," wrote Delvau, "even though he
was known to all of Paris."[68] "He kept within himself a crowd of secrets and
of melancholy thoughts," said Charles Coligny.[69] "Even though his name was
popular, perhaps even a little too much so," wrote Cochinat, "he did not live
happily." Noting that Privat, despite all his notorious storytelling, had not left
the world his own story before he died, Fournier declared that Privat's friends,
who had found their way so quickly to "the bottom of his heart," could not
dream of getting to "the bottom of his life."[70]

If one were to be the most complete bohemian, it seemed, one had to accept that his destiny would assume this form. As in the case of Holmes, one's
habit of disguise must prove inseparable from one's being. A storied being remains essentially unknown; to be the bond of society is to be essentially alone.
Too good to be real, one must suffer one's unreality.

Privat could appear as the fantasy figure of social unity in this era because
the role of the male bohemian had always been imagined as that of a prince
in disguise, a prince unjustly dispossessed of his realm. The role was that of an

outcast in whom, despite outward appearances, the real genius of society and hope for the future lived on. In fact, men who actually claimed to be fallen princes and other sorts of royalty and aristocracy lived in the bohemian society of Privat's day just as they did a decade or two later, in Guillemot's classification of bohemian types. Guillemot began his classification with "bohemian princes" who are "in quest of a vacant crown, or the means to reconquer that which they have lost," a category supplemented by his description of the "exotic bohemian," whose numbers include "dubious marquises," "louche counts," and "suspicious barons" from Italy, Spain, Brazil, Peru, and Mexico, among other places.[71] At the turn of the century Frank Wedekind was still having fun with this trope by way of the dubious titles of the characters in his play *The Marquis of Keith* (1900). These claimants and poseurs, however, merely made literal the sense of entitlement that had always characterized all bohemians.

As with so much else in this period, Johann Wolfgang von Goethe had created the model for this quasi-rebellious sense of entitlement. In the protagonist of *Wilhelm Meister's Apprenticeship* (1795–96) he provided a prototype for the image of oneself as a dethroned prince, an image through which he anticipated all the core themes of bohemia. These included a sense of dispossession from one's cultural patrimony, which in Wilhelm's case is represented by his grandfather's art collection; a father and son at odds with each other; conflicts between commerce and art; the association of the artistic life with sexual experimentation, intense friendship, unconventional forms of community, and gypsy vagabondage; and a conviction that one properly belongs to a higher social order, for which Goethe traces a distinguished cultural ancestry all the way back to William Shakespeare's Hamlet and Prince Hal. This Urtext would be recalled throughout this century, periodically resurfacing as a bohemian reference point, as in Wedekind's *Earth Spirit* (1895), in which the faithless Lulu is repeatedly identified with Goethe's entrancingly odd Mignon.[72] A decade before Wedekind wrote that play, it was not a good omen for the legal studies to which he was supposedly dedicating himself when he mentioned, in a letter to his mother, that he and his friends were entertaining themselves by reading aloud from Goethe's narrative of Wilhelm's adventures.[73]

Elaborating on Goethe's prescient model, the bohemian in nineteenth-century France was defined through multiple disinheritances, at once political, economic, social, and cultural. To begin with, repeated disillusionments with the revolutionary hopes generated in 1789, 1799, 1830, and 1848 helped shape the destiny of this figure. So Privat would exclaim—in the midst of a book about a dance hall!—"Come on, young men, get up, the time is ripe, listen to the cries of deliverance and liberty from all sides, add your voice to those of the people who are suffering, and prove to the world that you are still the worthy sons of those men who shattered tyranny, conquered Europe, and gave to the universe the grand and salutary example of two revolutions!" This outburst, however, seems to come out of nowhere and suddenly ends, resignedly and cynically, with Privat's reminder to himself that "the purpose here is not to issue a manifesto, but to try to amuse readers."[74] Abruptly interjected and then immediately set aside, this abortive call to action certainly reveals Privat's personal nostalgia for the Latin Quarter of his youth. At the same time, however, it captures the general predicament of mid-century bohemia, which was loosely associated with liberal and socialist aspirations but for the most part not politically engaged in any significant way.[75] Instead, as its name suggests, bohemia was generally conceived to be a country altogether different from the world of governments, parties, and politicians.

The political disappointments that helped make bohemia an "impossible land" were accompanied by the impression of economic disinheritance that created the stereotypical opposition between bohemians and philistines. In this regard, the princely sense of entitlement that characterized bohemians was a response to the conviction that the arts were being reduced, in modern society, from activities subject to enlightened upper-class patronage (as with Wilhelm Meister's grandfather) to degraded objects of commerce in a vulgar middle-class age. On the one hand, the status of art and artists was insulted by the way progress, under modern conditions, was defined in terms of "utility, the grand word inscribed on all the banners," as Privat put it.[76] On the other, such cultural space as was granted to the arts was widely viewed as being dominated by conservative officials and sclerotic institutions, frustrating aesthetic progress and youthful ambition. Suspect in their grasp of history, the resulting feelings of revolutionary disappointment and professional degradation were nonetheless vital to the desires that circulated among the Parisian students and artists who, together with their working-class lovers and various other more-or-less shady types, became the imaginary community of bohemia.

In letters that Privat addressed to the minister for public instruction, complaining of the difficult conditions of authorship and seeking support for his efforts, we glimpse this sense of disinheritance.[77] We see it even more strikingly expressed in a series of letters Privat wrote to Sue in 1843. While praising that "admirable book," *The Mysteries of Paris*, he hastens to point out that he is in a position very different from Sue's. Unlike the famous author—and, needless to say, his princely protagonist—Privat is "the bohemian," a figure whom the public does not take seriously.[78] He proposes, therefore, that Sue employ him as a ghostwriter, and one of the works he envisions is a novel that would tell the story of bohemians. He would describe "the life, of misery and hunger and rage, of that intelligent, hardworking, well-informed race— the problematic existence of all these young men who have been disabled by education and college, who have no position, and to whom our miserable civilization has left only two ways out, the gallows and the hospital. In these sorts of lives one finds marvelous eccentricity, unknown joys, and, above all else, prodigious resourcefulness. I know them, I've lived there with them, I live there still."[79]

Since another defining quality of bohemia was youth, these combined political and economic disinheritances were further overwritten with a sense of personal grievance typically directed at the head of the family, the father. In the stereotype of bohemia, as in Goethe's novel and Murger's life, the father appeared as the patriarch who fails to support the son's cultural ambitions. Baudelaire wonderfully dramatized this nexus of political, economic, and familial grievances. In the revolutionary days of 1848 he was seen carrying a gun and shouting that the insurgents should shoot General Aupick, who just happened to be his mother's second husband—the man who had usurped the place of his deceased father, as in a modernized version of *Hamlet*. Baudelaire's father had been an amateur artist; his stepfather had proven to be unsympathetic to his ambitions. With Aupick's support, the poet's mother had literally taken her son's inheritance out of his hands. The fact that he had been spending that inheritance at a breakneck pace was irrelevant, as far as Baudelaire was concerned. General Aupick was the disinheriting State, Economy, and Patriarch all rolled into one.

Of course, this is just an especially dramatic example of the many mundane instances of fathers opposing their sons' artistic ambitions, or of other figures cast into this punitive paternal role, such as Salomon Hamburg, Heine's rich uncle. There were certainly contrary cases, despite the widespread view of art as a sure pathway to poverty, but the stereotype was fixed on this point. In some sense the bohemian was always, as Louis Leroy mockingly said, an "unrecognized genius."[80]

Further contributing to the image of the bohemian was a metaphysical sense of disinheritance, in some part combining all these others, focused on the poetry of the past, vaguely specified ideals, and an aesthetic aura of spirituality or divinity. Bohemian blague may have been a send-up of sacredness in any and all aspects of society, but it could also suggest the nostalgia of latecomers to Romanticism for a world they presumed to have existed prior to its disenchantment under the materialist, utilitarian, democratic order of modernity.

Buoyed by these losses, bohemia, in the imagination of those who were sympathetic to it, was a land unto itself. It was effectively outside the boundaries of the state, situated in an existential realm wherein the triumphs of imagination could assuage disappointed revolutionary aspirations while still expressing hope for the future. It was also an economy unto itself, in which the workaday regime of business and industry gave way to reckless desire, spontaneity, improvisation, and sharing. At the same time it was a family unto itself, in which ad hoc friendships displaced kinship relations even as affairs with grisettes displaced the domestic and social expectations of marriage. Finally, and no less importantly, it was a time unto itself, the time of youth, conceived of as existing outside of chronology, like an eternal present, even though it was always shadowed by intimations that eternity might be much briefer than its reputation suggested. "My God, but what a beautiful thing youth is," Privat exclaimed when he was leaving his twenties behind, "and how much one is bound to miss it!"[81]

Under these conditions, who better to epitomize bohemia than a bastard mulatto from Guadeloupe—one who bore with him a personal, racial, and colonial background to magnify the multiple disinheritances that defined this form of life?[82] "The only fact that seemed to persist in all the versions" of Privat's stories about himself, said Banville, "is that he was the natural son of a great lord—an assertion confirmed by his invincibly aristocratic manner in the midst of the blackest miseries—and that he had a very rich brother in the colonies."[83] It might seem a striking fact that the most famous bohemian in mid-century Paris was a black man from the Antilles, but none of his contemporaries found this remarkable. After all, the metaphor of bohemia came from the popular habit of identifying the country of Bohemia with Gypsies, quintessential outcasts and vagabonds who were also considered racially distinct from other Europeans, and this racial association was reinforced by the commonplace invocation of the Wandering Jew as a bohemian prototype. (Privat himself was described as "a literary Wandering Jew.")[84] So it makes perfect sense that another exotic, a mulatto, should become the most legendary of bohemians, even if this fact should seem almost too perfect, too good to be true.

Besides, men and women of African ancestry belonged to all levels of Parisian society in this period. In addition to his acquaintanceship with Dumas and with Jeanne Duval, the mulatto actress who became Baudelaire's mistress,

Privat knew, or at least knew of, Guillaume Lethière, an artist who enjoyed the patronage of Lucien Bonaparte and who served as director of the French nation's school of art in Rome.[85] He also knew another countryman, the republican journalist and writer Melvil-Bloncourt, and is recorded as having frequented a café popular among mulattos.[86] He must at least have known of Eugene Warburg, an African-American artist who was beginning to make a name for himself before his untimely death.[87] The scholar David W. H. Pellow has pointed out as well that at the time when Privat attended Henry IV numerous students from the colonies attended Paris schools, including a fair number of students of color.[88] Also, among the poorest of the poor in Paris, living in "the camp of barbarians on the slope of Saint-Geneviève facing the Seine," Privat encountered "negroes from the coasts of the Congo, come to Paris as fugitive slaves."[89] There were others as well, in Privat's time as at the end of the century, when a popular American guide to Parisian bohemia took special note of the "big black Martinique negroes" at the Bal Bullier, which had been frequented decades earlier by Privat—and where one now might also see, in the adjoining arcade, boxing dummies, "wooden figures of negroes with pads" that patrons could punch so as to test their strength.[90] Among these various black emigrés, exiles, and images in Paris, Privat's race was less striking to his friends than was the extraordinary way he "wandered the streets of the great city, in search of the impossible, the strange, and the new."[91] He epitomized the bohemian, but he did so because he represented the stereotype in such a singular way. Always seeming to act, as Cochinat put it, "without self-interest, without calculation, and especially without profit," this arch-bohemian appeared to his friends as inimitable as those eccentrics he wrote about in his accounts of "unknown Paris."[92]

We might compare these writings not only to the novels of his age but also to Louis-Sébastien Mercier's multivolume *Tableau of Paris* (1782–88), Émile de La Bédollièrre's *The Industrial Trades and Professions in France* (1842), Henry Mayhew's *London Labour and London Poor* (1851), Jules Vallès's focus on down-and-out figures in *The Refractory Ones* (1865), Paolo Valera's *Unknown Milan* (1879), and even Lewis W. Hine's early twentieth-century documentary photographs of child laborers and other members of the poor working classes.[93] These men also investigated aspects of urban life that they knew would seem to belong to another world, as far as their genteel audience was concerned. Unlike these other authors, however, Privat did not write as an outsider seeking to inform his audience or to awaken the conscience of readers by exposing conditions among the poor that were all but incomprehensible to the upper orders of society. In his own way he was as brilliant as any of these other authors, and he was certainly as compassionate as the muckraking Mayhew and Hines, but he was also something that they were not: a compatriot of those about whom he wrote. This fact also differentiates his writings from the popular "physiologies" of this era with which they are otherwise affiliated: works that described commonly recognized urban social types, such as the grisette, the student, the bohemian, and the Parisian, as well as types defined by occupation, such as the clerk, the man of letters, the printer, and the thief. Instead of casting his reporting into this form of light literature or into sociological studies, interviews, or exposés, Privat wrote of this "other" Parisian world as if it were his own. He wrote as one who believed in the people who lived there. He even described this world in a lovingly upbeat way, portraying it as a grubby realm of enchantment in which mere survival was too good to be true and, therefore, extraordinarily beautiful. "I've seen more talent, wit, and erudition expended there to get one's dinner," he wrote, "than would have been required of all the diplomats to change the face of the world."[94]

Far in advance of the surrealist movement of the 1920s and the magic realism of the 1960s, Privat's writings found in the depths of Paris the most amazing persons, fantastic events, and weird topographies imaginable. Even when he wrote of the commonplace drudgery of ragpicking, he made something marvelous out of it—even as the ragpickers themselves did, in his account. If you have seen one ragpicker, you have not seen them all, as far as Privat was concerned. He subdivides those who live in this way into three types: the classic drunk; the modern "savage of Paris"; and "the artistic ragpicker," who is "the bohemian of his kind, the philosopher, the one who used to be something" but who now "lives amid the great family of the disinherited."[95] In his writings Privat is always aware of the particularities and idiosyncrasies of different ways of life, as when he calls attention to the argot, the "ancient idiom," of the farmers and peasants who come to sell their produce at Les Halles early in the morning, when respectable citizens are snoring in their beds. (This argot, he comments, must bear some relationship to that found among "the traders of the archipelago of the Antilles.")[96] When he writes of dance halls, he is careful to note their history and the fine distinctions among them, as well as the distinguishing features of the most famous grisettes among their habitués. Thus, it is important for us to know that La Closerie des Lilas, which was formerly La Grande-Chartreuse and is also known as the Bullier Gardens, serves as a kind of stepping-stone toward La Chaumière and Le Prado. "The young women whose modest dress prevented them from putting in an appearance at these two El Dorados, so dreamed of by grisettes, came there to try out the noble art of the dance."[97] From such sites and types, with which many of his readers might have at least a superficial acquaintance, he extends his range to "the exhibitors of monkeys" and to "all of vagabond Bohemia: strolling musicians, street singers, sword swallowers, egg dancers, balancing acts, teeth pullers, fire eaters"—and these are but the beginning.[98] Beyond these carnivalesque types exist even stranger sorts of ordinariness.

In an age in which work was being industrialized and standardized, Privat searched out the occupations that had arisen to fill in the smallest and oddest interstices in social reality; in a society whose rebellious youth used *grocer* as a generic insult for bourgeois types, he portrayed the provisioning of the metropolis with an unprecedented, painstaking, grotesque particularity. He wrote, for instance, of those who rent out good-looking cuts of meat to hang in the windows of cheap restaurants, just for show, while the patrons of these establishments are fed on inferior fare, which in some cases is assembled from scraps bought from dining places higher up the culinary chain.[99] Meanwhile, one man creates a thriving business by collecting and reselling the bread crusts that restaurants had been giving away to beggars; some people make their living by force-feeding pigeons; a shepherd stables his goats in a fifth-floor apartment.[100] A new industrial process threatens the livelihood of the tatterdemalions who used to earn their bread by walking up and down the docks while peacefully puffing on pipes, which thus would be nicely seasoned for the eventual customers of the merchant employing these men to break them in.[101] Some night owls hold body and soul together by serving as paid wakers, or human alarm clocks, for those whose occupations oblige them to get up and go to work in the middle of the night.[102] Others serve as "guardian angels," hiring themselves out to wine sellers and cabaret owners as bodyguards who will see that drunks—those willing to pay them an individual fee—will get home safely.[103] A bankrupt count takes up the job of "putative father," selling his name to women who would otherwise be unable to list anyone in that role on their child's birth certificate. (As the story goes, when news gets out that he has received an unexpected inheritance, the count is besieged by hundreds of his children from all over the country.)[104] Another man finds his niche by serving as a "universal Oedipus," selling his answers to the puzzles printed in newspapers to people who want to impress their families and neighbors by pretending that they have solved them.[105]

Delirious as they may seem, Privat's essays are written, as Banville accurately put it, in "a firm and sober style"—even when, as in the tale of the

count's inheritance, they seem pretty clearly to cross the line between journalism and fiction.[106] In and of themselves, these accounts make for fascinating
reading; it is ridiculous that such writings are not better known today. They
become even more fascinating when we recognize how Privat wrote himself
and his storied bohemian existence into his portrayal of Paris, as in the story
of the "putative father," written by a man whose very name pointed to the
tragic fact that his own father chose not to recognize him.[107] ("Here," wrote
Duchesne, in commenting on Privat's name, "I touch on a family drama that
is not rare across the sea, but the mystery of which it is not my place to un-
veil.")[108] By writing his life into his accounts of Paris, Privat bequeathed to us
an image of himself that is crucially different from, and even more compelling
than, the legend left to us by his friends.

Despite all their evident affection for him, his friends and acquaintances
invariably display a certain condescension toward Privat when recording their
memories of him. They do not find anything remarkable in the fact that the
most famous bohemian in nineteenth-century Paris should be a black man,
but they do associate certain aspects of his character with his colonial ("creole") origins.[109] Maillard, for instance, while praising his "wit" and his "real
talent for observation," adds that "the mere idea of any exertion made him
fearful; he was lazy, nonchalant, like the true creole he was and of which he
possessed all the insouciance and all the torpor."[110] Delvau's warm account of
this "insouciant creole" portrays him as living spontaneously, free of philosophical reflection, as happy "as birds are on their branches." Unlike his fellow
students at Henry IV, who "had become men," Privat, says Delvau, "remained
a child."[111] Duchesne, too, describes him as an overgrown child.[112] Cochinat
comments, "If Privat had known how to apply himself, if he had not had that
wretched fault of creoles, white or mulatto, the horror of disciplined organization, the exaggerated love of independence, and an invincible penchant for
fighting only as a volunteer, he would have, as one says, 'made his way.' "[113] The
casual, worldly-wise, ostensibly affectionate attitude we see in comments such
as these gives us a good sense of the subtly insulting milieu in which Privat
became a legend. One might recall Heine's clever poem "Imperfection," in
which a series of statements illustrating the titular concept includes the line
"And Alexandre Dumas is a mulatto," or Balzac's alleged habit of exclaiming, when Dumas's name was mentioned, "Eh, he's a nigger!"[114] In general his
friends portrayed Privat as a generous, amusing, lovable, pleasure-loving man
of great curiosity and inventiveness, but also as one whose pure bohemianism represented an infantile or instinctual nature. They viewed him as being

free of selfishness and calculation, but also as unreflective, moved by impulses rather than ideas. They associated his character with the freedom from care stereotypically identified with all creoles, "white or mulatto," and they also saw his independence, as a bohemian without a regular job, steady income, or permanent place of abode, as having some connection to his creole heritage. The popular image of creoles in this era did bear the impress of their closeness to non-European races, whose images were already stereotyped in terms of laziness and childishness. Although they noted it, however, Privat's comrades wrote as if his specific racial heritage was pretty much irrelevant, as far as they were concerned.

Privat, however, thought differently about all these matters. Whatever the motivations for his behavior with money may have been, his writings prove that they were not thoughtless. These writings, from beginning to end, focus on the microcosmic workings of economic rationality in the modern capitalist marketplace. They investigate the ways that poor people, whether they be counts or ragpickers, come to terms with this marketplace. His essays all tell of necessity: of the struggle to eke out a living, and to survive loneliness and despair, in an urban environment in which one's life appears obscure, small, and historically insignificant. Even as they delight in the imaginative resourcefulness of the poor, they all illustrate the unfreedom, the grotesque abjection, that structures the identity of anyone who can manage to adapt to this environment. If Privat himself did not successfully adapt to it, it was not because he was childishly unaware that his way of living would leave him vulnerable to necessity. In daring necessity to do its worst, he knew what he was doing. His financial recklessness was, in effect, a disciplined commitment to an alternative economy—a bohemian economy—of friendship, generosity, imagination, and chance. He had simply chosen to reject the definition of maturity that modernity was making a matter of common sense.

Unlike the various groups of socialists and utopians who tried systematically to reorganize the realm of possibility in this era, Privat sought immediately to live a seemingly impossible life. He took on this challenge at a time when the concept of bohemia had arisen to designate, among other things, a contradiction in the conditions of modern art, which was torn between the impulse to celebrate its economic irrationality, on the one hand, or to rationalize itself so as to be responsive to market logic, on the other. The tension between these impulses is the source of all the drama, including the sexual drama, in Murger's *Scenes of Bohemian Life*. Privat, however, seemed to walk right through such contradictions.

His contemporaries lauded Privat as the epitome of bohemia because he so fully lived in the impossibility of bohemia, with all its lies and fictions and deadly dares. Yet they had to condescend to him, too, so as to deny that he might possibly know more than they did about the logic of economic rationality. Otherwise, his life would have been a reproach to theirs. It was far easier to look at him as a creature of instinct, like a bird or a child, than to look at the abjection that defined their own successes in life; easier to picture him as irresponsible than themselves as craven; easier to see him as a typically thoughtless creole than themselves, in all their artistic pretensions, as slaves to the marketplace.

Privat also thought differently about his race than his friends did, as any careful reader of his writings will recognize. (That his friends did not read them with such care is another indication of the condescension that flourished within their amity.) He who was reproached by his friends for his supposed lack of a work ethic certainly knew the contemporary French idiom *travailler comme un nègre*, "to work like a nigger," just as he knew that the popular term for a ghostwriter, as in the position he had sought with Sue, was *nègre*. His rejection of what his friends called work was significant in terms of his racial origins, as well as in terms of his attitudes toward the commercial marketplace of the modernizing French nation.

We cannot know how serious Privat was in planning to write "a work treating of the histories of the colonies (Guadeloupe and Martinique) during the revolutionary period," although he wrote of his plans for such a history at various times in the 1840s.[115] What we can know, however, is that the most important works he did produce were all preoccupied with the history of colonialism and imperialism. He was a writer who, in an article on the gallery of American antiquities in the Louvre, would refer offhandedly in his opening paragraph to how "Pizarro and Cortez abolished at the same time the arts and the liberty of the American people."[116] In its most basic conception, his investigation into unknown Paris was a reversal of the projects that had sent Europeans out to explore "darkest Africa" or other lands considered to be exotic. Announcing his intention near the beginning of *Paris Anecdote*, Privat proposed that "the patriarchal customs of the golden age, the wiliness of the savage, the naiveté of the negro from the coast of Guinea are commonplace things. In their voyages to lands without names, Levaillant, Captain Cook, and René Caillé observed nothing more curious than what we have seen in certain quarters of Paris."[117] As one may infer from this passage, he was well aware of the images that came to Parisians' minds when they encountered persons such as himself, and he was capable of reciting these colonialist and racial stereotypes with wonderfully bland irony. So he wrote, about seeing a new grisette arrive on the scene, that "for poor girls as for negroes, liberty is quite simply the liberty to stroll around and do nothing."[118]

Like his tale of the thugs who tried to rob his friend, Banville's stories about Privat's love of grisettes take on a very different cast when they are seen in the light of this passage. Whenever Privat received an allowance from his brother, says Banville, he could not get it off his hands fast enough, and often he would hasten to spend it on meals for the poor women of the streets at some dive that would be willing to admit them, such as Le Boeuf Enragé. He would tell them all to come and to bring their friends, too, until the tavern where they gathered was packed to the rafters with pale, unhealthy, ill-dressed women holding their steaming plates while sitting in chairs, atop tables, on the floor, up the staircase, everywhere, "like flowers in a meadow."[119] In Banville's telling, this is a delirious scene of bohemian generosity, and surely it is that; but Privat lets us know that it was also a caring, willful, self-conscious act of defiance toward the very stereotype, of creole insouciance, that it seemed to fulfill.

It was also something more than that. Throughout his writings, as in the passage that relates poor girls to black people, Privat often seems to identify with grisettes, who come to represent for him the land of bohemia that he epitomized for others. The parallels he draws resemble similar comparisons in the works of Baudelaire and in many other writings of this time.[120] As Privat describes it, the Latin Quarter of his youth came to an end when grisettes began to consider affairs with students as beneath their dignity; and the students changed at the same time, losing their rebellious energies.[121] Nonetheless, he portrayed his own destiny, as a black man and as a bohemian, as forever intertwined with that of the grisettes. For instance, in the same letter in which he proposed a novel about young men such as himself, he also suggested one about them. "We would show the life of girls at first working in shops, from the age of six to sixteen, then as grisettes, roaming around the Latin Quarter, from seventeen to eighteen. From there they enter into brothels, become kept women, ballet dancers, or actresses in little theaters, and finally marry rich foreigners or die in the hospital." It would be, he said, a tale sometimes gay, sometimes terrible, giving the reader a panoramic view of vice. It would also show—and here we see his identification with them—"the horrible calculations of self-interest of which these unfortunates are victims." The suffering grisettes are like the suffering bohemians in their garrets, who, he tells Sue, must endure cold, hunger, and disease as they ghostwrite—and here again we may remember that the slang term for *ghostwriter* was *nègre*—most of the works supposed to have been written by famed savants. We may remember, too, that, like Privat, grisettes were famed for making up fantastic stories about their lives. Their two sorts of existence are allied: "the prostitutes of the body, and the prostitutes of the mind."[122]

To waste his money in throwing an extravagant feast for the grisettes and other miserable women of the streets, then, was not only a dramatic display of Privat's sense of identification with them. It was also an act of defiance hurled against the power of economic self-interest to define human beings. For Privat, kindness would be reckless or would not be. Either compassion would have the idealized freedom of art or it would go begging—or to the hospital. Through the grisette, as through all the downtrodden types of whom he wrote in describing his explorations into darkest Paris, Privat showed just how crucial his racial identity was to his shattering of all sorts of stereotypes, including that of modernity itself, founded as it was on the legacies of racism and colonialism.

Through his friendship with Privat, perhaps Banville did recognize something of what was at stake for his comrade in his role as the arch-bohemian. It is clear, at least, that Banville was aware of race as an issue of performance, not just of one's birth, being, or image. He tells a tale in his memoirs of a certain Prince Euryale "who flourished in the Latin Quarter, among the students, toward the end of the reign of Louis Philippe" (157).[123] One cannot judge how much of the story is historically true; the fact that Prince Euryale is the name of a character in Molière's *Princesse d'Élide* (1664), as well as a character in Greek mythology, certainly does not inspire confidence in its veracity. The way this story overlaps in some particulars with the known facts of Privat's legend also raises questions. In any case, Banville presents Euryale as a real character. "Son of a poor lockmaker in Guadeloupe, he had had the audacity to come to Paris without any money" (157). Once there, "without a profession, and neither wishing nor knowing how to make a living with his ten fingers," he decided to turn himself into a prince (157). This choice was made possible by "the only truly negroid talent that Euryale possessed: his ability, like that of all his kind, to intoxicate himself with his speaking and singing, without having drunk a single drop of any liquid whatsoever" (157).

Thus far, we are in the realm of stereotype. Immediately, however, matters of identity become more complicated. For Euryale's choice of his identity was occasioned by his attendance one night at a distinctively French institution,

the Opéra Comique. Euryale, who spoke perfect French and was well acquainted with all the argots of Paris, heard from its stage the stereotypical
dialect assigned to black characters, "the bizarre idiom that has never had any
existence except in musical comedies" (158). It was at that moment, according
to Banville, that he decided to become Prince Euryale, forever after greeting
people by exclaiming, "Me prince! Black prince in my country!" (159). He
began to buy clothes at expensive shops and meals at fancy restaurants without ever settling the bill, bluffing his way out the door by imperiously offering his card or by giving his address in lieu of payment. The manager of the
fashionable Café Anglais may have recognized the imposture, Banville thinks,
but chose to ignore it. "In the interest of Parisian commerce and the trade
in luxury items, it is indispensable that the fantasy legend of foreign princes
should maintain its glamour" (160–61). So it came to pass that "Euryale ended
up being universally accepted" before he died young of the inevitable consumption (161).

Banville presents Euryale as a clever, insouciant, clownish figure, "a veritable Harlequin" (157). He describes how this character's blackness is an act
that plays upon a ludicrous European image of his race, but at the same time
Banville portrays his acting out as actually being a racial characteristic. Such
monkeyshines go along with the taste for dancing and singing, and the dis-
taste for work, expected of such people. The story of the "fantasy legend of
foreign princes," when Privat turned his hand to it, could hardly have been
more different.

Privat told of "a poor savage from South America" that he encountered
"in one of the most sordid apartments in the rue d'Arras." This man "was a
great chief, a king," who "had been conveyed to Paris by one of those entre-
preneurs who exploit the curiosity of the public." Eventually, this showman
found that the public was losing interest in his freakish attraction. One day,
therefore, he "abandoned the unhappy descendent of the Incas without even
leaving him enough to clothe himself." Becoming aware of the king's situation, the public felt its compassion aroused, the case was talked about, and
finally "an evangelical missionary from London somehow learned, who knows
how, of the existence of this savage in the midst of Paris." Having intended
to preach the gospel to the savages of the new world, the missionary, with the
help of the king, instead set himself up in business in Paris. "Everyone profited
from this: the missionary did not have to face the dangers of an apostleship
in the Cordilleras, and the savage at least had a morsel of bread, some clothes,
and a roof to die under."[124] Here, as Privat presents it in this bitter story in

which everyone profits even as everyone and everything are degraded, we see
how so-called economic rationality works.

In such writings of his as survive, Privat never made any overt reference
to his identity as a man of color, a mulatto, who had spent his early childhood
in Guadeloupe. In that respect we must agree with those contemporaries who
judged that this man known to all remained, in an important sense, unknown.
Did not he himself say as much through the writings in which he identified himself with grisettes and other inhabitants of "unknown Paris"—with all
those people destined to live in their own country as if they were savages who
dwelt in wild lands where any claim to social recognition could not be other
than ridiculous?

So Privat knew he was unknown, and he also knew he was on display, not
only as the arch-bohemian but also as a black man.[125] If he was symbolically
disinherited in the former role, he was both literally and figuratively disinherited in the latter. A curiosity exhibited to the public, he knew that many
people, including even his friends, would see him as a kind of performing
monkey. It is likely that he had heard of other such displays, such as the "Carib
prince" who was exhibited in the Jardin des Capucines in the second decade
of the century, where he had amused the artists Théodore Géricault and Henri
Monnier, among others.[126] Perhaps he heard backhanded compliments such
as that which Nadar paid to Jeanne Duval when he said there was nothing
gauche about her, nothing of those "ape-like" characteristics "that pursue and
betray the blood of Ham." He may have read of how Jean-Pierre Dantan's
caricature of Dumas as a monkey made Augustin Jal laugh; perhaps he even
heard Nadar's sort snickering that Duval's hair, of whose perfumes Baudelaire
made such gorgeous poetry, actually stank like something "atrocious, abominable."[127] Since it was in circulation before he died, he may also have heard
what became a very famous story of Dumas's response to a dinner guest who
bluntly asked him if it was true that his father was a mulatto. "Yes," Dumas
is said to have answered, "my father was a mulatto, my grandfather a negro,
and my great-grandfather a monkey; my family begins where yours ends."[128]
Given how small a world the Parisian literary scene could be, it seems very
likely that he had heard of how Georges Dairnvaell had snidely characterized
him as a "charming bohemian" with "wooly hair" who "would be a charming writer if he were not lazy like a nigger."[129] It was surely with some reason
that Privat bitterly described man as "nothing but a perfected monkey," with
perfection in this case meaning that man was "much more malicious, traitor-
ous, and ugly, but infinitely less clever than the monkey."[130] It was in the early

years of the next century that the proudly bohemian Nicaraguan poet Rubén Darío would conclude an essay on the dismaying transformation of the Latin Quarter by describing how he had recently seen two men there, whom he described as a Negro and a mulatto, trying to mind their own business in a café while a pack of students harassed them with cries of "*chocolat! chocolat!*"; but the Paris even of Privat's day was not free of such scenes.[131] It was with good reason that in this age of the stereotyped newspaper Privat always remained aware of how images, when repeated often enough, function as facts in literature and society.

Stories, then, become even more necessary than facts. As his contemporary Philoxène Boyer put it, Privat mixed "perpetual fiction with perpetual truth."[132] For Privat, as Citron wrote, truth was "always veiled or travestied."[133] No one understood better than Privat himself the fact of his legend, just as no one understood better than he that to be a legendary type was also to be unknown. Turning unknowns into legends and legends, or stereotypes, into mockeries of knowledge, he demonstrated this understanding. Privat, he made clear, was not Privat, no matter how many persons identified him by this name, and even if one of those persons was he himself, swearing to it, repeatedly, to those supposed to be among the best of friends.

The story that most fully testifies to this understanding is one included in Privat's posthumously collected writings, a legend said to be Senegambian, "The Monkeys of God and the Men of the Devil."[134] In commenting on this story, Pellow has pointed out that it has antecedents in the Americas and in Africa, which Privat may be presumed to have heard during his childhood in Guadeloupe.[135] As Privat tells the tale, the legend was recounted to him by an African priest who was rescued from Portuguese slaveholders to whom he had been sold after his tribe was exterminated. Brought to France, he entertained Privat with "the most amusing stories in the world" (185), which included details of the best way to prepare a cannibal feast. Privat boasts, "I am perhaps the only French person, or at least the only French man of letters, who has had the honor of conversing with a priest of the minor god Papaye" (185). After these opening paragraphs, in which he introduces their first encounter and gives a brief initial description of his interlocuteur, most of the story is taken up with the legend of creation the priest recites when Privat questions him one day about how the world began (186). The legend is narrated with leaps forward and backward, as if it were indeed an oral account translated by Privat from the "horrible Creole tongue" (188) in which the priest strove to communicate with him. Yet the priest's system, says Privat, "did not appear to [him] any more or less absurd than all the other systems" (188), among which he includes historical and scientific theories, the stories of the Bible, and Greek mythology.

In brief, the story the priest tells is about the rivalry between God, who created the monkey, and the devil, who sought to imitate the deity's creation but who could produce only an inferior copy, or stereotype, of his work. Thus was man created. Then a day came when the devil, in the course of organizing his miserable creatures, decided to bring them to a river so that they might wash. Those who were greedy hurried to be first; the indifferent came next, when the small amount of water remaining was muddied; and finally there came those among the human race who had turned against the devil, wishing to confide their lot to God. By that time there was only enough water left to wet the palms of their hands and the soles of their feet. "And that is why we have white people who are evil," the priest told Privat, "and yellow people who are indolent, and black people who are good" (192). Having pity on the good black people, God then removed them from the company of their fellows and placed them "under a beautiful sun, in the country of the monkeys" (192). He abandoned them, however, when they sought to enslave the monkeys to help them combat the rest of humankind, whom the devil had spurred on to persecute them. "God took away the monkey's speech so that its conquerors could not subjugate it and make it work in their place" (187). There followed all of the devastations of human history, including the ruins, the tombs, the destruction of cultures, "the selling of one's brothers so that they might perish under the lash," the grotesque distinction between rich and poor: "only the devil is capable of thus abandoning his creatures" (188). We can then understand why throughout history "the poor negroes have always been sold, given over to slavery, transported out of their country: because men are the sons of the devil, and because white men, being the most cruel, are dearest to his heart" (193).

So the story goes.

But this at least seems to be a fact: that when he was in the Lariboisière Hospital, shortly before his final confinement in the Maison Dubois, the same institution where Murger would die a few years later, Privat expressed a desire to return to Sainte-Rose.[136] Did he remember at this time, when he was largely neglected by all those people he used to know, Villon's remark that "an old monkey is always displeasing"?[137]

Taking into account everything that we know and do not know about Privat, we cannot help but confirm that his legend was too good to be true.

To say so, however, is not to say that this legend falls short of truth. On the contrary, it means that truth never was and never could be good enough to hold within its image Privat, known to all, unknown. As Privat demonstrated so well, it would be devilish—which is to say, unbearably human—to believe otherwise.

CHAPTER 5

America, the Birthplace of Bohemia

Even today, people might be surprised to hear that bohemia had its origin in the United States. If we think about it at all, surely we know that *la vie de bohème* was born and bred on the banks of the Seine. Jules Barbey d'Aurevilly, however, knew better.

In 1858 Barbey anointed Edgar Allan Poe "the King of the Bohemians" (376).[1] He explained that this honor could have been won only by a citizen of the United States, the country Poe perfectly represented. "It was logical and just" (377), he wrote, that the greatest of all modern bohemians should have been born in the heart of America, the land in which the outcasts of all nations found refuge. In making this claim, however, Barbey was in no way anticipating the sentiments of Emma Lazarus—"Give me your tired, your poor, / Your huddled masses yearning to breathe free"—that would be taken to adorn the Statue of Liberty at the turn of the next century.[2] On the contrary, he saw America as a grotesque and godforsaken place whose immigrant population, in his mordant characterization, was "the cream of the scum of the earth" (377). Given the state of utter abjection into which he saw this country throwing itself ever more deeply every day, it was a fitting home to "the bohemian, which is to say, a man who lives at the mercy of his chance thoughts, sensations, or dreams, as he has lived socially in that mob of solitary individuals who resemble an immense penitentiary, the penitentiary of American industry and egoism" (384).

To some extent Barbey's image of the United States was a contemporary stereotype given credence in this era by many others, including, for instance, the *bohémienne* George Sand, whose views and values were otherwise about as different as different can be.[3] Barbey's opinion carried to its extreme the usual European grumbling over the rawness of American life. As he saw it, America brazenly celebrated in the plain light of day all that a thoughtful observer might glimpse in the shadowy depths of France's bohemia: soulless materialism, indiscriminate individualism, and the degradation of all values before the vulgar economic concerns of a democracy in which the rule of numbers is the only rule. Such being the case, Barbey obviously felt himself justified in correcting the historical accident that had made the term *bohemian*, in its modern sense, a French import to America. It did not matter, either, that Poe had died in 1849, before the modern sense of the bohemian had really established itself in this country, and so in his lifetime was not referred to by this term. In point of fact—in the *sensus spiritualis* of fact, at least—Poe was "the first and the best, in his way, of that lawless and solitary literature, without tradition and without ancestors . . . *prolem sine matre creatum*, which has stamped itself with the name of bohemia that will remain with it as its punishment!" (376).

Barbey was not alone in seeing the United States as deserving credit for inventing bohemianism.[4] In fact, his argument was voiced in America itself. The American version of this argument, though, turned Barbey's reactionary spleen into notes of joy, excitement, and pride. It transformed his carceral America, that disgusting and frightening "inn of the nations" (377), into a welcoming tavern, a place called Pfaff's, that drew bohemian royalty to the heart of Broadway in New York City. In doing so, this American argument also revised the admonitory image of Poe as the exemplar of bohemianism. While paying homage to the man whom Barbey saw as an "aristocratic spirit" (377) doomed to die in a gutter, so ill suited was his native land to his genius, this American argument singled out someone else as its symbolic native son. It celebrated the soaring song of Walt Whitman, in which even the filthiest refuse that ended up in the gutters of America could blossom into *fleurs du bien*.

At its most basic, the logic of the modern bohemian metaphor had arisen from the appropriation of a debased identity—in other words, from an action that Whitman's poetry, in its focus on common people and things, jubilantly extends throughout all of creation. At Pfaff's, the desire for this universalism was celebrated not only through the promotion of Whitman but also through the metaphorical coronation of the writer Ada Clare as Queen of Bohemia and of the newspaperman Henry Clapp Jr. as Prince or King. In and around Pfaff's, for a brief period in New York City just before the Civil War, these individuals and a number of others adopted *bohemian* as a term crucial to their identities and, they contended, to the definition of American identity in general. This small group saw this word as representing large personal, professional, and political matters that concerned all the citizens of their country and, indeed, all the people of the world. The fate of the word *bohemian* at this time, then, illuminates the possibilities of the social imagination in mid-nineteenth-century America. By examining Whitman's career in relation to Clapp, who promoted both him and Clare, and also in relation to Clare's life and work, we can delve into the making of modernity at a time when bohemia announced itself as a pure product of America.

From this American perspective, Barbey's conception of reality seemed actually to be standing on its head, in need of someone to turn it right side up again. Whitman's poetry might almost have been designed for the express purpose of seizing on Barbey's vicious description of America, point by point, and taking it as praise. Ah, the poet exclaims, so you think our nation a land of degradation? Very well, permit me to announce myself: "Walt Whitman, an American, one of the roughs, a kosmos" (["Song of Myself"] 1855, 1: 31).[5] You find materialism abhorrent? Then you must closely attend to my "word of reality . . . materialism first and last imbueing" (["Song of Myself"] 1855, 1: 30). You are appalled by the thought of a land in which all distinctions are leveled, all its mechanically enumerated persons crammed together into one vast mob? Let me then sing to you of "the divine average" and of the joy of being "equalized" ("As I Walk These Broad Majestic Days" 1860, 2: 318; "Salut au Monde!" 1860, 1: 175). You find the driving emphasis on utility in American industry destructive of all higher values? Stay—I will introduce you to the metaphysics of "ironworks or whitelead works . . the sugarhouse . . steam-saws, and the great mills and factories"—and then to all other industries, on and on and on, until you are utterly and sublimely exhausted (["Song for Occupations"] 1855, 1: 94). You think the New World a land "without tradition and without ancestors" and, therefore, empty of all redemptive meaning? Then hear my exclamation: "O I believe there is nothing real but America and freedom!" ("Apostrophe" 1860, 2: 290). You wrinkle your nose at our vulgarity? Then I will be pleased to hymn the smell of my armpits and the sizzling spray of my spunk, for "what is commonest and cheapest and nearest and easiest is Me" (["Song of Myself"] 1855, 1: 15). And as for the political spirit you think you oppose, you cannot oppose it; for "the sign of democracy" is "the password primeval" (["Song of Myself"] 1855, 1: 32). And as to your image of ours as a land that welcomes only despised outcasts, one "that gives refuge to and interbreeds all the revolts" of other countries (62), I respond by greeting you as "the huge composite of all other nations, cast in a fresher and brawnier matrix, passing adolescence, and needed this day, live and arrogant, to lead the marches of the world."[6] Our mixing is sweet, I tell you, and our migrations have only begun.

"I tramp a perpetual journey" (["Song of Myself"] 1855, 1: 74), and I am "not merely of the New World but of Africa Europe or Asia . . . a wandering savage" (["Song of Myself"] 1855, 1: 21). Like George Sand's Consuelo, I tell of "the wandering destiny, joyous and miserable, of the artists of the open road."[7] And as in your choler you find individualism damnable, I thank you for that song of yourself, I accept your every word, and I return to you (what you already have, and know, and believe, if only in glimmerings and quick sensations along your flesh and nerves), "the song of a great composite *democratic individual*, male or female."[8] And so on.

An abridged American translation of Henry Murger's *Scenes of Bohemian Life*, soon to be followed by other editions, appeared in *The Knickerbocker* magazine just two years after its publication in France in book form in 1851.[9] Even before such translations spread the word about this contemporary scene, however, other writers had been suggesting to Americans a new sense of bohemia that evoked the venturesome life of vagabond artists and their companions. With this new meaning of bohemia appearing as an element in her fiction since the 1830s, Sand was the most influential among these others. Major works in this vein, *Consuelo* (1842) and *The Countess of Rudolstadt* (1844), were translated and published in the United States within three years of their appearance in France. (Late in life, Whitman would say, "If it did not seem like treason to my old reverence for Walter Scott, I should call 'Consuelo' the greatest novel ever written.")[10] Another influence was Pierre-Jean de Béranger. With their romantic evocations of Gypsies and fun-loving grisettes, his songs came to be emblematic of bohemian life across the Atlantic in the 1830s and 1840s. Of his own life in the early 1850s, Whitman boasted, "I was myself called Béranger."[11]

Especially when dealing with his early years, it is difficult to know exactly what Whitman had read by any given date. It is clear, though, that the modernized meaning of *bohemian* was in the air all around him by the time that he was producing the first version of *Leaves of Grass* (1855), which embraced this meaning so fully as to make it seem quintessentially and aboriginally American. "It is, in the first place," his follower William Douglas O'Connor would later rhapsodize, "a work purely and entirely American, autochthonic, sprung from our own soil; no savor of Europe or of the past, nor of any other literature in it."[12] One can imagine Barbey sniffing, "I could not agree with you more."

As was well known, in France the word *bohemian* had traditionally referred most specifically to Gypsies and more generally to vagabonds, beggars, traveling showmen, exotic strangers, and similar types widely regarded as being morally and legally suspect. The modern usage of the word appropriated the identity of these socially marginal persons for the purposes of a metaphor, which then could serve to name a new class of the déclassé: that collocation of youthful students, artists, writers, intellectuals, journalists, and assorted others who began to be called bohemians in the 1830s. In this way the existence of those who used to be called bohemians, prior to this era, was aestheticized, even as they themselves were cast into the background of modernity. They had provided an outlaw image, suitable for romantic purposes, to young people who felt themselves at odds with the conservative commercial mentality of France under the July Monarchy—a mentality memorably captured in the exhortation of the government minister François Guizot, "Enrich yourselves!"[13] Having provided this image to struggling youth, however, those who used to be called bohemians were effectively banished into the prehistory of contemporary society. The word *bohemian* in its traditional sense would continue to be used right alongside its modernized version, as it is in *Consuelo* and *The Countess of Rudolstadt*, which also include, for good measure, references to those who are dubbed Bohemian by virtue of their nationality. Despite these concurrent usages, however, and despite whatever twists and turns of definition individual commentators might ascribe to modern bohemians, it remained the case that the appropriation of their name conveyed an attitude of identification, idealization, and dismissiveness, all at the same time, toward those who had formerly borne it. No matter what one may think of the rest of his analysis, Barbey was acutely sensitive to the conflicting motivations within this attitude when he sneered that modern bohemians would find in this name their own punishment.

Whitman's genius arose from the sureness with which he carried this bohemian appropriation of identity to its metaphysical extreme, where it became what D. H. Lawrence mockingly called "the awful pudding of One Identity."[14] Whitman, too, would romance the outcast, but he would not stop there. He would identify with everyone and, indeed, with everything, presenting himself as "Infinite and omnigenous" (["Song of Myself"] 1855, 1: 43). His enhanced self would encompass the likes of Murger, Sand, and Béranger, yes—"I am a real Parisian," he would write—but also everyone else, including "you, each and everywhere, whom I specify not, but include just the same!" ("Salut au Monde!" 1867, 1: 170, 173). In a barmy 1938 book, Esther Shephard went so far as to argue that Whitman had stolen the inspiration for his poetry from specific passages in the epilogue to Sand's *Countess of Rudolstadt*, but the truth is rather the opposite.[15] Far from being derived from any particular text,

Whitman's appropriation of identity was comprehensive and transformative, a synthesis of romanticism, bohemianism, and Emersonian transcendentalism. He so thoroughly identified with and idealized the bohemian that he could afford to dismiss this very word.[16] The French bohemian became an American original; the déclassé youth, a universally representative man reveling in the richness of his being; the outlaw, the very spirit of the laws of democracy.

"I will not have a single person slighted or left away," Whitman proclaimed (["Song of Myself"] 1855, 1: 24). This all-embracing sense of identity is one of the aspects of his poetry that sometimes led contemporary critics to write of his "oriental" philosophy.[17] Sweethearts and old maids, children and parents, policemen and criminals, the fat and the lean, farmers and sailors and trappers, galled slaves and beautiful bathers, butcher boys and blacksmiths and surgeons and deacons and lunatics . . . if he could not list them all, he would at least strive to indicate their unlimited totality through the extensive use of the list as a poetic device. Through their suggestion of encyclopedic comprehensiveness, his lists give form to the leveling and democratic sympathies in his work. In the furtherance of such sympathies, it is completely appropriate that lists are liable to seem arbitrary in nature, remaining open to potentially endless additions and revisions while granting no necessary priority to any items over any others. Indeed, the form of the list may seem an expression of a democratic ethos that insists on keeping in the foreground of one's perceptions a lively sense of the arbitrariness of all forms of representation or strictures of propriety. The panegoism served by this self-subverting form finds a parallel embodiment in Whitman's favorite device of anaphora. The repetitions in the beginnings of his lines—as in "If you are a workman or workwoman . . . / If you bestow gifts on your brother or dearest friend . . . / If your lover or husband or wife is welcome by day or night . . ." (["Song of Myself"] 1855, 1: 84)—suggests an unbounded accumulation of identities. As Daniel Hoffman has written, "His anaphoric line is an equalizing device, precisely appropriate to the presentation of Whitman's egalitarian feelings."[18] At the same time, like the paratactic tendencies of Whitman's writing in general, it serves to register an impression of the imperishable value of individuals within his panegoism.

These formal aspects of Whitman's work underlie and extend his thematic emphasis on comradeship. This goes well beyond the preexisting bohemian theme, as in Murger's work, of a camaraderie consequent to and compensatory for the miserable state of cultural, political, and economic dispossession symbolized by the artist's garret. Instead comradeship appears as an attachment that is fervently sexual as well as encouragingly social, comprising every part of the individual being, just as the poetic self comprises every sort of individual and every living thing in creation. "Perhaps the most illustrious culmination of the modern," Whitman would comment, "may thus prove to be a signal growth of joyous, more exalted bards of adhesiveness."[19] In carrying bohemianism to its metaphysical extreme, he also extended the unstable and often tempestuously competitive camaraderie of the *vie de bohème* to a physical, erotic, homosocial equanimity: "The institution of the dear love of comrades" ("I Hear It Was Charged Against Me" 1860, 2: 394). The voice of the poet may then finally seem to be that of desire itself: vagrant, vagabond, bohemian desire, careless of career and conventionalities. Pursuing the rich multiplicity of its ideal, it establishes its home, paradoxically, on the open road, where it may even tip its hat, linguistically, to the French bohemia it has encompassed and transcended: "Allons! whoever you are come travel with me!" ("Song of the Open Road" 1856, 1: 232).

Although Whitman left to others the business of identifying him with bohemia, they had solid grounds for this identification. From the opening lines of "Song of Myself" on through all of Whitman's other poems, *Leaves of Grass* is a compendium of bohemian tropes. Just to start with, what better way to recall the image of the bohemian than by opening one's work on a scene of idleness—"I lean and loafe at my ease" (["Song of Myself"] 1855, 1: 1)—and what better way to afflict the sensibilities of bourgeois philistines than by making a boast of that idleness?[20] He recalls all the drama of bohemian life, too: "He going with me goes often with spare diet, poverty, angry enemies, contentions" ("Song of the Open Road" 1856, 1: 237). Thus does Whitman, in effect, go beyond any and all reasons for explicitly referring to himself by the word *bohemian*. In extending to metaphysical extremes the act of appropriation that created this modernized term, he carried it to its vanishing point, made it all his own, and gave it into the keeping of America. The success with which he internalized bohemianism may be measured by the fact that nineteenth-century reviewers of his publications did not think to mention it even though bohemianism suffuses his poetry.[21]

Whitman's craft in writing and repeatedly revising his poems throughout the course of his life makes the word *bohemian* stand out by its very absence in his corpus of work. Its absence becomes even more markedly significant when one considers the historical circumstances under which Whitman did come to be hailed as a bohemian by the crowd at Pfaff's.

In criticizing what he considered to be Poe's debasement of his genius in the pursuit of cheap effects intended to win over a popular audience, Barbey had disdainfully noted that Poe failed to find for himself a P. T. Barnum, the vulgar impresario he needed in order to sell himself to an equally vulgar public.[22] Whitman, however, did find such a showman. The year in which Barbey published his poisoned tribute to Poe—whom Whitman once met, and whose reburial he attended, conscious of the woeful scarcity of mourners—was also the year in which Henry Clapp Jr. founded the *New-York Saturday Press*.[23] Every newspaperman worth his ink needs a good bar, and Clapp made Pfaff's, a basement tavern at 653 Broadway, near Bleecker Street, the favored hangout for his writers and friends. As William Winter remembered it, "The place was roughly furnished, containing a few chairs and tables, a counter, a row of shelves, a clock, and some barrels. At the east end of it, beneath the sidewalk of Broadway, there was a sort of cave, in which was a long table, and after Clapp had assumed the sceptre as Prince of Bohemia, that cave and that table were pre-empted by him and his votaries, at certain hours of the day and night, and no stranger ventured to intrude into the magic realm."[24] In the pages of the *Saturday Press*, which celebrated these gatherings at Pfaff's, Clapp also labored to promote Whitman as an honored figure in them, a great American writer, and an exemplary bohemian. With the aid of the *Saturday Press* and other publications, Pfaff's became something of a tourist attraction.[25] Decades later, therefore, when Henry James wanted quickly to sketch in the outlines of Basil Ransom's bohemianism in *The Bostonians* (1886), he wrote that Ransom "drank beer, in New York, in cellars, knew no ladies, and was familiar with a 'variety' actress."[26] Over the course of those decades Whitman would never forget Clapp's help; near the end of his life, he reminded his Boswell, Horace Traubel, "I've always told you it is essential for you to know about Henry Clapp if you want to really know me."[27]

To be sure, even apart from Clapp, Whitman had shown himself to be a dab hand at self-promotion. He more than earned the sly contempt shown by Norman Mailer a century later when this latter-day enfant terrible yawped at the author of "Enfans d'Adam" by travestying the title of Whitman's most famous poem, "Song of Myself," in the title of his own bid for bohemian renown, *Advertisements for Myself* (1959). Not until the photo of a languorous Truman Capote graced the back cover of *Other Voices, Other Rooms* (1948) would there be an authorial image so notorious as the one that Whitman chose for the frontispiece of the 1855 *Leaves of Grass*: an engraving by Samuel Hollyer, based on a daguerrotype by Gabriel Harrison, in which the poet appears in his shirtsleeves, collar open, hat slouched across his forehead, with

Figure 10. Photograph of Henry Clapp Jr., from William Winter, *Old Friends* (1909).

Figure 11. Samuel Hollyer, engraving of Walt Whitman,
based on a daguerreotype by Gabriel Harrison (1855)
(National Portrait Gallery, Smithsonian Institution/Art
Resource, NY).

his left hand stuck in his pocket and his right cocked on his hip. Dressed like
a workingman, he stands boldly at his ease; as an 1860 review put it, Whitman in this picture "appeared to be doing his best to look like a rowdy and a
vagabond, and with greater success, it must be admitted, than ordinarily falls
to poor human endeavor."[28] Throughout his life, negative reviews of his work
would take their cue from this image, calling Whitman a "Caliban," "a sort
of inspired rowdy," "a drunken Helot," "the Poet of the Roughs," a "tramp,"
a man "as ignorant of society as a Digger Indian," and thus, as William Dean
Howells summed up this matter, "not a man whom you would like to know."[29]
    Surviving daguerreotypes bear out the memory of Whitman's brother
George that the poet's clothes were stylish when he was young and that it was

not until after 1850 that he adopted the informal dress so famously identified with him.[30] Whitman's critics, however, did not wait until 1893, when George Whitman recalled this information for Traubel, to accuse Walt Whitman of being a poseur. In 1876, for instance, a writer for *Appleton's Journal* described Whitman gadding about New York City "as well attired as his precarious resources would allow" before he decided to "change his tactics" by adopting a rude mode of dress and consorting with roughs. This writer also cited an article in the *Contemporary Review* in which Peter Bayne described Whitman as "a mere trickster" who "entered upon the *rôle* of the loafer, dressed up accordingly, vulgarized his name"—shortened Walter, that is, the name under which he had previously published, to Walt—"and wrote a book filled with drivel and indecency."[31]

Notorious as it was, though, the publicity value of this engraving paled before the brazenness with which Whitman publicized a letter of praise Ralph Waldo Emerson had sent him, arranging for it to be printed in the *New York Tribune*, reproducing it in the 1856 edition of *Leaves of Grass*, and pulling a quote from it for the cover of his book. Although Emerson still met with Whitman afterward and so seemed to overcome his reported anger at this act, the offense could scarcely have been more flagrant; as Jerome Loving has pointed out, ten years earlier Whitman himself had editorialized in the *Brooklyn Daily Eagle* about the evil of publicizing private letters, saying that "the action of betraying a confidence in this way, whatever the provocation, is about as despicable and cowardly, as a man can possibly be guilty of."[32] Whitman sought to make his way by other methods, too, as when he published anonymous reviews of his own work, which, naturally enough, approved of it and, in addition, sought to purvey a provocative image of the author: "A rude child of the people!—No imitation—No foreigner—but a growth and idiom of America. No distant democrat—a man who is art-and-part with the commonalty, and with immediate life—loves the streets . . . is not prejudiced one mite against the Irish—talks readily with them—talks readily with niggers— does not make a stand on being a gentleman, nor on learning or manners."[33] Ironically, in presenting him as "one of the roughs," "disorderly, fleshy, and sensual," these self-authored reviews set the tone for the abusive rhetoric that would follow Whitman throughout his career.[34] In the short term, though, they reinforced the impression made by the frontispiece to that first edition of *Leaves of Grass*, especially when Whitman pasted extracts from them into copies of his work.

Whether Whitman's self-promotion fulfilled its intentions is a matter of judgment. His writing of anonymous reviews to sing his own praises was spotted almost immediately; his abuse of Emerson's private correspondence certainly attracted attention, but often quite negative attention, which not only affected him but also slopped over onto that eminent author, whose goodwill he desired; and he would spend much of his later life seeking to retreat from the image that he had spread through Hollyer's engraving and those self-written reviews.[35] By the 1867 edition of *Leaves of Grass*, "Walt Whitman, an American, one of the roughs, a kosmos," had been gentrified to "Whitman am I, of mighty Manhattan," and all subsequent editions would also forget that he had been one of the roughs. Of course, we can assume that there were multiple motivations for this cleaning up of Whitman's act, as there were for the avoidance he showed and denials he made in reference to the homoerotic aspects of his poetry. These would have included a well-justified fear of persecution, as well as his desire to extend his celebrity. His revision of his public image, in any event, was striking.

Both critics of his work and those whom Algernon Charles Swinburne called "Whitmaniacs" often agreed in regarding Whitman as simply being himself, expressing his nature, in his writings.[36] Nonetheless, whether canny, clumsy, or simply opportunistic in their effects, Whitman's efforts at self-promotion, which still continue to affect interpretations of his poetic self, became a consideration in the judgment of his work from the very beginning, when the first edition of *Leaves of Grass* was published in 1855. Many readers were attentive to the ways he had crafted his identity. In his 1885 *Poets of America*, for instance, Clarence Stedman judged that "the picture of Whitman in trousers and open shirt, with slouched hat, hand in pocket, and a defiant cast of manner, resolute as it was, had an air not wholly of one who protests against authority, but rather of him who opposes the gonfalon of a 'rough' conventionalism to the conventionalism of culture."[37] Even so fervent a devotee as his friend John Burroughs felt obliged, in his 1896 book on the poet, to allow that "Whitman showed just enough intention, or premeditation in his life, dress, manners, attitudes in his pictures, self-portrayals in his poems, etc., to give rise to the charge that he was a *poseur*." He judged, too, that "in the famous vestless and coatless portrait of himself prefixed to the first 'Leaves of Grass' he assumes an attitude and is in a sense a *poseur*." His conclusion, however, was that Whitman was a poseur only "in the sense, and to the extent, that any man is a *poseur* who tries to live up to a certain ideal and to realize it in his outward daily life."[38] Whitman's old acquaintance William Roscoe Thayer commented, "We must remember that he was a contemporary of P. T. Barnum and agreed with that master-showman's views of publicity."[39]

It was toward the end of the decade, as Whitman was preparing the third (1860) edition of his work, that Clapp entered his life, joined his cause, and became, until the outbreak of the Civil War, the impresario of bohemianism in America. Clapp had lived in Paris for three years and, on his return to the States, had spent some time as a translator of Charles Fourier, the utopian socialist whose works had helped to inspire the famous experiment in communal living at Brook Farm, among many other such efforts. In a fine bit of filigree for any tale of bohemian life, one anecdote has it that the *Saturday Press* was founded from the sale of the library of Edward Howland, who would eventually end up living in a socialist colony established by a group of Americans in Topolobampo, Mexico.[40] Be that as it may, the *Saturday Press* presented itself as "the independent organ of Bohemia," and Clapp used its pages to sponsor a debate about the place of bohemia in America. Like *Leaves of Grass* itself, this debate became a forum for exploring the very idea of America.[41] Clapp made a good job of it, too, as the debate reached beyond the *Saturday Press* to other papers and magazines across the nation.

Predictably, given Murger's famous declaration that "bohemia exists and is possible only in Paris," one of the major questions this debate raised was the fundamental issue of whether it even made sense to speak of bohemians in the United States.[42] Although he was known around Pfaff's as the Prince or King of Bohemia, Clapp saw the value of perpetuating this controversy, and so he was just as ready to devote his columns to writers who scorned the notion of an American bohemia as he was to print encomia to it. (It would not be surprising to learn that he himself had written arguments on both sides of the issue.) In 1860, for instance, he printed an article that declared the Parisian conception of bohemia to be "un-translatable and un-transferable," its author bluntly declaring, "Any one, therefore, who assumes the name of Bohemian in this country makes himself ridiculous."[43] Only three months later an article appeared in which bohemia was characterized, with a metaphysical reach reminiscent of Whitman's poetry, as "the universal land." "Bohemia is Kosmos," this contribution states, as it proceeds to sketch its history from the era of Adam and Eve ("The happy life they lived in Paradise was the pure Bohemianism that we, their descendents, dream of") on through to a multitude of historical and literary figures said to be bohemians—with the list of literary figures ending, of course, with the name of he who had written *Leaves of Grass*.

"The grand work of Bohemianism in our own day," the article maintains, "is our United States."[44]

Four years later, the argument was still going on, literally across the entire continent, despite the fact that the *Saturday Press* had died on the eve of the war. After the New York journal the *Round Table* published an article that inveighed against the *Saturday Press* crew at Pfaff's—"Ten or twelve years ago, there came here the twin abominations, Free Love and Bohemianism—the feculent product of Parisian low life"—a response that was printed originally in the *New York Leader* was reprinted in the *Golden Era*, a San Francisco newspaper whose contributors included some of those who had written for Clapp's paper, such as Artemus Ward (Charles Farrar Browne), Adah Isaacs Menken, Fitz Hugh Ludlow, and Clare.[45] The *Golden Era* added the Barnumesque title "The Siege of 'Bohemia': Slaughter of the Innocents!: A Monster Shell Thrown into Pfaff's: Everybody Wounded: Brilliant Sallies of the Heroic Besieged!: Etc., Etc., Etc.: Latest from the Seat of War!" Defending the reputation of bohemia, this article described it as "a name used to designate collectively those free and easy knights of the quill who are banded together in the bonds of good fellowship as the 'unterrified Democracy' of the Republic of Letters." At the same time, though, it argued that it would be "one of the greatest absurdities in the world" to call the habitués at Pfaff's bohemians, not only because they were responsible professionals but also because there was no such thing as an American bohemia. "The institution could not be in a country where, as Emerson says, the first question asked about a man is, 'What does he do for a living?'"[46] Right up to the end of the century, this reversal of Barbey's argument that America was bohemia's homeland, which maintained, on the contrary, that America could not possibly have a home-grown bohemia, continued to find proponents, including the journalist Charles Congden and such varied writers as Edward Everett Hale, Charles De Kay, Clyde Fitch, and Howells.[47]

In the antebellum years, the bohemian controversy that Clapp did so much to stir up did help to publicize Whitman's name and give his career a boost. "Did you see the Sunday Courier of April first?" his pal Frederick B. Vaughan wrote to Whitman in 1860. "It contains an article on 'Yankee Bards and New York Critics'. . . . It gives a good description of the Bohemian Club at Pfaffs in which you are set down as the grand master of ceremonies."[48] In addition to dedicating his own pages to Whitman's work—"What I can do for it, in the way of bringing it before the public, over and over again, I shall do, and do thoroughly"—Clapp persisted in encouraging Whitman in his tendency to see great value even in hostile critical notices.[49] (The excerpted reviews that Whitman had added to the 1856 edition of *Leaves of Grass* did, in fact, include some that were negative.) About criticism of a poem recently published in the *Atlantic*, Clapp wrote, "I take [it] to be good for you and your publishers, who if they move rapidly and concentrate their forces will make a Napoleonic thing of it."[50] In Whitman's words, Clapp was "a much needed ally at that time (having a paper of his own) when almost the whole press of America when it mentioned me at all treated me with derision or worse."[51] Clapp further contributed to the "any publicity is good publicity" aspect of this situation by printing negative reviews of Whitman's work in his own *Saturday Press* along with commendatory notices and poems. He also printed Whitman parodies, some of them quite funny, such as one that begins "I happify myself" and continues, in one passage,

> Women lay in wait for me, they do. Yes, Sir.
>   They rush upon me, seven women laying hold of one man: all
> the divine efflux that thrilled all living things before the nuptials of
> the saurious overflows, surrounds, and interpenetrates their souls,
> and they say, Walt, why don't you come and see us?[52]

Clapp even went so far as to expose his own publicity game, reprinting a review from the *London Leader* that pointed out how Whitman's "American puffers, in the disguise of critics, charge the author with irreligion and indecency: and these charges are unblushingly reprinted by his publishers, among the critical recommendations of his performances, as if thereby they would attract a numerous class of prurient readers."[53]

Christine Stansell has explained how Clapp's puffing of Whitman was distinctly related to the social and economic conditions of literary production in this period, to the cultural conditions of New York City in particular, and to the development of bohemian identity as a potential marketing vehicle for writers who did not enjoy, or who had lost or renounced, a privileged class status.[54] It may be added that Clapp's efforts were designed to move the moral and aesthetic issues on which Whitman's critics tended to concentrate into a more general debate about the definition of bohemia. By hailing Whitman as a bohemian, he gave the controversy over his work a broader cultural focus. In the context thus established, Whitman was not a lone figure but rather an index of modernity in the making. Clapp's publicity explicitly branded the desire embodied in *Leaves of Grass* as bohemian desire or, to be more precise, as the desire of bohemia for America, where it might find its true homeland and legitimate destiny.

So what did bohemia desire of America? It wished, first of all, not to be seen as an issue of class. In the France of the 1830s and 1840s, bohemianism was defined in reference to various types of disinheritance—generational, cultural, economic, and political—but the definiens that most strikingly set it forth involved matters of social position. To be bohemian was to accept, and even to seek out, the condition of being déclassé. As bohemianism was promoted in the *Saturday Press*, however, and in other publications that picked up on its portrayal, it was most saliently defined by the opposition it faced from "Mrs. Grundy."[55] Originally a character in Thomas Morton's *Speed the Plough* (1798), Mrs. Grundy had quickly become a byword for the most risibly narrow-minded sense of respectability. The difference between the bohemianism of France and the United States, then, could not have been made more clear. In France, its lack of respectability was of the essence, a standing insult to the powers-that-be contemptuously referred to as philistines or spoken of with an even more biting disdain as *épiciers*, grocers. America's bohemian ideologues might still occasionally refer to philistinism, but their dismissals of Mrs. Grundy gave even these references a different import. In America, contrary to the opinion of Emerson—who saw bohemians as "persons open to the suspicion of irregular and immoral living"—bohemia positively desired respectability.[56] Through the trope of Grundyism, it opposed itself only to an excessively restrictive, distorted, or factitious version of this quality. In this new world bohemians were not to be wild youths, scapegraces, or rebels; rather, they would be "men who ignore narrow views of things and who think broadly and freely—men who express opinions not offensively, but clearly and independently"—and thus the men who would compose (no matter what William Dean Howells might say) "our most respectable and progressive order."[57] "Bohemianism is social scepticism," said Moncure Daniel Conway in 1865, before going on to quote Whitman in illustration of his subject; but he also took care to note that New York City's bohemia "differs from that of London or Paris by being more in earnest."[58]

Naturally, those who made a cause of opposing any version of American bohemianism, such as the *Round Table*'s scribes, were oblivious to such distinctions, and the rowdy reputation of those who celebrated themselves at the long table under the sidewalk in Pfaff's tavern inspired some New York City journalists to establish, in the late 1860s, a Bohemian Club, "for the purpose of redeeming the name of Bohemian from the disrepute into which it had fallen."[59] Similarly, in 1873 a writer for the *Literary World* took time to remember the crowd at Pfaff's for the sole purpose of saying good riddance to them while congratulating literary New York for having better manners and leading "a more decorous life" than it had prior to the war.[60] In 1881, a writer in *Scribner's Monthly* would look back on Clapp's bohemian kingdom as "an outlawry," a "cisatlantic imitation of Béranger's or Mürger's *Bohème*," peopled by "aggressive, bold, unconventional young men."[61]

Some certainly agreed with these sorts of responses. One did not have to be a drunk, long-haired, wild-eyed apostle of free love, however, to find them disproportionate in relation to their alleged occasion. In 1859, for example, the editor of *Harper's* had already noted that, while "respectability is the converse of the Bohemian idea," there were, in fact, "plenty of men among [the bohemians] worthy of respect." He further noted that bohemians might sometimes be found "in fine houses and high society."[62] At the end of the century, in an account of the crowd at Pfaff's before the war, H. C. Bunner was not exaggerating by very much when he said that "Murger's Bohemians would have called them Philistines."[63] Like later popularized versions of their type in the next century, such as William Powell in the film *Double Wedding* (1937) or Gene Kelly in *An American in Paris* (1951), those promoted by the *Saturday Press* sought to make the world safe for bohemia by appearing to be essentially moral, tolerant, spiritually questing, and, above all else, unthreatening.

Having provided that abridged translation of Murger's work for the *Knickerbocker* under the pen name of Carl Benson, Charles Astor Bristed illustrated this tendency in his 1861 essay "A New Theory of Bohemians." In it he maintained that Murger's work conveyed "a limited and inadequate conception of Bohemianism." Bohemians were indeed unconventional, but poverty, immorality, and a defiance of respectability were neither requisite nor remarkably frequent attributes of their kind. "There are Bohemians with houses and lands and rent-rolls and government stocks. Nay, there are Bohemians who keep their accounts and their appointments with rarely deviating regularity." In Bristed's telling, even the drinking and smoking popularly associated with bohemian life are of negligible importance. The bohemian is simply "*a man with literary or artistic tastes, and an incurable proclivity to debt,*" he maintains, offering himself, with self-deprecating charm, as a case in point.[64] A few years later, Junius Henri Browne would offer a definition that would make even Bristed's sound unduly censorious. Explaining that "bohemians are found in the pulpit, on the bench, on the tripod"—that is, on the seat of oracular wisdom—he contended that "every day they are increasing the area of

Thought, the breadth of Charity, the depth of Love." In his portrayal, bohemians become virtually indistinguishable from reform-minded Protestants who reject Calvinism in favor of a sweeter Arminian faith. As with its disregard for class differences and its emphasis on nationalism, this marked concern for religion is another aspect in which the would-be respectability of bohemianism in America differed from its French version, in which religion had no role to play. "Children of Nature," wrote Browne of America's bohemians, "they go not about with solem[n] faces, declaring after the common fashion, the degeneracy of the age and the wickedness of humanity. They have a hope and creed born of reason and spiritual insight; believing that God and Good are identically the same; that Progress is onward and upward forever and ever." As if he had Bristed's essay at his elbow, he insisted, too, that "they honestly discharge every duty and every debt."[65] Other works, such as Lydia Leavitt's *Bohemian Society* (1889), would further develop this quasi-Whitmanian image of spirituality and progressivism.

Accounts such as these follow the general pattern established by the *Saturday Press*, in which a contributor who signed himself or herself "D.D." made bohemia the homeland, in one article, of Pericles, George Washington, Admiral Nelson, and Napoleon, among other notable figures.[66] (When Clapp briefly revived the *Saturday Press* after the Civil War, one correspondent made a point of adding Abraham Lincoln to the bohemian community.)[67] In another article, the same contributor, while contrasting bohemianism to sectarianism of all kinds, argued that "the nearer we approach Christianity, the nearer we approach Bohemianism."[68] In yet another, D.D., as reliably sententious as ever, argued that the bohemian was "the best Gentleman in the world" and described him in terms that made him sound more like Freddie Bartholomew in *Little Lord Fauntleroy* (1936) than a student in the Quartier Latin: "To be honest and brave, generous and just, to be charitable and courteous . . . is to be a Gentleman, and is to be so far a Bohemian."[69] Clare, who was otherwise a reliably witty contributor, wrote to a similar effect when she portrayed a bohémienne for the paper. A wealthy widow with two children, Clare's exemplar scorned "*useless* ceremony" and "*mere* convention," but only so that she might better fulfill "the dictates of high taste and kindly feeling." Clare opposed this domestic goddess to "the definition of the Bohemian with which our Sunday papers ring": poor, uncouth, drunken, debt-ridden, with a penchant for scorning women, wallowing in carnal degradation, and shocking others with his outrageous opinions.[70]

The laudatory references to Whitman in the *Saturday Press* followed a similar tack. While taking note of the *North American Review*'s criticism of some indelicate passages, one writer nonetheless praised Whitman as "a great Philosopher—perhaps a great Poet—in every way an original man." His work was said to recognize "the common brotherhood of mankind, and the same human nature repeated in every person."[71] Another presented him as "the people's poet," who, in this role, was fulfilling the cultural demand that "America must make her distinctive work."[72] In response to the widespread allegations of indecency levied against *Leaves of Grass*, a letter to the editor professedly written by a woman testified, "I have read it carefully, and in reading, have found no page which made me blush, and no sentiment which might not be expressed by a pure man."[73] Another article, signed "A Woman," alluded to an *Atlantic Monthly* essay on the "New World and the New Man," commenting, "We have a right to say that this National Genius, with a purely original body and soul, exists for us in this Poet, Walt Whitman."[74] Together with the wider debate carried on in the *Saturday Press*, references such as these emphasized democracy, individualism, nationalism, spiritual identity, manliness, moral decency, and tolerance as the distinctive qualities that defined bohemianism in America and, through America, in all the world. If one had to sum it up, one might call the attitude urged here one of patriotic cosmopolitanism.

Through such measures Clapp's paper sought to make bohemia respectable, both during its initial run and during its brief revival after the war, when it was happy to reprint Conway's opinion about New York's bohemia being distinguished by its earnestness.[75] This image of America's bohemia in the *Saturday Press* is comparable to the one Edith Wharton presented in *The Age of Innocence* (1920). In this novel the greatest scandal of such bohemia as America may find within its borders in the 1870s is simply, in Wharton's dry phrase, "the dread argument of the individual case." This presents itself in the form of Newland Archer's desire for the cosmopolitan Ellen Olenska, with her European taste for literature and her acquaintanceship with doubtful persons such as Dr. Agathon Carver, the founder of the Valley of Love Community in Kittasquattany, New York. Wharton's novel makes an excruciatingly ridiculous tragedy out of the conflict between the narrow notion of respectability in Archer's milieu, on the one hand, and the exquisite generosity of understanding represented by Madame Olenska, on the other. Barbey's dread bohemian is here a charming woman, like Clare's exemplary bohémienne, who errs only in being too moral and genteel for the stupid society in which she finds herself.[76]

Happy to keep alive the debate over bohemianism, Clapp nonetheless used his polemical tactics toward the strategic end of making bohemianism appear essentially innocuous: a representation of the American spirit, not a challenge to it, much less an offense against it. The most notable aspect of his strategy was how it anticipated and, perhaps, helped to shape Whitman's famous retreat away from the outrageous image he had cultivated in the mid-1850s and toward that of "the good gray poet" of O'Connor's 1883 hagiography.[77] By 1867 Whitman had already abandoned the provocative image—"disorderly, fleshy, and sensual"—he had once so assiduously cultivated. Drafting a letter for O'Connor to use, under O'Connor's own name, to influence William Michael Rossetti in his presentation of the forthcoming English edition of *Leaves of Grass*, Whitman now found it important to emphasize very different characteristics:

> That personally the author of Leaves of Grass is in no sense or sort whatever the "rough," the "eccentric," "vagabond" or queer person, that the commentators, (always bound for the intensest possible sensational statement,) persist in making him. He has moved, & moves still, along the path of his life's happenings & fortunes, as they befall or have befallen him, with entire serenity & decorum, never defiant even to the conventions, always bodily sweet & fresh, dressed plainly and cleanly, . . . and offering to the world, in himself, an American Personality, & real Democratic Presence. . . . The most delicate and even conventional lady only needs to know him to love him.[78]

The revelation of these sorts of machinations might make Whitman appear to have been just what some of his fiercest critics accused him of being: a poseur, a trickster, or, in more recent parlance, a publicity hound and careerist. Similarly, Clapp's tactic of giving Whitmanian desire the brand name *bohemian* might raise the suspicion that this term, perhaps even from its very beginning, had simply been a publicity device, as Edmond and Jules de Goncourt had suggested in portraying Murger and his associates as an ambitious cabal.[79] In both cases, the only sensible response is "So what?" It was nothing new, after all, for poets to try to make their way in the world by drawing attention to themselves. That is what writers and other sorts of artists always must do, in one way or another, if they wish their work to see the light of day. Whitman's tactics may have differed from those of the young Baudelaire, for example, when the latter wrote fawning letters to Victor Hugo, the literary colossus, and to the famous critic Charles Augustin Saint-Beuve, seeking to strike up a relationship with them; but the deceptions in the one case were no more shameful than the brownnosing in the other. In this respect, at least, Whitman was akin to Howells, who as a young man on the make eagerly sought to gain the acquaintance of those bohemians at Pfaff's whom he would later maul in print.[80]

One who sees anything exceptional in such behavior, socially or ethically speaking, would have to be in a state of sublime ignorance in relation to the conditions of artistic production not only in the nineteenth century but throughout modern history. The heirs to Whitman's song of the open road would all be commercial products, from Jack Kerouac and the free-wheelin' Robert Zimmerman to Willie Nelson and the tramps who were born to run out of New Jersey's Asbury Park into coliseums across the world; and so, too, was Walt Whitman—although, in his case, the commerce involved was on a decidedly smaller scale. Similarly, it would have been no news to Sand that her cross-dressing served to call attention to her as well as to disguise her, despite her protestations that she sought only to move through Paris in comfort and freedom. If there could ever have been any doubt in the matter, popular illustrations of her established that her clothes had this predictable effect. For his part, Murger, too, certainly knew what it meant to treat *bohemian* as a brand name as he continued to repackage his bohemian past in new texts throughout his life, despite his protests against being stereotyped by the general public.

To recognize such facts, however, does not lead to the conclusion that these figures were nothing but commercial products. Whitman was not merely a self-promoter, and *bohemian* was not just a brand name. As Jean-Paul Sartre famously said in another context, "Valéry is a petit-bourgeois intellectual, there is no room for doubt about that. But not every petit-bourgeois intellectual is Paul Valéry."[81] Once again, one would have to be sublimely ignorant to believe that taking these considerations into account must in any way diminish our sense of Whitman in particular or of bohemianism in general.

The question of the poseur does become significant, though, in relation to the logic that created the modern meaning of *bohemian*, which enables us to see the implications of Whitman's appropriation of bohemian identity from the beginning of his career right on through to the revisions he made, to his poems and his public image, throughout his life. In appearing to others as both the ultimate bohemian and the ultimate poseur, Whitman incarnated the historical contradiction that made bohemia a community always struggling with its own artifice. In France an analogous fate had befallen Alexandre

Privat d'Anglemont, as his status as the definitive bohemian had cast his life into the form of fiction; but in Whitman's case this contradiction was played out rather differently, in accordance with the differences that its American history brought to the concept of bohemia. There, because of its drive toward respectability, Whitman's career would seem destined to retrace the original sin of modern bohemia's origins, which was the bohemian's transcendence of the Gypsies and other dangerous sorts—the roughs, in a word—who had formerly borne his name.

As we have seen, in giving a positive value to a traditional term of derogation applied to marginal populations in France, modern bohemians had cast those populations aside all over again. Simultaneously identifying with them, idealizing them, and dismissing them from modernity, modern writers and artists had paid these outcasts a compliment, yes, but a decidedly backhanded one. Through her socialist commitments and her support of worker-poets, Sand labored quite intensively to counter this symbolic insult added to social injury, as Privat also did through his literary devotion to and life among the street people of Paris; but the very logic of the term *bohemia*, in its modernized usage, remained haunted by the equivocal politics of its appropriation. This logic did not unfold as Barbey had predicted, through the eventual fall of bohemians back into the state of base outlawry conveyed by their name, but, on the contrary, through their social rise. Modern bohemians could sustain their privileged status as outsiders only at the expense of other ritually excluded groups: poseurs in general, women in particular, non-European races of people as well, and, most casually and perhaps most consequentially, Jews.

The princely sense of entitlement that characterizes the modern bohemian, which leads Whitman to find his poetic self entitled to all of time, space, and creation, can be asserted only against a dramatic backdrop of dispossession to which others must be consigned if the bohemian is not to be. In the fate of these others we see perpetuated the founding act of nomination that created the modern bohemian. Submitting the material existence of bohemians (in the traditional derogatory application of that term) to the utopian will of bohemians (in the newly appropriated sense), this act subordinated social history to social and cultural ambition. This sacrificial logic was also played out in the romantic fatality of the themes that became the stereotypical tropes of bohemianism: that art will justify itself no matter what the cost, that love will lead to death, and that any bohemian's success will prove to be a betrayal. This ambiance was intensified in and through the ritual exclusions that

bohemians needed to sustain their identity. In these aspects of bohemian life
we see the contradictions to which modern bohemians bound themselves in
the act of identification, idealization, and dismissal that gave them their name.

In Whitman's case, as the logic of identification, idealization, and dismissal was taken to its metaphysical extreme, all "others" were absorbed within
the modern totality with which he identified his poetic self. A world without
otherness, however, must indeed be wholly metaphysical, a world cut off from
social history; and so it really ought to come as no surprise that the poet who
promoted himself as "one of the roughs" should later feel no qualms about
disavowing that portrayal in favor of an image of gentility. Just as the idealization of gypsy vagabonds had enabled French youths blithely to dismiss the life
of such persons in the present, along with the life of assorted others, including
that of women and Jews, so did absorbing all others into himself paradoxically
enable Whitman to exclude others at will.

Such contradictions were possible because, in the metaphysical context
of Leaves of Grass, neither roughs nor genteel persons retain any troublesome
reference to social reality. Even in those aspects in which Whitman's poetry
seems most topical, as in his sympathetic references to black Americans, such
as a fugitive slave, it is precisely the lack of distinction in his poetic embrace of
them that is crucial. Embracing all, one renders all unreal; and so one should
really not be surprised, either, to learn that in his private conversation the
poet should speak of the "nigger" as being, like "the Injun," of an inferior,
doomed race.[82] Discussing with Traubel one reason he "never went full on
the nigger question," he explained, "No! no! I should not like to see the nigger in the saddle—it seems unnatural; for he is only there when propped
there, and propping don't civilize. I have always had a latent sympathy for
the Southerner."[83]

It was not only in private or in old age that Whitman gave voice to such
sentiments. They were consistent with his free-soil but antiabolitionist politics;
with his sympathy toward the ideology of Manifest Destiny, which led him
to support the Mexican-American War; and with his racial views in general,
which placed nonwhites in a subordinate position, as when he condescended
to Hottentots, Australian aborigines, Bedouins, and Fijians, among others, in
"Salut au Monde!": "You will come forward in due time to my side" ("Salut au
Monde!" 1867, 1: 174). In "A Christmas Garland, in Prose and Verse" (1874) he
similarly wrote of the problem posed to "American Democracy" by "a powerful percentage of blacks, with about as much intellectual culture (in the mass)
as so many baboons." In this respect, too, a pattern was set for him by the

Saturday Press, which was always hospitable to casual racism and in which D.D., faithful at least in this respect to the French conception of bohemia, explained that "the Jewish characteristic of worshipping wealth, of following the letter and disregarding the spirit, of loving forms, and neglecting essences, their pride, cruelty, and lust of power, were all opposed to the spirit of Bohemianism, which is free, charitable, enlarged, honest."[84] These derogated others cannot be said to be exceptions to the bohemian ideal, either in Whitman's poetry or in the wider antebellum debate over bohemia. On the contrary, they are exemplary of the dispossession of social history out of which the modern conception of bohemia is created, just as the question of Whitman as a poseur arises from the rhetorical necessity, in the modern definition of bohemia, that its territory be defined through the ritual evocation and exclusion of artificial bohemians.

In carrying out this logic, Whitman's writing established the characteristic form of democracy as one of innocuous equivalence. In this respect his image of bohemia does turn Barbey's upside down, as previously noted, and yet finally may appear utterly irrelevant to it. It does not really matter, in terms of Whitman's bohemian desire, whether he is a rough, a gentleman, or any other type of person. He may be any of them. It follows, then, that the world of bohemia as embodied in his work might nourish the one described by Ada Cable, the publisher of the Bradford, Pennsylvania, *Sunday Herald*, in *Bohemia*, a luxury volume designed to benefit a charity for journalists: "Real Bohemia is to be found in the oil country. The rich man and the poor drill a well together, and their social relations are identical. The pauper of yesterday is the millionaire of to-day and he may be broke tomorrow. . . . All classes and nationalities flock to the oil regions, seekers after wealth. There is a community of interest. All are on a level as to social position if they are honest, decent and pleasant."[85] In this early twentieth-century representation, as in Whitman's, bohemianism is what is. Accepting all, one recognizes no others; social history drops out of reality; and the name of bohemia either disappears, as in Whitman's poetry, or becomes applicable to a sense of history, and literature, as just one thing after another—as in this publication, which included letters of support from Teddy Roosevelt and King Leopold of Belgium alongside contributions by such diverse persons as Edward Everett Hale, John Philip Sousa, John Boyle O'Reilly, Mary Baker Eddy, U.S. Senator Boes Penrose, Rear Admiral Winfield S. Schley, Archbishop P. J. Ryan, and B. W. Trafford, "Superintendent Contracts, Bell Telephone Company," writing of "the telephone of the future."[86] One might consider in this regard how rapidly the Bohemian Club founded in San Francisco in 1872 became a socially distinguished group; with this document before us, we can already look forward to the day when the likes of Henry Kissinger would join the hijinks at the Bohemian Grove.

Precisely because Whitman assigned bohemia such an exorbitant universality, then, it is important to remember that there was an actual community of bohemians in antebellum New York and that its members were embroiled in contentious debates, which resonated across the country, about what it all might mean. Whitman's poetic persona was that of a representative man, but the eagerness with which this community took him up should not lead one to conclude that he represented all that bohemia did mean, or that some thought it should mean, at this time. What bohemia desired of America looks very different, for instance, if we turn from the talismanic figure of Whitman to a very different one, that of the Queen of Bohemia, "the erratic but gifted Ada Clare," as the *New York Times* called her.[87]

The name with which she was born, to the planter aristocracy of South Carolina, was Jane McElhenney.[88] She legally changed it in 1857, borrowing the name of the Charles Dickens character in *Bleak House* (1852–53) who is engaged in a family struggle over an inheritance, as was McElhenney herself at the time.[89] An aspiring actress who began to establish a literary reputation with poems and articles in the *New-York Atlas*, Clare went on to become a columnist for the *New-York Saturday Press*, the *New York Leader*, and the San Francisco *Golden Era*. At the *Saturday Press*, Clare gained national attention and, accordingly, was sometimes associated with Whitman, as in an article in the *Cincinnati Commercial* on "Walt Whitman's New Poem," which adverted, in the course of its discussion, to "the charming piquancies of the *spirituelle* Ada Clare."[90] A gushing report from the *Philadelphia Dispatch*, which, like the one from Cincinnati, was reprinted in the *Saturday Press*, once compared Clare—"dashing in her appearance, gay, light-hearted, a genuine blond, and reported to have 'moneys' "—to George Sand.[91] Aside from their similar roles as prominent bohémiennes, though, these two had almost nothing in common beyond the scandal associated with their romances. Clare was the unwed mother of a boy, Aubrey, whose father was the musician and composer Louis Moreau Gottschalk. Anticipating Sarah Bernhardt's similarly bold actions some years later, when the child of this unmarried actress accompanied her on tour, Clare was said to have shocked hotel clerks by signing their registers as "Miss Ada Clare and son."[92]

During the Pfaff's era Clare's house at 86 West Forty-second Street was another gathering spot, on Sunday evenings, for this era's bohemians, whose numbers also included some other women, such as the writer Getty Gay (whom the *New York Times* described as "a talented bit of womanhood"); the artist Mary Freeman; the poet Ada Isaacs Menken; the actress and writer Dora Shaw; Clare's good friend Anna Ballard, with whom she is said to have dabbled in séances; and (again in the words of the *Times*) "Jenny Danforth, a wild, impulsive Western woman."[93] In addition to her work for the *Saturday Press* and other newspapers, Clare published one novel and eventually, after her inconclusive earlier attempts, became a working actress.[94] Her career ended with her notoriously gruesome death in 1874, at the age of thirty-nine, after a rabid dog bit her on the nose. A New York newspaper even spread the ridiculous story that in her dying agonies she "ran about the room on all-fours, barking and snapping at every thing within her reach."[95]

Outside the circle of Whitman scholars, Clare is now an almost entirely forgotten figure, and, barring the highly unlikely event of a Hollywood producer happening upon these pages and deciding to give her the biopic she so richly deserves, that situation will not change. Her newspaper writing is often lively and engaging, but it is also casual and unpolished—the work of a journalist writing in haste and concerned only with immediate effects. Her novel, too, while terrific in parts, is overall an ungainly beast that stumbles toward a ludicrous conclusion in which its main characters, shipwrecked and set adrift, die in each other's arms. A contemporary notice in the *Boston Review* described it, accurately enough, as a "rather clever combination of improbabilities and impossibilities . . . with the moral tone good on the whole."[96] For all its wittiness, her writing has none of the brilliance of conception, stylistic bravura, linguistic and thematic coherence, and resonant historical and aesthetic ambition that have made *Leaves of Grass* a classic. According to Charles Warren Stoddard, Clare wrote to him not long after the 1866 publication of her novel, saying, "I have been gradually separating myself from literature all Summer, and now am giving it up entirely for the present, honestly believing that I mistook my vocation when I attempted it."[97] It was then that she made the serious attempt to take to the stage that led to the career she pursued until her death.

Although Whitman seems to have bridled at her sexual freedom, he and Clare gave each other favorable notice in print and seem always to have spoken well of each other.[98] Clare once wrote, "Who knows whether I may not go down to posterity as the Love-Philosopher"; and Whitman, of course, was dedicated to becoming just such a figure.[99] Like Clare, too, Whitman was an outspoken supporter of women, demanding a culture that would recognize "the broad range of the women . . . of the middle and working strata" and ensure "the perfect equality of women, and of a grand and powerful motherhood."[100] Whereas Whitman's writing propels women into the liberation of an imagined future in which motherhood is their most sacred condition, however, Clare's focuses on the contested ground of sex and romance in the vexed present. In contrast to Whitman's metaphysical appropriation of identities, which gives them a common ground of desire, one can see just from the strategically understated title of her novel, *Only a Woman's Heart*, that Clare is concerned with the divisiveness of desire in the formation of identities and in the differing and conflicting fates of these identities. Even at its most theatrical, Whitman's voice is designed to convey an impression of an all-embracing sincerity; Clare's, as in the title of her novel, at once wry and sentimental, is characteristically ironic. Whitman seeks a language that can transcend social differences, Clare a language adequate to the experience of conflict. In other words, Clare's writing accomplishes something that Whitman's could not begin to do: it works to explain the power of Mrs. Grundy as the embodiment of all opposition to America's bohemians.

These differences are historically as well as biographically significant. The reality was that women had more to lose in bohemia than did men. This was especially true for middle-class women, for whom bohemia's rejection of convention generally entailed a decisive loss of their social position, not a vacation from it or a springboard for jumping higher in it, as was often the case with men. This point was still being made, complete with the melodramatic trappings of threatened seduction and rape, in Emilie Ruck de Schell's 1898 essay "Is Feminine Bohemianism a Failure?"[101] Ellen Glasgow, too, in her splendidly confused novel *The Descendant* (1900), would focus on this issue, which was by no means peculiar to the United States. One might think, for instance, of Thomas Mann's sister Carla, who killed herself when her bohemian history made it impossible for her to contract a respectable marriage; and there is also the example of Franziska zu Reventlow, who, like Clare, being an unwed mother, discovered how difficult life could be even in bohemia for one in her circumstances.[102] Unlike Clare, however, whose bravery stands out all the more clearly through the comparison, Reventlow would derive from her experiences a fiercely antifeminist attitude, arguing that women's natures unfitted them for the intellectual, professional, and physical pursuits of men.[103]

One's gender could make all the difference in the world, as Clare well knew. Her siblings had called her Tommy, for Tomboy, when she was young; and she would remember the implications of this family joke in her work as a

Figure 12. Photograph of Ada Clare (n.d.) (courtesy of the Harvard Theatre Collection).

critic, writing, of a volume entitled *Sea Kings and National Heroes*, "This book claims to be a book for boys. If that be the case I must be a boy, for I know it is a book for me."[104] It was with good reason that she introduced the protagonist of her novel, Laura Milsland, just as she is about to lose the freedom of her girlhood. Up to this time, while still remaining an exceptionally respectable figure in her family, school, and provincial community, she could be fiercely intelligent, wild, rebellious, ambitious, and even physically violent, fighting with other girls. ("And this," sneered the novel's reviewer in the *Round Table*, "is the Bohemian idea of the conduct of young ladies!")[105] She is, in fact, a proto-bohemian figure, with her complexion "almost as swarthy as a gipsey's" (57) and her moody, willful girlishness.[106] Soon, however, much as Ellen Olenska would arrive to shake the foundations of Newland Archer's life, a stranger enters hers. Foreign and seductive, Victor Doria, a bohemian still uncertain of the direction of his artistic calling, thoroughly upsets Laura's whole existence. Gender makes all the difference: his bohemianism abases hers, spelling the end to the freedom, pride, and honor of her youth.

The thoughts of Laura's father offer us the conventional opinion about persons such as Victor: "He was aware of the 'degradation' of Victor's professions, the drama, sculpture, and painting, all seeming to him to be so many forms of vagabondage, beyond which shiftlessness could not go" (67–78). Clare, meanwhile, is acute in her description of the bad-boy appeal that a man such as Victor can hold for a girl such as Laura. "If they are at all ambitious," she says of such girls, "their future lives look so narrow, they would willingly woo a heart-sorrow, as a means of widening the vista" (45). The "prospect of disappointment in love" is then "secretly seductive," the despair predictably consequent to it "a species of voluptuous grief" as it is anticipated in their youthful imagination (45). Despite the moralizing tone of this analysis, Clare's narrative at the same time completely justifies Laura's almost masochistic recklessness, given the likely alternative. "Laura would have been terrified at the idea of being drawn into a mutual attachment with a common-place, insignificant being," she says, "but the prospect of enjoying the stormy delights of a broken heart, quite raised her spirits to enthusiasm" (45). In this regard, it is notable that Victor is described as being slender, somewhat foppish, slightly effeminate—as different from this era's conventional American man as the tomboyish Laura is from its stereotype of the proper girl.

Victor toys with Laura and then drops her when he fears she might become an annoyance, and for the rest of the novel she feels bound to him, even as he resolutely avoids her. Bohemia is thus represented through him as bearing a thoroughly mixed character, at once attractive and punishing, liberating and imprisoning, for any woman of intelligence and spirit who comes into contact with it. "There are many more such 'Frankensteins' in the world," Clare comments, moralistically; but, once more, her moralism ends up supporting all the Lauras of creation against the dissatisfying society that looks forward to confining them again after they have been dumped by their dreams.

"Ah, me!" Clare exclaims, writing of Laura's infatuation, "how many such loves have been skillfully 'worked up,' and then thrown upon a world to which they were alien, in which they could find neither their place nor meaning. Thus are they doomed to stalk through life, lonely and incomprehensible spectres, objects of ridicule to most, or at best of curious pity" (69). One might take this for a description of the eternally lost victim of a vampire in an extravagant supernatural melodrama, not of a teenage girl with a crush on a visitor who did no more than ask her to pose for him so he could model her head in clay. Even if it is also one of its faults, though, it is one of the virtues of Clare's novel that its passionate apprehension of the conditions of women's lives spills through the boundaries of narrative tact, flooding the text with romantic desire even as the narrator's sense of irony seeks in vain to shape and order this gushing impulsiveness. Desire here is not, as in *Leaves of Grass*, self-rejoicing and serene and possessed of wisdom. In *Only a Woman's Heart*, desire is frustrating, and a mess, and as perfectly stupid as it is urgent and necessary.

In bohemian narratives, it is common for the author to take someone from the country, infected by the bohemian bug, to a cosmopolitan city, there to pursue risky artistic dreams. This is the pattern, for instance, in Henry James's *Roderick Hudson* (1875) and, on a decidedly different level of literary ambition, in Julia Frankau's *A Babe in Bohemia* (1889), the *Reefer Madness* of nineteenth-century works on this subject. As it became a myth in the nineteenth century, the life of Thomas Chatterton helped to establish this pattern, but it also corresponded to the social reality of bohemia as a distinctively urban and modern sense of community. Such a move from the country to the city occurs in this novel when Laura's father comes into some money and she persuades him to transport their family to the metropolis where she hopes to pursue the elusive Victor. Here, though, Clare introduces a twist into the narrative. Laura does not enter an atelier or set herself up in a garret with pen and ink. She becomes a different sort of artist altogether: an artist of respectability.

Having been "worked up" by a Frankenstein—we note that his name is *Victor* Dora—Laura internalizes that relationship and becomes a Frankenstein to herself. Imagining that Victor might never have turned away from her if she

had not been such a hoyden when they first met, she sets herself on an elaborate course of self-improvement designed to make her a lady. "Indeed she was,
in some sense of the word, herself an artist," says Clare, "and her own body
was the material out of which she was fashioning an image, fit to be shrined
on the altar of love" (121–22).

In this perverted form, however, the artist cannot find her place either
outside or inside society. Failing to win Victor's affection, Laura pursues a
series of "affectional experiments" (139) with men who resemble him. She is
"fearfully honest in her determination to love somebody" (138) but ultimately
unable to accept any of these substitutes when they do succumb to her charms.
"No wonder she fairly earned the reputation of being a thoroughly heartless
and dangerous flirt" (139). In place of the composed lover in *Leaves of Grass*,
who easily drifts from one scene to another, one man or woman to another,
with bohemian insouciance, we are given the paradoxical image of a frantic
coquette who is actually, if anyone could recognize the truth, completely un-
designing, so enthralled is she by her own desire. In contrast to Whitman's emphasis on manliness, a character seemingly rooted in the nature of one's flesh,
Laura's experience serves as an allegory of ladyishness, a character derived from
humiliating social and cultural demands. The promiscuity that might appear
as bohemian freedom, in the case of a man, appears in Laura's case as compulsion and shame.

In a further twist of the plot, and of the heart, the frantic fixation of her
desire for an alternative to conventional romance then comes to seem to Laura
a kind of wickedness. She feels she has made the mistake of thinking that she
"had a right to extract happiness out of the world" (183). In other words, she
has sinned in believing that a lady might still be free as a girl. Through complicated subplots involving her sisters and their husbands, the novel in fact
punishes her for this error, literally and figuratively disinheriting her, leaving
her "quite hopeless, to face the bleak, bitter world from which she expected
nothing but disappointment, contempt and forgetfulness" (203).

As always, though, the moralism through which Clare levies this punishment exists in an ambivalent relation to her desire fully to explain the logic of
Laura's position. Therefore, Laura is allowed to address her legal disinheritance
by saying, with obvious narrative justification, "The law is just a miniature of
the world; it's [*sic*] leanings are always on the man's side. The odds are always
against a woman. I sometimes fancy every force in this world prefers helping
a man to helping a woman" (216). Similarly, her abject conclusion, "I must
be the worst girl in the world" (217), is counterbalanced by the ending of the

novel, which takes her out of this world, in the melodramatic shipwreck, only after Victor finally falls in love with her and so joins her on that fatal voyage.

Moreover, none of this confused business happens before Clare further muddies the image of bohemianism by taking the opportunity of Laura's disinheritance to mock the popular image of bohemian poverty. "The idea of poverty, drawn entirely from novels," she writes, "was flattering to her imaginative and romantic tendency of mind. Little dreaming of the utter monotony of poverty, she looked to it for a certain measure of excitement and adventure." Having made this comment, Clare then draws attention once more to the masochism that ladyishness induces in its subjects: "Besides, being at the height of her self-depreciation and accusation, it gave her pleasure to materially punish herself" (218).

This description gives one a better appreciation for what was at stake in Clare's description, in the *Saturday Press*, of the bohémienne as a woman of means distinguished by her good taste. We might be inclined to draw the conclusion that this description reflects Clare's personal background, prior to the loss of her income after the Civil War, as a member of the slaveholding *rentier* class, just as we might attribute Whitman's decidedly different self-image to his northern working-class background. Clare does not in any way labor to fend off such a conclusion, which seems entirely legitimate, but she does indicate that it is incomplete. Like bohemia in general, she suggests, bohemian poverty in particular is a very different matter for women than it is for men. The life that Whitman boasted of to his friends—"I have a little room, & live a sort of German or Parisian student life—always get my breakfast in my room, (have a little spirit lamp) & rub on free & happy enough, untrammeled by business, for I make what little employment I have suit my moods"—is likely to be considerably less appealing to a woman who, like Laura, finds that she does not enjoy the same employment opportunities as men do. And this is not even to mention how it might appear to a woman such as Clare—one of those American mothers that Whitman glorified—who, in her early twenties, found herself with a child to support.

Bound to chance, the codes of romance, the demands of gentility, the inequitable exigencies of the law and other social institutions, female desire in *Only a Woman's Heart* cannot find its freedom on the open sea, much less on the open road; and Laura, unlike the extraordinary author of *Consuelo*, does not have the option of masquerading as a man. She has enough trouble, after all, masquerading as a woman.

Clare tries to expose this masquerade by showing her readers the

Frankensteinian manipulations, frustrations, displacements, and self-destructiveness that go into the making of a woman's heart. In doing so, she seeks to honor the bohemian dream, which, in the person of Victor, she will never totally renounce, even as she shows how for a woman this dream must be an experience radically different from what it is for a man. A subplot of the novel, in which one of Laura's sisters is disowned by her father when she goes onto the stage, stands in marked contrast to Victor's easy dabblings in various arts before he becomes successful as an actor.

Given this recognition, we can grasp the significance of the fact that American bohemia made Mrs. Grundy its *bête noire*—unlike, say, Milan's bohemia in the next two decades, where the "serious man" played this role. When people wrote of the bohemian in the nineteenth century, it was commonplace to say, "Hymen is an enemy to the character, and domesticity its ultimate destroyer"; and the very name of Mrs. Grundy suggests how women were stigmatized in America as being responsible for these unbohemian states of being.[107] Having been a tomboy, like her protagonist Laura, before she came under the power of "female relatives brought up in the old girl-slaughtering style," who trained her to be "that melancholy thing, a perfect lady," Clare had the basis for a more complex understanding of Mrs. Grundy than that enjoyed by the guys at Pfaff's who boasted of their independence from this bogeywoman.[108] Clare knew that the very profession of bohemian equality could mask continuing injustices. It was obvious, for example, that no matter how defiant she might be in living her life as she pleased, she was affected by her liaison with Gottschalk in a way that he was not, if only because he did not have to defy society in pursuing, ending, and living beyond their brief affair. She dealt with their differing fates with great bravery and sophistication; in 1862, long after the end of their relationship, Gottschalk attended the Sunday evenings at her house and even went to Pfaff's a number of times. *Only a Woman's Heart* shows, however, that she had not forgotten the spectacle she had made of herself, in publicly writing about her desire for Gottschalk, and that she remembered as well the masochistic poetry she wrote after their liaison, which featured lines such as "No mortal care shall shade thy rest; / All pain shall dwell with me alone."[109]

In a newspaper article a few years after her tortured run-in with Gottschalk, Clare courageously told herself and the world that "the type of women who fall in love with some irresponsive man and then go whining about him all their mortal lives, or perhaps retire to deserted places and weep themselves ugly and old for him, of course exists, but it is unworthy [of] being written about"; and then, three years later, she published a novel whose protagonist barely escapes ending up as just such a woman.[110] The divisions that mess up the narrative voice in *Only a Woman's Heart*, then, represent divisions in and among women with which she was thoroughly familiar. To one with such experience, the fact that antebellum bohemians found their defining antagonist in a specifically female figure might well suggest that American bohemia, despite its professed openness to the inclusion of women among its denizens, nonetheless remained a territory redolent of an overpowering manliness, such as that which Whitman preached, failing to register the contradiction this posed to his professed recognition of the equality of women.

It was precisely this suggestion that the Queen of Bohemia pursued in many of her newspaper writings. Rather than writing in opposition to Mrs. Grundy, she wrote in mockery of men's pretentions, as when she made fun of the character of Hilda, the virtuous copyist whom Nathaniel Hawthorne's *Marble Faun* (1860) contrasts to the darkly sensuous, sinful, and suspiciously Jewish artist Miriam. "This is no woman," she wrote; "'tis a piece of pale Italian marble, that cheats us with the semblance of life."[111] Her claim that Hawthorne's woman is no woman at all is of a piece with her repeated references to the ways that men, whenever they do happen to come into touch with a woman, refuse to credit her as such. For instance, taking the occasion of her inaugural column for the *Saturday Press* to praise Harriet Beecher Stowe's *Minister's Wooing* (1859), particularly for its criticism of Calvinism, she then anticipated how "the all-beholding critics" would yet manage to disparage such an outstanding writer: "Perchance they say, a woman may have gathered the materials for this work, but ah! certainly a man has tinkered them together. This scene is too vigorous, too bold, too learned, it comes upon us with too much force, we feel that it is a man's fist, that is taking our minds under the ribs. Keep, keep your soft fingers, madame, for stitching together the minor unessential parts of your story; your brother the preacher, who is never truly great except when he is writing surreptitiously under your name, shall work out for you all the vital and essential details of the same."[112] In a column published a month later, she continued the same line of criticism by parodying the language of masculine reviewing, reversing the stereotypical characterization of men and women. She begins, "I confess that though I often admire the writings of men, it always pains me to see a man exposing himself to general remark and to the gaze of women, by thus coming publicly forward." In what follows she dilates upon "the true male virtues," which make the home the sphere proper to them; graciously allows that men have had some literary successes; takes for granted that everyone knows men have never climbed the highest pinnacles of art; comments upon their endearing weakness, which makes the women in their lives so protective of them—and so on, through the predictable litany of derogation. The parody is uneven, sometimes turning to broad caricature and at other times virtually surrendering any pretence to ironic distance. For all its unevenness, though, it is a remarkably powerful expression of contempt for this sort of language, and powerful in part precisely because of its simplicity. Clare does not even make a pretence of arguing against, much less reasoning with, those who seek to deny the value of women's writing. Instead, she reproduces the self-indicting simplemindedness of their rhetoric, gives it a parodic twist, heightens it a bit for amusement's sake, and goes about her business: "Oh! what a heavenly thing, she inwardly cries, to have a stern husband, to be herself an invalid, to have just two—gracious heaven, I am but a woman, I ask not much—just two chronic diseases."[113] Obviously, as far as she is concerned, the attitudes evinced in such language do not deserve the compliment of a rational argument, and she will not lower herself to venture one. "When men argue about the incapacity of women, with the works of George Sand and Elizabeth Browning and Charlotte Brontë and Jane Austen and Rosa Bonheur under their eyes, of what avail will it be to argue with them? If a man insists that the sun shines not when he is at the very moment blinded by striving to look at it, there will be no logic strong enough to convey to him a ludicrous view of his unbelief."[114]

No doubt Hawthorne and his ilk would not have been amused by this sort of criticism, even though she often praised the author of *The Marble Faun* in her other writings. One can assert with a fair degree of assurance, too, that Hawthorne would have been disgusted by Clare's discussion of William Page's *Venus*, a painting that had caused something of a sensation as a result of its bold depiction, by the standards of the day, of the goddess's nakedness.[115] While finding fault with Page's portrayal—"It is a face that indicates to me bad grammar, and an antipathy to bathing, which, in Venus, to say the least, would be very inconvenient"—Clare was more interested in having some fun at the expense of the respectable, censorious, female museum goers who were evidently appalled by the suggestion "that a woman may be young, handsome, and seductive." Moreover, she asked, "If the *Herald*'s suggestion, that the Venus on exhibition outstepped the lines of modesty, caused such an influx of ladies to the Gallery, what multitudes would have flown there, in case there had been a hint that an immodest Apollo was to be seen?"[116] Her boldness in this case is in keeping with the argument about sex that she made in another column, one that virtually dared anyone who knew the gossip about her life to see in it a personal application. A woman, she said, "can hardly be said to be virtuous, in the active sense of the word, before she has fully loved, just as a man is brave only in the passive sense of the word, until that quality has led him to face danger." In case anyone might be uncertain about what she meant by having "fully loved," she went on to make it clear that she was addressing all those men who assume that there must be "a physical baseness of character" in a woman who has taken a lover: "The great body of men persist in believing, against all record and the witness of their own eyes, that the woman who can accept one man can accept all men."[117] She recurred to this topic in other writings, too, as when she took the opportunity of reviewing a performance of *Camille* (1856), an English adaptation of Alexandre Dumas *fils's* sensationally successful play about a courtesan, to remark that the popularity and undoubted excellence of this drama must dismay "the large class of people who hold it as an axiom in female life, that with a woman 'once impure is always impure.'"[118] On another occasion, she commented further on this issue in writing of the importance to a woman of maintaining a semblance of virtue. "But, in case of accidents," she wrote—thus referring, with scandalous nonchalance, to pregnancy—"above all, she must never listen to the accursed words of those who would persuade her, that, having made one error, there is nothing left for her but the paths of vice and degradation, she must fight against that idea with all the oneness of her soul."[119]

Nonetheless, Clare did understand abjection. Her sense of love was nothing like Whitman's mystic power of ecstatic expansion. She anticipated the image of romantic obsession that she dramatized in *Only a Woman's Heart* in an article in the *New York Leader* in which she argued that few people, "especially women," ever get over their first loves. The result, she said, is that all the loves that follow the first—"Jones, Brown, Grey, Smith, Simpkins, Thomkins, and Wiffles"—occupy the same secondary role, each one canceling out the last. "So, we cut away each plank behind us as we go."[120] As we see in this instance, though, as well as in the self-divided narration of *Only a Woman's Heart*, Clare, understanding abjection, opted for bravery. She makes such a joke of women's serial disregard for their lovers, after their first enthrallment, that she does not even bother to take note of how shocking that lengthy list, in and of itself, was bound to be even to many of those who sneered at Mrs. Grundy. She places herself above such pettiness.

She showed the same bold spirit in her reviews of others' writing. Unlike Whitman, who has often been seen, and not without reason, as humorless, she was quite the opposite. About an *Atlantic Monthly* article on John Keats by his acquaintance Joseph Severn, she observes, "There is internal evidence in the article that he caused the death of Keats, by boring him to destruction."[121] The opening line in her review of *Life in the Open Air* (1863) is "I am happy to learn from the preface of this book that this is the last volume of [Theodore] Winthrop's works."[122] In a thoroughly eviscerating review, as she paraphrases the theme of male trustworthiness in Anthony Trollope's *Rachel Ray* (1863), she writes, "Let it be allowed that the great mass of male affection is chaff, but it must be sustained that some wheat is to be found there, in order to excuse parents for letting their female children live, for otherwise we could learn a lesson of humanity from those savages who wisely murder the greater number of g[i]rls at birth."[123] Of Rebecca Harding's story "Paul Becker" (1863), she sighs, "I can only make out that two young and pretty girls love two seedy, shuffling old codgers, whose hands are violently hard, and who either can't or won't wear good clothes."[124] Reviewing the poetry of Adelaide Proctor, she comments, "There is a certain dignity and repose in her verses which causes her not to tell us too often that she desires to be incarcerated in an immediate mausoleum."[125] A volume entitled *The Every-Day Philosopher* (1863), written by "The Author of *The Recreations of a Country Parson*" (Andrew Kennedy Hutchison Boyd), forces her to conclude that only someone suffering from mumps could profit from it. "For in that malady any emotion, whether of pleasure or grief, makes the countenance to move, and causes great pain to the patient, and I will warrant that these essays will leave both the mind and the face in a state of complete vacuity."[126]

Meanwhile, Clare used her position at the *Leader* to give frequent notice to Mary A. Dodge, an advocate of women's rights who wrote under the name Gail Hamilton and who vigorously contested, for instance, the idea that women should sacrifice themselves for their children's sake. Clare called the essay in which Hamilton declared her opposition to this idea the best argument on the women's question she had ever read, and she termed Hamilton herself "the best essayist in America."[127] Playfully, she teased Hamilton for the criticism of dancing she had voiced in an essay for the *Atlantic Monthly*: "Idiocy in all intellectual matters is sweetly recommended to us as a beatific state by the majority of the male sex, especially by those who have tried it and know, but, as a general thing, they don't persecute us about our dancing."[128] Six months later, reviewing Henry David Thoreau's *Life Without Principle* (1863), she complimented his book by calling it "worthy of Miss Dodge, or Gail Hamilton, a lady gifted with the frivolous accomplishment of writing, although sadly deficient in the more serious art of dancing."[129]

For all her bravura, though, and for all her acclaim as, "so to speak, a queen," Clare well knew that there would be consequences for anyone who assumed a position as intransigent as hers in relation to the social organization and circulation of desire.[130] She might mock the stereotyped fate of the maiden literary lady—"O that she had a devoted husband, to abuse, to insult, to degrade her"—but she also experienced her fame as being rather more of a double-edged sword to her than Whitman's was to him. "For several years," she wrote in 1860, "my own private life and character have been made the subject of all manner of malicious and false statements. The most madly preposterous rumors, the most sickening hypocrisies have been labelled with my name, and sent to grovel through the provinces."[131]

Clare was as attuned as Whitman was to the development of modern advertising in the manufacture of celebrity. Of the saying "Good wine needs no bush," which refers to the branches inns used to hang outside their doors to notify travelers of the drink to be had within, she commented, "This proverb is opposed to the whole system of modern advertising"; and she went on to say, " 'Every man his own trumpeter,' is the popular motto of the day."[132] She could not take it to be true, however, as in this same era Whitman appeared to do, that any publicity was good publicity. If her name opened doors, as when the *Golden Era* introduced her to its readers in 1864 as "one whose name possesses a celebrity patent to all who are conversant with the more refined and polite current writing of the day," it could also be a burden.[133] She did not live to witness the condescension with which her bohemian fame at Pfaff's would be described by her literary acquaintance Edward Everett Hale: "Ada Clare experienced a melancholy and singular phase of life, which you may, perhaps, in some measure imagine, by supposing the lady in [John Milton's] Comus to accept the manners and morals of her company, and to assume a sort of leadership among them, but under the impression that the manners and morals were excellent and noble."[134] She did, however, take up her stage career under the name "Agnes Stanfield" in an apparent attempt to avoid the notoriety of "Ada Clare"—a decision that becomes especially interesting in light of Clare's paradoxical claim that it is only through acting a role that a woman can truly be herself.[135] "It is only on the stage," she wrote, "that the woman is taken out of the world's straight-jacket, and left with free limbs and free soul."[136]

For the men in the crowd with which Clare ran in those early years in

New York, to be bohemian suggested being oneself, without concern for the censorious world symbolized by Mrs. Grundy. Acting, in this context, was certainly appropriate to the stage but outside of its confines would suggest the poseur, the fake, or the confidence man, types inimical to the free and open manliness supposedly manifest both in *Leaves of Grass* and in the person of its author. As David S. Reynolds has written, in his analysis of Whitman's relation to the performance culture of his day, his life and work were suffused with theatricality; but in his comments on his own work and in his public persona, Whitman sought to emphasize an immediate relation between his words and his self, as in one of the most famous lines in his poetry: "Who touches this touches a man" ("So Long!" 1860, 2: 452).[137] Even when they could not help but recognize that there was something of the poseur about him, his most devoted readers, too, tended to regard his work in this way, as conveying the true nature of his being. For Clare, however, acting suggested the irreducible foundations in social and cultural structures of the very possibility of such a thing as a woman's true passion.

As the future author of *Only a Woman's Heart* heard that passion in 1860, it cried, "Give utterance, O give utterance to me: I am love, I am pain, I am pathos, I am passion. I am come from God to teach you, I am in anguish lest I die unheard!" Clare then commented, "Most women disregard this cry, this heart of life, crushing it within them, and so committing awful abortions upon their souls." Since she was feeling optimistic at that moment, or at least assuming that theatrical pose, she went on to say, "The struggles and pains that those women like me who have said 'I belong to myself and God' must pass through, are richly rewarded." At the same time, as if extending her sympathy to Mrs. Grundy, whom she could see recoiling from her words, she added, "I do not blame most women for sinking down into deceit and hardness of heart, they have so much against them."[138]

Even in this moment of self-assertion, Clare's voice is as self-divided as it is in the narration of her novel. Her proud claim that she is a soul alone with God is made with the utmost theatricality, through the prosopopoeia of the heart's speech and in the context of an argument that such speech is possible only on the stage, as an act of make-believe—as when friends refer to a woman as a queen, and even treat her as such, though all know that she has no kingdom and only such power as they may decide to pretend she has at any given time. Like the metaphysical universality in Whitman's assertion of bohemian identity, the imaginary singularity in Clare's may well be sincere, certainly constitutes a form of self-promotion, and is a fiction through and through. Thus, in historically telling ways, self-delusion—courageous, desperate, touching, and embarrassing—is written into the very structure of both these writers' acts of self-presentation.

Clare had played a minor role in John Brougham's stage adaptation of *Jane Eyre* in 1856, and in reading her assertion that she belongs to herself and God one might well think of Brontë's heroine at one of the most dramatic moments in that novel. This is when, having been teased by Edward Rochester about his supposed engagement to the beautiful and rich Blanche Ingram, Jane bursts out with a reply that gloriously violates the codes of decorum, deference, and feminine propriety that she has been obliged to observe. "I am not talking to you now," she exclaims, "through the medium of custom, conventionalities, nor even of mortal flesh: it is my spirit that addresses your spirit; just as if both had passed through the grave, and we stood at God's feet, equal—as we are!"[139] One might notice, though, that Clare's speech resembles Jane Eyre's in its irreality as well as in its transgressiveness. Both outbursts are couched in the hypothetical conditions of the imagination and so are structurally marked off, even in the act of their utterance, from social reality.

Thus, in contrast to Whitman's method of proclaiming, with dramatic assurance, the truth of his identity, Clare emphasized the fictionality of hers. Whereas he set his poetry off from the realm of artifice, she found her truest self within that realm. In Whitman the artifice excluded from and yet intrinsic to the definition of the modern bohemian reaches its acme: he appears to be at once genuine and manufactured, the ultimate bohemian and the ultimate poseur. Clare, on the other hand, elides these questions of genuineness and artificiality, since—as her mock title of queen indicates—she makes no serious claim to universal representation. Whereas Whitman appears as bohemian desire itself, she appears as but an instance of such desire. His domain of truth is metaphysical; hers, theatrical. In Whitman and Clare, despite their friendship and close association around the long table in Pfaff's basement, America was the birthplace of two very different bohemias.

In *Jane Eyre* Brontë showed a fierce concern with describing the almost supernatural pains and difficulties faced by a woman who desires to break through the barriers of irony between males and females, and such was also Clare's concern in her writings and in her life. It is no disservice to Whitman's genius to say that if we want to keep him honest, and to honor his inspiring example as a bohemian during his years among the crew sitting around in the basement of Pfaff's, it is good to keep in mind the "needle of repartee" (in Jane Eyre's words) that Clare brought to the table.[140]

CHAPTER 6

The Poverty of Nations

Narrowly regarded, the concept of bohemia was French in origin, but, as we have seen, it could not be held within this boundary. It had also arisen elsewhere—and nowhere in particular. At the same time that it was beginning to designate a way of life among certain residents of Paris in the 1830s and 1840s, bohemia proclaimed the international nature of its scenes. We hear this proclamation in the French word itself, *la bohème*, which alluded to the foreign kingdom of Bohemia and, more specifically, to the Gypsies whom the French associated with that land and yet viewed as stateless wanderers who formed a community unto themselves, one with no concern for national borders. Bohemia, then, was conceived of as a noncountry deliberately opposed to the organization of modern life through the identities, values, and institutional structures of the bourgeois nation-state. A ubiquitous countermodernity, an imaginary land that was gypsy-like even in the peregrinations of its name, bohemia was defined by displacement. The concept of bohemia itself shared the condition of the vagabond, of he who has *ni feu ni lieu*, neither hearth nor home. Its displacement in space mirrored its anachronism, governed as it was by a sense of simultaneous prematurity and belatedness. Outcast in time as well as geography, the concept of bohemia encouraged longings for a utopian future of the modern nation even as it sustained a nostalgic desire for a premodern era such as the Gypsies of romance were imagined to inhabit. Youths struggling to make their way in the contemporary metropolis thought of themselves as the disregarded heralds of days to come and as the disinherited legatees of a past in which they might have been the favorites of munificent princes, if not in fact princes themselves. A mode of existence without a proper place or time to call its own, a paradoxical invitation to revel in the riches of poverty, degradation, and misery, from the very beginning bohemia was a moveable famine to which like-minded souls everywhere were invited. One of the original members of Henry Murger's bohème, for instance, was a Polish patriot named Karol. Bohemia's defining sense of homelessness would stick even to those among its inhabitants who were fortunate enough to have fixed addresses; the tales of their tribe would make legendary just how precarious a roof may be when a neglectful world leaves youthful geniuses, their pockets full of tickets from the local *mont-de-piété*, with nothing more to pawn—and, despite all their heaps of manuscripts, canvases, or scintillating thoughts, nothing they can sell.

Despite his proclamation that it "exists and is possible only in Paris," Murger himself described bohemia in terms of this displacement of national boundaries in space and time.[1] As in the works of Honoré de Balzac, *Paris* in Murger's statement represents a modern urban life, enlivened by news, ideas, trade, and persons from all sorts of strange lands, which we are to see as standing in dramatic contrast to the unbearable heaviness of place among those immured in a provincial existence. Murger presents the modern metropolis as being the environment specific to bohemia in nineteenth-century France, as it must also be, we may infer, in any land where bohemians henceforth are to appear. As Murger presents it, however, bohemia is not an inherently French phenomenon, and thus is not limited to Paris. On the contrary, as he insists in the opening pages of the preface to his *Scenes of Bohemian Life* (1851), it has existed in all eras and locales and has numbered among its inhabitants not only vagabond Frenchmen of days gone by such as François Villon but also Greeks such as Homer, Italians such as Michelangelo and Raphael, and Englishmen such as William Shakespeare, to name but a few. Elaborating on his argument, we may see the international genealogy of bohemia even in its most profoundly French manifestations. We may note, for instance, not only Murger's own German background and his friend Karol's Polish identity, but also the fact that the most celebrated bohemian in mid-century Paris, Alexandre Privat d'Anglemont, was born in Guadeloupe of mixed African and European ancestry. As in this case, bohemia in general appeared as a nonplace, a wayward colony without a homeland, born between and beyond the lines laid down by modern nationalism.

Living up to the displacements in its etymology and fulfilling its conceptualization in Murger's writing, bohemia called attention to itself in countries such as England, the United States, and Germany soon after *Scenes of Bohemian Life* had popularized it in France, and not much later it appeared in such far-flung locales as Spain, Norway, and Peru. It drew attention to itself across the Apennines, too, where the best way to follow its displacements may be to examine how they showed up in the writings of one of the most extraordinary figures in the world of nineteenth-century bohemia, Iginio Ugo Tarchetti. To appreciate Tarchetti's labors, though, we must first consider how bohemia came to appear in the Italy of his time.[2]

In the Milan of the early 1860s, when Tarchetti was first dreaming of becoming a writer, *bohemia* was translated into a new word: *scapigliatura*. Writing under his anagrammatic pen name, Cletto Arrighi, Carlo Righetti bestowed this term upon a group of disaffected Milanese youth in *The Scapigliatura and the 6th of February* (1862), a novel set in 1853. The date in the title refers to the brief insurrection that year, inspired by Giuseppe Mazzini, against the Austrian occupation of Milan. At the novel's end several of Arrighi's characters die in the doomed revolt, which lends their story a heroic air and yet serves only to intensify the atmosphere of unproductive dissatisfaction that has enveloped them from the beginning. Prior to their ineffectual end, within a melodramatic plot in which Arrighi's protagonist discovers that the execrable husband of his married lover is his own father, the novel focuses on the genial companionship of these youths. We learn that they are informally joined in a group known as the *compagnia brusca* or, as this term might be translated, the rough crowd.

In the course of introducing his novel, Arrighi appropriated the term *scapigliatura* to designate this bohemian company and the other youth of their kind around the globe who suffer contradictions "between what they have in their heads and what they have in their pockets."[3] Derived from a term for disheveled hair that was used during the Renaissance to designate the outrageous young wastrels among the gentlemen of Florence, *scapigliatura* had come to signify disorderliness, dissoluteness, and libertinism in general. Arrighi rescued the word from obscurity when he first took it up in his 1857 novel *The Last Confetti*, but he expounded upon it much more prominently in his 1862 work.[4] It was not until the 1880 edition of this novel that he interjected into his definition of the scapigliatura an explicit recognition of its antecedents in France ("For a while now the French have called this *la bohème*"), but readers had immediately drawn the connection.[5] In a review published shortly after the novel appeared, for instance, Eugenio Camerini dubbed Arrighi Italy's "foremost and most felicitous colonizer" of bohemia, which he "rechristen[ed] in *Scapigliatura*."[6]

The two words generally were used interchangeably throughout the latter half of the 1860s and on into the 1870s. In fact, when Felice Cameroni translated Murger's signature work in 1872, he presented it under a title, *La Bohême: Scenes of the Parisian Scapigliatura*, that actually made the Parisian scene appear to be a copy of the Italian.[7] In this regard we might be reminded of how Jules Barbey d'Aurevilly had portrayed America, not France, as the homeland of bohemia.[8] France, as the Italians were concerned to make clear, did not own the copyright on this scene.

This parallel usage persisted despite the fact that Arrighi's novel had focused on an event specific to the Risorgimento, the movement for Italian independence and unification, thus leading Camerini to hazard that there was "a moral and patriotic element" in Italy's bohemia that was not evident in the French version.[9] In this respect it is notable that *The Scapigliatura and the 6th of February* was published almost a decade after the insurrection that furnishes its conclusion. In 1861 the kingdom of Italy had been established with Victor Emmanuel II at its head, and by the time Arrighi's novel was published young people like those he had portrayed were beginning to feel thoroughly disillusioned with the results of the nationalist struggle. Broadly speaking, they found themselves in a position analogous to that of the French youths who were dismayed by the way the July Revolution of 1830 had led to the "bourgeois monarchy" of Louis Philippe, frustrating hopes for more radical and republican transformations. In its lowest moments this disillusionment would lead to a weary cynicism like that which Tarchetti expressed in 1868: "Now we are also tired of politics."[10] More generally it led to a wide-ranging hostility to the established order of society of the sort that had led the same Tarchetti to write a novel, *A Noble Madness* (1866–67), boldly attacking the practice of military conscription, the institution of the standing army, and the conception of private property, among other things. As Arrighi himself would observe in 1868, in an exchange with the scapigliati of the leftist *Gazzettino rosa*, in his novel the revolt was directed against foreigners, whereas that of the present was "a continual rebellion against the *ordini stabiliti*."[11]

Its specifically Italian features aside, the scapigliatura of the 1860s and 1870s reiterated themes of the French bohemia of the 1830s and 1840s. The scapigliati idealized youth and youthfulness, romantically understood as being uniquely at odds with the established social order. They placed a high value on friendship, conceived of as promoting social ties outside of the domestic bounds of the family and free of the corrupting bonds of the nation's economic and political structures. Arrighi wrote of his scapigliatura as composing "a kind of mystical consortium, perhaps by way of the sympathetic force within the order of the universe that attracts similar substances to one another"; and in a series of exchanges with Arrighi carried on in the pages of the *Gazzettino rosa* six years later, Achille Bizzoni sought to underline the definitively displaced nature of the scapigliatura.[12] Unamused by Arrighi's presentation of himself as the "mamma" of the Milanese scapigliatura, he went so far as to rebuke the elder patron of his movement, contending that those involved in the *Gazzettino rosa* were "neither a caste nor a class," as Arrighi's formulations had made them out to be, and did not "aspire to constitute a legion or to form a party."[13] Rather, "united spontaneously and voluntarily," they were young men "who get along together without talking about it."[14] In other words, he wrote, they were youths who expressed "the ideas, the hopes, the convictions, and the aspirations of young Italians" and in doing so served as "fearless workers for the future."[15]

Despite this rebuke from his juniors, though, Arrighi was pretty much on the mark in the definition he had ventured to promote for this term before any persons were actually calling themselves by it. In Italy as in France, those joined in this quasi-mystical way typically could lay claim to more brains than coins, as Arrighi had remarked in his use of the venerable play on the words *testa* (head) and *tasca* (pocket). More than one commentator, therefore, termed the scapigliatura the "Proletariat of the Intellect"—a phrase that resonated as the century went on.[16] In Italy as in France, their youthful idealism and resistance to social conventions, together with their undisciplined nature even as a group, combined to establish among them a stereotype of idiosyncrasy, excessiveness, recklessness, and, in the end, fatality. Therefore, like the French bohemians, the scapigliati would have their martyrs. In 1876, cribbing from Murger's *Scenes of Bohemian Life* in his definition of bohemia as "the apprenticeship for the artistic life, the preface to the academy, the anteroom of the hospital, the vestibule of the mortuary," Francesco Giarelli offered a roll call: "And Rovani died in a sanatorium and Praga died in a sanatorium and Tellio died in a sanatorium and Tarchetti and Pinchetti and Pezza and D'Affre and Ciconi and Bezza and ten and a hundred others either ended up dependent on public charity or voluntarily opened the door of the sepulchre by themselves."[17] If he was not entirely accurate here—Tarchetti died in rooms he was sharing with his friend Salvatore Farina, neither seeking the grave nor appealing to charity—Giarelli nevertheless captured the general impression of how the lives of the scapigliati were often destined to be cut short. Lionello Patuzzi memorialized this pattern in the first lines of the epitaph that he composed for Tarchetti's tomb in 1869: "For the love of art to which he had sacrificed himself, he suffered daily pains and a premature death."[18]

The likely prospect of such a dolorous end did not overwhelm the scapigliati, however, any more than it did the bohemians in France. In their self-
portrayal, as in the public image of their doings, the sense of recklessness likely
to lead the scapigliati to the hospital or the morgue also seemed emblematic of
youthful romance, artistic experiment, and exuberant fearlessness in confronting economic, social, political, or merely quotidian obstacles. A representative
image would be that of Giuseppe Rovani, ensconced in a tavern, entertaining
his comrades with the defiantly silly jingle "It's incredible / just how terrible /
is the face, horrible! / of a creditor."[19] A novelist and critic, Rovani was a greatly
respected central figure in Milan's world of arts and letters. "His admirers and
all the artistic scapigliatura of the city," wrote Carlo Dossi, "rushed wherever
Rovani went," following him as he moved his base of operations from tavern
to tavern; and, as might be expected of any self-respecting scapigliato, Rovani
had about him more than one adage about the creditors who also trailed after
him.[20] "If bills were violins," he was quoted as remarking on another occasion,
"I'd be a Paganini."[21]

Some stories, such as many of those that Dossi collected about Rovani's
words and deeds, allow us to glimpse the especially strong influence that distinctive personalities are likely to carry in any cultural scene that is not otherwise bound together, like a caste or class or party, by a structured history,
hierarchy, agenda, and set of rules.[22] Consider, for example, Dossi's story of
the bar owner who reproved a young man who had dared to venture a comment about the habitual drunkenness of Rovani, who liked to refer to absinthe
as his "studio assistant." The indignant owner replied, "Drunk, he is able to
do things that you, sober, are not even capable of imagining."[23] Other stories
convey the sense of style that helped bring coherence to the culture of the
scapigliatura despite its defiance of social conventions and its reluctance to
impose any alternative strictures on itself. In them we might see, for instance,
Rovani imperturbably dining one day in the midst of a wintry garden, the
snow on the table serving as his tablecloth; or Cajo Tandardini, an assistant to
the sculptor Giuseppe Grandi, working in his windowed studio while wearing
nothing but a top hat and then, when the neighbors complain of his nakedness, donning a wool jacket that reaches only to his navel; or the libretticist
Fulvio Fulgono, having run up such a large account at a café that one evening
the proprietor finally refuses to serve him a cup of coffee, calmly responding
to this man, "Give me twenty centesmi then so I can go get one somewhere
else."[24] Still other stories convey this sense of style even within the darker
areas of the scapigliatura experience, such as Arrighi had indicated when he

wrote of the scapigliatura as "the personification of the madnesses that remain outside lunatic asylums."[25] We may learn, for instance, of how the friends of a certain poet and painter named Bossi, whose madness could no longer be managed outside of an asylum, regularly visited him there at dinner time, holding "lively philosophical, artistic, and medical discussions" to "break the monotony of his isolation and to dissipate the sadness of the place."[26] Another example of this kind, laying the stress this time on stereotypical bohemian poverty rather than stereotypical bohemian madness, allows us to glimpse the painter Tranquilo Cremona inviting an acquaintance into his house, pulling a piece of newspaper out of his shoe, and relieving himself in the middle of the room, unembarrassedly explaining all the while that for him "the paper serves three ends: first, as a book; second, a sock; and third, an asswipe."[27] Finally, as must also be expected in any tales of bohemia that recall Murger's model, we meet with some that are unrelievedly grim, as humor, melancholy, style, and inspiring force of personality all drop away to leave us face to face with a scene in which even the most ironic sense of romance can no longer be nourished. Such might be, for instance, the tale of Teresina, a model whom Dossi met in the studio of the painter Francesco Jacovacci. At the time Dossi makes her acquaintance, she is a nineteen-year-old beauty who looks to be thirty. She tells him that she has been a model since she was twelve; that her father sold her virginity for five hundred lire to a Roman aristocrat when she was thirteen; that he would beat her when she did not earn enough money. Dossi anticipates that in a short while she will no longer be able to make a living as a model and so will have to become a prostitute whose fee will gradually decrease from ten lire all the way down to two before she finally ends up in the hospital.[28]

Arising from these sorts of stories, as they circulated in Milan, and from the more general gossip, journalism, literature, and art identified with the scapigliatura, the collective image of this consortium might be described as carnivalesque, in keeping with Mikhail Bakhtin's account of the traditional pre-Lenten festival as an event characterized by the overturning of established social customs, institutions, hierarchies, and metaphysics.[29] Like the French bohemia before it, the scapigliatura certainly could look like a year-round carnival. Among other things, it was a community that displaced the conventional terms of caste, class, party, and nation while encouraging behavior that appeared excessive and licentious, not to mention imprudent, improvident, or downright mad, when viewed by the outsiders whom the scapigliati mocked as "serious men." It was with good reason that Murger had offered carnival as a summary image for bohemia in the final chapter of *Scenes of Bohemian Life*, as well as elsewhere in that text, and that it plays a major role as well in Arrighi's *The Last Confetti* and in the fantastic turn-of-the-century German bohemia in the novel *Mister Lady's Notes, or Incidents in a Remarkable District* (1913) by Franziska zu Reventlow. Despite his short and notoriously gloomy life, even Tarchetti turned his hand at one point to a brief description of the Society for Carnival Festivities; the image of carnival was always close to bohemian culture.[30]

To be sure, as Murger had emphasized, many of those who tried to make their lives an unending festival would end up in the hospital or the morgue, but had not such ever been the case? Yet the carnival goes on. So even when they set out quite seriously to define Italy's bohemia—for instance, as "republicanism in politics, reason in beliefs, realism in literature"—statements about this community, such as this one from Giarelli, were likely to conclude with a carnivalesque turn. Bohemia is also, Giarelli adds, "paradox in statistics" and "neologism in oratory."[31] It seems almost fated, then, that there should have had to come a time when someone like Luigi Perelli, a prominent man of letters who was a close friend of Rovani, would be enthroned as Rabadan, King of Carnival. To make the story even more perfect, in that role Perelli encountered Victor Emmanuel II, who was making his way home, and called out to him, in the Milanese dialect, "Ciao, cusin!" As Giarelli recounts, that "Farewell, cousin!" brought frowns to the foreheads of several of the illustrious persons accompanying the king of Italy, but the unperturbed monarch smiled, saluted the scapigliato king, and turned back to his entourage, saying, "We're in Carnival."[32]

As a summary image, the value of carnival is clear. It indicates a common ground among various nineteenth-century bohemias, and it captures something of their personality, style, and spirit. Inevitably, though, in pointing us toward those aspects of bohemia that were most easily popularized and translated across national borders, it oversimplifies the multiple conceptions, transformations, and migrations of bohemia in the nineteenth century. Beyond the more obvious similarities among these various bohemias, matters were more complicated.

In Italy in particular, even while *bohemia* and *scapigliatura* were used as near-synonyms, the very shuttling between the alternate terms suggested difficulties in pinning down one or the other, or both, in such a way as to make them adequate to the desires at stake in the social and cultural movement around them. Broadly speaking, the scapigliatura was associated with professions in journalism and the arts; with anticlericalism in religion; with democratic, republican, or socialist politics; and with realism, tinged with the influences of late romanticism, in aesthetics. In all these respects it did not erect any notable barriers to the word *bohemia* as it was customarily understood in France. Yet the Italian word *scapigliato* remained unsettled, uncertain, and in fact came to be jostled about not only by *bohemian* but also by other words that arose as cognate terms, *spostati, perduti,* and *refrattari* being the most common. (The other terms that came into play included *independenti,* the independent ones; *irregolari,* the irregular or abnormal ones; *avanguardia,* or the avant-garde; and, in reference to incendiary revolutionary destruction, *petrolieri,* for the fiery supporters of the Paris Commune of 1871.)[33] In this multiplication of terms we see further evidence that the translation of bohemia across the borders of Italy was a complex affair.

Within the word *bohemia* itself, of course, divisions already existed. Murger's bohemia differed from Gérard de Nerval's, and both of these from Sand's, Charles Baudelaire's, Privat's, or Courbet's. As in the exchanges between Arrighi and the *Gazzettino rosa,* such differences arose in Italy, too; contributors to the pages of the *Gazzettino rosa* and other journals filled them with contentious communications on issues ranging from electoral reform to aesthetic principles. An impoverished young enthusiast daring to write a letter to an established man of letters might observe, for example, "My *bohême* is *la bohême* of Murger; yours is that of [Giacomo] Leopardi," explaining, "You are serious, inexorably serious; I envy you, but I am not so; I laugh, or, better, sneer, get drunk, curse."[34]

The cognate terms that clustered around *scapigliatura* in Italy reveal still further differences. *Spostati,* for instance, literally means "the displaced ones" and more idiomatically designates those regarded as being maladjusted or misfits. As defined by Michele Uda and Leone Fortis in 1859, this term was associated with the scapigliatura from the start, so that a commentator in 1863 might refer to the "class of the *gente spostata,*" or misfit people, "that Cletto Arrighi called *Scapigliatura*" and whose members, he notes, "always stream into the great centers of population."[35] Similarly, in 1877 Fortis would refer to the quintessential "idealists of all idealisms, *spostati* of all the *spostature, scapigliati* of all the *scapigliature,*" treating these words as parallel and effectively equivalent.[36] This automatic association between *spostati* and *scapigliati* or *bohemians* would continue to the end of the century, as when a contributor to an 1888 book about Milan called the conductor Achille Panizza "the greatest *scapigliato* in Italy" while also referring to him as "this esteemed *spostato*" and as a "type of *bohême.*"[37] By 1895 a biographer of Napoleon could casually remark upon "the *spostati*, the *scapigliati*, the turbulent ones of every land."[38]

In conjunction with *scapigliatura*, the term *spostato* was open to a number of meanings. Sometimes, in identifying certain people as seeming out of place or, as we might say, at loose ends, it could convey a quite benign picture of them, as if they were no more disturbing than the hapless "little calves" of Federico Fellini's 1953 film *I vitelloni*. Consider, for example, the scholar who defined *scapigliatura* in terms of "the idle, irregular, thoughtless—without being sad—life of certain people, that life which chips away at the rules of good morals and of honest living, but does not go so far as to run into trouble with the penal code."[39] Perhaps not so benign but still sympathetic is the image of the spostato as one whose condition is owing to circumstances beyond his control: as one who has literally been displaced, through no fault of his own, from what ought to have been his proper post in society. The sociologist Gerolamo Boccardo suggested such an interpretation when he framed the issue of "these poor *spostati*" who populate bohemia as arising from a structural misfit between the continuing production of university-educated young men and the weak demand, in society, for their services. This interpretation, however, could also swing in a more ominous direction. "Woe to the society," exclaimed Boccardo, "that knowingly and systematically produces intellectual proletarians!"[40] From this turn in the meanings of *spostati* it was but a short step toward a more conservative viewpoint that drew knee-jerk analogies among "the unfortunate, the *spostati*, and the mad."[41] Critics might then completely reverse the more sympathetic understandings of the term so as to view the spostati as being totally responsible for their deplorable condition. "Milanese bohemia," one commentator observed in 1876, "is composed of off-key singers, talentless painters, and pretentious writers who have an instinctive horror of soap and grammar," whereas "true artists and writers are the most sober and systematic persons in the world," most of them working throughout the day "so that they might decently amuse themselves in the evening."[42] In 1883 another writer also made it clear that the spostati had no one to blame but themselves if they were so foolish as to model their idea of the artistic life "on jokes copied from *The Mysteries of Paris* or *The Life of Bohemia*." Such individuals deserved to be scorned for their failure to understand that "true artists work, are good and useful citizens and affectionate fathers of families, and find their strength in an orderly and tranquil life."[43]

This instability in the meaning of *spostati* helps to illustrate the diverse and often conflicting impulses in the scapigliatura as a phenomenon, as well

as in attitudes toward it among the broader populace. We see how restless and
unsettled the translation of bohemia could be—or, in other words, how endless were the displacements at work within the bohemian heritage. *Perduti*,
one of the other terms that kept company with *scapigliatura*, further illustrates
these complexities. Literally meaning "the lost ones," it might carry a sense of
challenge within its ironic pathos, as when a writer for the socialist journal *La
plebe* characterized his comrades in 1875 by saying, "We are the usual bohèmes
of literature whom the present conditions of society almost always condemn
to forced silence and uncongenial work; we are youths who have more faith
than they want to believe; we are *perduti* who engage in combat with the
intrepidity of the followers of Mazzini, with the tenacity of the Garibaldian,
with the patience of socialism."[44] Naturally, this word could also be used as an
insult, as could all the terms clustered around the scapigliatura, thus inviting
the boastful reply of Cameroni (one of whose pen names was "A Perduto"),
"With their pretentious ingenuity the so-called *serious men* think they can
insult the *perduti* of the republican press by titling them 'the Scapigliatura of
journalism, the *Bohème* of the pen.' Very well then, what they judge to be a
completely unflattering definition, we accept with pride."[45] This challenging
political edge to the scapigliatura was emphasized even more through the use
of the term *refrattari*, which was taken from Jules Vallès's well-known collection of sketches, originally published during the early 1860s in *Le Figaro*, *The
Refractory Ones* (1865). Although the characters of whom Vallès wrote were
a motley assortment of misfits, monomaniacs, and fools having in common
only that they struggled to make their way in the world because they did not
fit into ordinary social classifications—not having a "profession, a position,
a trade," as conventionally understood—this word clearly suggests a sense
of rebellion.[46] This suggestion was reinforced through the association of the
word with Vallès, who was famous (or infamous, depending on one's politics)
for his socialist activities, which culminated in his participation in the Paris
Commune. These actions led Amadeo Roux, for example, to refer to "the
insane and odious Jules Vallès" in the course of a commentary on the communards whom he identified as youthful spostati, bohemians, disciples of Balzac,
and *réfractaires*.[47]

The differing strains of meaning within this cluster of words were sometimes self-consciously or playfully delineated by the scapigliati, as when
Cameroni wrote, "Murger's *Bohème* is to Vallès's refrattari as a smile is to
an imprecation. The former is the dithyramb of the Scapigliatura; the latter

constitutes its martyrology."[48] Similarly, in an 1870 article entitled "Viva la Scapigliatura!" in which he also used the terms *Bohême* and *perduti*, Cameroni sought to distinguish between Heinrich Heine, whom the French had adopted as a revered bohemian, and Murger: "Viva the cynical grin of the former and the bitter smile of the latter!"[49] More usually these cognate words, especially when used by those distant from or opposed to Milan's bohemia, were tossed together higgledy-piggledy, as Cameroni indicated in one of his writings, a remembrance of Rovani. In this piece he adopted the presumed viewpoint of the Milanese establishment so as to refer to Rovani interchangeably, and with an ironic lack of discrimination, as a member of the scapigliatura, a bohême, and a refrattario.[50] By the end of the century the association among these terms had become so automatic that a sociologist could write of "that part of the bourgeois class in our city that welcomes within itself the *spostati*, the mad, the vagabonds, members of all sorts of professions, delinquent bank clerks, the bankrupt, the disgraced, the bohemian, the *refrattari*, and among these also some of good parts, who have no other fault save that of having made some error."[51]

This simultaneous multiplication of terms and tendency to run them all together resulted from the contrast between the definite impression the scapigliatura had made—there could be no question but that it existed as a social and cultural phenomenon—and the indefiniteness of its nature and goals. The rallying cries associated with it were so broad as to license a wide range of understandings and were, in any case, nothing like a party platform or unifying statement of principles. Those who offered definitions of this community pretty much ventured them on their own account, and these definitions tended to be impressionistic, as in Arrighi's original formulation in *The Scapigliatura and the 6th of February*, which had spoken of "advanced," "independent," "restless," "troubled," "turbulent" youth.[52] In 1870, for instance, the following was offered by a contributor to the *Gazzettino rosa*: "A lot of skepticism and a bit of discouragement; admiration for beauty and justice and indignation toward hypocrisy and wickedness; a smile on the lips and a frown on the brow; many remembrances, few hopes; ardent and crazy conspiracies, frequent and dolorous delusions: behold the Scapigliatura."[53]

The multiplication of terms testifies to the desire to pin down the class, or consortium, or fraction of the bourgeoisie, or whatever it was, and thus testifies also to the varied and sometimes conflicting impulses within the imagined community that was in question here. Meanwhile, the tendency to use these terms interchangeably or redundantly indicates the failure—or the irrelevance—of this desire to pin it down. Nonetheless, in a comparison with the French instance, certain features of the Italian do come into prominence.

In its Italian translation, bohemia left aside the wider reaches of the French term. It focused on educated young men, more or less bourgeois in origin, to the exclusion of the more motley assortment of individuals, ranging from criminals to gypsies, bottom dogs, buskers, acrobats, and oddball enthusiasts, that could fall within the scope of la bohème as understood in France. In Italy one misses the bohémienne, too; for all practical purposes, the scapigliatura was an all-male company, despite Arrighi's claim that it included both sexes.[54] Whereas political identifications in the French example tended to be at least vaguely republican and socialist (despite Murger's conservatism, and despite Karl Marx's sweeping condemnation of bohemia as reactionary), in Italy some writers made more marked attempts to claim for bohemia a radical essence and heritage. In this respect, it differed greatly from the bohemian scenes enjoyed by Arsène Houssaye in the 1830s, by the Pfaff's crowd in New York City in the 1850s, and by the enthusiasts in some other bohemian outposts as well, such as the one in Lima contemporaneous with Italy's scapigliatura.[55] "The pen of the bohème," wrote Cameroni, "prepares the barricade of the communard."[56] "That class of society, which the French call la Bohème," wrote Oreste Vaccari, "I cannot better define in our tongue than with the word Scapigliatura," which he then portrayed as signifying the motivating force present in all the revolutionary uprisings in nineteenth-century France and Italy: "It was still these same ones who made the revolution of '21, these same ones who fought in Paris in the days of July '31, these same ones who were responsible for the five days in Milan in '48, these same ones who were assassinated in Paris on the second of December in '52, in Aspromonte in '62, in Turin in '64, in Mentana in '67; it was still these same ones on March 18, 1871 who hoisted the red flag of the Commune in Paris and in all of southern France."[57]

Even with these notable traits, however, the scapigliatura remained a diffuse and multivalent phenomenon. Historians have tried to bring more definition to this phenomenon by distinguishing between a literary and a political scapigliatura (a *scapigliatura letteraria* and a *scapigliatura democratica*) and also by making reference to other types, such as an aristocratic or gilded scapigliatura, but this kind of distinction is not really adequate to the fluid interchanges among the cultural and political interests manifested by those identified as scapigliati. Cameroni, for instance, was a radical leftist, but at the same time he fully embraced the bohemianism of Murger, who was anything but that;

and the writings of Tarchetti, an impoverished journalist who nonetheless was accorded entrée to the salon of Countess Clara Maffei, veered wildly between a kind of moralized realism reminiscent of Eugène Sue, a literature of the fantastic evidently influenced by Edgar Allan Poe and E. T. A. Hoffmann, and the unclassifiable quasi-allegorical combination of realism and romance that drives his last and greatest work, *Fosca* (1869). As in the case of these two figures, what we see more generally in the phenomenon of the scapigliatura is a translation of bohemia across national borders that is not based on the task of establishing lexical identity but rather founded on a recognition that this word opens the possibility of exploring expressions of humanity, community, and society that exist in the contemporary order of things only in the form of spatial and temporal displacements. Disheveled, misfit, lost, refractory, gypsy: such was the condition of being figured through the language of Italy's bohemia. It was more an occasion for creative work, on one's self and on the society around one, than a signified concept. Cameroni announced, "In *la Bohème* the artist commands the man."[58] The divagations in the ways scapigliati imagined their community allow us to glimpse the variety of its instantiations, which then allow us to see how the term *scapigliatura* remained polemically energizing precisely because of its open-ended definition, not despite it. It was a vortex of displacements through which scapigliati took attitudes, themes, and tropes gathered from various sources and played with them, tried them on for size, tested them to see if they might be repurposed (as a newspaper might become a sock or an aid to hygiene), knowing all the while that they did not yet have what they desired, that for which they were still working, or that which was leading them to turn away from what others called work.

Contemporary critical views of the scapigliatura underlined the emphasis, among those who identified with it, on its diffuse, volatile, open-ended character. The reviewer who dubbed Arrighi's rough crowd the Proletariat of the Intellect, for instance, described them as being, if honest and talented, the liveliest and most productive part of the population, while warning that, if they were not so, they would become "the true cancer of society" and would "dishonor the country and the civil progress of humanity not only in Italy, but everywhere they might be."[59]

Other critics, meanwhile, condemned it entirely. In 1877, reviewing a book by the scapigliato Raffaelo Barbiera, Antonio Cima respectfully noted that Barbiera "distinguishes the true from the false bohème" but argued that he ought to have gone further and "not accepted at all that nomenclature, which, when it does not smell of misfortune, smells of poltroonery and quackery."[60] Better to sweep it all away—or to argue that it already had been swept away, as Eugenio Torelli Viollier did in the *Corriere della sera* the following year, contemptuously dismissing the young Italians who still identified with the idea of bohemia. He had once praised Tarchetti's writing and joined with him as a collaborator on a literary project, but that history no longer mattered, or mattered only insofar as it could be used to sneer at those who now refused to consider bohemia dead and gone.[61] "Like those little ladies in the provinces who flaunt themselves and believe that they are staying at the forefront of fashion, while dressing themselves in the dregs of the storerooms that Parisian merchants destine for export," these youths, he wrote, foolishly dream of recreating bohemia in Italy twenty years after it has faded away in France.[62] Arguing much as Torelli Viollier had, Oreste Cenacchi even made Tarchetti submit to the ultimate indignity of being used as a club to beat up a younger generation that Cenacchi deemed unworthy of assuming the bohemian mantle.[63]

Yet despite efforts to mock bohemia and all that appertained to it as nothing but an outmoded fad, it continued to inspire discussion. Other observers still worried about this mobile and flexible word and, not incidentally, about the unsettled population of urban youths who were associating themselves with it.[64] With these youths themselves speaking of their cultural stultification and inadequate employment, of being "condemned to forced silence and uncongenial work," many who identified with the established order of things felt threatened. In Italy and everywhere else that it was translated, observers of the bohemian phenomenon saw a challenge to capitalist ideologies that were supposed to rationalize and dignify labor while also naturalizing the economic system, rendering it impervious to question and debate—or, as Cameroni scathingly said, impervious to dreams, utopias, and fairy tales.[65] Boccardo, he who proclaimed the woe of any land that systematically produces intellectual proletarians, described this situation as one in which society learns that it must obey "all the great biological laws." Every year, he wrote in 1883, Italy's universities "throw into the marketplace a dense and numerous company of graduates, who come to swell the ranks of the legions of lawyers without clients, doctors without patients, architects and engineers without jobs. And then the town criers of the trashy journals, the filthy sheets of calumny and pornography, set themselves to propagating, in the life of our cities, the seed of the wasted wit of these unrecognized geniuses, these sons of *la Bohème* and of miseducation."[66]

Boccardo's imagery echoes that of a rabidly furious and widely influential essay by Elme-Marie Caro that was published in the *Revue des deux mondes* in the immediate aftermath of the Commune. Caro blamed that event on the satanic influence of bohemia, especially of the literary sort associated with small newspapers and journals. Popularizing a formula that may have originated in Émile Crozat's writing about *la maladie du siècle*, Caro included within his indictment of bohemia "doctors without clients," "lawyers without cases," "professors without students," and "all the déclassés of the liberal professions 'who carry a bachelor of arts diploma in the pockets of their worn-out coats.'"[67] From the way Boccardo's analysis in turn was echoed in the views of another critic, two years later, we can get a sense of the broad currency it had come to enjoy. As if to slap down the lament, as in the *Gazzetta di Milano*'s obituary for Tarchetti, about "times so hard for literature that is not commercial, for art that does not sell out," a writer identified by the initials G.P.A. sternly commanded, "When one reflects on the inexorable laws of demand, of supply, and of consumption, reconsidering the *irregolari*, Vallès's *refrattari*, one cannot exclaim, with any foundation in truth, 'Glory to the losers of the scapigliatura! The utopia of today is the reality of tomorrow.' There is an excess population in any land that does not produce enough for all: there is an excess of literati where the demand of the public is less than the supply of writers. Thence naturally follows a process of elimination as the weakest, the less fortunate, those unable to satisfy the demand, are inexorably eliminated."[68] The "desire for instruction," G.P.A. announces, is laudable "only as long as it does not give rise to a class that may one day prove dangerous to the society that has shown too much generosity of spirit" toward it. Economic rationality demands a stop to the production of this excess population of educated, or miseducated, youths, who else are bound to end up "selling their works, and their character along with them, to a journal."[69] Other writers, like Otto von Leixner in Germany, hastened to connect the dots between this population of loose youth and the threat of revolution; and Edmond Lepelletier, in France, extended this warning to the case of educated young women in Paris, those "bohemians in skirts" who, he said, were likely to become lesbians.[70] D. H. Lawrence's *The Rainbow* (1915), with its portrayal of Ursula Brangwen's relationship with Winifred Inger, is one of the more famous of the literary works that were to be influenced by this kind of warning.

Although Tarchetti died more than fifteen years before G.P.A.'s words were written, they help to represent the context in which he produced his entire oeuvre during just four hectic years, from 1865 to 1869. As all his major works of fiction show, he had already intuited the logic that would come to prevail in this critique of the scapigliatura. It was on this inexorable logic, not on the festiveness of carnival, that he focused his work. For him, the bohemian condition of homelessness was all-pervasive and, for that reason, excruciatingly difficult to translate into conventional terms, including what might seem to have become the conventional terms of bohemian community. He wrote of economic injustice and nationalist hysteria and the metaphysical politics of passion, not of cheerful recklessness, gypsy freedom, or the romance of youth. His work, therefore, better enables us to understand, even as it moves us beyond, the scapigliatura that Tarchetti was popularly taken to represent.

In its main outlines Tarchetti's life seemed so perfectly stereotypical of his kind that it led his biographer, Enrico Ghidetti, to assert that his story "offers the exemplary diagram of the culture of the scapigliatura."[71] He was born in 1839 and died in 1869, just shy of turning thirty—the age at which bohemians' enchanted transports were traditionally supposed to turn back into pumpkins. Tarchetti had the requisite tormented love affairs, most notably with a young woman named Carlotta Ponti, of which we have a record in his correspondence, which touches on the inevitable points of parental disapproval (hers) and suicidal ideation (both his and hers). After finishing his studies at the Collegio Trevisio in the Piedmont town of Casale Monferrato, situated between Turin and Milan, Tarchetti entered the military. He served for four increasingly discontented years, from 1861 to 1865, a period interrupted by an extended leave of absence on the grounds of his health, which would continue to be shaky throughout the brief time remaining to him. After getting himself back out into civilian life again, he scraped together a living in Milan, Turin, and San Salvatore Monferrato through his writing and editing for various journals.[72] Baptized Igino, he later preferred the spelling Iginio, and he added Ugo to his name in honor of Ugo Foscolo, whom he admired for his poetry, his fiction, and his translation of a work, *A Sentimental Journey Through France and Italy* (1768), by one of Tarchetti's favorite authors, Laurence Sterne. (According to Salvatore Farina, Tarchetti could recite entire pages of that book from memory.)[73] In addition to poetry and short stories, he published three novels, *Paolina* (1865–66), *A Noble Madness*, and—a work being serialized in *Il pungolo* as he lay in his bed dying of typhus—his incomplete masterpiece, *Fosca*. Each of these marks a startling advance over the preceding work, and *A Noble Madness* in particular received favorable critical attention in a number of journals, including Arrighi's *Cronaca grigia*, but none of them sold well. To reach anything like a popular audience, Tarchetti would have to await Ettore

Scola's 1981 film *Passion of Love*, which was based on *Fosca*, and the 1994 Stephen Sondheim musical, *Passion*, also derived from it.

Pressed for money, at one point during this period Tarchetti even set himself up as a teacher of English in Parma, despite the fact that his spoken English skills were said to be rudimentary.[74] He also managed to produce a serviceable translation of Charles Dickens's *Our Mutual Friend* (1864–65) and, in the midst of his other literary activities, found time for other recreations well suited to a bohemian, such as dabbling in mesmerism, with his sister Amalia serving as his subject.[75] It would seem, however, that such diversions were few. No one but Henry Murger, said one acquaintance, could have had the right to describe the final years of Tarchetti's life, in which he was often sad, weak, and impoverished. Tarchetti himself evidently kept Murger in mind, as when he used an allusion to the martyrology in the preface of *Scenes of Bohemian Life* to characterize the recently announced death of a young poet, Domenico Milelli. "The Gilberts, the Malfilâtres abound in Italy, more than elsewhere," he wrote.[76]

Ready reference to the so-called Bible of bohemia is certainly understandable in one who was so impoverished, as he struggled to survive as a man of letters, that for many days he had to subsist upon an unvarying diet of the only foodstuff in his lodgings: a hoard of beets. At once grim and absurdly comic, this is precisely the kind of incident out of which Murger constructed his work. Even at the best of times, though, and despite his attempts to protest against it, Tarchetti had a reputation as a lugubrious figure.[77] He is recorded as having dourly remarked to one of his brothers, "You are well adjusted, and I am not."[78] Farina recalled Tarchetti appearing, when he first met him, "tall, pale, melancholy, doomed."[79]

Others would memorialize quite different qualities in him, as Patuzzi did with the concluding words on his gravestone: "Honorably independent, respecting and sympathizing with others, he was loved and mourned; hurriedly, he put into books the part of his spirit desirous of infinity."[80] Ettore Soci, too, while citing him as "one of those *perduti* who waste away through the exuberance of their hearts," would go against this first tide of remembrance by remembering Tarchetti for his cheerful question, "Who can say how many ideas are in a flask of wine?"[81] For the most part, though, the reputation for melancholy stuck to him, with the writers for the *Gazzettino rosa* seeming to take particular amusement in it. In 1867, for instance, in an article satirizing a number of authors, Tarchetti was portrayed as saying, "I would like to be a hyena penetrating among the sepulchres and gnawing on the bones of the dead. . . . In the dark a loving maiden would seem to me a cadaver that rises up, like Galvani's frog, through the effect of magnetism, destined thereafter suddenly to fall under its lifeless weight."[82] In the same journal two months later Bizzoni joked that Tarchetti would like to write a novel entitled *The Emotions of a Worm in the Cemetery*.[83]

Especially given Tarchetti's public objections to this kind of portrayal, it was undoubtedly rather cruel of the *Gazzettino rosa* still to dwell on this reputation in his obituary, whose author claimed that Tarchetti had so assiduously haunted Milan's graveyards that their custodians grew to recognize and greet this habitué. "The tomb attracted him like a calamity," this notice said.[84] It must also be acknowledged, however, that the purveyors of this sort of gossip were not totally unprovoked. After all, the fact that Tarchetti had died so young had not prevented him from writing, when he was all of twenty-five years old, a poem that begins with the Murgeresque line "I sing the death of my youth."[85]

If the goods Tarchetti had to sell found few buyers during his lifetime, however, leaving him to be derided at times even within the restricted circles of the Milanese scapigliatura, he nonetheless became a notable symbol of the tragic scapigliato in the years after he passed away in the apartment of his friend Farina. Despite the desolate beginning to Farina's review, a year after Tarchetti's death, of two posthumous publications from his pen—"Who still speaks of Tarchetti?"—he acquired a reputation as a gifted writer cut down in his prime. For a while it came to seem that his first name had actually been "Poor," so frequently was he referred to in books and journals as "povero Tarchetti." Ironically, the very fact that he was said to be largely forgotten became part of his claim to fame.

In the words of Carlo Catanzaro, "He was an unfortunate genius, and his name has faded away as rapidly as the evening star; his life, like a meteor, shone forth and burnt out in a brief hour."[86] Pompeo G. Molmenti wrote, "He died young, still full of the spirit of an ingenuous faith; he died before a sick society could shrink his heart."[87] Having mentioned Tarchetti as being poetic, or unworldly, in disposition—as being one who, like Praga, was "refractory to the invitations of *reality*"—Sacchetti went on to describe how young people in 1880 remembered him with great tenderness. The custodian of the Cimetero Monumentale, he said, had told him of how Tarchetti's grave was frequently visited by people, youths, women—"and I have seen their great sorrow!" the custodian added.[88] Twenty-five years after Tarchetti's death, this kind of sentimental take on his life had become literary-historical boilerplate, as in the version offered by the historian Raffaelo Barbiera: "A Piedmontese novelist, discontented with everyone and everything; a melancholy intelligence, taken by death before his time, Iginio Ugo Tarchetti posed . . . as a rebel; but his pen released torrents of tender feelings."[89] Similarly, the historian Vittorio Bersezio wrote of him at this time as "a young man full of intelligence" and as "the most bizarre spirit, the most original character, the best soul in the world."[90]

Tarchetti was to remain what is generally called a minor figure in Italian literary history—or something even less than that, according to some.[91] Despite his relative obscurity, though, Tarchetti's image after his death had stabilized into that of a talented and sensitive young man who might stand as an example of the genius dying young, his promise suggested but not fulfilled. His tormented love affairs and the extremes of his reputed melancholy and misanthropy had largely been edited out of his remembrance, as had the intense economic and political critique that informs his fiction. He was still a minor figure, to be sure, but he had come a long way from the author whose death was accorded but thirty-one words in Turin's *Rivista contemporanea*, which concluded this obituary with the contemptuous observation that, as "a free thinker," Tarchetti had disdained the attendance of a priest.[92]

The efforts of his friends, especially Farina, who wrote of him with great affection throughout the rest of his own life, certainly helped to create this image of Tarchetti. Undoubtedly, too, this fashioning of Tarchetti as a symbol was helped along by myth-making cultural machinery that had been established at least since the days of Gilbert, Malfilâtre, and Thomas Chatterton. Like nineteenth-century bohemia more generally, the scapigliatura owed much of its formation to this machinery of conventions, topoi, and tropes centered upon the figure of the neglected genius; and Tarchetti, especially as time might seem to soften the edgier aspects of his life and work, fit the bill. In this regard, we might say that his posthumous reputation in the last three decades of the nineteenth century amounts to little more than one reiteration among many others of a nineteenth-century cliché. What makes this case particularly interesting, however, is that Tarchetti's novels give us a way to interpret cultural processes such as this, in which life is idealized through death. His fiction shows a fascination with the implication of death in life that goes far beyond the issues of character or temperament that his contemporaries noted through their gossipy references to Tarchetti's supposed melancholy, morbidity, or misanthropy; and, in doing so, it teaches us how to reconceive our entire perception of bohemia.

Figure 13. Photograph of Iginio Ugo Tarchetti (n.d.) (De Agostini Picture Library/Getty Images).

This is not to say that gossip may not also be instructive in its own right. Gossip can be as valuable as any other kind of fiction, and one report about a moment in Tarchetti's life is particularly telling in relation to his accomplishments as a novelist. Shortly before Tarchetti died, according to Giarelli, he was musing on the idea "that one day or another it would be necessary to find a way to make others suffer one's own pains, paying them, of course, in proportion to the quality and the quantity of what was delegated"—although he then went on to say of his own idea, "Ah, no! In practice it would be too difficult. . . . Let's not think about it!"[93]

At first glance, this might seem like the kernel of a narrative, a work of fantasy, in which one could trace out the potential consequences that would ensue if such a political economy of pain could ever actually be put into practice. This would then be the kind of thought that one might expect of an intelligent, imaginative, sensitive man of letters who rejected the invitations of reality so as to devote himself to art and who also happened to be personally acquainted with physical suffering. (Writing in 1868 to explain why his column in *L'emporio pittoresco* had been interrupted, Tarchetti exclaimed, "What a big ugly thing it is to be sick!")[94] What is most intriguing here, though, is Tarchetti's almost immediate rejection of his own idea on the grounds of impracticality. This is interesting because what we may also come to see here—if we did not see it from the first—is that he had suggested nothing more than the actual state of social affairs on which he had focused all his novels.

The rich, after all, do live at the expense of the poor, to whom they delegate their labors, their responsibilities, their battles, their needs, their desires, or, in a word, their pains—"paying them, of course," for their services. If there are limits to the extent of this sort of delegation, it is not for lack of attempts to abolish them among those with the wherewithal to pay, as we have seen, for instance, in the proposal by the eminent economist Gary Becker that the capitalist marketplace should be open to trafficking in human organs from both living and dead people.[95] This is but one of the more recent of the utterly fantastic systems that various social orders have created to establish proxies for the woes of their privileged subjects: systems of warfare, torture, sacrifice, slavery, conscription, taxation, subordination, imprisonment, banishment, indoctrination, penance, guilt, and pity, to name only some of the most prominent. At a certain point, no doubt, even the wealthiest persons are liable to find themselves suffering from an illness or injury that no amount of money can alleviate, but up to that time they will have contracted others to eat their pains for them, just as in some places one used to be able to hire "sin eaters" to consume one's transgressions. They will have contracted others to move, clean, coddle, and refresh their bodies; to receive the pleasure, the anger, or the pain that they wish to externalize; to serve as their fantasies, doubles, mirrors, ideals, conscience, or memory; to swallow their fear of death. Therefore, addressing how people look back at the cruelties of earlier times and then shake their heads at how terrible it would have been to live in those days, Tarchetti pointed out "that the same, and with reason, will be said one day of us," what with the meanness, misfortunes, wars, vices, and autocratic rulers of modern times—and not forgetting as well how people are compelled "to sell themselves every day."[96]

Tarchetti, perhaps, was especially conscious of the market in people with reference to the concerns of writers such as himself. So he raised the question "What does the man of letters sell?" and answered, "His thought." He characterized this bought thought as being consumed, like morsels of food, by a parasitic public. Today, he wrote, because people "no longer wish to think, we commission others to do it for us. What are men of letters? They are men who think for others."[97] As we can see from his comment the following year about how people sell themselves every day, however, his viewpoint on this matter was by no means limited to writers or even to the nation of Italy. Early in 1868, therefore, relaying reports of starvation from France, Algeria, Russia, Prussia, Finland, and England, he wrote of the condition of the poor in the world's most populous cities, in the wealthiest metropolitan centers, as being the most important question of the day.[98] To the political economy supposed to be responsible for the wealth of nations, he posed the question of the political economy of pain. Adopting and extending the heritage of the modern bohemian, he portrayed their production of wealth as a measure of the madness of modern nations.

No doubt matters are more complicated; it is in the nature of matters always to be more complicated, as it is in the nature of any unconventional vision of what is obviously real to seem impractical, "too difficult," and thus an unreal dream, utopia, or fairy tale. Tarchetti's rejection of his own thought— "Ah no!"—is the kind of unthinking denial that automatically assigns to the realm of imagination that which is humanly intolerable, not that which is untrue. The plaintiveness of his denial lies in the view it affords us of a writer who in the last days of his life seemed unable to recognize the reality of his own words. What he once saw and pursued, over and over again, in a series of increasingly amazing narratives, he could no longer see. Like a character out of the *ficciones* of Jorge Luis Borges, he no longer recognized himself as the author of his own works.

We do, however, have those three novels, if we can face up to them, in which to see something of Tarchetti's bohemian reality. A typical expression of sentiment in the first, *Paolina*, tells of "the laborer, that pariah of civil society, perpetually condemned to work like the animals that plow our fields, and condemned to perpetual scorn, and to perpetual poverty, like that of the delinquent. Who will ever bring themselves to believe that the worker has a heart, a will, desires, passions? He is born for forced labor, as the female worker is born for prostitution and for the pleasures of the rich. Let us praise riches!" (1: 267). As one may gather, this is a polemical novel that bears signs of being influenced by the ideas of Pierre-Joseph Proudhon, among others, such as Victor Hugo and Samuel Richardson.[99] It tells the story of an innocent and virtuous young worker who is raped by a marchese after a series of elaborate machinations designed to get her into his house and at his mercy. These machinations include, inter alia, arrangements to have her equally innocent, virtuous, and noble fiancé put into jail. This dreary plot, in which the grisette's death inevitably leads to the death of her betrothed, who, mourning her, joins Garibaldi's forces and perishes in battle, is also twisted with Gothic perversity. We learn that the marchese who ravishes Paolina had years before seduced, betrayed, and abandoned her mother, who died in giving birth to her. As if alluding to the Oedipal drama thrown into the mix of Arrighi's *The Scapigliatura and the 6th of February*, where it underlined the generational antagonisms in which the scapigliatura was rooted, Paolina's oppressor, deceiver, and rapist turns out also to be her own father.

After such a summary, it need scarcely be added that this is a crude work of sentimental melodrama. In a letter to his friend Albino Ronco, Tarchetti described it as a "wretched little thing" that he wrote only for the money it would bring him (2: 692), and one would not wish to dispute his description. The very fact that he excused himself in this way, though, may lead us to consider seriously the questions this piece of hackwork raises about the possibility of doing anything at all without being driven by money. In the figure of the marchese, money in this text is an unaccountable and invincible power identified with historical tradition, social structures, and cultural distinction. As such, it would seem to leave no room for a literature or art outside its grasp, putting culture in a situation like that which Tarchetti would suggest when he wrote of the man of letters as a hireling of rich people for whom his thoughts are nothing but fashionable commodities that make it easier for them to avoid thinking. Immanent in *Paolina*, despite the fact that it is a crudely simplistic work in virtually every respect—style, characterization, plot, theme, and so on—is a complex apprehension of the modern market in human beings that Tarchetti would represent in his next novel, *A Noble Madness*.

This work begins with a narrator, Ugo, hearing from an old friend whom he has not seen for some fifteen years, since he was twelve years old. The narrative then shifts to the voice of the friend, of whose last name we are given only the initial letter: he is known as Vicenzo D. He explains that he has spent much of the time since Ugo has last seen him doing nothing but dissipating his inheritance, living aimlessly, save for such direction as was given him by his love for a woman named Teresa. Recently his life took a turn, however, through his chance meeting with a neighbor. As fate would have it, this neighbor was also known as Vicenzo D, and his story occupies the rest of the narrative.

The madman of the title, this alter ego of Vicenzo D is the same age, about twenty-seven. He tells of his conscription into the military and of the brutalizing effects of military life, thought, and statecraft, as exemplified in particular by the Crimean War. After providing his namesake with vivid descriptions of battles in this conflict, he tells of how he ended up deserting the army (an act that led to his adoption of Vicenzo D as a pseudonym under which to conceal himself). As the other Vicenzo has his Teresa, so had this Vicenzo his Margherita, whose death drove him to become a solitary wanderer and misanthrope. Although at times he would seem perfectly sane in his interactions with others, at others he was quite mad—or at least what the world commonly judges to be mad. This is a novel in the Romantic tradition, and the distinction is crucial.

From our wastrel narrator we then learn that this second Vicenda D finally put an end to their acquaintanceship by committing suicide. He did so in a spectacularly ghastly way, shooting himself not simply in the head but in the face, and not once but twice, totally obliterating his features. As a message he left for the first Vicenzo D explains, he took this action because he knew his suicide would allow his impoverished and indebted friend, since he bears the same name, to be accounted dead. With the aid of a job his alter ego arranged for him before blowing his face off, along with some savings he left him, Vicenzo D will be able to start life afresh while secretly repaying the debts from his old life. He will be able to wed his beloved Teresa, whom the other Vicenzo had also come to love. Out of the death of this other will come the stability of a marriage, an end to his irresponsible aimlessness, and a future invested with the wisdom, or noble madness, that he has gleaned from the deserter's words.

Tarchetti uses the two Vicenzos to distinguish and yet bring together a number of bohemian types. There is the dissolute scapigliato, famed for his improvidence and creditors; the perduto (as both Vicenzos have been "lost," the one from the knowledge of his old friend Ugo and the other from the army and his original identity); the refrattario at his most political (in the views expressed by the second Vicenzo in the course of his antimilitary diatribes); the madman who has managed not to be incarcerated in an asylum; the bohemian lover who regards his beloved as all that he has to hold, and all that he desires to have, in a world in which the generality of men are preoccupied with buying, selling, and profit taking; and, of course, the martyr who either dies or, as in this case, commits suicide before he is thirty. In this compendium of bohemian types, Proudhon makes his influence felt. "Property is theft," we are told, and thievery therefore may be adjudged noble, given a world in which law is "nothing other than the immoral defense of the original usurpation that has forced all of us to confront one another in the roles of creditors and debtors" (1: 399). This critique is then extended to various aspects of human life. We learn that one result of the cruel injustice at the heart of society is that education is designed to produce a particular kind of cruelty, which takes the form of egoism. The deserter illustrates this by referring to the patriotic stories taught in schools, which bring children to reverence "the Romans, who were the greatest thieves and assassins in the world" (1: 402), along with other figures such as Alexander the Great and "that great villain Napoleon" (1: 401). The logic that elevates historical figures such as these, not to mention vicious characters from the Bible such as Jacob ("who usurped the inheritance of his brother with a plate of beans" [1: 401]), leads directly to the practice of snatching men away from their families, agriculture, and industry "to make them murderers" in the military (1: 402).

Admittedly, it may seem that the incisiveness of this argument is attenuated when its speaker furiously breaks it off and rushes away, accusing the first Vicenzo D of being an assassin because he has unthinkingly killed a bug that had been buzzing underfoot. Such a reaction does bespeak insanity of a sort, and the deserter later sends a note apologizing for his temporary loss of reason. In the context of A Noble Madness as a whole, however, this reaction represents perfect poetic and philosophical sense. The afflicted Vicenzo D is not a militant vegetarian, a Buddhist who would spare the life of the mosquito feeding on his arm, or anything of that sort, and so as a matter of practical morality his reaction must seem disordered, as he himself admits almost immediately thereafter. Nonetheless, this reaction is true to the relentless focus in this novel on the violence that has structured human relationships throughout history and that has been sustained and idealized through cultural tradition, nationalism, and marketplace capitalism. As the deserter explains, his madness takes the form of an obsession with the destruction that draws humankind, along with all living creatures, into its orbit. Reflecting on "war, hunting, the tyrannical and ferocious customs of men," and all other sorts of violence, he becomes horribly fascinated with his own guilt not only in the Crimea, where he had killed a soldier of one of the nations opposed to his in this conflict, but also in general. As if anticipating characters in Thomas Hardy's fiction, such as young Jude Fawley in the opening pages of *Jude the Obscure* (1895), he realized that even his most innocent stroll killed "thousands of tiny organized beings, all of them living, happy, and having a right to life and prosperity." It was because he recognized that he was "compelled to prolong [his] existence through the destruction and enslavement of other creatures" (1: 416) that he chose to retire from the world. Rather than bringing him any relief, however, his isolation only delivered him into an agony of uncertainty over judgments about good and evil, guilt and virtue, and the nature of reason, leaving him wondering whether all of human life might not be an absurdity.

In other words, he recognized that every human being, merely by living—apart from any questions of intentionality, morality, ethics, or rationality—conscripts others to suffer for him. To contemporary readers, the most striking aspect of *A Noble Madness* was its attack on the standing army as an institution, and the narrative does elaborate at considerable length and in considerable detail on the evils of military life; but the violence done to Vicenzo D when he was impressed into the army and the brutal actions he subsequently performed at the army's behest come to seem to him exemplary, not exceptional, in terms of human relations. Despite his feeling for his lost Margherita, for instance, he comes to think of love as existing only transcendently, with God, while on earth, as he writes in the journal that he gives to the first Vicenzo D to read, the meaning given that name "is but an echo and a shadow." Thinking of how lovers may kill their rivals "because they perceive that their existence is an obstacle to the achieving of their aspirations," he concludes, "The idea and the need of death lie hidden in the idea and the need of love" (1: 523). Alternatively, he considers that we may find the truth of our words not outside humanity, with God, but inside it, within the unfathomable will of the human body: "Faith is an internal organ, love is an internal organ;

your conscience is completely hidden away in an intestine" (1: 519). Words in general seem fully implicated in the violence that structures human existence, according to his journal, which in some passages seems almost to be quoting Friedrich Nietzsche. "I see in words," he writes, "in their absolutism, in the abuse that they do to thought, so many tyrants of whom we have become the victims.—We must remake the human vocabulary. The history of a word is yet to be written" (1: 518). In the mind of Vicenzo D, then, as in his life, there is no getting away from our abusive employment of others to serve our ends, whether through outright violence and victimization or through the sweetest rhetoric. Subject to language and to our own bodies, we are also proxies exploited by ourselves. We are incapable of knowing ourselves, mad beings that we are, whether we are labeled as such or not. In his review of *A Noble Madness*, Torrelli Viollier summarized these aspects of the novel by calling Tarchetti an "absolutely modern" writer, a "contemporary of Leopardi, of Byron, and of Musset" who represented "the uneasiness, the weariness, the feverish and inexplicable impatience that torments the modern generation."[100]

In a sense, between *Paolina* and *A Noble Madness* nothing has changed. As the marchese could lord it over the common people, toying with them for the sake of his own pleasure, here the established order of nations will also shove a little guy around until, like Paolina's betrothed, his only way out is through the dubious satisfaction of martyrdom. It is also true, however, that in *A Noble Madness* everything is different. In this novel there is not even a whiff of heroism to be won through military action, as there is in the earlier narrative. In *A Noble Madness* martyrdom is wholly a private affair and, as such, capricious and grotesque. The nation that seemed to serve, in *Paolina*, as at least a symbol of noble aspirations is viewed here as a school that manufactures murderers so that it may feed them into its own killing machine. It seems that the best for which one can hope is to lead an out-of-the-way bohemian life, avoiding responsibilities and piling up debts, on the off-chance that for no good reason one might eventually be offered a way out. Only through a fantastic doubling of one's identity—in other words, through imposture, crime, and madness— can one hope for a loophole in the economy that makes creditors and debtors of us all. If such a thing as love might live among us, it would have to consist of this imposture, crime, and madness. In other words, it would have to be a thing of multiple and irreducible displacements—and thus, as the triply framed story within a story within a story that is *A Noble Madness* makes clear, a thing of art. Even one's hope for this thing, though, must be modest at best. After one Vicenzo D figuratively and the other literally dies to the world, what emerges in this novel is simply the stereotypical end of all bohemians who manage to survive their twenties: marriage and a job. Even as a thing of art, lasting love seems to be imaginable only under the sign of submission to the hateful and deathly economy of bourgeois life.

In *Paolina* and *A Noble Madness*, Tarchetti represented as a reality the society he imagined on his deathbed when he mused about the possibility of people paying others to bear their sufferings. Perhaps, dying, he raised this issue casually, distractedly, and so missed the obvious connection it had to his writings over the previous four years, or perhaps he privately savored the irony of telling his visitor that such a state of affairs would be impractical and then watching him nod in agreement. (To begin to appreciate this possibility, one need only imagine a former Occupy Wall Street demonstrator saying, on his deathbed, "Wouldn't it be nice if people with money could pay poor people to do their will?—but no, that would never work," and then seeing those around him smile and nod in agreement.) It is impossible, of course, to know what Tarchetti was thinking. As we see in his first two novels, however, he was obsessed with developing an incisive image of the social totality, despite Torelli Viollier's characterization of him as a psychological novelist unconcerned with the outer world.

This kind of summary image of society also appeared, among other places, in his story "Riccardo Waitzen" (1867), in which the titular figure is a struggling, debt-ridden artist, a composer, in the bohemian era of the 1840s. He falls in love with a dying woman, Anna, who not only returns his love but also pays his debts. She both inspires his art and frees him to compose, thus leading him forward to what will eventually be a successful career in Paris. What she asks in return is that he pledge that he will continue to love her for the rest of his life, even after her death. He agrees, of course; and, of course, he breaks his promise a couple of years after she dies, ceasing to love and mourn her. He then enjoys his prosperity until a vision of his betrayed Anna shows up to scare him to death. In the meantime, Tarchetti has the opportunity to comment, "Nothing is more serious and painful, nothing is more insufferable to the majority of men, than the burden of gratefulness. It is a tremendous debt that everyone quietly carries away. . . . The trivial satisfactions, the little victories that we bring back every day, every hour, in that unrelenting war between soul and soul, between creature and creature, in those constant and pitiless battles of egoism, are the only sensations that comfort us, in our human pettiness, for the great and real evils of life. All of that is sweet, but nothing is sweeter and more consoling than the undoing of the bond of gratitude"

(1: 621). Precipitated through hatred, rejection, and denial of indebtedness, the ego here is the fiction of the autonomous individual that sustained the political economy of this century and that continues to be the basis of neo-liberal economics today. A figure of the bohemian who has made good—like Murger, when he literally and figuratively moved from the Left to the Right Bank—Riccardo Waitzen allows Tarchetti to expose how the logic of economics infiltrates every dimension of human relations: psychological, perceptual, emotional, social, moral, and, not the least among these, aesthetic. By universalizing the image of burdensome gratitude across these dimensions, Tarchetti provides a summary image of a society in which mutuality figures as enslavement, reciprocity as assault, commonality as war, and identity as the weaponry of self-deception by which we strive to subject others to a will that we must be deluded even to claim as our own. As we have seen how we may go berserk with sexual desire, in *Paolina*, or with nationalism, in *A Noble Madness*, so here we find an excoriating view of how we may go crazy with the cruelty that lies hidden within the most innocent delights of everyday life.

At times Tarchetti used this technique of creating a summary image in an offhand way, as when he took advantage of the topic of books designed for a popular audience to draw his readers into rejecting egoism and recognizing the responsibility that comes with their privileges: "And all of us to whom falls the good fortune of a more or less distinguished education will always be responsible for the immorality and poverty by which we are surrounded until we prove that we have done as much as we can to dissipate ignorance, the primary cause of both poverty and immorality."[101] As in this case, such summary images may sometimes seem too casual or too easy, at least if one believes that someone who goes this far ought then also to accept a responsibility for laying out a program of action. Tarchetti does nothing of that sort here, and he was almost as silent on this score when he wrote of poverty as the major issue confronting European nations and then concluded merely by urging those who were well off to be more charitable. At such moments, despite all his Proudhonian allusions, one might be tempted to find him wanting in political consciousness. In their generality, do not such calls to responsibility end up addressing readers entirely in personal and individual terms, thus reinforcing the very egoism that Tarchetti had set out to criticize?

To read him thus, however, would be to read too simply. Since he has identified hunger as a national and international crisis, the most important one currently facing Europe, it is obvious that he believes it demands to be addressed through governmental action—or, as *A Noble Madness* intimates, through radical changes in government. In this context, to conclude a newspaper article with a call for charity does not represent any evasion of or obliviousness to politics. What it does represent, in its telling silence on the conduct of national institutions, is Tarchetti's unsparing estimation of the likelihood of any such political change.

We should remember, then, that political commitment does not require, or at least ought not to require, a commitment to stupidity. Instead of condemning him as politically inefficacious, we might view the gloominess for which Tarchetti was attacked by his socialist comrades as showing how much greater than theirs was his sense of responsibility. The very words with which Ferdinando Martini criticized his writings in 1874 might be taken as providing the grounds for valuing them: "Tarchetti tends to see and represent human acts and feelings in their brutish aspect; an often prejudiced, always melancholy observer, he curses and despairs; he is an artist whom art does not console, wholly intent on excavating within himself the perilous abysses of philosophy."[102] Nicely capturing the possibility of such a revaluation, in 1893 an anonymous critric writing about *A Noble Madness* referred to Tarchetti's "humanitarian pessimism."[103]

It would be pretty to think that bohemians could all comport themselves like those in Enrique Perez Escrich's *The Blue Dress Coat* (1864), whose share-and-share-alike ethos ensures that even the most impoverished members of the group have a sufficiency of "coffee and rum; two liquids, or, to put it better, two necessities for all dreamers."[104] But which holds up better, we might ask: the *Gazzettino rosa*'s glowing evocations of the revolutionary happiness that awaited its editors just up the road or Tarchetti's pitiless dissections of the human beings for whom he nonetheless demanded social justice? Does Tarchetti's *Noble Madness*, in all its impractical extremity, really need the note of moderation that even so sympathetic a reviewer as Felice Cavallotti felt obliged to introduce into his praise of this book: "I certainly do not need to persuade my friend Tarchetti that he has exaggerated, caricatured, the colors of his book through an excessive pessimism"?[105] Should we adopt the commonplace assumption, on the part of both leftist and conservative critics, that one can draw clear distinctions between the ideal and the real, morality and brutishness, optimism and pessimism, and similar categories, or should we pick up on Tarchetti's challenge to the ways these abstractions are defined and set in opposition to one another in the first place?

Given how people conventionally use words, one could hardly expect anything else than that people should have portrayed Tarchetti as a gloomy, melancholy, death-haunted figure. As previously noted, they did have some good reasons for doing so. As his writings show, however, Tarchetti had even better reasons for objecting to this portrayal—one of which stemmed from his implicit critique of the conventional usage of words such as *gloom, melancholy, pessimism*, and *reality*. Tarchetti argued, for instance, in his supposedly gloomy, melancholy, and pessimistic manner, that what we call happiness arises out of the reality of our economic and social relations in such a way as to be indelibly marked by our antagonism toward others:

> I do not know if others have ever put their minds to that singular
> rivalry over happiness that exists among men. It is a strange and
> stubborn rivalry, into which they often put a force of perseverance
> and self-respect that they rarely or never exert in the most noble
> affairs of life. Everyone wants to be happier than all the rest,
> and at the expense of all the rest; and one may say that the
> public and private works of every man, beneath their apparent
> disinterestedness, are directed only at this essential goal. But since
> no one can be happy, and everyone knows it, everything is then
> reduced to considering as a greater or lesser happiness the certainty
> of being less or more wretched than another, and satisfying oneself
> with that.[106]

If we would have any meaningful happiness, he intimates here, as he also suggested in *A Noble Madness*, then we must remake our entire vocabulary.

Tarchetti worked and reworked this kind of summary image of human affairs throughout his brief career, but it was in *Fosca* that he developed it most brilliantly. Set in 1863 and narrated by its protagonist some five years after the events of which it tells, *Fosca* is the story of an army officer, Giorgio, in his late twenties. On leave because of illness—heart trouble, significantly enough—he chances to meet and fall in love with a young woman, Clara, in Milan. Married and the mother of a son, she falls for him, too; and theirs becomes an ultraromantic, self-absorbed, self-pitying passion. Their idyll is interrupted when Giorgio is recalled to duty and assigned to a new post, where the colonel in charge kindly takes him under his wing, extending to him a standing invitation to have his meals at his house. There he meets the colonel's dependent female cousin, who is the same age as Clara but otherwise her opposite in virtually every respect, including her name. Instead of being "clara," bright or clear, she is "fosca," dark or gloomy. Skeletal in appearance and extremely ugly, she is also mortally ill.

The colonel describes his cousin as "sickness personified, hysteria made woman" (2: 271). Fosca's doctor, another regular at the colonel's dinners, asks Giorgio to show her attention, since her illness, though it still must doom her, seems to be alleviated through his influence. Giorgio then allows himself to be drawn ever closer to this dark and deathly woman, who becomes passionately attached to him almost immediately. After a few weeks, the relationship has become so tortuous to him that his own health is in danger, as he and the doctor both recognize, and so Giorgio tries to extricate himself from it by obtaining a leave that will enable him to go to see Clara in Milan. His plan is thwarted, however, when Fosca learns of it and stealthily follows him onto his train, where she appears so obviously ill that he feels obliged to take her back home. Unaware of this episode and oblivious, also, to the nightly visits that Fosca has demanded Giorgio make to her room, where he tries to soothe her, the colonel continues to regard him with patronizing affection. This situation changes completely, however, when Giorgio, with the aid of the doctor, again tries to escape it by obtaining a transfer to another post. When the news of his imminent departure is announced at dinner, Fosca bursts out with the truth of their relationship; and, to make a very bad night even worse, Giorgio subsequently reads a letter from Clara saying that she must sacrifice their love so that she can devote herself to her son and to her husband, who has lost his money. This inexcusable betrayal, as he sees it, leads Giorgio to a revelation about Fosca's obsessive attachment to him: "She alone has truly loved me" (2: 413). In what was to have been a crucial chapter in the novel, which Tarchetti was unable to complete because of his own sickness, Giorgio was supposed to have completely accepted Fosca's love at last, spending a night having sex with her before leaving to face the duel with the colonel that had become inevitable after Fosca's shocking outburst at dinner. In the duel the colonel is wounded but recovers; Giorgio later learns that Fosca died three months after these events; five years later he recounts the story, trying to sort out his experiences.

Sickness, then, in this final novel, becomes the summary image through which Tarchetti seeks to portray life. From the very beginning, with his history of sickness, Giorgio is a kind of misfit, a spostato in the lineage of the scapigliatura and bohemia. Though not explicitly labeled as such, he bears the telltale signs. Holding traditional village life in contempt, he is a young man of the modern metropolis. He does not really fit in even there, though, this youth who uses the phrase "the solitude of society" (2: 242) to describe his sense of things. He tells of being born with "extraordinary passions," adding, "I have never known how to hate or to love by halves; I have not been able to lower my feelings down to the level of those of other men. Nature had made me a rebel to common measures and common laws" (2: 242). In putting him at odds with society, his temperament leads him to feel naturally allied with all the losers, "all the unhappy ones" (2: 277), in society. Sickened morally as well as physically, he is always inclined to find "a good man in every unfortunate one, a wicked man in every prosperous one" (277). His condition recalls bohemians' paradigmatic association with illness, which traditionally serves to evoke their existence on the margins of society, their alienation from respectably "healthy" ways of life, the tragedy that is the likely consequence of their recklessness, the exceptional intensity and volatility of their passions, and their tendency to madness.

In *Paolina* Tarchetti had represented love as leaving one vulnerable to suffering and loss, in *A Noble Madness* as an occasion for violence, but ultimately, in both cases, while still granting at least some respect to the romantic image of love as a divinely redemptive feeling. In *Fosca*, however, it is something else again. "Rather than the analysis of a feeling," says Giorgio, "rather than the account of an amorous passion, I produce here, perhaps, the diagnosis of a sickness" (2: 243).

Superficially, of course, there is nothing new in such a characterization of love, which has ample precedents in literary and cultural tradition. In a note that he tosses to Clara after he first chances to see her—"I am unhappy, I am sick, I suffer" (2: 253)—Giorgio simply repeats clichés that have a history extending back hundreds and thousands of years. The same kinds of clichés, in fact, are strewn throughout Tarchetti's own love letters to Carlotta Ponti. As the novel continues, however, it becomes evident that it is going far beyond conventional uses of the trope of lovesickness. We see, first of all, a rather disturbing self-consciousness about this conception of love, as if Giorgio and Clara were aware of the tradition behind it and were driven more to satisfy that than each other. "We almost desired to suffer," he writes, "to pose our love as an obstacle to our happiness, to our future, in order to render it praiseworthy. We felt ourselves struggle with the frenzy to sacrifice something to one another" (2: 256). This kind of frenzied desire, which calls our attention to the sickness of the trope of lovesickness, is then grotesquely repeated in the passion that Fosca contracts for Giorgio. Her passion is such, the doctor tells Giorgio, that rejection from him would literally kill her. "It's the sickness of love, it's sensitivity elevated to the ultimate power," he says (2: 312). Self-consciousness about love as a highly artificial kind of performance is then evoked even more emphatically as Giorgio, at the doctor's urging, agrees to meet with Fosca, to spend time with her, and to promise to love her. Much like that worked up by the Boffins and John Rokesmith in order to draw love out of Bella Wilfer in Dickens's *Our Mutual Friend*, this deliberate and self-conscious performance seems weirdly motivated, spooky, and excessive, as if Giorgio's assent to the situation is not really voluntary. When he says, "The fear of killing her rendered me capable of any sacrifice" (2: 356), we may remember how he and Clara longed for the opportunity of a sacrifice adequate to the status they desired for their desire; and so we have some reason to suspect that, in agreeing to play the role of Fosca's lover, he has already been infected by the disease of love. Even if we do not know that Tarchetti admired the work of Hoffmann and Poe, we may guess that soon enough it is the role of the lover that will be playing him.

His relationship with Fosca serves to underline for us how much Giorgio's affair with Clara had already been premised upon the image of love as a sickness in which two people become parasitic upon one another. "As I had foreseen," he wrote of the earlier affair, "my health was revived . . . but it seemed that I had taken from her all that I had added to myself. She was not withering, but she was slowly declining" (2: 257). The gifts and sacrifices of love, it seems, never balance out; modern love is a sickness precisely because it establishes a creditor-debtor relationship that can be neither rationalized nor escaped. It is not an alternative to an economy in which anything and everything can be capitalized; it is this economy's triumph. "Even if you were to repudiate me, repulse me," Giorgio writes to Clara, "I feel that you could never disavow this debt" (2: 264)—and we see that his words are as threatening as they are caring.

Only hinted at in Clara's gentle decline, the literal import of this figure of speech about the economy of love becomes clear—and dark—in Giorgio's relationship with Fosca. This relationship threatens him with death in direct proportion to the extent to which it enlivens her. "Twenty days after the convalescence of Fosca," he records, "I no longer had either health, or courage, or a hope of surviving this calamity" (2: 359). You now have the germs of her illness in you, the doctor tells him, adding, "Think: it is necessary that you choose between her life and yours; either you or her, that is the dilemma" (370). Giorgio's inability to extricate himself from this zero-sum game then leads to his duel with the colonel, which marks the ultimate end of his love-sickness. Of the instant when his saber felled the colonel, he comments, "The sickness of Fosca was transfused into me: I had won in that moment the sad inheritance of my failure and of my love" (2: 425–26).

Structured by the economic and social order of the world that sustains it, love in *Fosca* is ultimately an impulse that pits everyone against every other one—the dilemma the doctor sums up as "either you or her." As a sickness, love reproduces the unhealthy relations of society as a whole, and so equality is no more to be found in love than it is in the world around it. What accrues to one must be subtracted from, or delegated to, another. The notion that sacrifice might be glorious turns out to be a prescription for self-deception, victimization, or martyrdom; the notion that one's indebtedness to another might be uplifting turns out to be a prescription for betrayal, exploitation, and resentment. It is as if Tarchetti were utterly perverting the sentimental conception of love in *Our Mutual Friend*, but doing so by paying utterly faithful attention to all the creepy manipulations of personal relations that are designed dramatically to rationalize the relation between money and love in that novel.

Tarchetti traces the parasitism of love on economic and social structures straight through the bodies of Clara and Fosca. The historical background to Giorgio's relationship with the former goes back at least to the twelfth century, to the *Art of Courtly Love*, in which Andreas Capellanus hypothesized that true love could exist only in an adulterous or extramarital liaison, since a husband's and wife's legal possession of each other in matrimony eliminated the quality of gratuitousness necessary to the definition of this feeling. Although Capellanus would eventually disavow it, this hypothesis proved to be immensely influential in conceptions of medieval and Renaissance romance, in the history of the novel, and in the mores of bohemia; and Tarchetti drew out this influence by fashioning Clara as a married woman with a child. Although the clarity of her freely loving relationship with Giorgio is already somewhat disturbed even before he is recalled from leave and sent to his new post, it is notable that a downturn in her family's economic fortunes is what puts a definite stop to it. Slyly, Tarchetti points out to his readers the historical truth of idealized adulterous love: that it was essentially aristocratic. Gratuitous only in relation to those who can afford to imagine themselves as being above economic concerns, it cannot survive the alteration in her family's economic condition, which therefore serves to emphasize that it was never in any meaningful sense free, independent, pure, or "true" in the first place.

When Clara and Giorgio took a clandestine trip to the countryside and enjoyed themselves there as if it were their own private park, as when they met in the lodgings he rented so they could get together in the city, the freedom of their love was an image that they could afford to purchase. Not to put too fine a point on it, their freedom depended on their imaginary elevation above others, such as the peasants for whom that countryside was a place of work, not of leisure; and we may remember Giorgio's disdain for village life and his proudly rivalrous words, "I have not been able to lower my feelings down to the level of those of other men." Just as people who are poor are given to saying things like "I can't afford to be sick," Clara, once her husband loses his money, can no longer afford to be in love. The same class distinctions that gave rise to the concept of love she once practiced have now put an end to it. In effect, as Giorgio obliquely recognizes in his furious response to her letter, she has never really loved him at all, and that is because it is never a question of who but rather of what loves anybody. What loved Giorgio, Tarchetti makes clear, was a cultural fantasy that can move a woman of privilege but that must have very different effects on those for whom words such as *truth* and *reality* must have a different meaning.

It is a confrontation with the logic of economic and social relations, then, that turns Clara to Fosca, the idyllic light of love to its Gothic obscurity, beauty to ugliness. It is not incidental, therefore, that Fosca is dependent on the colonel, her cousin, not only because she is his infirm female relative but also because she has been rendered impecunious as a result of a bad marriage to a supposed count who turned out to be an adventurer interested only in the money he could squeeze out of her parents. He succeeded in bleeding them dry and, incidentally, in hastening their deaths before he took his leave, leaving Fosca pregnant with a child that, to her despair, she was unable to carry to term. In every respect, then, Fosca appears as Clara's double, not as the opposite that readers have often taken her to be. Here as elsewhere, Tarchetti's writing confounds conventional oppositions. Whereas Clara finds herself in a marriage that does not fully satisfy her, Fosca finds herself married to a man who does not care for her at all. The reduced circumstances to which Clara must adapt as a result of "serious and sudden reversals of fortune" (2: 404) become Fosca's utter dependence on her cousin as a result of the deliberate machinations of a sleazy con man with whom she had believed herself in love. The son to whom Clara feels obligated to devote herself in her difficult situation becomes the child mourned by Fosca, who had joyfully anticipated the devotion she might give it. Clara's capacity for self-sacrifice, in her decision to abandon her love for Giorgio, becomes Fosca's drive to sacrifice for him not only her virtue and reputation but her very life. We are thus brought to see how love emerges from and is sustained, structured, and perverted in accordance with the logic of a specific matrix of economic and social conditions. Had Clara remained prosperous, she and Giorgio could have carried on, with the world being none the wiser, as before; or had she not been socially and economically dependent on her male guardian, just as Fosca is on her father, husband, and cousin in turn, their love might have turned out differently. To drive this point home, in one of her letters to Giorgio Fosca distinguishes the condition of women from that of men. "You do not know what it means for a woman not to be beautiful," she says. "For us beauty is everything. Living only to be loved, and unable to be so except on the condition of being attractive, the existence of an ugly woman becomes the most terrible, the most anguished of tortures" (2: 332). In contrast, she says, a man, even if deformed, can focus his existence on worldly ambitions. She notes, too, that matters are different for women of a lower class than hers, who are not bound by the same codes of etiquette and honor. They are freer to love and need not have the same fears of being taken in or hurt by an illicit passion.

Thus, through Fosca's words, as through the structure of this narrative, Tarchetti analyzes how love is established in and through the institutions of gender, class, courtship, marriage, and wealth. It is a vortex of displacements. We come to see that the individual in love is less a human being than an abstraction: a prescribed set of expectations, conventions, and rules that play themselves out in a historically, socially, and culturally determined human form. The role plays the person, and all there is to the person over and above the role is another abstraction: the ego that exists in a rivalry with all other egos. *Fosca* takes on the design of a Gothic allegory because of the designs that the modern nation has upon everyone, which all are ultimately focused on stripping away distinguishing personal characteristics—temperaments, characters, and desires as well as appearances, status, and money—so as to leave people as nothing but abstractly equivalent profit-seeking agents in a universe wholly defined by creditor-debtor relationships. "I am distrustful of love," writes Giorgio, "because the more profound it is, the more monstrously egoistic it is" (2: 325). Perhaps remembering the brash maxim of Sébastien-Roch-Nicolas Chamfort, "Love, as it exists in society, is nothing but the exchange of two fantasies and the contact of two epidermises," Giorgio concludes, with feline subtlety, "Love is the fusion and the conciliation of two egoisms that satisfy one another" (2: 325).[107] Like his narrative as a whole, this line mimics the conventional rhetoric of love—"fusion" and so on—so as to show it as

nothing but so much mimicry, as if carrying to its logical extreme the comment of another Frenchman, La Rochefoucauld, that "there are men who
would never have fallen in love if they had not heard love talked about."[108]

It follows that to take love otherwise, to take it seriously, as if it represented one's own nature, will, and feelings, must inevitably lead one to experience it as a sickness, an attack upon oneself by something outside oneself.
Thus does the egoistic competition at the root of it all make itself felt, even if it
is not understood. Accordingly, even as she denies that in "good and generous
natures" love is egoistic, Fosca's argument that it is actually "a need to make
others happy . . . a frenzy to sacrifice oneself for the happiness of others" (2:
335) merely serves to emphasize all the more the excruciating violence in which
love originates and to which it returns. As Tarchetti noted elsewhere, and as
this narrative so exquisitely dramatizes, such sacrifices are not easily forgiven.
In the guise of mutuality, they establish dependency; in the guise of generosity,
debt; in the guise of tender feeling, demands. They might as well be assaults—
and, in fact, they reveal themselves as such when they lead with seemingly
logical inevitability to the duel between the abstracted egos of Giorgio and the
colonel. As Tarchetti makes clear, Giorgio has no wish to fight, no personal
investment of any sort in this battle; and the colonel's participation in this
ritual peculiar to his era, class, and profession is equally senseless, given that
he had shown nothing but love for Giorgio and little else but contempt for his
cousin right up to the moment at which the revelation of their relationship
forced upon him the obligation to be mortally offended.

Fosca further elaborates this summary image of love as a sickness through
Giorgio's speculations upon medical science, which, as he considers it, in a
theme continued from *A Noble Madness*, seems to be leading humanity to
judge its most intimate and personal passions as nothing but mindless dis-
turbances of matter. It is a doctor, after all, who brings Giorgio and Fosca
together in the first place, and in playing this intermediary role he treats love
as a physical condition subject to scientific analysis, diagnosis, and treatment.
Love is thus yanked out of the medieval spirituality of Capellanus and into the
modern world of nineteenth-century positivism, even as Clara is jerked out of
the poetic world of her romantic idylls and into the world of bourgeois realism, centered on the material realities of home, family, and morality, in which
she must henceforth exert herself. Given his own romantic temperament,
Giorgio must claim to abhor "materialistic theories" (2: 312), and yet he cannot
help but feel driven toward them by his experiences. "It is not true that love is
a question of sentiments," he writes, going on to say that "it is only a question

of nerves, of fluids, of animal harmonies" (2: 309). Viewed culturally, socially, and historically, love is an abstracted role; viewed scientifically, an impersonal physical phenomenon; viewed by any given individual through whom this role or this phenomenon manifests itself, a feeling of disequilibrium, an attack, a sickness, more or less dramatic, depending on one's circumstances.

"Who would not wish to grant love a more spiritual and more noble origin?" Giorgio asks. "But that is not possible," he concludes (2: 309). So he writes elsewhere, "I was born for love, and I have loved; had I been born for murder, I would have murdered" (2: 326). The terms of his comparison are significant: as we see in the murder to which it almost leads in this novel, as a result of the duel between Giorgio and the colonel, love does not represent a harmonious individuality, much less a harmonious fusion or reconciliation of individuals. It is rather a churning effect of the constituent antagonisms among the egos demanded by modern social life. It is the sickness that must define affective relationships that aspire to an imaginary mutuality in a society in which nature is defined by laws of supply and demand. It is self-loathing *à deux*; it is the confounding of the ideal and real in economic relations; it is the frenzied copulation of death-driven abstractions. Through the doubling of Clara's economic fall in Fosca's, which ultimately makes Giorgio feel compelled angrily to transfer his affections from the one to the other, we see the irreducible deprivation, antagonism, and masochism of modern love.[109] Through these figures we see capital writhing with desire.

It was with a kind of terrible poetic justice, then, that Tarchetti's final illness prevented him from writing the chapter of *Fosca* in which he was to have described Giorgio and the colonel's cousin finally engaged in lovemaking, despite the doctor's earlier warning to Giorgio that such an act would surely kill her. Dying and in desperate need of money, Tarchetti had managed to sell *Fosca* to Leone Fortis, the editor of *Il pungolo*, by neglecting to mention that the manuscript he was delivering had a missing chapter. Publishing the novel in serial installments, Fortis did not realize how he had been hoodwinked until it was almost time for chapter 48, the missing one, to appear. Tarchetti was unable to provide it, and so his friend Farina, himself a novelist, hastily composed an episode, based on what he understood of Tarchetti's intentions, to fill the gap. Telling of Giorgio's grotesque night in Fosca's embrace, Farina's pages do adequately fill out the narrative, but one cannot help but wonder what Tarchetti would have produced if he had been able to finish his work. According to Farina, the chapter was actually Tarchetti's "sole pretext for writing *Fosca*" and was to have taken up a full quarter of the book.[110] As it stands, this maimed work instead must physically embody, as well as represent, Tarchetti's vision of the economic pressures of modernity that eventuate in the production of sick subjects loving themselves to death.

In *Fosca*, the sentimentality in Murger's bohemian scenes, which are borne aloft by gusts of youthful enthusiasm despite the weight of irony that hangs upon their narration, becomes an utter nightmare. Love becomes an unqualified disaster, a kind of perverse dependence. A sticky mess of self-delusion, betrayal, and exploitation, it not only ends but also begins in loss: in a vortex of displacements in which one cannot hope to find an original ground of nature, truth, or reality. In effect, Tarchetti took the socially and culturally situated bohemia of Murger's work—the bohemian *scene*—and represented it as a metaphysical *condition* arising from economic and political inequity. Murger's bohemia arose from an artistic spirit manifested in particular characters, Tarchetti's from the spirit of the modern nation as manifested in the dissolution of character in general. (*Fosca*, we may recall, is set in 1863, just after the unification of Italy under Victor Emmanuel II.) In this novel, as in Tarchetti's other writings, the writhing of unhuman competition at the heart of things takes various forms—conflicts between the sexes, the bafflement of desire over its own unaccountability, the implication of death in life, historical pessimism, social decadence, psychological despair, misanthropy—that no carnival could hope even momentarily to redress. The protagonist of this sentimental journey has no home to which he can return.

The defining homelessness of bohemia was a sign of its dissatisfaction with the origins of the modern nation. In Italy as in France, bohemia was a symptom of modernity attempting to be a respite, escape, or cure. As Murger had taken care to note, it was not headed in only one direction: it was a preface to the Académie française, as well as to the hospital or the morgue. As a symptom, then, it bore reference to a socioeconomic alteration in the conditions of art and to the parlousness of those conditions for individuals engaged in art and all that appertains to it. As respite, bohemia might be a way to ecstasy, transcendence, or the insights of genius; or it might be little more than the fun of going slumming, of taking a gang of grisettes to a dance, or of wasting mummy's and daddy's money until such time as they tightened the purse strings and one finally had to slip into a respectable career, leaving art behind. As an escape, it might be an exaltation of *l'art pour l'art* and an idealization of the artist's life, or it might be merely a playing at these things and, perhaps, a similar playing at politics. And as for bohemia serving as a cure for modernity—well, here is where matters become more complicated still.

Despite those who claimed for bohemia the lineage of nineteenth-century rebellions and revolutions, it was obviously not a cure for modernity in the sense of putting an end to it or radically transforming it. A colony without a homeland, multiplying across borders and potentially spreading everywhere, bohemia did not become anything like a nation in its own right. It crossed national borders, but there was never such a thing as a Bohemian International. This fact, however, which some might take as spelling out bohemia's failure, might instead be a sign of its value. For what bohemia did become, if only occasionally, incompletely, and inconsistently, was a dramatic exception to the drive toward the disciplinary organization of power that Michel Foucault, in *Discipline and Punish* (1975), has identified with the modern nation. Like art, bohemia could not progress; and in a century defining itself in terms of a teleological development from a hypostatized state of tradition to an idealized goal of modernity, this was its greatest value. It could not be held accountable in the language of productivity; it either could not or would not work, in the terms demanded by the modern world; but its idleness did labor to keep the health of the world in question.

"They reproach the scapigliatura for its disorder," wrote Cameroni. "The accusation is logical, as long as one calls *order* the silence imposed through asphyxiation."[111] Even more pithily, another scapigliato said of bohemia, "The lack of discipline unites it."[112] Insofar as bohemia may have been a cure for modernity, then, what made it such was its heritage of resistance to the disciplinary ordering of its motivations and measuring of its achievements. In this regard it defied the progress of the modern nation tacitly or passively but also, at times, deliberately and self-consciously, as in Tarchetti's melancholy criticism of how the logic of economics is with us even in our happiness, even—or especially—in our beds. From this viewpoint, charity may not be sufficient to our needs, but we certainly need all the charity we can get.

To illustrate further the sense of charity that Tarchetti urged upon his readers when he wrote about desperate sex, melancholy, and the poverty of nations, one might think of the defiant evocation of "Our Dead" that Giarelli published in *La farfalla* at the same time when writers such as Torelli Viollier were eager to consign bohemia to the dustbin of history:

The cemetery in which our dead sleep has no boundaries. It extends
itself, intrusively, through the whole world. Wherever someone
falls for an idea, for a protest, for a madness—if you will—there
is the sod over which we grieve, there the sod on which we base,

sadly and reverently, the spirit of cosmopolitan humanity. . . . And
you bohemians of Paris . . . you communards . . . you socialists,
deported by the czar . . . and thou, great army of the proletariat,
thou, cannon fodder, thou, blessed rabble—that extends so far
across the earth—today—without distinctions among names—
nationality—motives—and sacrifices—we commemorate you—
we—the perduti of *La farfalla*.[113]

If, when, and where bohemia was a cure for modernity, it became so
as a sense of community dispersed in space and time and encompassing all
sorts of people who would never meet except through the assertion of their
undisciplined allegiances. Dying, yet struggling to work, as Tarchetti did; feeling overwhelmed by one's own despairing destiny, yet trying to divine how
that destiny might find common cause in the existence of others; struggling
with conventional ideas and physical limitations and yet writing one's way
through them; gathering a sense of camaraderie from the literature of various nations and striving to reproduce that imaginary community even while
testing it all the way to the extremes of its own tendencies to corruption, violence, and death—if all this is not some kind of cure, a bohemian might say,
then we moderns are even more desperately sick than anyone could ever have
imagined.

CHAPTER 7

Sherlock Holmes Meets Dracula

Bram Stoker and Arthur Conan Doyle did not know each other well, although they shared an acquaintanceship, having encountered each other in the waning years of the nineteenth century. Both were of Irish descent, but Conan Doyle's immediate relatives had long been settled in England. As literary men they moved in some of the same social circles, and in 1907 Stoker would interview Conan Doyle for the *New York World*, but they were not especially close at this time or any other. Nonetheless, as if acting in concert, these two wrote tales that summed up the mythic life of the bohemian as a modern cultural figure. The first adventure of Sherlock Holmes, *A Study in Scarlet*, appeared in 1887, *Dracula* in 1897; and just as Dracula represents the fantasized origin of the bohemian, Holmes is this figure's fantastic end. In the convergence of the twain, we can see how the modern archetype of the bohemian had come to sustain the possibilities and impossibilities of nineteenth-century life.

It need hardly be said that Stoker's and Conan Doyle's protagonists never literally met, but this is not only because they happen to be fictional. The tales in which they live have incompatible premises, which represent two strains of Gothic tradition. With Dracula, we have an exploitation of otherworldly terrors in the tradition of Horace Walpole and Matthew Lewis, whereas Holmes updates the heritage of Ann Radcliffe, whose works dramatize eerie mysteries that are then all submitted to a rational explanation as her narratives draw to a close. No matter how accidental it may appear, however, the meeting of Holmes and Dracula within the cultural world of the late nineteenth century provides us with a telling reevaluation of the struggles that were played out through the conception of the bohemian from the 1830s on to the final decades of that century and the beginning of the next. As the fate of modern civilization is put at risk in the careers of these characters, their meeting suggests that the definitively marginal figure of the bohemian is central to the history of modernity.

In this regard, it is notable that both are superhuman figures, Holmes in his astonishing ratiocination no less than Dracula in his death-defying diablerie. Yet civilization must take note, too, that both remain subject to mortality and to certain mortifying limits of nature. For all his extraordinary abilities, Dracula can live only if he maintains a highly specialized diet, can enter only where he is invited, and can exert his powers only in the darkness of night (211).[1] Similarly, although Holmes's gifts seem to put him beyond humanity, we see him reaching his own limits when he falls prey to a sense of ennui that sometimes threatens to disable him, as when he partakes of his own peculiar diet of cocaine. Without these weaknesses, these characters could not be identified with bohemia, that land both utopian and haunted by its inhabitants' mortality.

Dracula, of course, is the bohemian as atavism. He represents the prehistory of this figure, its existence before it took on its modern definition. As Count Dracula, an aristocrat, he recalls the long-established image of the bohemian as one who bears a sense of entitlement that an imperceptive world fails to honor. In the modernized version of the bohemian, this sense of entitlement occasionally took the form of actual claims to a social position lost through usurpation or disinheritance, but for the most part it was registered imagistically in the popular identification of bohemians with vagabond restlessness, contempt for bourgeois respectability, impatience with the established gatekeepers of literature and art, an exalted sense of self, and a devotion to parasitic idleness and self-indulgence. These terms of the modern bohemian's definition were already rehearsed in the stereotypical portrayal of bohemians in the older sense of the word, which referred to those who were called Gypsies and other marginal types: people who were treated as being responsible for their own stigmatization in the eyes of the dominant orders of society throughout Europe. Along with the other outcasts associated with them, Gypsies were looked upon as if they held themselves above the law and so deserved to be treated as inferiors by law-abiding folk. Supposed to have their own kings and queens, they seemed to live in a parodic version of an aristocracy, breeding as a distinct race, disdaining ordinary work, and maintaining their own code of honor among thieves while acting as if mendicancy and larceny were privileges they inherited in the same way that others inherited landed estates. They were seen as flouting any middle-class sense of decency with their licentious ways, flaunting a taste for extravagantly improvident display, and, in general, refusing to become dutiful subjects, much less citizens, of the modern nation.

Dracula, to be sure, is no ordinary bohemian idler. As Stoker's Jonathan Harker learns to his chagrin, however, when he is imprisoned in the count's castle and makes a vain attempt at bribing a Gypsy to smuggle out a letter, Dracula is the supreme leader of these bohemians and, as such, their atavistic type writ large. He is the premodern bohemian blown up to mythological proportions and given the stigmatized attributes of his kind in what Harker and his comrades must view as the most extreme form imaginable. In Dracula, for instance, the bohemian sense of entitlement becomes a claim to empire that potentially extends over all the world; in an inversion of the course of European imperialism, his efforts to enforce this claim begin in London, which at this time was often regarded as the most advanced metropolitan center of modern civilization.[2] Bohemian vagabondism is similarly transformed in Stoker's narrative, expanding to Dracula's travels not only through physical space but also through diverse natural phenomena. Professor von Helsing explains, "He can transform himself to wolf . . . he can be as bat. . . . He can come in mist. . . . He come on moonlight rays as elemental dust. . . . He can, when once he find his way, come out from anything or into anything" (211). The other qualities of the bohemian find a comparable expansion in the count. As Stoker indicates through the case of R. M. Renfield, who, imprisoned in Dr. John Seward's asylum, yearns for the count's arrival as his Master, the bohemian contempt for the philistine becomes Dracula's commanding air of superiority and claim to power over all of humanity, as in a parody of divinity. In this Master's realm, bohemian impatience with cultural authorities becomes disregard for Western culture *in toto*. Should Dracula achieve his ends, this culture will be replaced by a mode of governance that comes from the categorically alien East and, as if that were not bad enough, from that territory as reconstituted in a supra-alien form beyond the bounds of life. Transylvania lies beyond even the historical kingdom of Bohemia, and in this novel it is less a real place than "the centre of some sort of imaginative whirlpool" (10), as Harker writes early on, not yet realizing the profundity of his words.

In his version of the bohemian's exalted sense of self, too, Dracula goes beyond all bounds. He is so outrageously self-aggrandizing that anyone who does not simply bow to his mastery, as Renfield does, must struggle even to know how to refer to him—or to "It" (84)—or to "this Thing" (202). The bohemian condition of parasitism is literalized in his unquenchable thirst for human blood, while the sense of being forever young that moves the modern bohemian, as in Enrique Gómez Carrillo's description of a kiss "made of youth and infinity," becomes the condemnation to eternity conveyed by this vampire's bite.[3] The stereotypical bohemian nostalgia for the good old days of one's miserable youth—for "the dear old horrors," as George Gissing put it—is terrifically heightened in the horror story of *Dracula*, driving this trope of joyful misery about as far as it can go.[4] Rather than being confined to the nostalgic retrospective that youth presents to maturity, the ambivalence inspired by Dracula's capacity for rejuvenation is limitless, potentially confounding all perspectives on life. The horror of the undead youthfulness associated with Dracula may justly remind us of Thomas Mann's *Death in Venice* (1912), in which the bohemianism Gustav von Aschenbach has repressed in his life and art returns in the tragically perverse form of his desire for Tadzio, a beautiful young boy. In Stoker's novel, too, the desire to seduce children for purposes of rejuvenation will testify to a repressed bohemianism struggling to set itself free in the world.

Bohemians' fabled mendicancy and idleness, meanwhile, are represented in Dracula's determination always to take what he wants, rather than labor for it, and also in the reversal within his being of the usual human hours of wakefulness and rest. The bohemian, as the critic Friedrich Carl Peterssen put it, "takes day for night, and night for day"; and in *Dracula* this reversal magnifies the nocturnal dissipations popularly associated with the bohemian tribe into the growing threat of a literal and figurative power of darkness.[5] For Stoker's late nineteenth-century readership, this dark threat of licentiousness was manifested most spectacularly through Dracula's blood-sucking assaults on women, which made a travesty of the sanctified Victorian icon of the nurturing mother. "Your girls that you all love are mine already," Dracula boasts at one point to the band of heroic men allied in opposition to his desires, adding, "and through them you and others shall yet be mine—my creatures, to do my bidding and to be my jackals when I want to feed" (267).

Dracula's identification with the Gypsy race, as it was viewed in the nineteenth century as constituting the prehistory of modern bohemia, does not simply bring to life its traditional image. Undead, demonized, as if alchemically reduced to its metaphysical roots in a primordial inscription of otherness that is also, paradoxically, the creation of identity, this seemingly anachronistic image becomes supremely threatening in the here and now of modern times. It is this ominous inscription of otherness that we read in the proliferation of diverse forms of writing—diary entries, newspaper articles, a ship's log, stenographed reports, letters, invoices, and so on—that compose the text of Stoker's novel.

As a premodern bohemian, then, Dracula stands in stark contrast to Stoker's hero, Walt Whitman, who saw his Irish admirer as having treated him "like a best son."[6] Whereas Whitman so fully embraced otherness that he seemed to erase it, together with the very word *bohemian*, Dracula, the unreconstructed product of Bohemia, the Ur-Bohemian, threatens to reclaim, with a vengeance, the original meaning of this word. He is poised to destroy the modernity with which Whitman identified himself, together with the democracy he glorified and the healthy sexuality for which he proclaimed himself a spokesman. The secret threat Dracula and his minions pose to modernity appears as a nightmarish mockery of the enlightened group of "Invisibles" that Whitman's beloved George Sand described as the agency of modern republican bohemianism in her *Countess of Rudolstadt* (1844), thereby revising the similar plot device in Johann Wolfgang von Goethe's *Wilhelm Meister's Apprenticeship* (1796).[7] In fact, Dracula might well be seen as a bogeyman cobbled together less from the folklore of vampires than from the rhetoric of those in the mid-nineteenth century who most fervently denounced the modernized version of the bohemian. Early on Félix Pyat had frantically inveighed against young men of this bohemian kind as constituting "a rage, a furor, a contagious, epidemic, endemic malady, a scourge worse than cholera, a veritable plague from the Orient": his words could serve as a précis of Stoker's narrative, which also luxuriates in the imagery of disease.[8] The conspiracy theory of Edmond and Jules de Goncourt, which saw in Henry Murger's *bohème* a form of socialism firing "red-hot shot at the preeminent literary man," explodes into Dracula's violent attack on all the representative cultural figures—doctor, lawyer, entrepeneur, professor, lord, innocent wife—in Stoker's narrative.[9] *Épater le bourgeois* becomes, in this novel, the literal draining of his veins and transforming of his being to the semblance of the other he had scorned. Equally à propos to Stoker's creation is the fervid invective of Jules Barbey d'Aurevilly, in which the portrait of bohemian America as a welcoming inn "that tomorrow will be a cut-throat" perfectly encapsulates the beginning of *Dracula*, in which Harker's welcome into the count's castle quickly turns into an ominous imprisonment that sets the stage for all the bloodletting that is to follow.[10]

The parallels do not end there. The soulless matter that is the count's nature, native element, and command—the "brute world," as Van Helsing terms it (223)—recalls Enlightenment materialism, with its associated revolutionary

Figure 14. Photograph of Bram Stoker (n.d.) (Stringer/Hulton Archive/Getty Images).

energies, and thus the more important target Barbey and the Goncourts were aiming to strike through their criticism of bohemians. Karl Marx's radically divergent critique of bohemians as a counterrevolutionary *lumpenproletariat*— "the whole indefinite, disintegrated mass, thrown hither and thither, which the French term *la bohème*"—is also encompassed in the design of *Dracula*, which raises the specter of an entirely new species taking over the earth, a species not only déclassé, like bohemians, but unclassifiable in the conventional terms of humanity.[11] In Harker's desperate nonce definition, this is "a new and ever-widening circle of semi-demons to batten on the helpless" (53–54). The antihero of Stoker's novel has in mind a revolution that would mock Marx's dream of historical progress while simultaneously making the Reign of Terror in France at the end of the previous century look like child's play. The crime involved here goes beyond crime, into the realm of the unnamable.

Under both the older and the newer meanings of *bohemia*, this imaginary land had always been associated with criminality. The association was direct, as in allusions to Gypsy thievery and in Marx's identification of bohemians with criminal types, and figurative as well, as in bohemians' general image as outlaws, either despised or romanticized, as the case might be.[12] In English literature, one may think of shady bohemian characters such as Sancho de Saumarez in Robert B. Brough's *Marston Lynch* (1860) or, more famously, Becky Sharpe in *Vanity Fair* (1848) as occupying what Theodor Mundt, writing in 1858, referred to as the "boundary-line of the criminal world" on which stand "the bohemians . . . of which the newest French literature is full."[13] This criminality, however, had generally been a partial, incidental, or metaphorical aspect of bohemian identity. Even in Marx's furious and rather idiosyncratic denunciation, it is not criminality as such but what he takes to be political opportunism, bolstered by disgusting moral laxity and social irresponsibility, that distinguishes the bohemian. It is owing to this broader characterization that he could identify Louis Bonaparte, oxymoronically, as a "princely lumpen bohemian," consigning him to the unsavory crowd of vagabonds, rogues, mountebanks, beggars, literati, and other types with which he filled out this category.[14]

With Dracula, the situation has changed. As all the other characterizations of the bohemian are magnified in him, so, too, is criminality, which becomes so great in his case as to escape all conventional definition. In Dracula the inscription of otherness is no longer allowed to be occasionally, figuratively, or even habitually criminal. Instead, the count is just such an arch-criminal as Honoré-Antoine Frégier, in his study *Of the Dangerous Classes of the Population in the Large Cities, and Of the Means to Improve Them* (1840), perceived in the nineteenth-century vagabond: a figure whose very being is a crime, prior to and independent of any particular acts that he might commit.

In *Dracula* bohemian otherness becomes a violation of the very concept of law. Stoker's novel allegorically returns us to the origin of the bohemian by bringing the distinction between legality and criminality into crisis. The confounding of this distinction is manifested in virtually every topic of concern broached by this narrative. We see it in the confusions that arise between Protestant and Catholic religious practices; between monogamy and promiscuity (in the case of Lucy Westenra, whose several suitors lead her naively to express a wish that society might "let a girl marry three men, or as many as want her" [60]); between heterosexuality and the homosexuality evoked by the fervid Whitmanian camaraderie enjoyed by Harker, Seward, Van Helsing, their American friend Quincey P. Morris, and Arthur Holmwood, who assumes his late father's title of Lord Godalming in the course of the narrative; and between masculinity and femininity, with the stereotypical attributes of each sex being mixed up between them, as when Godalming breaks into hysterics (203) shortly before Van Helsing finds a "man's brain" in Mina Harker, née Murray (207).[15] This confusion also arises between purity and impurity, beauty and ugliness, past and present, pain and pleasure, and a host of related concepts. It only makes sense, then, that the band of men opposed to Dracula's criminality must themselves resort to criminal activities, ranging from housebreaking to what legal authorities would be obliged to call murder, in order to pursue their ends.

To law-abiding folk, an ordinary criminal will be threatening to a greater or lesser degree. An arch-criminal, however, is not only threatening but also attractive. It is the strange attraction associated with Dracula that most profoundly violates the very conception of law in Stoker's novel. This violation is dramatically represented through the crucial turning points in the plot of the novel in which ambivalence, the feeling that scandalizes all conventional logic and rationality, rises up out of the text, monstrously and undeniably, as if to recall Charles Baudelaire's definition of bohemianism as a "cult of multiplied sensation."[16] Dracula bears a weird and yet commanding presence from the very beginning, but during Harker's stay in the count's castle, where he has come to perform the legal business of his employer, the ambivalence his host evokes is really brought home to him when he is visited by three women. These women have "something about them" that makes him feel "longing" and, at the same time, "deadly fear" (42). This unnamable "something" is the crime of crime itself: a category for which this novel finds no secure foundation either in or beyond the world of humanity.

In his self-contradictory desires—his exalted abjection, his yearning fear, and so on—Harker, the man of law, finds that criminal violations of the civilized conception of law are actually intrinsic to that conception. Helplessly, languorously, he undergoes a kind of philosophy lesson, and this Sadean philosophy in the bedroom teaches him what similar incidents throughout the novel are designed to teach its readers: that law and crime are coeval, one and the other simultaneously created through a metaphysical inscription of otherness that is also the inscription of identity. The scene of Harker's seduction is written so as to tantalize readers in the same way as the women tease the lawyer, teaching us that there is no such thing as an inaugural moment in the establishment of law, which could then be threatened by crime arriving from beyond its borders only after the fact. Instead, marking at once the possibility of law and its undoing, ambivalence appears as the unsurpassable condition of one's being: the unhuman impetus of human civilization. In the specific case of Harker, the inference we are offered is that he is implicated, body and soul, in Dracula's bohemian horrors, as are all the admiring members of the human race whom he serves to represent, including the readers of his story.

It is no wonder, then, that Harker's "delightful anticipation" of the women's approach should also be "an agony"; that he should find one of the seductive three, as she bends over him, "both thrilling and repulsive"; or that the erotic perversity of the whole experience should be underlined by his stereotypically feminine posture, supine and passive, as the vamps boldly seek to have their way with him (42). The experience is sensual, overpowering, and unquestionable. Having in his own person become a "something" completely immersed in its strangeness to itself, Harker trembles with the luscious senselessness of it all until Dracula bursts in to scatter the women, frustrate the hypocrite reader, and force desire again to recognize the lesson of its perversity, which binds law to crime. "This man belongs to me!" he yells (43). As the fantasized origin of the bohemian, there in the wilderness of the Transylvanian mountains, he leaps in where Harker's conscience fails to, in a parody of the role that middle-class morality is supposed to play in such situations. Since Harker's rescue is such a mockery of deliverance from temptation, the ambivalence out of which this scene is built is reinstated even as the man of law comes to his senses, feels unqualified "horror" (44), and collapses into the state of unconsciousness that signals his reentry into the modern, conventional, decidedly unerotic understanding of law.

The strange attractions that prove compelling in the other sexual scenes of this novel, involving Lucy and Mina, are of a piece with what we see in this one, although each adds a distinctive something to the mix. For instance, after Dracula's kiss transforms Mina's best friend into a voluptuous, carnal, and passionate "nightmare of Lucy" (190), Lucy's fiancé, Arthur, volunteers to kill her. The opportunity is thus afforded us to envision her body shaking, quivering, and twisting "in wild contortions" as Arthur, "like a figure of Thor," leans over her to drive "deeper and deeper the mercy-bearing stake" that lays her to rest for good (192). In this sadomasochistic portrayal of "high duty" (192), middle-class law becomes all but indistinguishable from vicious vampiric desire. Placing a distinctive emphasis on the image of law as being established by men in and through the female body, Stoker reveals law's passion: the embracing otherness that both enables and undoes its institutionalization. All the men share in this profoundly ambivalent scene, with his comrades encouraging Arthur in his task and looking on as he performs it. The female body here appears vampiric insofar as it expresses sexual desire, in contrast to which logic, rationality, and natural order ritually assert themselves through violence that transforms the sexual body, as if by miracle or magic, into "sweetness and purity" (192).[17] In effect, Stoker presents us with an anthropology lesson about how the very ceremonies meant to demonstrate our transcendence of primitive unreason actually reveal the hold it maintains upon us.

With this sort of prompting, we may remember that bohemians, both traditional and modern, were associated with sexual license. Some commentators argued that this did not exceed in any way the discreet practices of those identified with respectable society, but it nonetheless proved a consistently fascinating abomination to persons supposed to be respectable. We may remember, too, that despite its notable female participants, nineteenth-century bohemia was always an overwhelmingly male affair, just as it is under Dracula's leadership in Stocker's novel. The case is no different whenever Van Helsing or the other opponents of Dracula are in command. The gang-rape scene of Lucy's deliverance, for instance, is prefigured in the narrative by a series of episodes in which all the men volunteer to transfuse their blood into her body in an attempt to save her. By representing women as figures that allow men to bind themselves together even while, because of Dracula, men also strive against one another over these women's bodies, Stoker gave the constitutive ambivalence in his text an emphasis at one and the same time homosocial, homoerotic, and patriarchal.[18] This emphasis finds its logically perverse culmination in the moment in the novel in which Mina, rendered "unclean" by

Dracula's embrace, finds herself identifying with him, weeping with pity for him, and bringing the men to join her in this feeling (269) as if they, too, must be helplessly drawn to him.

In this instance and elsewhere, vampirism plays the role in this novel that mesmerism plays in contemporary portrayals of bohemian life such as Fitz-James O'Brien's "The Bohemian" (1855), Léon Cladel's *The Ridiculous Martyrs* (1862), and George du Maurier's *Trilby* (1894). In fact, Stoker associates a form of mesmerism with Dracula, whose violation of Mina establishes a psychic connection between them that allows her male associates to track him down. As a quasi-scientific practice invented in the late eighteenth century and maintained, with extensive but varying degrees of social and intellectual acceptance, by way of diverse theories, practitioners, and modes of presentation, mesmerism in general was a phenomenon very different from vampirism, which existed only as a zoological curiosity and popular source of literary and visual imagery. In these narratives, though, as it confounds the senses, the fascination of mesmerism, like that of Stoker's vampirism, bodies forth the inability of law logically to account for its own existence. Through this compelling and yet senseless fascination, the power of law comes to appear virtually equivalent to the power of imagination. No longer confined to religion, aesthetics, or similar categories of cultural activity, imagination appears to be at the bottom of everything. The boundaries of all such categories, then, must themselves be thoroughly confused, as when Protestants in their pursuit of Dracula avail themselves of Catholic paraphernalia and ritual, of both modern technology and ancient folklore, and of theories of psychology, physics, and metaphysics that they make up as they go along. Bohemia, it would appear (but could we ever have had any doubts in this matter?), is a realm of the imagination. It is the domain in which law as regarded from any viewpoint—Marxist, reactionary, liberal, democratic, scientific, Catholic, Protestant, Western, Eastern, and so on—is imaginary.

This is not to say that nineteenth-century bohemia made law out to be unreal but rather to point out that it served to encourage a view of law as being of the nature of images, not of formal logic, natural order, providential design, or anything similar to such frameworks of understanding except as these, too, might be understood to be fundamentally imaginary. Among other things, bohemia was a "something" that encouraged the recognition of ambivalence, just as *Dracula* does. In modern bohemia, this is why nonsensical *blague* could serve as the most characteristic mode of communication, why outwitting lawful creditors could be treated as a game, and why living with a grisette could

be regarded as a "marriage of the thirteenth arrondissement," in a simultaneous imitation and rejection of the law.[19] The imaginary nature of law is even
asserted in the closest "something" we have to a founding moment of modern
bohemia, which is the act—anonymous, communal, impossible to assign to
a precise place and time—that gave this word its modernized meaning in the
1830s, transferring it from the Gypsies and other marginal types traditionally
designated *bohémiens* to the young urban gypsies—students, artists, journalists, and such—who henceforth would be recognized under this name. In
the imaginary act of vampirism we see both a revelation and a reversal of
the historical act that created this modern sense of *bohemia*: the act, that is,
of the metaphorical appropriation, idealization, and dismissal of the identity
of those formerly referred to by this term. As in a dark parody, the vampire's
bite of Stoker's novel displaces this process in favor of one defined by mastery, demonization, and incorporation. As a result of this displacement, the
representatives of modern civilization are sucked back into the crime of its
conception, whence they must strive violently to disavow, once and for all, all
that they have learned of this crime in the course of the narrative. Jonathan
Harker's "Note" at the end of the narrative, which tells us that there scarcely
remain any authenticated documents in the mass of materials out of which his
record is composed (326), so that we have no "proofs of so wild a story" (327),
completes this process of disavowal. The traditional figure of the bohemian
has been returned to the prehistoric realm whence he came, and so modernity
can return to its imaginary power.

This is where Sherlock Holmes comes in. To grasp the significance of his
arrival on the modern scene, however, it is necessary to know how bohemia
had become available for Stoker's fantasy of its premodern origins. Born in
the 1830s, by the last decades of the nineteenth century the modern bohemian
had wandered into a wide variety of lives. From the 1860s through the 1880s,
for instance, many people in the United States treated *bohemian* as simply another word for *reporter*.[20] Although he would write feelingly of the Murgerian
form of bohemia in a later story, "Married Abroad" (1860), this was the sense
of the word that George Alfred Townsend took for granted in his 1861 play *The
Bohemians; Or, Life in a Newspaper*. This equation of bohemian and reporter
appeared in works ranging from Philip Allison's *The Boy Bohemian; Or, The
Adventures of a Young Reporter* (1879)—a crude novella published in Frank
Tonsey's "Five Cent Wide Awake Library" series—to Milton Noble's comedic
drama *Interviews; Or, Bright Bohemia* (1881). In William Dean Howells's *A
Modern Instance* (1882) being a freelance journalist living in a rooming house

is sufficient to qualify one as a bohemian even though the man in question is respectably married, living with his wife, and, at the time, not given to any irregular habits. This identification with journalism also appeared in newspaper articles themselves, such as one in the *Brooklyn Daily Eagle* that portrayed as "A Typical Bohemian" a man who had promoted a politician through his writings and then sued his subject for refusing to fork over the dough he supposedly owed him for this puffery.[21] "People in every day life call all reporters Bohemians," one scribe noted in 1884.[22]

This conception of bohemians as journalists stands in contrast to the one that gained predominance in England near the end of the century, which viewed the bohemian as a figure most closely associated with the theatrical world, which, as it happens, was Stoker's home after he took a position as manager in 1878 for the famous actor Henry Irving, whom some have seen as a model for Dracula. This is the definition that appears, for instance, in an 1893 novel by Florence Warden, *Passage Through Bohemia* (1893): an amusingly outlandish farrago that sweeps its protagonist through the world of low-rent theatrical companies and vulgar entertainments, such as freak shows. Robert Blatchford's *A Bohemian Girl and McGinnis* (1889), Warden's later *Bohemian Girls* (1899), and James Clarence Harvey's *In Bohemia* (1905) use this same definition, to which that famed oracle, Mr. Punch, gave his imprimatur when he described the inhabitants of bohemia as "our artists, our men of letters, our musicians, and, above all, our actors."[23]

During the same decades when these definitions were taking hold, however, others quite different from them were also circulating. In Gissing's *New Grub Street* (1891), for instance, the word *bohemian* simply designates poor, struggling, would-be writers, with no special reference to either journalism or theater, and in his *Odd Women* (1893) bohemianism is given the even broader meaning of that which stands on the other side of "wealth and position."[24] The same New York newspaper that definitively identified bohemians with hack reporters in 1872 would later, in 1885, instance a Bowery songwriter as an archetype of this kind and, in an 1889 article entitled "Bohemians and Bohemians: One Set Counteracting the Movements of Another," would illustrate "three shadings" of bohemians by taking as exemplars the eminent Victorians Matthew Arnold, Thomas Carlyle, and John Ruskin.[25]

The definition was simply all over the place, sometimes even in the same work. For instance, in *The Bohemians of London* (1857), by the Irish journalist Edward M. Whitty, "Bohemia, as we suppose every one is aware, is a cant term for a section of London, the part inhabited by clever fellows with much reputation, and pretty women with very little, by the classes who are said to 'live on their wits'—journalists and politicians, artists and dancers."[26] Over the course of the novel, though, this snappy and already rather expansive definition has been stretched to include both low life and middle-class life, including that of rich industrialists, until the only people left out are aristocrats or "swells." One may note, too, that the same scribe who recorded the popular identification of bohemians with reporters also contradicted this definition, preferring one that identified an individual's involvement with arts and letters and concomitant disgust with mundane life.[27] Some would draw their distinctions more finely, as Vernon Lee did in distinguishing a "little clique of more mystical and Bohemian pre-Raphaelites" from the rest of their ilk on the basis of this crowd's more louche, lively, and cosmopolitan gatherings, while others would boldly strike through such distinctions entirely, as when one of Florence Brooks Emerson's characters announces that a bohemian in New York "may be anyone from a man of the world with an artistic bias, to the foreign beggar, trying to live by his brush and pen. The opulent publisher may cherish threadbare ideals by the side of the Bohemian Jew who lavishes his rich store of life on romance."[28]

Indeterminate and contested to begin with, by the turn of the century the word *bohemia* had become a vessel into which one could pour almost anything. In his story "A Bohemian" (1886) the Spanish writer Rafael Altamira identifies it with a devotion to literature that is pure and idealistic; in his novel *Kristiana-Bohème* (1885) the Norwegian writer Hans Jäger identifies it with a commonplace devotion to sexual satisfaction among young men torn between the innocent young girls for whom they long and the prostitutes who will sleep with them. Despite the fact that Eugenio Torelli Viollier, in 1878, had claimed that in Italy "the word *Bohème* no longer has any meaning except as an insult," in 1891 the German critic Hermann Bahr said that only in bohemia had he found "the seed of a national and modern future"; but then again, in that same year, Rubén Darío opined that in Mexico, Havana, Chile, and Buenos Aires any honorable man of letters would totally scorn this term, which was fit only for beggars and drunks.[29] In 1894 Bruno Wille gladly named "the literary bohemia" with which he had mixed in Germany as one source of his grandiose philosophy of emancipation, which also drew upon doctrines of Nietzschean individualism, religious mysticism, Tolstoyan pacifism, Buddhism, vegetarianism, socialism, and free love; in 1898 Frank Norris rebuked all of Wille's sort, sneering that "it is only the small men, the 'minor' people among the writers of books who indulge in eccentricities that are only immoralities under a different skin; who do not pay their debts; who borrow without idea of returning, who live loose, 'irregular,' wretched, vicious lives, and call it 'Bohemianism.'"[30] In a period when writers as varied as the esteemed Henry James, Franziska zu Reventlow (Munich's "Queen of Bohemia"), and Julia Ward Howe (author of "Battle Hymn of the Republic") were declaring that bohemia had become thoroughly genteel, an English review of a performance of Giacomo Puccini's *La Bohème* (1896) saw no change at all. "There is not much difference between Bohemianism in the thirties of this century and in the present day," this anonymous reviewer stated flatly, "nor is smug 'respectability' much improved."[31] This was a minority opinion, but it by no means stood alone. Moreover, whereas Otto von Leixner, in 1888, said that the bohemia of contemporary Berlin was testimony to "simple poverty" unrelieved by Murgerian poetry, Camille Mauclair argued in 1899 that "the lack of money" never had anything to do with bohemianism, which arose instead from "the lack of moral education."[32]

Even when writers shared many of the same premises, the portrayals of bohemia that emerged from their works could be wildly incompatible. For instance, Alejandro Sawa's *Declaration of a Loser* (1887) and Paul Heyse's *Adventure of a Bluestocking* (1897) both tell of young provincials with literary ambitions moving to the big city—Madrid and Munich, respectively. Thus far they follow the well established paradigm for narratives of bohemia, and both feature protagonists who are self-consciously rebellious and who end up in an ironic relation to the bohemian tradition they self-consciously seek to enter. In keeping with this tradition, these characters find romantic and sexual complications intertwined with the difficulties they face in trying to establish careers for themselves. Their stories are alike, too, in their concern to evoke the contemporary aesthetics of naturalism, à la Zola, as the latest thing in literary circles. In addition, Heyse's novel offers to its female protagonist, Toni Vetterlein, something very like what Sawa's protagonist and first-person narrator, Carlos Alvarado Rodríguez, presents to us: "a veritable moral trial that, while being subjective in form, in its overall synthesis is nothing other than the psychological trial of all the youth of his time" (80).[33] So much having been noted, however, one must add that these two works could hardly be more different from each other.

Sawa came of Andalusian and Greek ancestry. Before his life ended in an all-too-bohemian fashion, immiserated in poverty, blindness, and neglect, he had served as Darío's guide to Paris, having been introduced to him by Gómez Carrillo. "He was a writer of great talent and always lived in a dream," Darío would remember.[34] Regarded by his friends as being drawn from his own life, Sawa's *Declaration* presents itself as a response to specifically Spanish realities. Written with a doom-laden, febrile, quasi-allegorical intensity, it opens with a fierce denunciation of the Spanish nation, which had a "War of Independence against Napoleon . . . but no war of Independence against the monarchy and the Church; no war of Independence against the degradation of everyone, those up high and those down low; no war of purification against the repugnant leprosy that eats away the national body from the toes of the feet to the top of the head" (90). After a brief honeymoon with the city when he first arrives in Madrid, Carlos Alvarado suffers one punishing disillusionment after another. The opposition journal at which he was excited to obtain a position turns out to be corrupt; his affair with a married woman sours; the editors, publishers, and theaters to which he tries to sell his writings treat him like a beggar; he falls into desperate poverty, takes up with a prostitute named Carmen, becomes her pimp, abuses her when she cannot give him enough money, and finally makes a philosophical decision to commit suicide. Ambitious, self-consciously literary, and yet slapdash in its passionate construction, his tale expels from itself the clichés of nineteenth-century bohemianism. Carmen is no Mimi Pinson or Musette, he notes (166), referring to the adorable characters made famous by Alfred de Musset and Henry Murger, and "anyone lies who assures us that love in our modern societies is compatible with poverty" (152). As his title announces, Sawa translated the bohemian dreamer—precisely what he himself was supposed to be, as viewed by his friends in Madrid and Paris—into a hopelessly defeated figure.

Sawa's bohemia, in short, is as serious as a heart attack. Heyse's bemused, worldly-wise entertainment, *Adventure of a Bluestocking*, with its carefully contrived toy-like construction, is something else again. Although she is engaged to be married, his heroine, Toni, is determined to gain the experience in life that she feels she will need as a writer. To this end, she has left home to come to Munich, where she has arranged to stay with her aunt. Fritz Rempler, the head of a local group of bohemians, is pleased to take her interest in a literary career as a sign that she is prepared to have him seduce her. He promptly advises her to read *Madame Bovary*, to leave her aunt's house, and to come live with him, "like a younger artist in the atelier of a master" (48).[35] Despite her theoretical respect for all things bohemian, she finds that Rempler's icky appearance is better suited to smoky, gaslit rooms than to the clear light of day, and she is not sure whether a bride-to-be ought to be quite so free in her living arrangements as he advises. Musing over such questions, she visits two school friends now also living in Munich and finds that they exemplify two possible fates for her: to be cynically married to a rich old nobleman, on the one hand, or to a be a lower-middle-class mother contentedly reduced to caring for her babies, on the other. When Tino, a painter she has met, asks to do her portrait, she is still irresolute, but she feels duty bound to enter into the milieu of the studio that she had hitherto encountered only in novels about artists. Her experience with him is unremarkable enough until one day when she is shocked to find herself almost letting him kiss her. "Had this harmless little 'artist novel' with which she had occupied herself just for fun led to such a tragic dramatic end?" (111). Returning home, confused, to find that her fiancé, Max, has just arrived, she confesses what has happened and then fears that Max will challenge Tino to a duel. Instead, Max restores normalcy to her world by going to Tino's studio and insisting on buying the portrait even after Tino has offered it as a gift. Max thus puts their relation with Tino back on a purely economic basis while reaffirming his conventional relationship with Toni and laughing away the notion that the world of bohemia could disturb them in any way. Pleased and penitent, she decides to surrender her hopes for a career. "I still have a great, great deal to learn of what life is all about," she tells Max, "but for that I will go to your school" (128).

Considering that Heyse came from a prominent, prosperous, urbane family and was a highly educated and successful writer who would be awarded the Nobel Prize in Literature in 1910, it might seem that we could let the great stormy blast of authenticity in Sawa's writing blow Heyse's *Adventure* away. Surely his is a bourgeois view of bohemia, a cheap tourist relic, and dismissible as such. Such a conclusion, however, would be completely misguided. For one thing, it would ignore the subtleties in Heyse's antifeminist comedy, which make it considerably more interesting than antibohemian screeds such as Mauclair's article on Puccini. (The painter, for example, is portrayed as a serious youth who is sincerely attracted to Toni, and even the sleazy bohemian leader, Rempler, is made out to be passionately caught up in his own risible seriousness.) We would also have to overlook other relevant considerations, such as the fact that women are not treated with any more respect in Sawa's novel, or, for that matter, in bohemian discourse throughout the second half of the nineteenth century, than they are in Heyse's *Adventure*. (Reventlow, for instance, the most famous woman in Munich's bohemian scene at the turn of the century, was notably antifeminist in her own writings.)[36] The most important reason an invocation of authenticity would be misguided, though, is that it would require us to forget how the authority to define and describe bohemia had been in question from its very beginning, in the 1830s.

In 1878 George Saintsbury was complaining, with considerable justification, "Of all the words which, by dint of clumsy repetition and misuse, have become unwelcome to the ears of Englishmen, there are perhaps few that are more unwelcome than the words Bohemia and Bohemianism"; but this sort of complaint had always belonged to the discourse of bohemia.[37] Félix Pyat had lodged a similar objection in expressing his detestation for the bohemian students in the Latin Quarter in 1834, and Henry Murger began his preface to *Scenes of Bohemian Life* (1851) by grouching about supposed misuses of his key word.[38] The divergences between Sawa's and Heyse's narratives simply illustrate the fact that quarrels over the possession of this word, which were precisely what gave life to the modern conception of the bohemian, were still far from being resolved by the end of the century.

By that time the death of the bohemian, in France, Italy, the United States, England, and other countries, had been announced over and over again, from the time of Murger's initial success on to the aftermath of the Civil War in America and then in turn-of-the-century works such as Morley Roberts's *Immortal Youth* (1902), in the opening pages of which its protagonist exclaims, "Bohemia is quite extinct!"[39] As might be expected under these circumstances, the novel goes on to contradict him with the argument that "Bohemia is a mental state, and as such only a reality to those who are conscious of it"; but this argument was no more conclusive, historically speaking, than any of the others.[40] The aestheticist turn Roberts gave to the notion of bohemia was simultaneously being contradicted, for instance, by the democratic, socialist, modernist sense being ascribed to the term in Spain by the manifestos of Ernesto Bark, a Polish-Russian emigré.[41]

No universal conclusion could arise out of such a welter of definitions, but one general impression did emerge in discussions of the bohemian in France, England, Germany, Spain, and America during the latter decades of the nineteenth century. Matters may have been different in Cuba, Mexico, and South America, as Darío averred, but in Europe and the United States it had become commonplace to see a change in bohemia. Often reiterated, this was that a bohemian need not necessarily be a déclassé type at odds with respectable society. In reply to the public image of Édouard Manet as "a kind of bohemian," for instance, Émile Zola would write, "The life of an artist, in our correct and civilized times, is that of any peaceful bourgeois, painting pictures in his studio as others sell pepper from behind their counter."[42] So much for the way bohemians used to spit out "grocer!" as an insult directed at the philistines of their society. Pío Baroja wrote of the "vague aspiration toward the white glove" of the turn-of-the-century bohemia he knew in Madrid, in contrast to the tavern-centered bohemia of earlier years.[43] Outside observers such as Henry Bacon, in *A Parisian Year* (1882), came away with similar impressions, noting "the growth in respectability of the profession of art since those days when Thackeray wrote 'The Newcomes' and Bierstadt's transparent lantern hung out on Beacon Street, in Boston, notifying the passers of 'drawing taught here;' when artists were obliged to affect broad-brimmed hats and red-lined cloaks, and to cut their flowing locks would have been fatal. Now, [the artist] is often mistaken for a gentleman of leisure."[44] In London, too, the self-proclaimed bohemianism of the Savage Club was sufficiently respectable for Queen Victoria, Prince Albert, and other members of the royal family to be willing to attend its amateur performances at the Lyceum Theater of Richard Brinsley Sheridan's *School for Scandal* (1777).[45] As S. J. Adair Fitzgerald reported, far from being the "shady and shabby community" it had been fifty years earlier, the bohemia of 1890 might appear an altogether different place, "looked up to with that respect and veneration that is ever the due of those who strive to inculcate the principles of beauty in all matters artistic and aesthetic."[46] In a novel of the same year, *In Low Relief: A Bohemian Transcript*, Morley Roberts agreed. In opposition to the "religious odium to the old notions of Bohemian art-land which have not died out," he maintained that just as "artists may nowadays be gentlemen, so they are not all libertines"—and so the parents of the young ladies who pose for them, he was pleased to report, may breathe a sigh of relief.[47] "In a word," said Mr. Punch, "it is now respectable."[48]

The Savage Club's fashionable performance took place in 1860, and in the *New-York Saturday Press* this newly respectable character had been asserted since the 1850s. While some would still use *bohemian* as a term of abuse, on this or that occasion, on the whole this characterization had carried the day by the closing decades of the century. The fact that *Harper's Weekly* would title one of its regular columns "Bohemian Walks and Talks" (1857–58) is a good measure of just how quickly the bohemian metaphor could become innocuous in this era. For another such measure, we need only turn to W. C. Morrow's observation that by the end of the century bohemia had become a popular Parisian attraction, with the tourist "'doing' Bohemian Paris as he would the famous art galleries, or Notre-Dame, or the Madeleine, or the cafés on the boulevards."[49]

This, too, was hardly a new development. Mark Twain had had his eye out for grisettes, as a Parisian sight-to-see, in 1869, and the bohemian phenomenon in England and America also had functioned as a tourist attraction of sorts. The bohemian redoubt of Pfaff's restaurant on Broadway had drawn curiosity seekers in the late 1850s, for instance, and bohemia was still such a hot topic in 1876 that a newspaper editor, William H. Muldoon, could advertise a lecture about it at the Brooklyn Academy of Music. The promised entertainment—his talk on "that generally jolly, sometimes unhappy, though exceedingly useful creature, 'the Bohemian'"—"will be varied," said one notice, "with some most excellent vocal music by Mr. Clark Ackerman, the well known tenor, assisted by a double quartet of male voices, and Miss Ida Haddon will recite an original Centennial ode written by Mr. Kenward Philp."[50]

By the last decades of the nineteenth century, in other words, it had become possible for even such a respectable specimen of British manhood as Arthur Conan Doyle, that bluff, hearty, moralistic, rugby-loving defender of empire, home, and family, to view himself as a bohemian. True, he did come from a family in which his father, three of his uncles, and one of his grandfathers were artists, and his years as a student of medicine bring to mind the frequent identification of medical students with bohemians in 1830s and 1840s Paris. Conan Doyle certainly knew some of the literature on this subject, too; he had read Twain's comically disillusioned account of grisettes, and in 1883 he warmly recommended to his mother G. L. M. Strauss's recently published *Reminiscences of an Old Bohemian*.[51] In the case of this earnest and diligent young medical practitioner, though, who dutifully attended to his mother and worked hard to provide for his sisters, bohemianism clearly signified unconventionality only in the loosest possible sense.

In his autobiographical novel *The Stark-Munro Letters* (1895), for instance, an old military man who is friendly but rather rough in his manners and inclined to drink can be dubbed bohemian. So, too, can pleasant evenings at a married friend's apartment, solely on the grounds that it is scantily furnished and smells of cheese.[52] The definition is even more diluted in Conan Doyle's *Memories and Adventures* (1924), in which he declares, about a stay of some weeks with relatives when he was a young man, "I fear that I was too Bohemian for them and they too conventional for me."[53] It is clear from the context that nothing more scandalous than a bachelor's relaxed domestic manners is to be inferred here, and Conan Doyle's personal letters from the era in question bear out this portrayal.

In identifying himself as a bohemian, the young Conan Doyle clearly meant to suggest only the life of a young man at the outset of his career who has a limited income and who, therefore, lives rather more informally than is the norm among more settled members of the respectable middle classes. No reference is made to disdain for middle-class respectability, much less to bohemians' legendary tendencies toward idleness, improvidence, sexual license, and passion for the arts. When vagabondism comes into play in his correspondence, prompting Conan Doyle to assert that he has "a strong Bohemian element" in him, it is in the form of his most respectable service as a dedicated ship's surgeon aboard the *Hope*, a whaling ship bound for six months in the Arctic.[54] Like almost all educated Victorians of his era, Conan Doyle struggled over questions of religious belief, and he was capable of hijinks such as submitting a hoax letter to the *Lancet*, but that was about as much rebelliousness as he ever showed when he was a young man.[55] Conan Doyle was a bohemian pretty much in the way that every sister's brother is a bohemian.

By the time that the future author of *A Study in Scarlet* was boasting of being too bohemian for his relatives, then, the term had wandered so far in its meaning that it might signify only the most superficial unconventionality, of a sort that might be welcomed with a tolerant smile at the dinner table of even the prissiest Mrs. Grundy. In the literature of his day, this is what we see, for instance, in the mild comedy of the stories in *In and About Bohemia* (1892), by Charles James Wills. In his creation of Sherlock Holmes, however, Conan Doyle gave a more vigorous sense to the term. In contrast to the atavism that Stoker would make of the bohemian, identifying him with the powers of a past "which mere 'modernity' cannot kill" (41), Conan Doyle made his bohemian absolutely modern.

Professedly logical and scientific from the top of his hat to the toes of his boots, Holmes is liable to appear to Dr. John Watson as "positively inhuman." "You really are an automaton—a calculating machine," the good doctor comments (*The Sign of Four* [1890] 100).[56] Holmes is as monstrous in his own way as Stoker's vampire is in his, and in the detective's case, too, this monstrosity is especially marked in relation to women—the subject of the conversation that spurs his companion to call him a machine. Holmes's misogyny is frequently attested to by Watson, though it may be most exquisitely represented when he speaks disdainfully of "the usual feminine ululation" to be expected of a wife who finds herself in the vicinity of her murdered husband (*The Valley of Fear* [1915] 942). Holmes's attitude, however, differs from Dracula's. Whereas the count's way with women serves to emphasize his bohemian licentiousness and disregard for private property, as represented by affianced or married females,

Figure 15. Photograph of Arthur Conan Doyle (1896) (HIP/Art Resource, NY).

Holmes's misogyny exaggerates his character in a very different direction. He respects private property and shows little, if any, interest in sex.

In the case of Holmes, misogyny represents the bohemian opposition to married domesticity taken to its modern limit, at the opposite extreme from the gypsy vagabondage incarnate in Dracula. Holmes represents abstract mind, not marauding body, and intellectual ambition, not a thirst for the mystic power of blood. The definitively undomesticated condition of the modern bohemian in the first half of the nineteenth century, to whose adventure marriage spells an end, becomes in Holmes the scientist's resistance to female interference with his pursuits that we also see in contemporary characters such as Tertius Lydgate in George Eliot's *Middlemarch* (1871–72) and Swithin St. Cleeve in Thomas Hardy's *Two on a Tower* (1882). Holmes's misogyny, in other words, is not a personal matter with him, as everything, including his treatment of women, is with Dracula. Instead, Holmes's misogyny is entirely modern: strictly professional.

Given the legendary association of bohemians with grisettes in particular and romance in general, it might be difficult to see how such a denatured version of the species could still be said to belong to it. This, however, is precisely the point of Conan Doyle's invention of Sherlock Holmes: to show us the end of the bohemian. As Britain entered the final years of a century in which, it had become clear, virtually anyone could be dubbed a bohemian, with the consequence that this figure could go no further, Holmes represents this bohemian at the end of his tether: singular, irreplaceable, and bored almost to death. Only sporadically capable of experiencing any emotional attachment to the society to which he is absolutely necessary, Holmes lives out the heritage of the bohemian both before and after his adventure at the Reichenbach Falls, where he survives his own death, just as Dracula did his.

More than anything else, Holmes represents art to a philistine society, epitomized by Scotland Yard's detectives, which is unable to recognize its value and importance. On this score he is comparable to Mann's Tonio Kröger, that bourgeois who, having "gone astray in art," dresses like a gentleman and yet feels that his bohemian soul makes him "unhuman."[57] Holmes, however, is a much more daring conception. Whereas Mann ends "Tonio Kröger" with its protagonist seeking to bring art back toward the bliss of ordinary life, there is no way back, even in imagination, for Holmes. As Conan Doyle presents it, there is no way back, either, from the middle-class civilization whose bliss, as far as Holmes is concerned, is a combination of ignorance, hypocrisy, and stupidity. For Holmes, even art is pretty much just a game, and a wearying

Figure 16. Bernard Partridge, "Arthur Conan Doyle with Sherlock Holmes" (Art Resource, NY).

game at that, in which he at times finds it difficult to feign any interest. It is ironically beautiful, then, and just, that Conan Doyle came to feel this character's popularity to be a burden on him, sought to break the public's unrequited emotional attachment to Holmes by killing him, and only reluctantly brought him back to life for a further course of adventures, pressured by the public's appreciation of Holmes's unhuman necessity to society.

In the narratives of both Stoker and Conan Doyle, the bohemian becomes a superman, a pulp version of Nietzsche's *Übermensch*, in relation to whom society as a whole must reconceive itself. In contrast to Stoker's Dracula, the atavistic bohemian who threatens to destroy all of Western culture, Conan Doyle makes the modern version of the bohemian, the artistic soul who journeys toward respectability, culture's savior. Just as Dracula's fascinating power draws his opponents into an ambivalent engagement with his crimes, though, so does Holmes's draw his supporters into a similar complicity with the crimes he is dedicated to solving. In fact, though he is a modern artist whose procedures are scientific and whose dress is that of a gentleman, Holmes himself is not entirely certain that he might not prefer to be some kind of demon.

Prior to his marriage, Watson calls himself a bohemian, too; but he is a bohemian, as Conan Doyle himself was, only in the loosest possible understanding of the word. A medical professional and a military veteran, he lays claim to a "natural Bohemianism of disposition" ("Musgrave Ritual" [1893] 444) on the basis of his bachelorhood and his ability to adapt to informal and impromptu circumstances. Once married, he never speaks of himself in such terms again. The case of Sherlock Holmes is decidedly different.

Conan Doyle assigns Holmes two classical attributes of the bohemian, a violin and a pipe. We are also told, by Holmes himself, that he is often inclined to the definitive bohemian vice of idleness—indeed, that he is "the most incurably lazy devil that ever stood in shoe leather" (*A Study in Scarlet* 17). In case these clues should escape our attention, Conan Doyle introduces him as a man of artistic sensibilities. The Whistlerian title of *A Study in Scarlet*, which is meant to fit the crime scene in the narrative, is created by Holmes himself. "Why shouldn't we use a little art jargon," he comments, admiring this scene as "the finest study" he has ever viewed (28) even as he looks forward to going out to hear some Chopin played by a well-known violinist, Wilhelmina Norman-Neruda. Watson's bloodless, innocuous, hand-me-down bohemianism is evidenced by his reading: "I sat stolidly puffing at my pipe and skipping over the pages of Henri Murger's *Vie de Bohème*" (*A Study in Scarlet* 32). As we see in his aesthetic appreciation of crime, however, which recalls Thomas De Quincey's wonderful essay "On Murder Considered as One of the Fine Arts" (1827, rev. 1839 and 1854), bohemianism is much more vital to Holmes's identity. Everyone can see it; Athelney Jones, a Scotland Yard detective, tells him in *The Sign of Four* (1890), "We all know that you are a connoisseur of crime" (172).

Holmes is so much of an aesthete, in fact, that he offers us a book review of Watson's narrative about their initial adventure, *A Study in Scarlet*. "Honestly," he tells Watson, "I cannot congratulate you upon it. Detection is, or ought to be, an exact science and should be treated in the same cold and unemotional manner. You have attempted to tinge it with romanticism" (*The Sign of Four* 92). Watson replies, "But the romance was there . . . I could not tamper with the facts" (92). The obvious irony here is that Holmes, in identifying himself with science, still shows himself to be more of an artist than does Watson, the writer. Like the most doltish of creative writing students, Watson defends his work on the basis of its supposed fidelity to life, whereas Holmes demands, first and foremost, the hard, gemlike flame of a sophisticated sense of style. From this exchange alone we might almost predict that Watson will soon be happily married, abandoning his pretence of bohemianism in favor of "the home-centred interests which rise up around the man who first finds himself master of his own establishment," leaving Holmes, "who loathed every form of society with his whole Bohemian soul . . . buried among his old books, and alternating from week to week between cocaine and ambition" ("A Scandal in Bohemia" [1891] 177).

Conan Doyle did not always labor to emphasize the aesthetic sensibilities of Holmes as much as he did in *A Study in Scarlet*. Overall, though, the character established in that first narrative is maintained in the subsequent novels and stories. Sometimes it is maintained by artist "jargon," as Holmes would term it, as in "The Adventure of the Red Circle" (1911), in which Holmes answers Watson's query about his pursuit of a case that holds no financial interest for him by saying, "It is art for art's sake, Watson" (1066). Holmes's habit of dropping literary quotes and allusions into his conversation also serves this purpose; in *The Sign of Four*, he quotes Jean Paul, Johann Wolfgang von Goethe (twice), and Stendhal. We also have those moments in which the aesthetic nature of his detective science is explicitly discussed, as when Holmes says, in *The Valley of Fear*, "Some touch of the artist wells up within me, and calls insistently for a well-staged performance" (951). These features of the Sherlockian corpus all help to reinforce his image as an inveterate bohemian, even when Watson manages sometimes to persuade him "to forego his

Bohemian habits" long enough to visit him and his wife ("Adventure of the Engineer's Thumb" [1892] 311).

It is because he is such an artist that Holmes, the respectable bohemian gentleman, is also a demon. The recurrent problem that Conan Doyle's narratives organize for us actually has very little to do with the solving of crimes on the basis of clues; all that business of telltale cigarette ash, tire marks, scratches, callouses, telling gestures, and whatnot is ridiculous as forensic instruction and, if taken literally, tedious as the basis of a plot. (In this regard, one can understand why Conan Doyle soon tired of the Holmes narratives and resented how much more popular they were than his other works of fiction, such as his historical novels.) In this business, as Holmes tells us, it is style that is all important. Holmes's supposedly scientific deductions in these narratives play the same stylistic role as the signature references within them to supposedly famous events for which there is no extratextual referent, such as "the singular tragedy of the Atkinson brothers at Trincomalee" ("A Scandal in Bohemia" 177). Like the pipe, the violin, and the other traits of our protagonist, they simply tell us that we are in a Sherlock Holmes story, which is following the formula of the others; and it is this reiteration of sameness that yields the pleasure in reading about this evidence, not the supposed surprise of the discoveries to which they lead, which, being so formulaic, will never really be a surprise at all. It is not his pseudo-science that makes Sherlock Holmes such a generative figure, culturally speaking. Rather, it is the question that Conan Doyle organized in and through all the reiterated features of his signature style: what will the end of the bohemian signify?

Crucial to Holmes's identity as a bohemian is his dandyish resolve not to enjoy himself, which, in its most extreme form, becomes his "inhuman," as Watson terms it, devotion to cold-blooded scientific reasoning. This is a characteristic that Conan Doyle borrowed from the image of the modern bohemian, now evolved into the figure of the aesthete, as one who could not rest satisfied with the pleasures of ordinary life and so must seek out new sensations, whether these be in the world of art inimical to middle-class values or in the dissipations associated with the lives of artists, including indulgence in drugs. For Baudelaire and others, such as Fitz Hugh Ludlow, the American bohemian who wrote *The Hasheesh Eater* (1857), De Quincey had helped to set a standard of sorts through his account of his indulgence in opium. Getting into this spirit of things, the gypsy figure of Will Ladislaw in George Eliot's *Middlemarch* (1871–72) dutifully tries the effects of both wine and opium on his system; and Strauss, the "Old Bohemian" whose book impressed Conan

Doyle, boasts of having experimented not only with hashish, opium, and large quantities of wine, but also with laughing gas, ether, and chloroform.[58] In *The Sign of Four*, Holmes explains his own drug use by saying, "I abhor the dull routine of existence. I crave for mental exaltation. That is why I have chosen my own particular profession, or rather created it, for I am the only one in the world" (92). Sounding like a dyspeptic Oscar Wilde, an aesthete too world-weary even for wit, he later elaborates on his statement for Watson's benefit: "I cannot live without brainwork. What else is there to live for? Stand at the window here. Was ever such a dreary, dismal, unprofitable world? See how the yellow fog swirls down the street and drifts across the dun-coloured houses. What could be more hopelessly prosaic and material? What is the use of having powers, Doctor, when one has no field upon which to exert them? Crime is commonplace, existence is commonplace, and no qualities save those which are commonplace have any function upon earth" (96). Having closed a case in another narrative, "The Red-Headed League" (1891), he shrugs off Watson's praise and refers him to a motto from a letter Gustave Flaubert wrote to George Sand: "*L'homme c'est rien—l'oeuvre c'est tout*" (212).

As Conan Doyle reported, it is an odd coincidence of literary history that the fame of Sherlock Holmes had its origins in a social occasion that also inspired Wilde to write one of his most famous works.[59] In 1889 J. Marshall Stoddart, the managing editor of *Lippincott's Monthly*, had both Wilde and Conan Doyle to dinner in London, with the result that both agreed to write books for the magazine, which turned out to be *The Picture of Dorian Gray* (1890/1891) and *The Sign of Four*. After the disappointing reception of *A Study in Scarlet*, it was this second work that really began the sensational success of Conan Doyle's creation; and, though it is a coincidence, its genesis at the same time, place, and table as Wilde's tour de force of aestheticism could not have been more appropriate if the Fates had deliberately conspired to arrange the matter. For Holmes is in certain respects Dorian Gray's twin. He, too, lives for certain multiplied sensations, and his vitality, too, is dependent on an artwork that represents corruption formally displaced from himself. In his case, of course, this art is the work of crime.

"A true Bohemian has a natural love of licence," said James Glass Bertram, "and an intense hatred of law and order."[60] The formula that launched Sherlock Holmes into the realm of popular mythology made him just such a bohemian, but in the paradoxical position of fighting what he loves and upholding what he hates. Like Stoker's Dracula, in other words, he is designed to represent and inspire ambivalence, as even so dull a blade as Watson is compelled to recognize when he says, "I could not but think what a terrible criminal he would have made had he turned his energy and sagacity against the law instead of exerting them in its defence" (*The Sign of Four* 119). As Holmes openly admits and Watson at least half recognizes, crime plays exactly the same role for the detective as cocaine does. Crime is his drug, not his duty or crusade. He acts for the good of home, family, and empire only because he obtains personal gratification in doing so, just as he does when shooting up. It is no wonder that Watson's nervous observation is reiterated by Inspector Gregson ("It is a mercy that you are on the side of the force, and not against it, Mr. Holmes" ["The Greek Interpreter" (1893) 573]) and by Holmes himself: "You know, Watson, I don't mind confessing to you that I have always had an idea that I would have made a highly efficient criminal" ("The Adventure of Charles Augustus Milverton" [1904] 673). As everyone who has a close look at him can see, the behavior of Holmes is, in the most rigorous sense of the term, perverse. By upholding law and order, he is able to indulge his pleasure in crime.

Strictly speaking, Holmes has so arranged his life that it is only himself that he need please. The fact that he solves crimes that upstanding citizens, the police, or the government want solved is but an incidental byproduct, a pragmatic rationalization, of his commitment to achieving the kind of intellectual stimulation that he needs to stave off ennui. Like Dracula, he feeds off the body of respectable society.

Watson should not really be reassured, then, when Holmes says, of a letter from a noble client, "I assure you, Watson, without affectation, that the status of my client is a matter of less moment to me than the interest of his case" ("The Adventure of the Noble Bachelor" [1892] 328). At first glance, Holmes may seem to be asserting, with a modest disclaimer of any special virtue on his part, that he is not what his contemporaries would call a tufthunter. An elementary deduction, though, will tell us that Holmes certainly does have no reason to plume himself on his attitude, but not because he thereby shows himself to be free of snobbery. What he shows, rather, is the perverse pleasure he takes from the prospect of a suitably interesting crime, for the victim of which he could not care less.

When Holmes says, in "The Final Problem" (1893), "Of late I have been tempted to look into the problems furnished by nature rather than those more superficial ones for which our artificial state of society is responsible" (552), we see again the general contempt for society that is on display through all his adventures, together with his only motive for having anything at all to do with it: his addiction to "problems." These failing him or, over time, finally proving too "superficial" to excite him, he has no reason to be concerned with human-kind. Therefore, although he serves as a useful plot device, the arch-criminal Moriarty is a totally uninteresting character in the Sherlockian universe, for everyone can see that he simply mirrors Holmes himself—or, to put it more precisely, mirrors Holmes's perversity. (Mycroft, Sherlock's smarter brother, is not even an interesting plot device, since he conveys nothing of the bohemian outlawry that makes Holmes's intelligence interesting in the first place.) It makes perfect sense that a description of Moriarty in "The Final Problem" as one who "pervades London" (543) from a secret position in which he "sits mo-tionless, like a spider in the centre of its web" (544), should be recycled from a story published earlier in the same year, "The Adventure of the Cardboard Box" (1893), in which it describes Holmes himself: "He loved to lie in the very centre of five millions of people, with his filaments stretching out and run-ning through them, responsive to every little rumour or suspicion of unsolved crime" (1044). It makes sense, too, then, that in some of Conan Doyle's narra-tives, such as "The Adventure of the Abbey Grange" (1904), Holmes shows no compunction about making extralegal judgments, deliberately foiling the of-ficial course of justice, when he considers himself better qualified in the matter than the police or courts might be. He is not only, as he boasts, "the last court of appeal" for persons who cannot find solutions to their cases elsewhere ("The Five Orange Pips" [1891] 246); when he so chooses, he is detective, prosecutor, defense, judge, and jury. In this regard, Watson's remark about "the egotism which [he] had more than once observed to be a strong factor in [his] friend's singular character" ("The Adventure of the Copper Beeches" [1892] 362) is, to put it mildly, rather mild. When Holmes knows he is right, he knows he is right, and not in the grievous manner of Anthony Trollope's obsessed protago-nist in *He Knew He Was Right* (1869). The narratives bear him out, supporting his extralegal judgments and, in addition, his illegal behavior. "You don't mind breaking the law?" he asks Watson, breezily, in "A Scandal in Bohemia," and Watson immediately replies, "Not in the least" (187).

The stroke of brilliance in Conan Doyle's conception of the Sherlockian universe was his decision to make an antisocial, misogynistic, drug-addicted, perverted bohemian the only person able to know society. No one else can enter into, communicate with, and comprehend all parts of society as can he. Unpredictable and irreplicable, he marks the end of the individual's adequacy in social representation. In this regard Conan Doyle anticipated Mann's judg-ment, in *Buddenbrooks* (1901), that the bohemian represents the grotesque decline, the decadence, of the bourgeois. Conan Doyle's most famous character illustrates society's total lack of confidence in itself.

Most literally, we see Holmes as the only subject who knows in the signature situation, recurrent through all his adventures, in which he is privy to a truth that he withholds from others, for a greater or lesser period of time, even though that truth is necessary to complete society's image of itself as an essentially orderly and ultimately just world. In *A Study in Scarlet*, for instance, in which London appears as a counterpart to the bohemian whirlpool of imagination that is Stoker's Transylvania—"London, that great cesspool into which all the loungers and idlers of the Empire are irresistibly drained" (4)—Holmes deduces the identity of a murderer but for a time refuses to divulge it to Inspectors Lestrade and Gregson, or even to Watson. He can trust no one but himself with this knowledge: "As long as this man has no idea that anyone can have a clue there is some chance of securing him; but if he had the slightest suspicion, he would change his name, and vanish in an instant among the four million inhabitants of this great city" (45). More generally, Holmes's position of knowledge is conveyed by his familiarity with all levels of society and his ability to move freely in and out of them. His uncanny skill in disguising himself as all sorts of characters, male and female, young and old, poor and prosperous, is another means by which Conan Doyle specifies his role as the only figure in and through whom society as a whole can be comprehended. Meanwhile, his tribe of Baker Street Irregulars, the "street Arabs" upon whom he calls to aid him in his work, are the modern urban equivalent to the Gypsies that serve as Dracula's minions in the hinterlands of the East. They exemplify Holmes's ability to communicate with everyone, high or low, no matter how disparate their individual worlds may be from the one of genteel bohemianism that he nominally inhabits. He suffers these children to come unto him, and, like all the other types with whom we see him, from prizefighters to peers, they acknowledge his superior position of understanding.

In this respect, as previously noted, Holmes recalls the proto-Sherlockian figure of Rodolphe, in Eugène Sue's much-imitated *Mysteries of Paris* (1842–43), who also disguises himself so he can delve into the underside of society, solve crimes, and right wrongs, generally accompanied by his own version of Watson, the Englishman Walter Murph. Unlike the Providence that Rodolphe explicitly represents, though, Holmes does not have divinity to back him up. The plotting of Sue's novel still followed an eighteenth-century pattern; with Holmes, we dwell within the intellectual universe of late Victorian England. In this respect, Holmes occupies the bohemian role that Alexandre Privat d'Anglemont played for the Paris of the 1830s and 1840s, as a legendary figure who supposedly knows and is known by everyone and who, therefore, effectively holds society together. Unlike Privat, though, who was famous for carrying his unselfish devotion to others to the point of recklessness, Holmes, like Stoker's vamp-entranced Harker, is always after a certain "something." He serves society only because he gets something out of it. Through the conception of this latter-day bohemian, then, Conan Doyle made society dependent on a social parasite, a perverse parasite at that. It is rather as if Queen Victoria had invited Dracula across the threshold of Buckingham Palace so that he might assume the place Albert had vacated (may he rest in peace!) as her trusted adviser.

By Conan Doyle's time, the crisis of faith had become something of a cliché, almost a mandatory *rite de passage* for anyone with pretentions to intellectual seriousness, as Thomas Hardy indicated by the way Sue Bridehead mocks Jude Fawley's earnest stumblings after religious conviction: "You are in the Tractarian stage just now, are you not? . . . Let me see—when was I there?—In the year eighteen hundred and—."[61] With Holmes, however, Conan Doyle arguably came up with a more disillusioned view of the operations behind the scenes of life than we get even in Hardy's mythology of a blindly acting First Mover in relation to which human reason, desires, and ambitions are farcical. Conan Doyle made society, in all its workings as in its desire for self-comprehension, dependent on one who is not simply unconcerned, like Hardy's nature, but who is forced to make himself seem to love what he loathes. While recalling the expansive bohemianism of Whitman as, with his knack for disguise, he encloses multitudes, Holmes simultaneously embodies the utter estrangement of Dracula from humanity.

It is conventional to compare Holmes to other detectives, such as Eugène-François Vidocq or Edgar Allan Poe's Arsène Dupin, but the more apt comparison in this respect is again to Wilde's Dorian Gray or, for example, to his bohemian contemporary George Moore. Like Privat, Dorian Gray, and Holmes, the young man that Moore described himself to have been is distinguished by his pleasure in moving through and being able to communicate with all levels of society. Like Holmes, too, he presents himself as one who knows: "And you, my dear, my exquisite reader, . . . admit that if you ever thought you would like to know me that it is because I know a good deal that you probably don't."[62] He is dedicated to an aesthetic sense of life and fully recognizes that he needs interesting crimes to keep him interested in this life: "Injustice we worship; all that lifts us out of the miseries of life is the sublime fruit of injustice. Every immortal deed was an act of fearful injustice; the world of grandeur, of triumph, of courage, of lofty aspiration, was built up on injustice . . . Oh, for excess, for crime!"[63] In short, he is, as he says, "perverse": "almost everything perverse interests, fascinates me."[64]

Marking the end of the line for bohemianism, Holmes also marks the end of any confidence in the very existence of the social order against which the figure of the bohemian had been historically articulated. It is notable, for instance, that in *The Sign of Four* the criminal Jonathan Small shows a greater sense of justice than does Major Sholto, the ostensibly respectable figure of the British authority that has imprisoned Small. Having joined in a conspiracy with three Indians to steal a fabulous treasure, Small needs the major's help to retrieve it; and, when he offers to cut him in on their deal, Sholto's first suggestions is that they cut out the others. "What have three black fellows to do with our agreement?" he asks (168). Small, however, stands firm; and he is equally loyal to the native of the Andaman Islands, Tonga, who is viewed by Watson as a primitive horror. Even though Conan Doyle elsewhere is capable of being conventionally racist, not to mention a forthright imperialist, in this novel "the Four" are clearly portrayed as honorably holding to a social order, criminal though it may be, in a bohemian style of honor among thieves that puts to shame those on whose behalf Holmes works. The rhetoric, redolent of racism and primitivism, that Watson elsewhere applies to the world of criminals—"I knew not what wild beast we were about to hunt down in the dark jungle of criminal London" ("The Adventure of the Empty House" [1903] 566)—would apply better, in this novel, to Sholto and his ilk.

Other Sherlockian narratives, such as "The Boscombe Valley Mystery" (1891), "The *Gloria Scott*" (1893), and "The Crooked Man" (1893), also turn upon plots in which respectability proves to be a mask for a history of betrayal, as in *The Sign of Four*. The point here, though, is not that Conan Doyle constructs a fictional universe in which the criminal underworld is always or even usually more just than respectable society, for that he assuredly does not. (Holmes does not pretend to be at all sympathetic to Small or Tonga.) What Conan Doyle does is rather more unsettling: he makes his hero fundamentally uninterested in the question of justice altogether. He will certainly show earnestness or sympathy on various occasions, and he never uses his powers "upon the wrong side," as he says ("The Final Problem" [1893] 552), but it is always a matter of taste that determines his involvement in any particular case. Like art as described in Wilde's preface to *The Picture of Dorian Gray*, Holmes's crime solving has nothing to do with justice.

Dracula gives us a fantasy of the origin of the bohemian in which this figure battens on the health of society; the Sherlock Holmes narratives give us a fantasy of the end of the bohemian in which this figure battens on social corruption. If we consider these works together, we see the bohemian begin in gladness—exuberant, megalomaniacal, woman-devouring gladness—and end in the despondency and madness evidenced in Holmes's ennui, egotistical isolation, and misogyny. Once cast out from a social order that he mocks, in the end the bohemian takes his place within that order, upholds it, and all the more clearly shows it to be meretricious. No longer a figure of the unknown, the bohemian now serves the cynical function of making society seem knowable. Emerging from a prehistory of demonic irrationality, overflowing imagination has become the emptiness of law, and a carnivalesque alternative to society has become the figure of a self-contained individual faithlessly serving a world he disdains, which, it is clear, must expect to be hopeless without him. Spiritually speaking, it is already lifeless, though undead. Thanks to the extraordinary interventions of Holmes, it just doesn't know it yet. In short, what Privat called the "impossible land" of the bohemian has become the impossible life of the modern world.[65]

In the character of Sherlock Holmes, having been transformed from social outcast to a figure absolutely central to social order, the career of the bohemian thus comes to an end. Murger's template for bohemian experience would continue to be reproduced, in narratives such as Enrique Gómez Carrillo's *Sentimental Bohemia* (1899) and August Strindberg's *Swedish Bohemia* (1908) as well as in daily life, as in the cultural center that was developing in New York's Greenwich Village while Conan Doyle was still alive.[66] The word *bohemian* would live on and might continue to be inspirational, but its possibilities had been mapped and its exhaustion marked. By the end of the nineteenth century, bohemia had been conceptualized as the experience of a generation, of a class fraction, or of an isolated individual; as a geographically and historically bounded phenomenon and as one that is universal and ever recurrent; as a social formation, a cultural style, a stage of life, and a psychological disposition or temperament; as a sanctuary from hypocrisy and a cloud-cuckooland of phonies; as an affair of artists (who might be geniuses or poseurs, joyful or suicidal, innocents or con men) or as a community of journalists, professionals, riffraff, or members of high society; as a territory populated by ambitious bourgeois; as a nest of political radicals, reactionaries, utopians, progressives, or conservatives; as a man's world or a woman's; as a world white, black, native, foreign, patriotic, and subversive; as a world distinctively French, American, English, German, Spanish, Norwegian, or cosmopolitan; as a homoerotic paradise, a haven for heterosexual freedom, or a hotbed of sexual exploitation; as a scene of romance, of realism, of experimentation, of idleness; as a destination for the young and the superannuated, for layabouts and careerists, for whores and ladies and angels. It is not possible to comprehend all at once the diverse permutations of nineteenth-century bohemia; but even if it were, Dracula and Sherlock Holmes would still stand out. As a figure defiantly marginal to society, challenging its pieties, no future bohemian could go further than Dracula already had gone; and as a figure asserting its centrality to society, no future bohemian could be greater than Sherlock Holmes. In Dracula's seeming desire to cover the entire earth with his race of vampires, Stoker created a powerful picture of the ambivalence with which the dream of bohemian community had been received throughout the nineteenth century; in the melancholy self-possession of Sherlock Holmes, Conan Doyle forecast the perverse end of that dream of community in the instrumental rationality that would turn out to be the modern world's preferred nightmare.

Conclusion

In all its migrations among nations, in all the tumultuous life of its diverse local scenes, in all the transformations wrought within it as the decades went on—including its translation into other terms, such as *scapigliato* and *Schlawiner*—the vagabond word *bohemian* made itself at home in the nineteenth century. Famed for living on the margins of society, or even completely outside it, what Fitz-James O'Brien called "that modern mystery, the bohemian," in the end turned out to be inseparable from the social life of this time.[1]

In the nineteenth century bohemia was much more than one would gather from the received idea of it that has been passed down to us by Giacomo Puccini's *La Bohème* and all its offshoots in popular culture, such as the television ads for paintings in "Starving Artist Art Sales" that may be purchased either in modest dimensions or in "sofa size." Bohemia was a literary invention, a makeshift community, a rallying cry, a dream, a delusion; a time of carnivalesque license and a space of intense social commitment; a seedbed of revolution and a cheap tourist attraction; a site of vibrant experimentation, calculated ambition, reactionary accommodation, and fatal recklessness; a spontaneous invention, a hoary myth, a cliché; a movement of friends and strangers, a moving spirit of desire—bohemia was all this and more. While Queen Victoria reigned in England, while revolutions convulsed the Continent and a civil war the United States, this label that a handful of Parisians had slapped onto themselves in the 1830s and 1840s became an occasion for general amusement, contempt, inspiration, idealization, historical reconstruction, and polemical reformulation. "The winds that blow from Bohemia" were indeed, as Théophile Gautier said, "capricious."[2] The ranks of those known as bohemians did include impoverished artists, but they also included journalists, businessmen, socialists, mesmerists, vegetarians, aristocrats, drug addicts, pacifists, suffragists, proletarians, advocates of free love, criminals, entertainers, and, according to contemporary testimonies, public figures ranging from Adam and Eve to Abraham Lincoln and Vladimir Ilyich Lenin.

Although the crucible of bohemia refined images of the artist that still pervade popular culture, in the nineteenth century bohemia was never identified exclusively with the artist's life. One reason bohemia came to be such an exceptionally flexible term is that from its beginnings it signified an informal and improvisatory sense of community.[3] In contrast to contemporary artistic brotherhoods such as the Nazarenes, the Pre-Raphaelites, and Henry Murger's Water Drinkers, bohemia had never designated a restricted set of persons. It differed also from other organizations with which it was often associated, such as those of the St. Simonians and the Fourierists and other sorts of socialists, and even from loosely defined cultural movements such as the table-rapping "Modern Spiritualism" that arose at the same time his *Scenes of Bohemian Life* (1851) was bringing Murger international fame. Unlike these social and cultural formations, bohemia did not really have an established ground from which it might venture out to seek converts and extend its dominion. Paris was proclaimed its homeland, but many persons who gave voice to this idea also insisted that it could not be and never had been contained solely by that city.

In George Sand's novels of the 1830s and 1840s, as in the preface to Murger's widely translated and immensely influential *Scenes*, bohemia was conceived to be an international affair; and so it proved to be throughout the second half of the century. The "singular spectacle" that Ernesto Quesada described, of a group of young men in Buenos Aires in the 1880s who passionately identified with the bohemian scene that had existed decades earlier in Paris, was in fact not singular at all.[4] The career of bohemia carried it to many such outposts, where it colonized new locales and, in doing so, underwent all sorts of fantastic transformations. As François Truffaut recognized in the international bohemian fellowship proclaimed in the title of *Jules and Jim* (1962), geographical freedoms defined bohemia as much as did those that were cultural, social, political, and economic.

A territory of the imagination lacking any central body, structure, or genealogy, bohemia did not readily lend itself to any kind of institutional discipline. It could be evangelical only through the lure of its wandering example, not through any sort of formal enrollment. It was this organizational marginality that enabled it to become central to nineteenth-century social and cultural history. Bohemia's weakness as an organized community was its strength as an inspiring metaphor.

In Hans Wachenhusen's popularized portrayal of bohemians in 1857, they appeared as urban gypsies who were as completely "harmless" as they were "careless," and many others were happy to reproduce this image throughout this century and on into the next. We might think, for instance, of how playing around with bohemian tropes leads to harmless farce in René Clair's film *Le million* (1931) or of how, in *Double Wedding* (1937), William Powell's bohemian is portrayed as a swell guy despite his unconventional living situation in a trailer parked next to a cheap tavern that serves as his second home.[5]

Yet matters were never quite that simple. In fact, as "the class of individuals whose existence is a problem," bohemians often appeared to be throwing all of life into question.[6] Accordingly, writing in 1904, Julius Bab portrayed these "defiantly genial outsiders" as "the *centrifugal element of humanity*," from the study of which he proposed to develop the new scholarly discipline of "Asociology."[7] Hermann Eek, the protagonist of Hans Jäger's *Kristiana-Bohème* (1885), might have looked forward to the advent of this new science when he bemoaned his life in late nineteenth-century Norway, complaining, "I was and remain socially impossible."[8] Bab's proposal, however, spoke to people in general, not just to those seemingly excluded from the general company. He saw the bohemian as a form of life whose recognition might demand that the concept of society be fundamentally reconceived. "For what is 'la bohème' at bottom," he wrote, "other than a peaceful experiment in *practical anarchism*, i.e., in the development of an ungoverned zone of life outside the nationally organized society?!"[9] Throughout the nineteenth century, as critical observers indicted it as a refuge for lazy do-nothings, social misfits, crackpot thinkers, and all sorts of irresponsible seducers of youth, bohemia was widely regarded as a troubling affair. As Bab saw, though, one had to consider also that the bohemian's problem might well be everyone's. Bohemian life was not simply a problem, then; as Erich Mühsam said, it was "a damned serious problem."[10]

Most obviously, it was modern capitalist society that the bohemian seemed to stand outside, question, or threaten. The figure for whom the marketplace does not work, or who refuses to work for it, or whose so-called work—whose art—is for all practical purposes an anarchistic assault on the notions of utility, productivity, morality, and value governing the political economy of this era, the bohemian often rose up as a reproach to the middle classes and the philistinism for which they stood. Social Darwinist critics of these "intellectual proletarians," as they were sometimes called at the time, condemned this image of bohemians; and many others, whether any kind of Darwinist or not, agreed with them. Charles Dickens, for instance, although yielding to no one in his criticism of the philistine middle classes, portrayed Harold Skimpole in *Bleak House* (1853) as one whose bohemian charm was merely an instrument of his utterly irresponsible and conscienceless self-regard. Others, meanwhile, saw things differently. The socialist aesthete Oscar Wilde was delighted to cultivate this image of the bohemian as a standing reproach to the bourgeoisie, and other thinkers also took this image as a sign pointing to the need for fundamental political change. The more a bohemian is an "enthusiast or idealist," lamented Fritz Kunert in the early 1890s, "the faster the teeth of society's gears will tear him to pieces." Such a state of affairs then calls for "a social reorganization that will allow the struggle for individual existence to vanish" in favor of a system of production "that guarantees an adequate livelihood to every member of society."[11]

Like the stereotype of the happy-go-lucky bohemian goof-off, this image of the bohemian as a reproach to the middle classes is all too well known—is, in fact, paradigmatic of another received idea of the bohemian that grotesquely oversimplifies this figure's history. For the moment, however, we need only observe its demonstrable power, which portrays the bohemian as an outsider to society in general and to the capitalist marketplace in particular. Bohemia in this conception is not the nineteenth century as we are generally supposed to know it but rather another nineteenth century entirely, an underground or unofficial society of this era, which gathers into itself all the eccentricities of the time: tonsorial, sartorial, political, dietary, sexual, criminal, and so on. Here we may think of the response—"Whaddayagot?"—that Marlon Brando's hipster outlaw in *The Wild One* (1953) gives to the girl who asks him, "Hey, Johnny, what are you rebelling against?" Long before Brando ever shrugged on a leather jacket, though, at the end of the 1800s, some bohemians were already styling themselves as "modern pagans" who had thrown off two thousand years of Christendom together with the totality of modern commercial and industrial society. Perhaps most famously represented among the "Kosmikers," the Cosmic ones, of the poet Stefan George's circle in turn-of-the-century Germany, this identification also appeared in Jäger's *Kristiana-Bohème* and was suggested as well in works as diverse as Algernon Charles Swinburne's *Poems and Ballads* (1866), Friedrich Nietzsche's philosophy, Thomas Hardy's *Jude the Obscure* (1895), Isadora Duncan's "dance of the future," Henry James's *The Ambassadors* (1903), and Vaslav Nijinsky's choreography of *L'après-midi d'un faune* (1912).

This emphasis on a state of bohemian being that was paradoxical, at once modern and pagan, and hence marvelously exceptional, would continue to be reproduced in the years that followed. If only in a tragically attenuated form, bohemian antecedents are recognizable, for instance, in Virginia Woolf's focus in *Mrs. Dalloway* (1925) on the aesthetics of the exceptional "moment" and on the transient ecstasy, and pathos, of Clarissa Dalloway's youthful romance with Sally Seton, in which socialist theories, carefree manners, and unconventional sexuality combined to bring this future wife of a member of Parliament such pleasure as she would never know again.

Short of a revolution, though, bohemia would seem to be condemned to just such transience. From the time of Murger to the present day, bohemia's stereotypical career, from youth to maturity, was set. Philibert Audebrand quoted the Swiss poet Etienne Eggis as explaining that he was going to Paris to "do bohemia" ("faire ma Bohême"), as other young men might speak of their plans to do rhetoric or philosophy.[12] In the words of the bumbling protagonist, Elias, in a humorous novel of Madrid's bohemia by Enrique Perez Escrich, *The Blue Dress Coat* (1864), "At twenty years of age, he dreams and sees everything through rose-colored glasses . . . —a happy age, when he has no fears, neither of men, nor of hunger, nor of cold, nor of the rude blows of misfortune. A lucky interval of life in which he always sings because dangers do not recognize him; in which the mind is effervescence, the soul enthusiasm, and the heart fire. At the age of thirty-three things assume a different complexion."[13]

As the stereotype is generally understood, the temporary nature of this interval is due to its essential unreality. "It seems," wrote Oscar A. H. Schmitz in his journal in 1897, in the midst of his own bohemian years, "that we all at some time *pour épater le bourgeois* strike a pose for a while, but gradually we become ever more ordinary."[14] Since it cannot last, the conclusion is drawn that this moment must have been an illusion from the beginning. It is then seen as a period of time that bespeaks immaturity, a temperament or state of being that can be so delightful only because it is out of touch with the true nature, and dangers, of things. Appropriately, then, Escrich's novel is structured as a cautionary tale that its protagonist narrates to a young enthusiast who, by its end, has been persuaded to turn aside from the bohemian way of life he had been planning to enter.

Transience, however, does not necessarily imply unreality or falseness. "One is sometimes right at the age of twenty-five," Gautier observed, "and wrong at sixty. There is no need to disavow one's youth."[15] Woolf drew a similar lesson by portraying the fleeting time shared by Clarissa Dalloway and Sally Seton as having culminated in a kiss like that described by the Guatemalan writer Enrique Gómez Carrillo in his *Sentimental Bohemia* (1899): a kiss "made of youth and infinity."[16] As Woolf describes it, this had been and has remained, in the face of all the changes and dangers that her passage through the many years since then would bring her, the most exquisite moment of Mrs. Dalloway's life.

That such a situation could be suggests a terrible discontent in the organization of life, and this suggestion also pervaded the discourse on bohemia in the nineteenth century. If some might judge its ecstasies to be essentially unreal, others might regard them as diagnostic of a dreadful unreality in the societies that sought thus to dismiss them. If bohemia could not survive the realities of social life, then so much the worse for that life. If a fearless happiness was to be available only to men and women in the brief time of their youth, and if this lesson was to be steadily reinforced by the sight of each new generation of bohemians fulfilling the popular stereotype by bending their necks to the yoke as they passed the age of thirty, then one might even decide to trust no one over thirty; one might even hope to die before getting old. In other words, one might conclude that this circumstance did not amount to a disconfirmation of bohemian desire but rather to an urgently compelling motive for seeking to persist in one's bohemianism against all reason.

Some, such as Alexandre Privat d'Anglemont, did just that, while others, such as Kunert, sought to address this situation by interpreting the temporality of the bohemian experience as a corrigible issue of politics, not a generalizable lesson in the nature of truth, reality, psychology, or sociology. As if drawing from both their examples, Mühsam in turn-of-the-century Munich and Berlin committed himself to a progressive conception of bohemia that embraced all of society's so-called outsiders: "Criminal, vagrant, prostitute, and artist—that is the bohême that knows the pathways of a new culture." Bohemia, he argued, "is rooted deep in the essence of humanity." Far from being asocial, as Bab had claimed, in most cases the bohemian displays "a blunt refusal of existing conditions in all their characteristic forms" together with "a very social yearning toward an ideal culture of humanity."[17] With slightly different emphases but to a similar effect, bohemia had been given a progressive face by the *scapigliatura* in Italy during the 1860s and 1870s; by John Boyle O'Reilly, the Irish patriot who ended up in Boston after being transported to Australia, in the last decades of the century; and by Ernesto Bark, a Russian-Polish refugee who agitated for a reformist, anticlerical, feminist socialism in late nineteenth- and early twentieth-century Spain.

Where this kind of political confidence was unimaginable or in abeyance, however, bohemia might appear as the symptom of a distress for which there was no evident cure. It then became heir to *le mal du siècle*, the vaguely defined sense of disillusionment and unhappiness associated with the Romanticism of the first decades of the nineteenth century and taken to its extreme in the cult of decadence that arose near its end, as among writers such as Joris-Karl Huysmans. Alphonse Lemonnier, for instance, remembered Murger as once saying, "Bohemia isn't a country, it's a sickness that's killing me"; and at the century's end one finds this sickness still being narcissistically cultivated in the words of the young Ludwig Klages, with not a little help from his reading of Friedrich Nietzsche, and with a boost as well as from the legacies of his bohemian and Romantic predecessors.[18] In Klages's adulatory study of Stefan George, "every deep-living contemporary" has felt himself to be a quasi-Romantic, quasi-bohemian, quasi-Nietzschean "wanderer." He is "one who in unknown seas spreads his sails toward questionable coasts" until the light of his "wasting fire of yearning" has glimmered "even unto feverishness, even unto madness," and glimmered "the more wildly the more the life of the crowd and of the nations died into an ever more insensible coarseness."[19]

More generally, of course, bohemianism was publicized as a way of life characterized by laughter in the face of all the miseries that life in general, and poverty in particular, could throw at one. "We were unhappy; those were the good times," wrote Théodore Muret in 1834, giving voice to a sentiment that lived on to become a cliché reiterated throughout Murger's writings and far beyond them, as in the epigraph to *Army of Shadows* (1969) that Jean-Pierre Melville borrowed from Georges Courteline: "Bad memories, you are welcome nonetheless . . . you are my distant youth."[20] As in these instances, the emphasis on carefree gaiety was generally shadowed by a perverse idealization of morbid states of being. So famed for his moroseness that he was said to have envied the worms in graveyard tombs, Iginio Ugo Tarchetti may have been an unusual case, but we still must remember that the climax of Murger's dramatized *Scenes of Bohemian Life*, reiterated in Puccini's *La Bohème*, is the exquisitely wrenching death of Mimi, that symbol of, and delicious sacrifice to, the youthful aesthetic sensibility of her author.

As it suggests a state of alienation from the grounds of health, this emphasis on morbidity represents physiologically the sociological status of the bohemian, in the popular imagination, as a prince in exile—or, in other words, an unrecognized genius. When Johann Wolfgang von Goethe wrote his proto-bohemian bildungsroman *Wilhelm Meister's Apprenticeship* (1795–96), his protagonist found an apt image for his condition in the drama of William

Shakespeare's *Henry IV Part 1* (1596–97). In this drama, the heir apparent to the throne of England, Hal, bides his time by roistering among commoners and thieves in taverns, in exile from the splendors of his courtly privileges; and a comparable sense of dispossession showed itself in the recklessness of the pleasures and in the deliciousness of the pains pursued by bohemians. In both cases we see expressed a sense of grievance, a sense of being owed a much more adequate living than that with which they currently make do.

The fact that bohemians were notorious for the lightheartedness with which they ignored their debts to landlords and creditors suggests much the same idea: that in the greater scheme of things it was the world that was in their debt, not vice versa. Bohemians' unpaid bills were the reverse image of the unredeemed promises of the modern marketplace. If the only way bohemians' sense of entitlement to a higher status could be displayed was through their utter disregard for their déclassé state of being, even to the point of endangering their health and their very lives, then so be it. Deprived of the luxuries that were their due, they could yet defy the world by adopting an utterly negligent attitude toward it. They could refuse to portion out their pleasures in accordance with the world's trifling reckonings; and when pains came, as worldly individuals always predicted they must to those who carelessly ignored the truth, reality, and psychology of political economy, they could defiantly luxuriate even in their suffering.

Rebellion, after all, can take an aesthetic as well as a political form, even if complacent philistines contend that the political is the only meaningful pathway for discontent, in relation to which the aesthetic represents at best an irrelevant detour and at worst a total loss of direction. Mühsam, moving between the worlds of the bohemian arts, on the one hand, and of anarchist and socialist politics, on the other, knew better. Bohemians in general were not content to wait for the revolution in order to begin living revolutionary lives; and if the materials ready to hand included the somewhat dubious heritage of Romanticism, with its shopworn tropes of the *poète maudit*, insurgent desire, quasi-aristocratic sensibility, and morbid affections, then it was with these that bohemians would seek to make their way. For is it not true that any road to the future must run through the past?

Bohemia, in fact, always made a strength of its attachment to the past, as in Stefan George's lyric evocation of "the former time where I was still king."[21] With its sense of dispossession and exile came a corresponding sense of nostalgia, which pervades every manifestation of bohemia in the nineteenth century and against which the forward-looking aesthetics of Woolf and other modernists would seek to redefine what art, aesthetics, and the life of the artist ought to be. Lambert Strether in *The Ambassadors* is the ironically defined figure of this nostalgia. In his case this is a nostalgia for a youth he never had; for a bohemia for which he was (as one must ever be) too late; and for a world of aesthetic values made ideally desirable, but ultimately ungraspable, among the products of modernity in which these values are found. Strether's great task in this novel is to return a wayward youth, Chad Newsome, to his proper place in the Newsome family's industrial concern in the United States, and James's great joke in the novel arises from the fact that he never names the product made by this family business, as if to imply that any such commodity must be aesthetically obscene. In the end, Strether's nostalgia is for a bohemia that is neither as depraved as those outside it may suppose it to be nor as ideal as it may seem to those within it: a bohemia as essentially unfixed, mobile, and morally ambiguous as art itself.

In this novel as a whole, as in one notable scene of "innocent friendly Bohemia" into which Strether stumbles when he unexpectedly encounters Chad in the company of Madame de Vionnet, Chad's married lover, James's irony seeks to counter what might be called the core fantasy of bohemia.[22] This fantasy is that one's resistance to the rationality defined by political economy, if sufficiently intense, may create, not *despite* but *because of* its ultimate failure, a triumph over that rationality—a triumph that takes the form of nostalgic memorialization.

From this perspective, one might say that in the discourse of bohemia throughout the nineteenth century we see the nostalgia for one's youth peculiar to the young: the effort to incorporate a past that is already lost even though it has scarcely begun. It is as if one's ongoing youth were somehow not really what it ought to be, as would be the case if one were in exile, disinherited, pitiably unrecognized, or generally at the mercy of a world that refuses to pay what it owes. This nostalgia can then serve as a driving motivation for experiment and adventure. A sense of loss, bohemia discovered, can be liberating; and perhaps the youth of this time could discover itself only by recognizing and accepting, from the first moment of its self-consciousness, its death. After all, if G. W. F. Hegel were to be trusted, it would not be the first time that such a recognition had made masters out of those who might otherwise have been slaves. This land of bohemia, as a contemporary pamphlet put it, "bordered, to the north and the south, to the east and the west, by necessity, is situated under all the latitudes of hope."[23]

From its beginnings, the modern concept of bohemia took its life out of death, out of the martyrdom of its defining figures, from poets such as Thomas Chatterton all the way forward to dodgy types such as Teddy, Cathy, Bobby, and the other beautiful losers in Jim Carroll's "People Who Died" (1980)—and yet further forward, all the way to the present day. This bohemian nostalgia was usually described, conventionally enough, as a retrospective emotion, as when the critic and historian Theodor Mundt wrote in 1858 of the courtesan who "at the side of rich lords always recalls, with the most heartfelt longing," the relationship with the poor bohemian that served as the "introductory course" to her way of life.[24] The image of this emotion contributes to the biggest cliché of bohemia, which is that whenever it is met with it is always already a thing of the past. "For whatever else Bohemia may be," wrote Arthur Bartlett Maurice in 1916, "it is almost always yesterday."[25] This is the kind of nostalgia, of glad youth recollected in chastened maturity, that we see reproduced, for instance, in works such as the conventionally unconventional *Ballads of a Bohemian* (1921), in which Robert Service showed his keen eye for the marketable commonplace.

In the second half of the nineteenth century critics sometimes gave voice to a more specialized version of this nostalgia, which arises when observers view a particular social and cultural scene as a pathetic imitation of the supposedly original bohemia of days gone by. In 1878, for example, the same year in which the journalist Eugenio Torelli Viollier was mocking the young men in Italy who were calling themselves bohemians, Max Nordau, the cultural critic who would later distinguish himself as a theorist of degeneration, characterized the so-called bohemia in contemporary Paris as nothing but an "aftereffect," dismissing the whole affair by stating that "there are no more misunderstood geniuses."[26] Similarly, in a 1912 article the Nicaraguan poet Rubén Darío described how he had been obliged to disappoint a visiting friend who was eager to see the bohemia of the Latin Quarter, telling the naive visitor that all had changed since he had written of it twelve years before. "My beloved Mister Murger is now as old as Villon," he said; and as for the bohemian Quarter, "that doesn't exist."[27] James L. Ford, in 1921, similarly lamented the fact that the real bohemians of his own youth had been replaced by the "professional bohemian," who "performs for the benefit of visitors from the suburbs and the upper west side . . . in the purlieus of Washington Square and Greenwich Village."[28] Right up to our own time, bohemia is still, always, being pronounced dead.[29]

Observers such as Nordau, Darío, and Ford did correctly perceive that a sense of nostalgia suffused the bohemian phenomenon, both in its most general and in its most localized manifestations. They failed only to see that there had never been and could never have been an original or true bohemia, lived fully, in the present tense.

From the beginning, written into the bohemian celebration of youth was an anticipation of its death, just as written into its recklessness was an anticipation of a time of reckoning that would surely come once bohemia's "long succession of todays," in Privat's phrase, turned to tomorrow.[30] Since the modern figure of the urban gypsy was from the very first an imitation bohemian—as the borrowed name of this figure reminds us—the assumption of this identity always bespoke a commitment to a sense of nostalgia. The idea of being bohemian, in the modern meaning of the word, was premised upon an identification with loss, as represented by despised stateless wanderers thought of as belonging essentially to the past. Therefore, it was also premised upon an anticipation of rejection, suffering, and death not only in the future but even in one's joyous, hopeful, resolutely cheerful present existence. Bohemian nostalgia, then, does not necessarily represent delusion or disavowal, just as servitude does not necessarily represent recognition of a higher order of being. Whatever else it was, for this or that individual, nostalgia was also the framework that enabled bohemians to persist in seeking a life that the common sense of their day judged to be impossible. It was while writing in the mode of nostalgia, after all, that Mühsam was able to strive after a freedom that would not be the attribute of an individual "but rather the form of life of the community of all humankind."[31] As he turned fifty, just a few years before his death in a concentration camp, "No one will begrudge me the vanity," he wrote, "of feeling myself to belong to the young generation."[32]

One need not articulate an ethos of living for today, after all, if one's sense of history has not convincingly foretold a future in which that present day will be recoverable only in the bittersweet form of nostalgia. Insofar as bohemia's reckless nostalgia is also its defiance of the greater recklessness of social conventions—of the violence of marketplace rationality—it is never an end in itself. Instead, at least for many of those who identified with bohemia, its recklessness functioned as a critique, a tactic, and a strategic goal. As a critique, it insisted on the value of desires unaccountable to established institutions of dress, manners, class, marriage, education, and art; as a tactic, on the power of lively friendships and impromptu associations to reform or perhaps even to revolutionize social reality; and as a strategic goal, on the utopian spontaneity to which one must entrust the making of the future every single day.

Nostalgia in bohemia, then, marked the refusal to allow economic reason

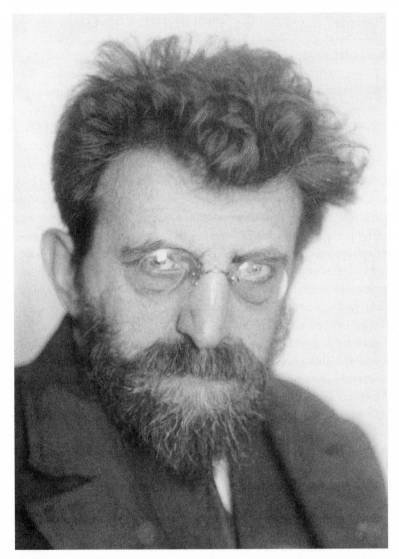

Figure 17. O. Ang, "Porträt Erich Mühsam" (c. 1928) (Bundesarchiv).

to be managed by the prospect of death. To idealize the power of youth, in the nostalgic manner of the bohemian, as if this time of one's life were practically dead already, could serve to set the image of youth free to learn whether the world might not still be an adventure even, or especially, amid the deadly new realities of modern life. Therefore, as one of the paths to the future blazed by bohemians led to aesthetic responses such as the modernist creed developed by Woolf and others in her Bloomsbury gang, another led (by way of Gérard de Nerval and Charles Baudelaire, among others) to the revolutionary experiments in life of the surrealists between the world wars. Bohemia was never a simple and unified phenomenon, and neither were its legacies.

So it would be wrong to say that those who aged out of bohemia mourned a world and time that never really existed. Bohemia was certainly real enough even though its reality was always made out of nostalgia, its youth always destined to be preserved in amber. Precisely so that they may be the bohemians they are, bohemians always learn too late, die too young, betray their ideals, and remember with regret. A bohemian who is not something of a poseur— belated, imitative, anachronistic, dislocated, and thus, in a word, nostalgic— would be a contradiction in terms.

Given this defining emphasis on liberating the time of youth from the grip of death and all its institutional promoters, it only makes sense that the commingling of art and life was taken for granted in bohemia. As Roger Shattuck put it, "Toward the middle of the nineteenth century a few artists began to 'live up to' their art, to live on a level with it."[33] The response of Murger's friends to his *Scenes of Bohemian Life*, in seeing it as being based on their lives as well as his own, was typical. The slogan of *l'art pour l'art* was sometimes picked up by this or that cohort of bohemians throughout the century, but even in such cases bohemianism still existed in the interplay of works and lives. Gustave Flaubert's famous injunction, "Be regular and ordinary in your life, like a bourgeois, so that you may be violent and original in your works," was a cautionary response to this bohemian legacy, in which, as in a Wildean paradox, life turned into art and art into life.[34] Those who identified with bohemia generally described it in terms of the value of this interplay, which crossed the boundaries of specific scenes, cities, and nations to make an international affair of living. Accordingly, in an 1894 tale John Henry MacKay would tell of one character's "charming little stories, which he had heard from young rakes in Piccadilly or from the students of the Latin Quarter or in the artistic bohème in Munich, or which he himself had experienced in his restless travels through the world, charming little stories such as Maupassant has left us."[35] It was in opposition to the likes of Sand, Murger, Privat, Walt Whitman, Ada Clare, and Iginio Ugo Tarchetti, who did not seek to distinguish themselves from their writings, instead lending themselves to the common assumption in this era that one could and should look to find authors' lives in their works, that modernists such as James, Woolf, and James Joyce would articulate an aesthetic in which the author is supposed to stand clear of his or her creation, like a God "paring his fingernails," as Joyce's Stephen Daedalus puts it.[36] Among bohemians, however, as among their heirs in later social and cultural formations, such as the surrealists of the twenties and thirties or the Beats of the 1950s, no such punctilio was observed.

This commingling of art and life did undoubtedly lead at times to laughable eccentricities. One might instance the morning when Alfred Schuler, a truly crackpot thinker of bewildering influence in the turn-of-the-century bohemia of the Schwabing district in Munich, emerged from a morning bout of masturbation to ask his friend Klages if the bluish rings he had seen in the course of this activity perhaps constituted a cosmic experience of the sort that the members of their circle were forever seeking in their life and art.[37] At other times this obliviousness to the distinctions between art and life might encourage more dire consequences, as in those cases in which the bohemian emphasis on reckless youth could develop into an almost cult-like encouragement of self-destruction. The theme of Aimé Millet's monument in the Montmartre cemetery for the author of *Scenes of Bohemian Life*, "Youth throwing flowers on the tomb of Henry Murger," could easily be taken to be a metaphor for young people throwing themselves in the grave. Otto Julius Bierbaum seized upon this tendency in his comic novel *Stilpe* (1897), in which the title character ends up playing the role of a suicidal bohemian artist as part of a cabaret act, in which, as the climax of the act, he pretends to hang himself—until one night, without warning, the act is not feigned.

In Munich, at about the same time Bierbaum was writing this novel, those in the circle around George, Schuler, and Klages were seriously cultivating the notion that "it was a particular duty . . . to die young" so as not to lose their youthful fire.[38] From Chatterton on, the martyrology of bohemia was so filled with suicides that at times it might have seemed that the desire to distance oneself from a hostile society must logically end in the ultimate exile of the grave, and it cannot be denied that drowning himself during a rainstorm in the pond of Plessis-Piquet, his umbrella open, certainly did make a striking, proto-surrealist image of Espérance Blanchon, one of Murger's circle.[39] One doubts, however, that this image was inspiring to his father, the prosperous butcher whose life his son had scorned, or to others who cared for him, if such there were; and the same might be said of the last images left by the others who took this way out of the future.

Between comical cosmic self-abuse and decidedly unfunny self-destruction, though, lay a great expanse of potential experience. The interplay of art and life in bohemia emboldened many people to act more thoughtfully, bravely, generously, and joyfully than they otherwise would have. It taught them to seek fulfillment in ways that would have seemed unthinkable before a certain story of bohemianism (from a book, from a friend, from a passing stranger, from a turn in their own lives . . .) made more reality available to them. It led them to find meaning in conditions of life that they would otherwise have scorned. Without this interplay, they might not have felt free to think and act in ways for which they invented their own ad hoc rationale without worrying about the judgments of established authorities and institutions. Without it, they might not have been drawn to recognize the truth to be found in masquerade, with Sand; the ignobility of work, with Murger; the foreign lands and races at the heart of European cities, with Privat; the democratic passions of words, with Whitman; the Frankensteinian manufacture of women's hearts, with Clare; and the economics and politics of desire, with Tarchetti. All of this and much more might have remained invisible if not for the international career of the word *bohemia* over the course of the nineteenth century, which so famously brought Bram Stoker to learn of the life that begins precisely where life seems to leave off—where we have nothing but dubious writings, popular legends, and fantastic reports of ambivalent desire—even as it brought Arthur Conan Doyle to learn that what happens when art ceases to mix things up with life, when bohemia becomes entirely rational, is truly a crime beyond imagining.

This is not to say that the modern concept of bohemia was always a source of rebellion or even that it should be seen as having played such a role more often than not. Bohemia was the self-nominated margin of nineteenth-century culture and society, a supposed "oasis in a world of humbugs," as a German reviewer put it in her account of August Strindberg's novel *The Red Room* (1879); but that very fact should alert us that its claim to fame deserves critical scrutiny.[40] Its proudly self-professed marginality, for instance, could and did serve at times to reinforce the marginalization of others: the uneducated poor, the working classes, women, Jews, the nonwhite races. If not inevitable within bohemia, the denigration of these sorts of people was not merely incidental to it, either. Although bohemians often displayed democratic, socialist, or feminist sympathies, as in the works of notable figures such as Sand, Privat, Gustave Courbet, Jules Vallès, Clare, Tarchetti, Alejandro Sawa, and Müh-sam, it could also define itself through its déclassé pride in standing outside the working classes; through its frequently misogynistic idealization of the grisette; through its ostensibly friendly demeaning of the African heritage of Privat; through its use of the Romantic image of the vagabond Gypsy to per-petuate the poisonous stereotype of the money-grubbing Jew.

Its supposed marginality could also obscure in other ways the extent to which bohemia was complicit with the same social orders to which it seemed to be opposed. Even as it became a summary figure in the popular imagina-tion for art itself, conceived of as suffering in exile from the modern capitalist society inimical to it, bohemia helped to define and consolidate a conception of art perfectly adapted to that society. In *The Bostonians*, with his portrayal of Selah Tarrant as a would-be trafficker in exotic selfhood, James may have given a picture of the bohemia of 1870s America that needs to be enjoyed more for its splendidly bilious style than for its historical accuracy, but still this work is shot through with some telling insights into this phenomenon. The more the discourse of bohemia insisted upon its disinterested pursuit of the ideal and its obliviousness to marketplace concerns, the more it helped to reorganize the political economy of aesthetics in accordance with the formula that Immanuel Kant had sketched out in the late eighteenth century, in which art was to be rigorously distinguished from and raised above crafts and commodities—and thus to become, despite Kant, a peculiarly valuable craft and commodity.[41] Whether or not they meant to do so, every time bohemians such as Baudelaire and Tarchetti railed against the utilitarian ethos of their age they contributed to this ideology of art. They helped make it a quasi-sacred realm that was sup-posed to glorify the nation by transcending social, historical, economic, and political contexts, and thus they helped to define art in a way that perfectly complemented one of the defining inventions of the nineteenth century, the public museum of art: the temple of culture. Bohemia's dirty garret was the anteroom to the immaculate white cube of modern exhibition spaces.

Accusations that this or that bohemian might have sold out, as Murger was accused of doing, simply appear silly once one recognizes the extent to which the discourse of bohemian marginality served as an adaptation, not an opposition, to the history of this time. As Jerrold Seigel has written, bohemia "was at once a form of life and a dramatized interpretation, both of itself and of the society to which it was a response."[42] In a sense, bohemians were doing the bidding of the philistine bourgeois even as they insulted him. They did not recognize that by proclaiming the independence of art from the commercial marketplace they might simply be making it innocuous. Personal conflicts such as those between Murger and his father, public kerfluffles over events such as the 1863 *Salon des refusés*, and the myriad motivations that made bohemians "unconventional" all may appear, retrospectively, as having helped to make the arts safe for capitalism. The very qualities on which bohemians prided themselves—their independence and rebelliousness—might then be, ironically, precisely what qualified them for institutionalization, as evidenced by the long history of *embourgeoisement* that has seen the art world capitalize on every avant-garde that raised its fist in the nineteenth and twentieth centuries.

What is more, this process—as in Whitman's self-promotion—often did not even leave any room for irony around it. We may remember that almost as soon as bohemia acquired its modern definition, bohemian scenes arose—in the New York City of Whitman's era, in turn-of-the-century London, and elsewhere—that insisted on its gentility. We may remember, too, that these scenes and others also became tourist destinations, even as the bohemian phenomenon in general was being commodified by the books, plays, images, operas, songs, and cabarets dedicated to it. In 1907, the Viennese satirist Karl Kraus, "perhaps the last bohemian of any artistic necessity and consequence," bitterly characterized as trained dogs the bohemian artists that impresarios advertised as such so as to attract paying customers to their establishments.[43] This state of affairs seemed to Kraus a comedown from "the spirit of the Parisian bohème," but only because he, too, despite his redoubtable capacity for satire, could not help but be inclined to nostalgia in this matter.[44] As the readiness with which it lent itself to commodification showed, bohemian marginality was often all too central to the modern world in which it arose.

It is not only from a distant and retrospective view that bohemia appears in this character. Individual bohemians did disappoint one another, sell out, become serious men and practical women seemingly oblivious to the fervor of their youth; and even prior to such disappointments, bohemia was often far from being the rebellious counterculture its nostalgic historians liked to picture it as having been. The *rapin* or art student, for instance, whose bohemian carelessness writers such as Baudelaire would evoke, was often more like a nineteenth-century frat boy than anything else: a kid living on an allowance from *maman* and *papa*, hazing new entrants into the atelier, and partying as hard as possible, all the while harboring careerist ambitions and getting ready to grab at the main chance when it should offer itself.[45] Alexandre Schanne, the Schaunard of *Scenes of Bohemian Life*, seemed content enough to take over his father's toy factory; Champfleury became a specialist in porcelain manufactures, employed by Sèvres as chief of collections; and the list of such nonsuicides goes on.

There should be no surprise about such developments. People tend to remember that Murger described bohemia as the preface to the hospital and the morgue, but he did not fail to note that it was also the preface to the Académie française, to which he, in fact, would have been delighted to be elected.[46] If it was always easy to oversell the rebelliousness of bohemia, Murger was not among the deluded customers of that image. Similarly, the same Franziska zu Reventlow who described bohemian Munich as a "fantastic dreamland" in *Ellen Olestjerne* (1903) also portrayed it, elsewhere in this novel and in her diary and other writings, as a realm governed by much more down-to-earth concerns: trying to earn enough to feed and house oneself, dealing with unreliable men, coping with depression, and managing life as an unwed mother.[47] Similarly astute observers, with similarly disillusioning insights, can be identified in all of bohemia's international scenes.

All such allowances having been made, however, it remains true that the bohemian phenomenon did offer many people a way forward that was better than any they could otherwise have dreamed. The emphasis in recent scholarship on the extent to which bohemia was a kind of mirror image of bourgeois society, representing its driving impulses, values, conflicts, and needs, has been a salutary corrective to romanticized accounts of bohemians as rebellious outsiders, wild, beautiful, and free, defying an uncomprehending world.[48] This is also, however, an emphasis symptomatic of an era when there may appear to be no outside to the capitalist marketplace or to the triumphant hegemony of the middle classes in it. Taken too far, this would become an approach that saves no argument for ideas, passions, fantasies, movements, and works that did not reach their desired end; for people who took risks without any guarantees that they would pay off and often, in the end, without any publicly recognized return; for the honor of reckless commitments to imprudent convictions. We would then be in a situation in which our own compromises with what we have taken to be unassailable historical forces would lead us to discredit the possibility of any experience that does not affirm our own cherished disappointments. Unlike the stereotypical philistine who sees art as idleness and the artist as nothing but a do-nothing, we would then be seeing in them nothing but the market, nothing but the production of history, nothing but . . . our own acceptance of ourselves as dismal stereotypes.

In this book, I have tried to analyze the bohemian as (to quote a Mexican journalist writing in the early 1860s) "a *drama* in action, a complicated, variable, difficult, foreign, sometimes terrible drama."[49] As a symptom of modernity, bohemia was also an attempted alternative, escape, and cure, and it has to be evaluated in all these aspects if we are to begin to understand what its reason for being may have been, and what might yet be our own.

NOTES

CHAPTER 1. BOHEMIAN POSEUR JEW

1. George Sand, *Histoire de ma vie*, ed. Martine Reid (Paris: Éditions Gallimard, 2004 [orig. 1854–55]), 1199.

2. Sand, *Histoire de ma vie*, 1212.

3. Sand, *Histoire de ma vie*, 1212.

4. Émile de la Bédollière, "L'étudiant en droit," *Les français peints par eux-mêmes: Encyclopédie morale du dix-neuvième siècle*, 10 vols. (Paris: L. Curmer, 1840–42), 1: 20.

5. See the reproduction of one such certificate in Dore Ashton, *Rosa Bonheur: A Life and a Legend* (New York: Viking Press, 1981), 57.

6. In her *Histoire de ma vie* Sand does refer to her mother's rather disreputable past, which she described elsewhere as placing her mother among "the vagabond and disparaged race of the bohemians of the world." (See Sand, "À Charles Poncy" [23 December 1843], *Correspondance*, ed. Georges Lubin, 26 vols. [Paris: Garnier Frères, 1964–95], 6: 327.) This reference might seem to call into question her mother's parental authority in issues of social conventions such as this one, but this past is not presented as bearing any relation to her mother's judgment in this instance.

7. The editor of Sand's correspondence points out that a letter to Jules Boucoiran (4 March 1831) shows that it was Boucoiran who gave her the idea of cross-dressing, not her mother. See Sand, *Correspondance*, 1: 818n. Also, in 1835, while objecting to another correspondent's suggestion that her dress was carnivalesque and sexually suggestive, Sand referred to it as her "habit de *bousingot*," thus associating it with the rebellious republican students whom she would later portray in *Horace* (1842). She told the same correspondent that she had at times attached "some tender superstitions and the secret of certain profound memories to this disguise." (Sand, "À Adolphe Guéroult" [6 May 1835], *Correspondance*, 2: 880.) These comments, obviously, differ from the emphasis in her autobiography on the utilitarian aspect of her costume.

8. Sand, *Histoire de ma vie*, 1231.

9. Cf. the comparison drawn between Pyat's and Sand's conceptions of bohemia in Jerrold Seigel, *Bohemian Paris: Culture, Politics, and the Boundaries of Bourgeois Life, 1830–1930* (Baltimore: Johns Hopkins University Press, 1986), 16–19.

10. John Reed, *The Day in Bohemia, or Life Among the Artists* (New York: Hillacre, 1913), 33.

11. Sand, "À Pierre Bocage" (21 February 1845), *Correspondance*, 6: 803; and "À Émile Regnault" (13 June 1831), *Correspondance*, 1: 895.

12. See Robert Darnton, "Introduction," in Anne Gédéon Lafitte, Marquis de Pelleport, *The Bohemians: A Novel* (1790), trans. Vivian Folkenflik (Philadelphia: University of Pennsylvania Press, 2010), ix. On this point see also George Levitine's description of the image of the artist in the late eighteenth century in *The Dawn of Bohemianism: The* Barbu *Rebellion and Primitivism in Neoclassical France* (University Park: Pennsylvania State University Press, 1978), 31–32. One also sees *bohemian* begin to take on its modern meaning in a booklet that J. P. R. Cuisin published under the pseudonym "A Curious Bohemian." See *Un bohème curieux, La vie de garçon dans les hotels garnis, ou l'amour à la minute: Scènes de la vie joyeuse entre étudiants, grisettes, rapins, courtisanes et truqueuses* (Paris: Chez tous les libraires, 1823 [orig. 1820]).

13. Jules Barbey d'Aurevilly, "Edgar Poe" (1856), *Les oeuvres et les hommes*, 26 vols. (Paris: Alphonse Lemerre, 1860–90; rep. Geneva: Slatkine Reprints, 1968), 12: 377.

14. Julius Bab, *Die Berliner Bohème*, ed. M. M. Schardt (Paderborn: Igel Verlag Literatur, 1994 [orig. 1904]), 23.

15. But see Arthur Symons's passing mention of "the Jews" as bohemian antagonists in his "Introduction" to Henry Murger, *The Latin Quarter*, trans. Ellen Marriage and John Selwyn (New York: Doubleday Page, 1901), viii. More obliquely, Israel Zangwill suggested an antagonism between bohemia and Jews in his story "The Jewish Trinity," in *Ghetto Comedies* (New York: Macmillan, 1907), 105–36. Seigel briefly discusses a connection between anti-Semitism and antibohemianism, while also noting how bohemia was sometimes joined "with anti-Semitic activists," in *Bohemian Paris*, 178–80, 291. On the more recognized relation between the bohemian and the bourgeois, Seigel's work in its entirety is vital. See also, e.g., Christine Stansell's analysis of how bohemians "always existed in symbiotic relation to bourgeois culture rather than in opposition to it" in *American Moderns: Bohemian New York and the Creation of a New Century* (New York: Henry Holt, 2000), 18; and Marilyn R. Brown's argument that "the bohemian was bourgeois from the outset" in *Gypsies and Other Bohemians: The Myth of the Artist in Nineteenth-Century France* (Ann Arbor, Mich.: UMI Research Press, 1985), 100. Brown's important work in its entirety is relevant to my argument in this chapter. See also Helmut Kreuzer's description of bohemia as the "antagonistic complement" of the bourgeoisie in *Die Boheme: Analyse und Dokumentation der Intellektuellen Subkultur vom 19. Jahrhundert bis zur Gegenwart* (Stuttgart: J. B. Metzlersche Verlagsbuchhandlung, 1971), 45; and César Graña, *Bohemian Versus Bourgeois: French Society and the French Man of Letters in the Nineteenth Century* (New York: Basic Books, 1964).

16. Jeffrey Mehlman, *Legacies of Anti-Semitism in France* (Minneapolis: University of Minnesota Press, 1983), 4. For the continuation of the figurative association between bohemians and Jews in France in the early decades of the twentieth century, see Pierre Birnbaum, *Anti-Semitism in France: A Political History from Léon Blum to the Present*, trans. Miriam Kochan (Oxford: Basil Blackwell, 1992 [orig. 1988]), 153–57.

17. Félix Pyat, "Les artistes," in *Nouveau tableau de Paris au XIXme siècle* [ed. Henri

Martin], 7 vols. (Paris: Madame Charles-Béchet, 1834–35), 4: 9. For a comparable but much more sympathetic account of this medievalist fad among the youth of the Latin Quarter, see Alexandre Privat d'Anglemont, *Paris anecdote*, ed. Charles Monselet (Paris: P. Rouquette, 1885 [orig. 1854]), 141–62.

18. Pyat, "Les artistes," *Nouveau tableau*, 4: 8–9.

19. On Sand's first meeting with Pyat, see Sand, "À Félix Pyat" (December 1830 [?]), *Correspondance*, 1: 761–63. Sand's disagreement with Pyat may also have had some personal basis; see "À Félix Pyat" (28 [?] March 1833), *Correspondance*, 2: 283–84. She also refers to some unspecified animus Pyat expressed toward her, among others, c. 1834–35 in her *Journal intime* (Paris: Seuil, 1995 [orig. 1833–68]), 90.

20. Sand, *La dernière Aldini* (Paris: J. Hetzel, 1855 [orig. 1838]), 172.

21. Sand, *La dernière Aldini*, 6.

22. Sand, *La dernière Aldini*, 77.

23. Sand, *La dernière Aldini*, 200.

24. Sand, *Horace*, ed. Nicole Courrier and Thierry Bodin (Meylan: Les Éditions de l'Aurore, 1982 [orig. 1842]), 276.

25. Sand, "À Ferdinand François" (23 [?] January 1844), *Correspondance*, 6: 401. Sand's characterization of Leroux in this instance is touched with irony, in light of his inconstant enthusiasms and the drain he put on her finances, but it is serious as well. It is worth noting that Sand had begun to refer to herself as a bohemian as early as 1835; see "À Jean-Joseph Bidault" (29 June 1835), *Correspondance*, 2: 905. Of particular interest in this regard is an extended account that she wrote of her conception of herself as a bohemian artist, around the time of the composition of *La dernière Aldini* and while she was glorying in her affair with Frédéric Chopin, in a letter to Eugène Delacroix. See "À Eugène Delacroix" (7 [?] September 1838), *Correspondance*, 4: 482–84.

26. See Privat d'Anglemont, *Voyage à travers Paris, 1: Le Prado* (Paris: Chez Paulier, 1846), 38.

27. Pyat, "Les artistes," *Nouveau tableau*, 4: 18.

28. Gabriel Guillemot, *Le bohême* (Paris: A. Le Chevalier, 1868), 90.

29. In this regard the new definition was still patterned on the old: in its fifth (1798) and subsequent editions, the dictionary of the French Academy included in its entry for *bohême* the expression *foi de bohême*, referring to the good faith, or honor among thieves, that bohemians were reputed to keep among themselves.

30. Charles Monselet, "Alexandre Privat d'Anglemont," in Privat d'Anglemont, *Paris anecdote*, 6.

31. An anonymous commentator quoted in Theodore de Banville, *Mes souvenirs* (Paris: Chapentier, 1882), 65. One might hazard that the commentator was Banville himself.

32. Alfred Delvau, "Alexandre Privat d'Anglemont," in Privat d'Anglemont, *Paris inconnu* (Paris: Adolphe Delahays, 1861), 10.

33. See Anon., *Almanach des grisettes et des bals de Paris pour 1848: Lions, étudiants, reines de Mabille, lorettes* (Paris: Librairie littéraire et politique, 1848), 20. It is notable in this regard that in *La vie de garçon dans les hotels garnis*, "Un bohème curieux" presents himself on the first page (i) as a "parasite."

34. For the discourse on gypsies as the "real bohemians" in this time, see Brown, *Gypsies and Other Bohemians*, 17.

35. James Clarence Harvey, "Introduction," *In Bohemia* (New York: H. M. Caldwell, 1905), xii. See also Kreuzer's characterization of the issue of true versus false bohemians in *Die Boheme*, 17–20 and 175–77; Elizabeth Wilson's argument that "the bohemian stereotype seeks to conceal, but inadvertently exposes the uncertainty at its core, for it characterizes the artist simultaneously as an authentic and dedicated creator, and as a poseur" in *Bohemians: The Glamorous Outcasts* (New Brunswick, N.J.: Rutgers University Press, 2000), 9; and Peter Brooker's argument that "role-playing was not an alternative to a bohemian life style . . . so much as its very essence" in *Bohemia in London: The Social Scene of Early Modernism* (New York: Palgrave Macmillan, 2004), 13.

36. William Dean Howells, *The Coast of Bohemia* (New York: Harper and Row, 1893), 216–17.

37. Charles De Kay, *The Bohemian: A Tragedy of Modern Life* (New York: Charles Scribner's Sons, 1878), 26.

38. See Albert Parry's description of how one of Whitman's great promoters, Henry Clapp Jr., was wont to fulminate against bohemians, in *Garrets and Pretenders: A History of Bohemianism in America*, rev. ed. (New York: Dover, 1960 [orig. 1933]), 46. On this subject of Whitman's pose see also the outstanding study by Joanna Levin, *Bohemia in America, 1858–1920* (Stanford: Stanford University Press, 2010), 13–69.

39. See George Matoré, *Le vocabulaire et la société sous Louis-Philippe*, 2nd ed. (Geneva: Slatkine Reprints, 1967 [orig. 1951]), 67–68.

40. Achille Bizzoni, "Due parole alla 'Frusta'" (1868), in Giuseppe Farinelli, *La Scapigliatura: Profilo storico, protagonisti, documenti* (Rome: Carocci editore, 2003), 228. "Scapigliatura" is loosely translatable as "the disheveled ones." On behalf of himself and his comrades, Bizzoni was responding to an article of Righetti's in a paper he edited, the *Cronaca grigia*.

41. Roberto Sacchetti, *Cesare Mariani: Racconto*, ed. Gabriele Catalano (Florence: Vallechi editore, 1973 [orig. 1876]), 114.

42. See Enrique Perez Escrich, *El frac azul: Episodios de un jóven flaco* (Madrid: Manini Hermanos, 1864), 127.

43. Emilio Carrere, *Retablillo grotesco y sentimental* (Madrid: Editorial "Mundo Latino" [1921]), 11.

44. Junius Henri Browne, *The Great Metropolis: A Mirror of New York* (Hartford, Conn.: American Publishing, 1869), 157–58; G. J. M., "Bohemianism: A Fast Fading Phase of Literary and Artistic Life," *Brooklyn Daily Eagle* (20 April 1884): 4.

45. Raffaello Barbiera, "Uno scapigliato," *Simpatie: Studi letterari* (Milan: N. Battezzati and B. Saldini, 1877), 49; Bab, *Die Berliner Bohème*, 90; Julio Camba, quoted in Ernesto Bark, *La santa bohemia y otros artículos* (Madrid: Biblioteca de la Bohemia, 1999 [orig. 1913]), 27.

46. H. C. Bunner, "Urban and Suburban Sketches: The Bowery and Bohemia," *Scribner's Magazine* 15 (April 1894): 454.

47. Anton Kuh, "Ich bin Bohemien," *Simplicissimus* 33 (21 May 1928): 103.

48. Alexander Schanne, *Souvenirs de Schaunard* (Paris: G. Charpentier, 1887), 259.

49. Henry Murger, *Scènes de la vie de bohème*, ed. Loïc Chotard and Graham Robb (Paris: Gallimard, 1988 [orig. 1851]), 39–40.

50. Murger, *Scènes de la vie de bohème*, 376.

51. Murger, "Le manchon de Francine," *Oeuvres complètes*, 12 vols. in 6 (Paris: [Michel Lévy], 1855–61; rep. Geneva: Slatkine Reprints, 1971), 9: 240.

52. Murger, *Les buveurs d'eau*, *Oeuvres complètes*, 1: vi.

53. Murger, "Le manchon de Francine," *Oeuvres complètes*, 9: 270. The members of this group called themselves "Water Drinkers" because they had decided not to serve wine at their gatherings, lest they embarrass those unable to afford it.

54. Pierre Larousse, *Grand dictionnaire universel du XIXe siècle*, 17 vols. (Paris: Administration du Grand Dictionnaire Universel, 1866), 2: 866–67.

55. Adrien Lélioux, in Trois Buveurs d'Eau [Adrien Lélioux, Léon Noël, and Nadar], *Histoire de Mürger pour servir à l'histoire de la vraie Bohème*, 2nd ed. (Paris: J. Hetzel [1862]), 71.

56. Nadar [Gaspard-Félix Tournachon, pseud.], *Charles Baudelaire intime: Le poète vierge* ([Paris]: Obsidiane, 1985 [orig. 1911]), 57.

57. Edmond and Jules de Goncourt, *Manette Salomon* (Paris: Union Générale d'Éditions, 1979), 32.

58. Alfred Delvau, *Henry Murger et la bohème* (Paris: Bachelin-Deflorenne, 1866), 69, 30.

59. Jules Vallès, *L'insurgé* (Paris: Bibliothèque-Charpentier, 1923 [orig. 1886]), 22, 31.

60. Pío Baroja, *Los últimos románticos* (Barcelona: Editorial Planeta, 1954 [orig. 1906]), 139–40.

61. See Erich Mühsam, "Bohème," *Die Fackel* 8 (30 April 1906): 7.

62. Camille Mauclair, "Le préjugé de la 'Vie de Bohème' et les moeurs de l'artiste actuel," *La revue des revues* 31 (December 1899): 464.

63. Guy de Maupassant, *Bel-Ami*, ed. Gérard Delaisement (Paris: Éditions Garnier Frères, 1959 [orig. 1885]), 47.

64. O[reste] Cenacchi, "Il primo Elzevir dello Zanichelli," *Teatro e romanzo: Note e ricerche* (Bologna: Nicola Zanichelli, 1886), 166.

65. On this topic see Gabriel P. Weisberg, ed., *Montmartre and the Making of Mass Culture* (New Brunswick, N.J.: Rutgers University Press, 2001).

66. Arthur Bartlett Maurice, *The New York of the Novelists* (New York: Dodd, Mead, 1916), 115.

67. See Emilio Carrere, "El dolor de llegar" (1909), *Mis mejores cuentos* (Madrid: Prensa Popular, [1920]): 123–72.

68. See Th[éodore] Barrière and H[enry] Murger, *La vie de bohème*, rev. ed. (Paris: Calmann Lévy, 1896 [orig. 1849]), in which this refrain appears in songs throughout the play.

69. Théodore Pelloquet, *Henry Murger* (Paris: Librarie Nouvelle, 1861), 18.

70. Gustave Courbet, "À Francis et Marie Wey" (31 July 1850), *Correspondance de Courbet*, ed. Petra ten-Doesschate Chu (Paris: Flammarion, 1996), 92.

71. Sawa's dog is mentioned in Emilio Carrere, "La casa de Álex Sawa," in José Esteban and Anthony N. Zahareas, *Los proletarios del arte: Introducción a la bohemia* ([Madrid]:

Celeste Ediciones, 1998), 64. On the topic of Courbet's poses, see ten-Doesschate Chu, *The Most Arrogant Man in France: Gustave Courbet and the Nineteenth-Century Media Culture* (Princeton: Princeton University Press, 2007).

72. Courbet, "À Alfred Bruyas" (3 May 1854), *Correspondance de Courbet*, 113–14.

73. James McNeill Whistler, "JW to Mario Proth" (June/August 1859), *The Correspondence of James McNeill Whistler, 1855–1903*, ed. Margaret F. MacDonald, Patricia de Montfort, and Nigel Thorpe; including *The Correspondence of Anna McNeill Whistler, 1855–1880*, ed. Georgia Toutziari (on-line edition, University of Glasgow: http://www.whistler.arts.gla .ac.uk/correspondence/), The Pierpont Morgan Library, New York, Call Number MA 4500; Glasgow University: Whistler (GUW) System Number 11559 (2012-6-16).

74. E[lizabeth] R[obins] and J[oseph] Pennell, *The Life of James McNeill Whistler*, 6th ed. (Philadelphia: J. B. Lippincott, 1919), 37.

75. Alphonse Duchesne, "Alexandre Privat d'Anglemont," *Le Figaro* (9 August 1859): 3.

76. Charles Baudelaire, "Préface," in Léon Cladel, *Les martyrs ridicules: Roman parisien* (Plan de la Tour: Éditions d'Aujourd'hui [1979—orig. 1862]), 3, 9.

77. Théophile Gautier, from a contemporary review quoted in Schanne, *Souvenirs de Schaunard*, 261.

78. On this point concerning the impressionists, see Alexander Sturgis, Rupert Christiansen, Lois Oliver, and Michael Wilson, *Rebels and Martyrs: The Image of the Artist in the Nineteenth Century* (London: National Gallery Company, 2006), 108. On the interrelationship of dandies and bohemians, see Seigel, *Bohemian Paris*, 97–124, 284–86.

79. Philibert Audebrand, "La grande Bohême," *Le Figaro* (26 July 1859): 3. Perhaps thinking of Hugo, Audebrand also gives "gilded Bohemia" as a synonym for "la grande Bohême." In contrast to Hugo's portrayal, though, see the distinction Mario Proth draws between a negligible "little bohemia" and a genuine and admirable "great bohemia" in *Les vagabonds* (Paris: Michel Lévy Frères, 1865).

80. Charles Asselineau, *Charles Baudelaire: Sa vie et son oeuvre* (1868), in *Baudelaire et Asselineau*, ed. Jacques Crépet and Claude Pichois (Paris: Librarie Nizet, 1953), 80.

81. G[ustav] L[ouis] M[aurice] Strauss, *Reminiscences of an Old Bohemian*, new ed. (London: Downey, 1895 [orig. 1883]), 215.

82. Barbey d'Aurevilly, *Du dandysme et de George Brummel*, ed. Marie-Christine Natta (Bassac: Plein Chant, 1989 [orig. 1845]), 152.

83. See Paul de Saint Victoire, quoted in Schanne, *Souvenirs de Schaunard*, 263.

84. T. J. Clark, *Image of the People: Gustave Courbet and the Second French Republic 1848–1851* (Greenwich, Conn.: New York Graphic Society, 1973), 94.

85. C[arl] Ploetz, "Henri Murger: Eine litterarische Skizze," *Archiv für das Studium der neueren Sprachen und Literaturen* 31, ed. Ludwig Herrig (Braunschweig: George Westermann, 1862), 415.

86. See Alexandre Dumas, *Les Mohicans de Paris*, 19 vols. (Paris: Dufour, Mulat et Boulanger, 1859–62), I: 192.

87. Proth, *Les vagabonds*, iii.

88. H[onoré]-A[ntoine] Frégier, *Des classes dangereuses de la population dans les grands villes, et des moyens de les rendre meilleures*, 2 vols. (Paris: J.-B. Baillière, 1840), I: 50, I: 192.

89. See Pierre Bourdieu's reference to the "normative, or, better, performative enunciations" that established *la bohème* in *Les règles de l'art: Genèse et structure du champ littéraire* (Paris: Éditions du Seuil, 1992), 87.

90. On this process, see Brown's richly informative *Gypsies and Other Bohemians*.

91. Anon., "Bohémiens," *Magasin pittoresque* 19 (1851): 394.

92. Quoted in François de Vaux de Foletier, *Les bohémiens en France au 19e siècle* (Paris: Éditions J.-C. Lattès, 1981), 223; the journal in question appeared in 1854. On this point see also Seigel, *Bohemian Paris*, 131–33.

93. See José Cubero, *Histoire du vagabondage du Moyen Âge à nos jours* (Paris: Éditions Imago, 1998), esp. 48–51; and Vaux de Foletier, *Les bohémiens en France au 19e siècle*, especially his reproduction of an 1864 letter (111–13) summarizing relevant legal articles and declarations from 1790, 1849, 1851, 1858, and 1863.

94. Quoted in Jean-Pierre Liegeois, "Bohémiens et pouvoirs publics en France du XVe au XIXe siècle," *Études Tsiganes* 24 (Dec. 1978): 20, 28.

95. See Schanne, *Souvenirs de Schaunard*, 319.

96. See Walter Benjamin, "Paris, the Capital of the Nineteenth Century" (1935), trans. Howard Eiland, ed. Howard Eiland and Michael W. Jennings, in *Selected Writings*, ed. Michael W. Jennings, 4 vols. (Cambridge, Mass.: Harvard University Press, 1996–2003), 3: 40. See also, especially in relation to the *bohémienne*, Aruna D'Souza and Tom McDonough, eds., *The Invisible Flâneuse?: Gender, Public Space, and Visual Culture in Nineteenth-Century Paris* (Manchester: Manchester University Press, 2006).

97. Hans R. Fischer, *Berliner Zigeunerleben: Bilder aus der Welt der Schriftsteller, Künstler und des Proletariats* (Berlin: S. Fischer, 1890), 92.

98. See Georg Queri, *Kraftbayrisch: Wörterbuch der erotischen und skatalogischen Redensarten der Altbayern* (Munich: Deutscher Taschenbuch Verlag, 1981 [orig. 1912]), 43.

99. Fritz von Ostini, "Eugen Kirchner," *Velhagen & Klasings Monatshefte* 29 (September 1914): 134. See also Ostini's speculation, in an article published a year later, that this term had originally made reference to Russian exiles, who were seen as leading a shadowy and unwholesome existence, in "München in der Kriegszeit," *Deutsche Kraft* 12 (1915): 5–6. In *Wo die Geister wandern: Literarische Spaziergänge durch Schwabing* (Munich: Verlag C. H. Beck, 2008), 11, Dirk Heißerer traces this word to Austria and Bavaria circa 1900, suggesting that it bore special reference to Slovenian peddlers.

100. See, for example, Michael Doeberl's reference to "the artistic and literary bohemian, the *Schlawiner*," in *Sozialismus, sozial Revolution, sozialer Volkstaat* (Munich: Allgemeine Zeitung, 1920), 34; and the reference to the "'*Schlawiner*' (the Bohème of Schwabing)" in Max Hildebert Boehm, *Volkskunde* (Berlin: Weidmann, 1937), 43.

101. René Prévot, *Du mein Schwabing! Kreislauf romantischer Ironie* (Munich: Rösl, 1921), 8.

102. Carl von Ossietzky, "Vor Sonnenaufgang," *Die Weltbühne* 36 (16 September 1930): 426; Konrad Heiden, *Adolf Hitler: Das Zeitalter der Verantwortungslosigkeit*, 2 vols. (Zurich: Europa Verlag, 1936), 1: 350.

103. Julius Petersen, "Die Sehnsucht nach dem Dritten Reich in deutscher Sage und Dichtung II," *Dichtung und Volkstum* 35 (1934): 174.

104. Privat d'Anglemont, *Voyage à travers Paris, 1: Le Prado*, 49–50.

105. Champfleury, "Confessions de Sylvius," *Chien-Callou* (Paris: Michel Lévy Frères, 1860), 138.

106. See P[ierre]-J[oseph] Proudhon, *La pornocratie ou les femmes dans les temps modernes* (Paris: A. Lacroix, 1875), 226–27.

107. Henry James, *The American* (1877), *The Novels and Tales of Henry James*, 26 vols. (New York: Charles Scribner's Sons, 1922), 2: 83.

108. Sand, *Le Compagnon du Tour de France*, ed. René Bourgeois, with Bernadette Chouvelou, Jean Courrier, and Jean-Pierre Maque (Grenoble: Presses Universitaires de Grenoble, 1979 [orig. 1841]), 114. On this issue of bohemia in relation to women, see Wilson, *Bohemians: The Glamorous Outcasts*, 85–138; and Brooker, *Bohemia in London*, 102–12.

109. See Friedrich Carl Peterssen's comments on this issue in "Der Zigeuner," *Genrebilder aus dem modernen Babel* (Stuttgart: M. Kröner, 1870), 22.

110. Ludwig Meidner, "An alle Künstler, Dichter, Musiker," in Joh[annes] R[obert] Becher et al., *An alle Künstler!* (Berlin: [Fackelträger-Verlag], 1919), 8.

111. See also the distinction Sand drew between bohemian behavior and proletarian identity, in a discussion of Pierre Leroux, in "À Charles Poncy" (25 November 1845), *Correspondance*, 7: 194.

112. Proudhon, *France et Rhin*, 2nd ed. (Paris: Librarie Internationale, 1867), 258.

113. Proth, *Les vagabonds*, 6.

114. See Sand, "À Saint-Beuve" (10 March 1835), *Correspondance*, 2: 824 and *Journal intime*, 148; and Schanne, *Souvenirs de Schaunard*, 96.

115. On this topic see George K. Anderson, *The Legend of the Wandering Jew* (Providence: Brown University Press, 1965).

116. See Linda Nochlin, "Gustave Courbet's *Meeting*: A Portrait of the Artist as a Wandering Jew," *Courbet* (New York: Thames and Hudson, 2007), 29–54; and see also Jack Lindsay, *Gustave Courbet: His Life and Art* (New York: Harper and Row, 1973), 119, 193; and Clark, *Image of the People*, 139, 157.

117. Courbet himself identified one of the figures in this painting as a lucre-loving Jew. See the letter to Champfleury of 1854–55 reproduced in "Appendix II" in James Henry Rubin, *Realism and Social Vision in Courbet and Proudhon* (Princeton: Princeton University Press, 1980), 110–12. See also the discussion of the possible relation between this figure in *The Artist's Studio* and the description of Jews in Flora Tristan's *Les promenades dans Londres* (1840) suggested by Lindsay, *Gustave Courbet*, 129–30.

118. Ch[arles] de Ricault d'Héricault, *Murger et son coin: Souvenirs très vagabonds et très personnels* (Paris: Louis Tremaux, 1896), 21; Paul Lafargue, *Le droit à la paresse*, ed. Maurice Dommanget (Paris: François Maspero, 1970 [orig. 1880]), 131.

119. Nathaniel Hawthorne, *The Marble Faun: Or, The Romance of Monte Beni* (1860), ed. Fredson Bowers, *The Centenary Edition of the Works of Nathaniel Hawthorne*, ed. William Charvat, Roy Harvey Pearce, Claude M. Simpson, and Matthew J. Bruccoli, 23 vols. (Columbus: Ohio State University Press, 1968), 4: 388, 22.

120. Hawthorne, *The Marble Faun*, *Works*, 4: 460.

121. Hawthorne, *The Marble Faun*, *Works*, 4: 429.

122. D. D., "Bohemia," *The New-York Saturday Press* 3 (16 June 1860): 2. "Rachel" was the internationally famous stage name of the actress Rachel Félix. See also, for example, the contrast drawn between bohemians and "a Jew tailor" in Carl Benson [Charles Astor Bristed, pseud.], "A New Theory of Bohemians," *The Knickerbocker* 57 (March 1861): 316.

123. William Makepeace Thackeray, *The Newcomes: Memoirs of a Most Respectable Family* (New York: William L. Allison, n.d. [orig. 1855]), 218.

124. [Fitz-James O'Brien], "A Paper of All Sorts," *Harper's New Monthly Magazine* 16 (March 1858): 515. O'Brien is identified as the author of this anonymous article in Francis Wolle, *Fitz-James O'Brien: A Literary Bohemian of the Eighteen Fifties* (Boulder: University of Colorado Studies, 1944), 157.

125. Champfleury, "Cadamour," *Les excentriques* (Paris: Calmann Lévy, 1890 [orig. 1852]; rep. Geneva: Slatkine Reprints, 1967), 256. See also the portrayal of Jewish models in a booklet written by Taxile Delord, Arnould Frémy, and Edmond Texier, *Paris-Bohème* (Paris: Librairie d'Alphonse Taride, 1854), 57. For an analysis of *Manette Salomon* in the context of the history and representation of Jewish models in nineteenth-century France, see Marie Lathers, *Bodies of Art: French Literary Realism and the Artist's Model* (Lincoln: University of Lincoln Press, 2001), esp. 21–59 and 142–68.

126. See Édouard Drumont, *La France Juive: Essai d'histoire*, 2 vols., 43rd ed. (Paris: C. Marpon and E. Flammarion, 1886), 1: 22n.

127. For the casual anti-Semitism in Sand's letters, see, for example, "À Gustave Papet" (27 [?] April 1837), *Correspondance*, 3: 809, and "À Sainte-Beuve" (15 [?] January 1842), *Correspondance* 5: 569. See also the description of the *bohémienne* in *Consuelo*, who, Sand comments—even as she disclaims any desire to insult other races—does not have "the insinuating curiosity or the tenacious mendicity of an indigent *ebbrea*." Sand, *Consuelo* (1842), in *Consuelo/La Comtesse de Rudolstadt*, ed. Léon Cellier and Léon Guichard, 3 vols. (Paris: Garnier Frères, 1959), 1: 14.

128. Murger, *Scènes de la vie de bohème*, 247.

129. Murger, *Scènes de la vie de bohème*, 247.

130. Murger, *Scènes de la vie de bohème*, 247. Cf. the analysis of Medicis as "the pure and abstract production and movement of profit, reified profit," in Adrian Rifkin, "Parvenu or Palimpsest: Some Tracings of the Jew in Modern France," in *The Jew in the Text: Modernity and the Construction of Identity*, ed. Linda Nochlin and Tamar Garb (London: Thames and Hudson, 1995), 279.

131. Cladel, *Les martyrs ridicules*, 137.

132. Alfred de Vigny, *Chatterton* (1834), in *Théâtre* (Paris: Alphonse Lemerre, 1885), 287.

133. For other examples of this attitude in bohemian circles in turn-of-the-century Madrid, see, for instance, Ernesto Bark's comment, as he cites a work he had written in 1889, that "the Spanish press [at that time] was not, like the German and Austrian, corrupted through and through by Jewish gold, the *Jewry*," in "Estadística social," *La Santa Bohemia y otros artículos* (Madrid: Celeste Editions, 1999), 72. See also the moment in Ramón del Valle-Inclán's *Luces de Bohemia* (1924) in which Max Estrella, a character based

on Alejandro Sawa, jokes around with another character about beginning a revolution by destroying the Jews of Barcelona. Valle-Inclán, *Luces de Bohemia*, in *Obras completas*, 2 vols. (Madrid: Editorial Plenitud, 1954), 1: 915.

134. Bab, *Die Berliner Bohème*, 39.

135. See also how this author toys with the image of Jews in bohemia in his stories "Ein aufrechter Edelmann" (153–99) and "Schofeles und Bofeles" (201–28) in *Der Topf der Danaiden und andere Geschichten aus der deutschen Bohême* (Berlin: Vita, 1906).

136. Oscar Wilde, *The Picture of Dorian Gray*, ed. Donald L. Lawler (New York: W. W. Norton, 2007 [orig. 1890/91]), 44; Robert W. Chambers, *In the Quarter* (Teddington, Middlesex: Echo Library, 2007 [orig. 1894]), 23.

137. Henry James, *The Tragic Muse* (1890), *The Novels and Tales of Henry James*. Volume and page numbers are given within the text.

138. Philarète Chasles, *Mémoires, Oeuvres de Philarète Chasles*, 2 vols., 2nd ed. (Paris: G. Charpentier, 1876), 327–28.

139. Viktor Mann, *Wir waren fünf: Bildnis der Familie Mann* (Konstanz: Südverlag, 1949), 147.

140. For his view of gypsies as but a pale reflection of the paganism of old, see the passage from his 1903 "Hestia" quoted by Hans Eggert Schröder, *Ludwig Klages: Die Geschichte Seines Lebens/Erster Teil: Die Jugend*, in Ludwig Klages, *Sämtliche Werke*, ed. Ernst Frauchiger, Gerhard Funke, Karl J. Groffmann, Robert Heiss, and Hans Eggert Schröder, 10 vols. (Bonn: H. Bouvier, 1964–69), 1: 340. (This biography appears as a two-volume *Supplement* to the *Werke*.)

141. Schröder, *Ludwig Klages, Sämtliche Werke*, 1: 242. On how Klages customarily used the word *Jew* see Theodor Lessing, *Einmal und nie wieder* (Gütersloh: Bertelsmann, 1969 [orig. 1935]), 421–22. See also Robert E. Norton's portrayal of Klages and his associates throughout *Secret Germany: Stefan George and His Circle* (Ithaca: Cornell University Press, 2002).

142. Max Horkheimer and Theodor W. Adorno, *Dialectic of Enlightenment: Philosophical Fragments*, ed. Gunzelin Schmid Noerr, trans. Edmund Jephcott (Stanford: Stanford University Press, 2002 [orig. 1944]), 165.

143. Mühsam, "Ascona" (1905), in *Ascona: Vereinigte Texte aus den Jahren 1905, 1930, und 1931* (Zurich: Sanssouci Verlag, 1979), 67–68.

CHAPTER 2. MAGGIE, NOT A CHILD OF THE STREETS

1. Auguste Ricard, *La grisette: Roman de moeurs*, 4 vols. (Paris: Lecointe and Durey, 1827; rep. Stuttgart: Belser Verlag, 1989), 2: 177.

2. See Théophile Gautier, *Mademoiselle de Maupin* (1835), *Oeuvres complètes*, 5 vols. (Paris: Charpentier, 1877–94; rep. Geneva: Slatkine Reprints, 1978), 5: 56.

3. See Louis Honoré Fréchette, *Les amours et aventures galantes des grisettes* (Paris: A. Mie, n.d.).

4. Frank Wedekind, *Die Tagebücher: Ein erotisches Leben*, ed. Gerhard Hay (Frankfurt am Main: Athenäum, 1986), 143. This entry is dated July 3, 1892.

5. On this topic see François Gasnault, *Guinguettes et lorettes: Bals publics et danse sociale à Paris entre 1830 et 1870* (Paris: Aubier, 1986). For other discussions of the grisette not otherwise cited below, see also Joëlle Guillais-Maury, "La grisette," in *Madame ou Mademoiselle? Itinéraires de la solitude féminine XVIIIe—XXe siècle*, ed. Arlette Farge and Chrisiane Klapisch-Zuber (Mayenne: Éditions Montalba, 1984); and Paul Jarry, *Étudiants et grisettes romantiques* (Paris: Le Goupy, 1927).

6. Edith Wharton, *The House of Mirth* (1905), in *Novels*, ed. R. W. B. Lewis (New York: Library of America, 1985), 301.

7. Karl Marx, *Grundrisse: Foundations of the Critique of Political Economy*, trans. Martin Nicolaus (New York: Random House, 1973 [orig. 1857–58]), 611.

8. Alexandre Privat d'Anglemont, *Voyage à travers Paris, 1: Le Prado* (Paris: Chez Paulier, 1846), 58, 81. Cited hereafter as *Le Prado*. For my translation of Privat's use of "nègres" as "negroes," see note 89 in Chapter 4.

9. Privat d'Anglemont, *Le Prado*, 79.

10. S[imon]-J[ude] Honnorat, *Dictionnaire Provençal-Français, ou dictionnaire de la langue d'oc*, 3 vols. (Digne: Repos, 1846–48), 2: 380.

11. Thomas Hardy, *Jude the Obscure*, ed. Norman Page, 2nd ed. (New York: W. W. Norton, 1999 [orig. 1895]), 96.

12. See Ernest Desprez, "Les grisettes à Paris," in Jules Janin et al., *Paris, ou le livre des cent-et-un* (Paris: Ladvocat, 1831–34), 6: 211–12.

13. Jean de la Fontaine, "Joconde," *Contes et nouvelles en vers*, 4 vols. (London: N.p., 1778 [orig. 1665]), 1: 14.

14. G[ustav] L[ouis] M[aurice] Strauss, *Reminiscences of an Old Bohemian*, new ed. (London: Downey, 1895 [orig. 1883]), 122.

15. Honoré de Balzac, "La grisette" (1831), *Paris: Morceaux choisis* (Hibouc, 2007), 38, at http://www.hibouc.net/lib/balzac-paris.swf.

16. Louis Huart, *Physiologie de la grisette* (Paris: Aubert [1841]), 46–47.

17. Louis-Sébastien Mercier, *Tableau de Paris*, rev. ed., 12 vols. (Amsterdam: N.p., 1782–88), 8: 133.

18. See Hans Wachenhusen, *Die Grisette: Ein Pariser Sittenbild*, 3rd ed. (Berlin: Verlags Comptoir, 1855), 8.

19. On this point and others related to this essay, see the important work of Jean-Claude Caron, *Générations romantiques: Les étudiants de Paris et le Quartier Latin (1814–1851)* (Paris: Armand Colin, 1991), esp. 197–222.

20. Deux étudiants, *Physiologie de la Chaumière, suivi de l'hymne sacré* (Paris: Bohaire, 1841), 6.

21. In this regard, the changes *grisette* underwent in successive editions of the *Dictionnaire de l'Académie française* are instructive. In 1694 this word is defined as a contemptuous term for a young woman from a low station in life; in 1740 and 1762, this reference to a young woman (now of *mediocre* rather than *basse* station) is no longer associated with

contempt; and in 1835 the entry specifies that in its "familiar" meaning *grisette* refers to "a coquettish and gay young female worker."

22. See Privat d'Anglemont, *Le Prado*, 37.

23. P[ierre]-J[ean] de Béranger, "Les infidélités de Lisette" (1813), *Oeuvres*, new ed., 2 vols. (Paris: Garnier Frères, 1876), 1: 112.

24. See Mary Gluck's discussion of the identification of the grisette with popular literature in *Popular Bohemia: Modernism and Urban Culture in Nineteenth-Century Paris* (Cambridge, Mass.: Harvard University Press, 2005), 40–41.

25. See Wachenhusen, *Die Grisette*, 5. For a contemporary account that seeks to debunk this storied romance of the student and the grisette, see F.-F. A. Béraud, *Les filles publiques de Paris, et la police qui les régit*, 2 vols. in 1 (Paris: Desforges, 1839), 2: 310.

26. Champfleury [Jules Fleury-Husson, pseud.], *Les aventures de Mademoiselle Mariette*, new ed. (Paris: Michel Lévy Frères, 1863 [orig. 1853]), 160, 108. See also Louis Lurine, *La treizième arrondissement de Paris* (Paris: Lamiche, 1850).

27. Alfred de Musset, *La confession d'un enfant du siècle*, ed. Gérard Barrier (Paris: Gallimard, 1973 [orig. 1836]), 28.

28. Wachenhusen, *Schmetterlinge* (Berlin: J. C. Huber, 1857), 88.

29. Mark Twain, *The Innocents Abroad, or the New Pilgrim's Progress*, 2 vols. (New York: P. F. Collier and Son, 1911 [orig. 1869]), 1: 147.

30. Paul Lindau, *Alfred de Musset* (Berlin: A. Hofmann, 1877), 230. Lindau's analysis was far from novel; in 1861 Antonio Watripon was already objecting to those who claimed grisettes had never really existed in his *Souvenirs du Quartier Latin* (Paris: Lucien Marpon, 1861), 13–14.

31. Henry Murger, *Scènes de la vie de bohème*, ed. Loïc Chotard and Graham Robb (Paris: Gallimard, 1988), 121.

32. Th[éodore] Barrière and H[enry] Murger, *La vie de Bohème*, rev. ed. (Paris: Calmann Lévy, 1896 [orig. 1849]), 94.

33. Champfleury, "L'homme aux figures de cire," *Les excentriques*, 2nd ed. (Paris: Calmann Lévy, 1890 [orig. 1852]; rep. Geneva: Slatkine Reprints, 1967), 318.

34. Mercier, *Tableau de Paris*, 8: 134.

35. Murger, *Scènes de la vie de bohème*, 311.

36. Émile Souvestre, *L'échelle des femmes*, new ed. (Paris: Calmann Lévy, 1884 [orig. 1835]), 131.

37. Janin, *Un hiver à Paris* (Paris: L. Curmer and Aubert, 1843), 266.

38. Balzac, *La Duchesse de Langeais* (1834), in *La comédie humaine*, ed. Pierre-Georges Castex, 12 vols. (Paris: Éditions Gallimard, 1977), 5: 1000.

39. See Caron, *Générations romantiques*, 206.

40. Émile de La Bédollièrre, "L'étudiant en droit," in *Les français peints par eux-mêmes: Encyclopédie morale du dix-neuvième siècle*, ed. Léon Curmer and Pierre Bouttier (Paris: Omnibus, 2003 [orig. 1840–42]), 46.

41. Deux étudiants, *Physiologie de la Chaumière*, 3; A[uguste] Luchet, "Physiologie du quartier Latin," in Anon., *Almanach des grisettes et des bals de Paris pour 1848: Lions, étudiants, reines de Mabille, lorettes* (Paris: Librarie littéraire et politique, 1848), 33.

42. Balzac, "Un prince de la bohème," ed. Patrick Berthier, *La Comédie humaine*, 7: 809.

43. Paul de Kock, "Les grisettes," *Nouveau tableau de Paris au XIXme siècle* [ed. Henri Martin], 7 vols. (Paris: Madame Charles-Béchet, 1834–35), 1: 178.

44. Wedekind, "An Armin Wedekind" (14 March 1892), *Gesammelte Briefe*, ed. Fritz Strich, 2 vols. (Munich: Georg Müller, 1924), 1: 231.

45. See Henry Murger, *Scènes de la vie de bohème*, 236–37. Murger also showed, however, that this boast might prove difficult to maintain, as with the friends divided by a woman in "Le dernière rendez-vous" (1851) and "Le bonhomme jadis" (1856).

46. It is notable in this regard, however, that, in addition to providing a sly sketch of a Murger-like character, *The Adventures of Mademoiselle Mariette* also includes a moment in which the heroine is brought to say of her lover, "Gérard doesn't notice his own contradictions and his perpetual lies." See Champfleury, *Les aventures de Mademoiselle Mariette*, 209.

47. Murger, *Les buveurs d'eau* (1855), *Oeuvres complètes*, 12 vols. in 6 (Paris: [Michel Lévy], 1855–61; rep. Geneva: Slatkine Reprints, 1971), 1: 13.

48. Murger, *Le pays Latin* (1855), *Oeuvres complètes*, 4: 126.

49. Nadar [Gaspard-Félix Tournachon, pseud.], in Trois Buveurs d'Eau [Adrien François Lelioux, Léon Noël, and Félix Nadar], *Histoire de Mürger pour servir à l'histoire de la vraie Bohème* (Paris: J. Hetzel, 1862), 240. Murger had earlier used this line in "Le manchon de Francine," which first appeared as an episode of his *Scènes de la bohème* in *Le Corsaire-Satan* in 1847.

50. Nadar, *Histoire de Mürger*, 241. For this line in the play, see Murger and Barrière, *La vie de bohème*, 104. Lucile, who died of consumption, is identified as the original of Mimi by Alexander Schanne, one of Murger's intimates from his early days, although Schanne also says that Mimi was a composite of all the women Murger had known, including a childhood love. See Schanne, *Souvenirs de Schaunard* (Paris: G. Charpentier, 1887), 176.

51. Théodore Muret, "Le Quartier Latin," *Nouveau tableau de Paris au XIXme siècle*, 189.

52. Souvestre, *L'échelle des femmes*, 126.

53. Murger, *Scènes de la vie de bohème*, 363.

54. Janin, "La grisette," in *Les français peints par eux-mêmes*, ed. Curmer and Bouttier, 36.

55. Janin, "La grisette," in *Les français peints par eux-mêmes*, ed. Curmer and Bouttier, 38.

56. Victor Rozier, *Les bals publics à Paris* (Paris: Gustave Havard, 1855), 63; Lurine, *Le treizième arrondissement de Paris*, 37.

57. De Kock and Charles Labie, *Le commis et la grisette* (Paris: Chez Marchant, 1834), 8.

58. Charles Coligny, "Henry Murger et la Bohème," *L'artiste*, n.s., 11 (15 February 1861): 75.

59. Giacomo Puccini, *La Bohème: An Opera in Four Acts* (New York: G. Ricordi, 1917 [orig. 1896]), 28.

60. Deux étudiants, *Physiologie de la Chaumière*, 61.

61. Murger, *Scènes de la vie de bohème*, 234.

62. Charles Fourier, *Théorie des quatres mouvements et des destinées générales* (1808), in *Théorie des quatres mouvements et des destinées générales suivi du Nouveau monde amoureux*, ed. Simone Debout-Oleszkiewicz (Paris: Les Presses du réel, 1998), 183, 184.

63. Theodor Adorno, *Aesthetic Theory*, ed. Gretel Adorno and Rolf Tiedemann, trans. Robert Hullot-Kentor (Minneapolis: University of Minnesota Press, 1997), 136.

64. See, for instance, the outburst on lost revolutionary energies interjected into a pamphlet describing a dance hall and the grisettes who flock there in Privat d'Anglemont, *La Closerie des Lilas: Quadrille en prose* (Paris: J. Frey, 1848), 38–39; and the comparable chapter—bitter, self-mocking, and satirical—entitled "De l'indifférence de la Chaumière en matières politiques" in Deux étudiants, *Physiologie de la Chaumière*, 19–28.

65. Ricard, *La grisette*, 3: 7.

66. Privat d'Anglemont, *Le Prado*, 82.

67. Privat d'Anglemont, *La Closerie des Lilas*, 63.

68. Privat d'Anglemont, *Le Prado*, 81. This expression seems to have been, or to have become, something of a commonplace; Wedekind, for instance, used it in *Pandora's Box* (1904). See Wedekind, *Die Büchse der Pandora*, *Gesammelte Werke*, 9 vols. (Munich: G. Müller, 1920–21), 3: 175.

69. Privat d'Anglemont, "Quatre lettres à Eugène Sue," ed. Pierre Citron, *Revue des sciences humaines* 103 (1961): 393. This letter was written in 1843.

70. Edmond and Jules de Goncourt, *Journal: Mémoires de la vie littéraire*, ed. Robert Ricatte, 22 vols. (Monaco: Les Éditions de l'Imprimerie Nationale de Monaco, 1956), 2: 72.

71. Friedrich Nietzsche, *Jenseits von Gut und Böse: Vorspiel einer Philosophie der Zukunft* (Leipzig: C. G. Naumann, 1886), 189. Nietzsche pointedly uses the masculine form of the French term *commis*, "clerk," rather than the female *commise*.

72. See Nadar, "La vie et la mort de Lequeux," *Quand j'étais étudiant*, 2nd ed. (Paris: Michel Lévy Frères, 1858 [orig. 1856]), 87–88.

73. For his dating of the death of the grisette, see Watripon, *Souvenirs du Quartier Latin* (Paris: Lucien Marpon, 1861), 14. For "Mon Vieux Quarter Latin," see Nadar, *Chants et chansons de la bohême* (Paris: J. Bry Aîné, 1853), 56–58; and Watripon, *Les trois âges du pays Latin* (Paris: C. Noblet, [1863]), 21–23. Under the title "Le vieux Quartier Latin" this also appears in Jules Thelmier, ed., *La chanson du vieux Quartier Latin* (Paris: Sous les Galeries de l'Odéon, 1891), 2. In *La cité des intellectuels: Scènes cruelles et plaisantes de la vie littéraire des gens de lettres au XIXe siècle*, 3rd ed. (Paris: H. Daragon, [1905]), 468–69, Firmin Maillard wrote about Antonio Watripon and Jules Choux quarreling over their rival claims to authorship of this song, claiming that they both contributed to it but that the real author was Charles Lepère, the future minister of the interior.

74. See Privat d'Anglemont, *Le Prado*, 33; Murger, *Scènes de la vie de bohème*, 311; Louise Colet, *Lui: Roman contemporain* (Paris: Michel Lévy Frères, 1864 [orig. 1860]; rep. Geneva: Slatkine Reprints, 1973), 74; and De Kock, *La reine des grisettes* (Paris: Arnauld de Vresse, 1864), 7. See also Eugène Vermersch's claim that in 1864 one can still meet with at least "the debris of a race that is tending more and more to disappear, that of the grisettes," in *Le Latium moderne: Lettre à un étudiant en droit* (Paris: E. Sausset, 1864), 17.

75. See Diego Vicente Tejera, "Celia," *Poesías*, 3rd ed., rev. (Paris: Maréchal and Montorier, 1893), 225–39. For *Trilby*, see below. On the advancing figure of the female bohemian, see, e.g., the alarmed article by E[dmond] Lepelletier, "La bohème féminine," *L'Écho de Paris* (11 August 1884): 1.

76. Champfleury, *Souvenirs et portraits de jeunesse* (Paris: [E. Dentu], 1872 [orig. 1863]; rep. Geneva: Slatkin Reprints, 1970), 296.

77. See E[lme-Marie] Caro, "La fin de la bohème," *Revue des deux mondes* 94 (15 July 1871): 256.

78. See P[ierre]-J[oseph] Proudhon, *La pornocratie ou les femmes dans les temps modernes* (Paris: A. Lacroix, 1875), 162–63 and 229. Also, on this question of the woman in public in this era, see Aruna D'Souza and Tom McDonough, eds., *The Invisible Flâneuse? Gender, Public Space, and Visual Culture in Nineteenth-Century Paris* (Manchester: Manchester University Press, 2006).

79. Proudhon, *La pornocratie*, 227.

80. Edmond and Jules de Goncourt, *Manette Salomon* (Paris: Union Générale d'Éditions, 1979 [orig. 1867]), 194, 394. On the relation between Proudhon's attitudes toward women and those of other French writers of his time, see Charles Bernheimer, *Figures of Ill Repute: Representing Prostitution in Nineteenth-Century France* (Cambridge, Mass.: Harvard University Press, 1989), esp. 200–233.

81. Béraud, *Les filles publiques de Paris*, 2: 303.

82. J. Fitzgerald Molloy, *It Is No Wonder: A Story of Bohemian Life*, 3 vols. (London: Hurst and Blackett, 1882), 1: 50.

83. Alexandre Schanne, *Souvenirs de Schaunard* (Paris: G. Charpentier, 1887), 319.

84. Lily Curry, *A Bohemian Tragedy* (Philadelphia: T. B. Peterson and Brothers, 1886), 254.

85. Henry S. Brooks, "A Catastrophe in Bohemia," *A Catastrophe in Bohemia and Other Stories* (New York: Charles L. Webster, 1893), 27.

86. See Marie Le Baron, *The Villa Bohemia* (New York: Kochendoerfer and Urie, 1882).

87. William Dean Howells, *The Coast of Bohemia* (New York: Harper and Brothers, 1893), 48.

88. Margaret Sherwood, *A Puritan Bohemia* (New York: Macmillan, 1896), 11, 12.

89. Mercier, *Tableau de Paris*, 8: 135.

90. Charlotte Brontë, *The Professor* (New York: Harper and Brothers, 1900 [orig. 1857]; rep. New York: AMS Press, 1973), 239.

91. Brontë, *The Professor*, 192.

92. William Makepeace Thackeray, *Vanity Fair*, ed. John Sutherland (Oxford: Oxford University Press, 1983 [orig. 1848]), 369.

93. Critics who see Sue Bridehead as Hardy's botched or biased portrayal of the "New Woman" of this period mistake her cultural type, I believe, although this is not to say that contemporary discourse about the New Woman is irrelevant to the interpretation of this novel.

94. See the disdainful, smirking portrayal of grisettes as money-hungry amateur whores in J.-B. Ambs-Dalès, *Amours et intrigues des grisettes de Paris, ou revue des belles dites de la petite vertue*, 3rd ed. (Paris: Roy-Terry, 1830). A leftist counterpart to this conservative portrayal appears in Eliphas Lévi's Fourierist tract *Paris dansant, ou les filles d'Héroiade* (Paris: Chez tous les marchands de nouveautés, 1845). Similar portrayals appear in Satan [Georges-Marie Mathieu-Dairnvaell, pseud.], *Physiologie des étudiants, des grisettes et des bals de Paris*

([Paris]: G. Dairnvaell, 1849); Louis de Montchamp, *Les bohémiennes de l'amour: Scènes de la vie parisienne* (Paris: Fruchard, 1859); and Germain Picard, *La vérité sur le Quartier Latin* (Paris: Chez tous les libraires, 1865).

95. Murger, "Le dernier rendez-vous," *Oeuvres complètes*, 2: 103.

96. Ricard, *La grisette*, 4: 21.

97. George Eliot, *The Mill on the Floss*, ed. Gordon S. Haight (Oxford: Oxford University Press, 1980 [orig. 1860]). Page numbers to this work are given within the text.

98. Eliot, *The Journals of George Eliot*, ed. Margaret Harris and Judith Johnson (Cambridge: Cambridge University Press, 1998), 71.

99. See Eliot, "Pictures of Life in French Novels," *Saturday Review* 2 (17 May 1856): 69–70.

100. Franziska Gräfin zu Reventlow, *Ellen Olestjerne* (1903), in *Autobiographisches*, ed. Else Reventlow (Munich: Albert Langen, 1980), 220.

101. Huart, *Physiologie de la grisette*, 27.

102. See "GE to John Blackwood" (3 January 1860), in Eliot, *The George Eliot Letters*, ed. Gordon S. Haight, 9 vols. (New Haven: Yale University Press, 1978), 3: 240. Hereafter referred to as *Letters*.

103. Edward M. Whitty, *The Bohemians of London* (Philadelphia: T. B. Peterson and Brothers, 1864 [orig. 1857]), 152.

104. For the proposal Eliot rejected, see Gordon S. Haight, *George Eliot: A Biography* (New York: Oxford University Press, 1968), 56. I am also indebted to Haight for some of the other information in this paragraph.

105. Eliot, "The Morality of Wilhelm Meister" (1855), *Essays of George Eliot*, ed. Thomas Pinney (New York: Columbia University Press, 1963), 146.

106. For Eliot's public image, see, for instance, the invocations of her name in Curry, *A Bohemian Tragedy*, 221; George Moore, *Confessions of a Young Man*, ed. Susan Dick (Montreal: McGill–Queen's University Press, 1972 [orig. 1888]), 138; and Robert Appleton [Roman Ivanovitch Zubof, pseud.], *Violet: The American Sappho: A Realistic Novel of Bohemia* (Boston: Franklin, 1894), 150.

107. "GE to Mrs. Nassau John Senior" (4 October 1869), in Eliot, *Letters*, 5: 58.

108. "Mme Eugène Bodichon to GE" (26 April 1859) in Eliot, *Letters*, 3: 56.

109. "Charles Eliot Norton to George William Curtis" (29 January 1869) in Eliot, *Letters*, 5: 7.

110. "Mrs. Elizabeth Gaskell to GE" (10 November 1859) in Eliot, *Letters*, 3: 197.

111. "GE to Vincent Holbeche" (13 June 1857) in Eliot, *Letters*, 2: 349.

112. "GE to Mrs. Charles Bray" (4 September 1855) in Eliot, *Letters*, 2: 214.

113. "GE to Mme Eugène Bodichon" (16 December 1860) in Eliot, *Letters*, 3: 366.

114. Christian Reid [Frances Christine Fisher, pseud.], *A Daughter of Bohemia* (New York: D. Appleton, 1874). Page numbers are given within the text.

115. Ada Clare, "The Question of Humor," *The Golden Era* (17 April 1864): 4.

116. George Alfred Townsend, "Married Abroad," *Bohemian Days: Three American Tales* (New York: H. Campbell, 1880). Page references are given within the text.

117. Cf. Eliot's description, in her discussion of the limit to "the sphere of the artist," of Balzac as "perhaps the most wonderful writer of fiction the world has ever seen" but one who "in many of his novels has overstepped this limit." Eliot, "The Morality of Wilhelm Meister," *Essays of George Eliot*, 146.

CHAPTER 3. THE INDIGNITY OF LABOR

1. See Trois Buveurs d'Eau [Adrien François Lélioux, Léon Noël, Nadar (Félix Tour-nachon, pseud.)], *Histoire de Mürger pour servir à l'histoire de la vraie bohème*, 2nd ed. (Paris: J. Hetzel, [1862]). Hereafter referred to as *Histoire de Mürger*. The biographical de-tails that I give here are adapted from the accounts of Lélioux and Noël in this volume and from Eugène de Mirecourt, *Henry Murger* (Paris: Gustave Havard, 1856); Théodore Pelloquet, *Henry Murger* (Paris: Librarie Nouvelle, 1861); Alfred Delvau, *Henry Murger et la bohème* (Paris: Bachelin-Deflorenne, 1866); Ch[arles] de Ricault d'Héricault, *Murger et son coin: Souvenirs très vagabonds et très personnels* (Paris: Louis Trémaux, 1896); Georges Montorgueil, *Henry Murger: Romancier de la bohème*, 7th ed. ([Paris]: Bernard Grasset, 1928); and Robert Baldick, *The First Bohemian: The Life of Henry Murger* (London: Hamish Hamilton, 1961). Murger's name was originally Henri Murger; when he began to publish he took to spelling it Henry Mürger, thinking the *y* and the *tréma* made it more stylish. For the sake of consistency, except when citing others I reproduce it in this work in the form in which it most often appeared in his own time.

2. The topic of worker poets was much discussed at this time. See, for instance, the article by Eugène Lerminier, "De la littérature des ouvriers," *Revue des deux mondes* 28 (15 December 1841): 955–76, and the articles written in response by George Sand, "Dialogue familier sur la poésie des prolétaires," *La revue indépendante* (January 1842): 37–65, and "Second dialogue familier sur la poésie des prolétaires," *La revue indépendante* (September 1842): 597–619. Louis Veuillot showed his knowledge of this discussion, and of Murger's background, when he chose to include in an insulting commentary on his work, and on bo-hemia in general, a characterization of Murger's poetry as the "true verse of an artisan-poet, according to the classic taste of 1840." See Veuillot, *Les odeurs de Paris*, 2nd. ed. ([Paris]: Palmé, 1867), 90.

3. Léon Noël, in Trois Buveurs, *Histoire de Mürger*, 90.

4. A slightly different account is given by Montorgueil (*Henry Murger*, 80), who says the break happened when the police visited Murger's home with questions about his girlfriend, a married woman who, with her husband, was being pursued for theft and other crimes.

5. The original title of this work, when it appeared at irregular intervals in *Le Corsaire-Satan*, was *Scènes de la bohème*. It acquired its present title, under which it is best known, with the third edition of its book publication. My quotations from this work are from Henry Murger, *Scènes de la vie de bohème*, ed. Loïc Chotard and Graham Robb (Paris: Gal-limard, 1988 [orig. 1851]). For its dramatic adaptation I quote from Th[éodore] Barrière and

Murger, *La vie de bohème* (Paris: Calmann Lévy, 1896 [orig. 1849]). For all other works by Murger citations are from his *Oeuvres complètes*, 12 vols. in 6 (Paris: [Michel Lévy], 1855–61; rep. Geneva: Slatkine Reprints, 1971). Page numbers are given within the text.

6. Henry Murger, from a letter dated 22 September 1842, reproduced in Trois Buveurs, *Histoire de Mürger*, 140.

7. Murger, from a letter dated 30 July 1844, reproduced in Trois Buveurs, *Histoire de Mürger*, 164.

8. For a contemporary essay that describes the "Bohemians of today" (4: 9) with contempt, but in images close to those that Murger would help to popularize, see Félix Pyat, "Les artistes," in [Henry Martin, ed.], *Nouveau tableau de Paris au XIXme siècle*, 7 vols. (Paris: Madame Charles-Béchat, 1834–35), 4: 1–22.

9. For Murger's description of great artists of all ages as bohemians, see the "Préface" to his *Scènes de la vie de bohème*, 29–30; for his mention of Balzac's novel as the text imitated in the founding of his bohemian "Water Drinkers," see *Scènes*, 290.

10. Armand de Pontmartin, "Un jeune écrivain: Étude morale: Henry Murger et ses oeuvres," *Revue des deux mondes* 35 (1 October 1861): 703, 711.

11. See also, for instance, the account of the model Sarah Brown, the "Queen of Bohemia" in the Paris of the 1880s and 1890s, in Marie Lathers, *Bodies of Art: French Literary Realism and the Artist's Model* (Lincoln: University of Nebraska Press, 2001), 243–48.

12. Alexandre Privat d'Anglemont, "Quatre lettres à Eugène Sue," ed. Pierre Citron, *Revue des sciences humaines* 103 (July–September 1961): 393. For nineteenth-century analyses similar to Privat's, see, for instance, L[ouis] Clément de Ris, *Portraits à la plume* (Paris: Eugène Didier, 1853 [orig. 1851]), 43; Alphonse de Calonne, *Voyage au pays de Bohême* (Paris: E. Brière, 1852), 12; F. L. [Frédéric Loliée?], "Bohème," *Dictionnaire des dictionnaires: Encyclopédie universelle des lettres, des sciences, et des arts*, ed. Paul Guérin, 4 vols. ([Paris] A. Picard, 1884), 2: 75; and G. P. A., "Il vero nei libri, negli scrittori ed i suoi effetti," *La rassegna nazionale* 23 (1885): 201.

13. See E[lme-Marie] Caro, "La fin de la bohème," *Revue des deux mondes* 94 (15 July 1871): 241–67. On bohemians and leftist politics, see Jerrold Seigel, *Bohemian Paris: Culture, Politics, and the Boundaries of Bourgeois Life, 1830–1930* (Baltimore: Johns Hopkins University Press, 1986), esp. 181–212. See also Philibert Audebrand's description of Murger's reactionary response to the events of 1848, and of his lodgings at the time in the same apartment house where Proudhon resided, in *Soldats, poètes et tribuns: Petits mémoires du XIXe siècle* (Paris: Calmann Lévy, 1899), 295.

14. See Montorgueil, *Henry Murger*, 202–4. The chapter in question was entitled "Son Excellence Colline" and was replaced by "La toilette des graces."

15. Seigel, *Bohemian Paris*, 291.

16. Quoted in B. Mirkine-Guetzevitch, "Henri Murger, agent secret de la Russie pendant la Revolution de 48," *Nouvelles litteraires, artistiques et scientifiques* 265 (11 December 1927). "The organization of work" was a catchphrase during this period, due in large part to Louis Blanc's *Organisation du travail* (1840).

17. George du Maurier, *Trilby*, *Harper's New Monthly Magazine* 88 (March 1894): 577.

18. Anon., "The Big Rock Candy Mountain," American folk song (traditional).

19. See Iginio Ugo Tarchetti, "Pagini di romanzo" (1868), *Tutte le opere*, ed. Enrico Ghidetti, 2 vols. ([Bologna]: Cappelli Editore, 1967), 2: 548.

20. Thomas Carlyle, *Past and Present* (1843), *The Works of Thomas Carlyle*, 30 vols. (London: Chapman and Hall, 1899), 10: 205. This edition is hereafter cited as *Works*.

21. Léon Faucher, *De la réforme des prisons* (Paris: Angé, 1838), 64.

22. H[onoré]-A[ntoine] Frégier, *Des classes dangereuses de la population dans les grandes villes, et des moyens de les rendre meilleures*, 2 vols. (Paris: J.-B. Baillière, 1840), 1: 281.

23. Carlyle, *Past and Present, Works*, 10: 208.

24. Carlyle, *Sartor Resartus: The Life and Opinions of Herr Teufelsdröckh, Works*, 1: 157.

25. John Ruskin, *Unto This Last*, in *Essays and Belles Lettres* (London: J. M. Dent and Sons, 1907), 162n.

26. Ruskin, *Unto This Last*, in *Essays and Belles Lettres*, 112.

27. Nathaniel Hawthorne, *The Blithedale Romance* (1852), ed. Fredson Bowers, Matthew J. Bruccoli, and L. Neal Smith, *The Centenary Edition of the Works of Nathaniel Hawthorne*, ed. William Charvat and Roy Harvey Pearce, 23 vols. (Columbus: Ohio State University Press, 1962–97), 3: 65.

28. See, e.g., Charles Fourier, *Le nouveau monde industriel et sociétaire, ou invention du procédé d'industrie attrayante et naturelle distribuée en séries passionnées* (Paris: Bossange Père, 1829), 12; and Marx, *The German Ideology* (1845–46), in Marx and Friedrich Engels, *Collected Works*, trans. Richard Dixon et al. (New York: International Publishers, 1975–), 5: 47.

29. Carlyle, "Chartism" (1839), *Works*, 29: 132.

30. George Orwell, *Down and Out in Paris and London* (1933), *The Complete Works of George Orwell*, ed. Peter Hobley Davison, Ian Angus, and Sheila Davison, 20 vols. (London: Secker and Warburg, 1997–98), 1: 102.

31. Paul Lafargue, *Le droit à la paresse* (Paris: François Maspero, 1970 [orig. 1880]). Page references to this work are given within the text. On Lafargue's identification with bohemia, see Seigel, *Bohemian Paris*, 188–89.

32. Marx, *The Communist Manifesto* (1848), *Collected Works*, 6: 500; and Marx, *Capital, Collected Works*, 35: 510.

33. Alejandro Sawa, *Declaración de un vencido* (1887), in *Declaración de un vencido y Criadero de curas*, ed. Francisco Guttiérrez Carbajo (Madrid: Ediciones Atlas, 1999), 166.

34. [George William Curtis], "Editor's Easy Chair," *Harper's New Monthly Magazine* 19 (October 1859): 705.

35. Nadar, *Charles Baudelaire intime: Le poète vierge* (Paris: Obsidiane, 1985 [orig. 1911]), 90. "Saint-Simon" refers to the Comte de Saint-Simon, who began a small but influential socialist movement in the early nineteenth century. "Phalansteries" and "familisteries" are Fourierist terms designating certain forms of communal living arrangements. It is notable in this regard that Henry Clapp Jr., the "King of Bohemia" in antebellum New York City, had earlier worked as a translator of Fourier's writings.

36. Edmond and Jules de Goncourt, *Journal: Mémoires de la vie littéraire*, ed. Robert Ricatte, 22 vols. (Monaco: Les Éditions de l'Imprimerie Nationale de Monaco, 1956), 1: 236. This entry was written in 1856. See also their characterization of "new elements" in the literary world, "without ancestors, without knowledge, without a fatherland in the

past, unconfined by any education, free of all tradition," in their novel *Les hommes de lettres* (Paris: E. Dentu, 1860), 21.

37. See Charles Hugo, *La bohême dorée* (Paris: Michel Lévy Frères, 1859).

38. See, e.g., Henry Brown, *A Parisian Year* (Boston: Roberts Brothers, 1882), 53; and S. J. Adair Fitzgerald, *Sketches from Bohemia: Stories of the Stage, the Study, and the Studio* (London: Tarstow, Denver, 1890), 157–58. Louis Émile Edmond Duranty inserts a joke on this subject in one of his stories, in which a minor academic painter who is outraged by Edouard Manet's *Déjeuner sur l'herbe* (1863) assumes that the artist must be a horrible bohemian dressed in rags, only to be dumbfounded when he sees the elegantly dressed artist. See Duranty, "La simple vie du peintre Louis Martin," in *Les séductions du Chevalier Navoni* (Paris: Librarie de la Société des Gens de Lettres, 1877), 338.

39. Edmond and Jules de Goncourt, *Journal*, 1: 236.

40. E[ugenio] Torelli Viollier, "La bohème" (1878) in *La pubblicistica nel periodo della scapigliatura*, ed. Giuseppe Farinelli (Milan: Istituto Propaganda Libraria, 1984), 131.

41. Adolphe d'Ennery and [Eugène] Grangé, *Les bohémiens de Paris*, in *Magasin théatral: Choix des pièces nouvelles jouées sur tous les théatres de Paris, v. 30* (Paris: Marchant, 1846 [orig. 1843]), 8–9. This play was almost immediately translated into English, presented as the work of Charles Zachary Barnett, and put on stage in London; see Barnett, *The Bohemians of Paris! Or, The Mysteries of Crime!* (London: John Duncombe [1843]).

42. Auguste Vitu, "Notice géographique, historique, politique et littéraire sur la Bohême" (1849), in *Les mille et une nuits du théâtre*, 8th ser. (Paris: Paul Ollendorff, 1891), 17. See also the description of how the word *bohemia*, "invented, some twenty years ago, by six or seven witty men, has been disfigured by vaudeville-writers and playwrights" in Anon. [Taxile Delord, Arnould Frémy, and Edmond Texier], *Paris-Bohème* (Paris: Librairie d'Alphonse Taride, 1854), 6.

43. In a narrative in *Les excentriques*, "L'élève de Moreau" (1846), Champfleury similarly disparaged the title *Bohémiens de Paris* in relation to the meaning and to the spelling—*Bohèmes*, with the *accent grave*—preferred by his crowd. See Champfleury [Jules Fleury-Husson, pseud.], "L'élève de Moreau," *Les excentriques*, 2nd ed. (Paris: Calman Lévy, 1890 [orig. 1852]; rep. Geneva: Slatkine Reprints, 1967), 215.

44. See also Francisque Michel and Édouard Fournier's reference, in *La grande bohême: Histoire des royaumes d'argot et de thunes du duché d'Egypte, des enfants de la matte, des races maudites et des classes réprouvées depuis les temps les plus reculés jusqu'à nos jours* (Paris: Rue du Pont-de-Lodi, [1850]), to "those *plebeians* of the great cities, . . . that populace, sovereign in vice, always the same in its disorders, always stampeding toward the same objects of desire, floundering in the same mire of impure morals" (3). A similar sense of the word appears in Theodor Mundt, *Paris und Louis Napoleon: Neue Skizzen aus dem französischen Kaiserreich*, 2 vols. (Paris: Otto Janke, 1858), in which he writes of "these bohemians, these *Viveurs*, these Mohicans, of which the newest French literature is full," all of whom live on "the borderline of the criminal world" (168–69). "*Viveurs*" is a reference to Xavier de Montépin's *Les viveurs de Paris* (1852), "Mohicans" to the novel by Alexandre Dumas, *Les Mohicans de Paris* (1854).

45. A[lexandre] Privat d'Anglemont, *Paris inconnu* (Paris: Adolphe Delahays, 1861), 100.

46. See Peter Paterson [James Glass Bertram, pseud.], *Glimpses of Real Life as Seen in the Theatrical World and in Bohemia: Being the Confessions of Peter Paterson, a Strolling Comedian* (Edinburgh: W. P. Nimmo, 1864; rep. Hamden, Conn.: Archon Books, 1979).

47. Marx, *The Eighteenth Brumaire of Louis Bonaparte, Collected Works*, 1: 149, 157. The formulation evidently enjoyed some popularity; see Friedrich Szarvady's description of Louis Bonaparte as "a princely Bohemian" in *Paris: Politische und unpolitische Studien und Bilder, 1848–52* (Berlin: Franz Dunder, 1852), 1: 146. (Vol. 1 was the only volume to appear.) See also the description of "professional conspirators" as "democratic bohemians of proletarian origin" in Marx and Friedrich Engels, "*Les Conspirateurs* par A. Chenu . . ." (1850), *Collected Works*, 10: 317.

48. Carlyle, "The Nigger Question" (1849), *Works*, 29: 367; and "Model Prisons" (1850), *Works*, 20: 80.

49. Ruskin, *Time and Tide* (1867), in *Time and Tide* and *Munera Pulveris* (New York: Macmillan, 1928), 40.

50. Champfleury, *Souvenirs et portraits de jeunesse* (Paris: [E. Dentu], 1872; rep. Geneva: Slatkine Reprints, 1970), 94.

51. G[eorge] Gregory, *The Life of Thomas Chatterton, with Criticisms of his Genius and Writings, and a Concise View of the Controversy Surrounding Rowley's Poems* (London: G. Kearsley, 1789), 25.

52. Quoted in John Dix, *The Life of Thomas Chatterton* (London: Hamilton, Adams, 1837), 237.

53. Thomas Chatterton, from a letter to his sister, Mary Newton, quoted in Sir Herbert Croft, *Love and Madness: In a Series of Letters, One of which Contains the Original Account of Chatterton*, rev. ed. (London: G. Kearsley, 1786), 199.

54. Gregory, *The Life of Thomas Chatterton*, 100.

55. Mrs. Edkins, quoted in Dix, *The Life of Thomas Chatterton*, 314. The quotation is taken from an appendix, "Mrs. Edkin's Account," that provides the testimony of a friend of Chatterton's mother.

56. Thomas Warton, *The History of English Poetry, from the Close of the Eleventh to the Commencement of the Eighteenth Century*, 4 vols. (London: J. Dodsley, 1774–81), 2: 539–40.

57. J.B., "Preface," in Thomas Chatterton, *Miscellanies in Prose and Verse* (London: Fielding and Walker, 1778), xviii.

58. Croft, *Love and Madness*, 222.

59. Gregory, *The Life of Thomas Chatterton*, 107, 48–49.

60. See the letter from Horace Walpole reproduced in Gregory, *The Life of Thomas Chatterton*, 61n.

61. William Wordsworth, "Resolution and Independence," in *The Poetical Writings of Wordsworth*, ed. Paul D. Sheats (Boston: Houghton Mifflin, 1982), 281.

62. Chatterton, from a letter to an acquaintance, Mr. Barret, quoted in Dix, *The Life of Thomas Chatterton*, 243.

63. Chatterton, from a letter dated 14 May 1770, reproduced in Croft, *Love and Madness*, 198.

64. Alfred de Vigny, "Préface," *Chatterton*, in *Théâtre* (Paris: Alphonse Lemerre, 1885), 258. Further page references to this preface and this play are given within the text.

65. Hawthorne, *The Blithedale Romance*, *Works*, 3: 66.

66. A[ugustin] Jal, "L'école de peinture, 1800–1834," *Nouveau tableau de Paris au XIXme siècle*, 3: 277.

67. Franz Liszt, "De la situation des artistes et de leur condition dans la société" (1835), in *Artiste et société*, ed. Rémy Stricker ([Paris]: Flammarion, 1995), 22, 27.

68. See James H. Rubin's comment on the outlawing of artists' guilds during the French Revolution and on the concurrent opening of the profession to the free market in *Courbet* (London: Phaidon, 1997), 31: "As a result, from 1789 to 1838, the number of individuals declaring themselves to be artists in the Paris census records leapt from 354 to 2,159."

69. Alfred Delvau, "Alexandre Privat d'Anglemont," in Privat d'Anglemont, *Paris inconnu*, 6.

70. Nadar, in Trois Buveurs d'Eau, *Histoire de Mürger*, 246–47.

71. Edmond and Jules de Goncourt, *Journal*, 4: 155.

72. Gustave Courbet, "À Pierre-Joseph Proudhon" (July–August 1863), *Correspondance de Courbet*, ed. Petra ten-Doesschate Chu (Paris: Flammarion, 1996), 206. See also the analysis of the relationship of Courbet to Hegel and Proudhon in James Henry Rubin, *Realism and Social Vision in Courbet and Proudhon* (Princeton: Princeton University Press, 1980), 29–37. This entire book is valuable for its analysis of the relation between work and art in this age.

73. Ernesto Bark, "La santa bohemia" (1913), in *La santa bohemia y otros artículos* (Madrid: Biblioteca de la Bohemia, 1999), 36.

74. See, e.g., Fourier, *Le nouveau monde industriel et sociétaire*, 54.

75. See Jacques Lethève, *La vie quotidienne des artistes français au XIXe siècle* (Paris: Hachette, 1968), 158.

76. See Montorgueil, *Henry Murger*, 173.

77. See Philip Mansel, *Paris Between Empires: 1814–1852* (London: John Murray, 2001), 311.

78. Gérard Monnier, *L'art et ses institutions en France: De la révolution à nos jours* (Paris: Gallimard, 1995), 208.

79. See Immanuel Kant, *Critique of the Power of Judgment* (1790), ed. Paul Guyer, trans. Paul Guyer and Eric Matthews (Cambridge: Cambridge University Press, 2000), 183; George Wilhelm Friedrich Hegel, *Aesthetics: Lectures on Fine Art* (1835), trans. T. M. Knox, 2 vols. (Oxford: Oxford University Press, 1998), 1: 11; and Percy Bysshe Shelley, "A Defence of Poetry," in *Shelley's Poetry and Prose*, ed. Donald H. Reiman and Sharon B. Powers (New York: W. W. Norton, 1977), 508. See also Liszt's distinction between artisans and artists in "De la situation des artistes et de leur condition dans la société," *Artiste et société*, 21.

80. Enrique Perez Escrich, *El frac azul: Episodios de un jóven flaco* (Madrid: Manini Hermanos, 1864), 126.

81. Marilyn Brown, *Gypsies and Other Bohemians: The Myth of the Artist in Nineteenth-Century France* (Ann Arbor: UMI Research Press, 1985), 100.

82. Liszt, "De la situation des artistes et de leur condition dans la société," in *Artiste et société*, 29.

83. Charles Asselineau, *Charles Baudelaire: Sa vie et son oeuvre* (1868), in *Baudelaire et Asselineau*, ed. Jacques Crépet and Claude Pichois (Paris: Librarie Nizet, 1953), 100.

84. Anon., "L'esposizione di belle arti in roma," *Nuova antologia di scienze, lettere et arti* 37, 2nd ser. (1883): 534.

85. Privat d'Anglemont, from an 1853 letter to Eugène Sue, in "Quatre lettres à Eugène Sue," ed. Pierre Citron, *Revue des sciences humaines* 103 (July–September 1961): 394.

86. Walter Benjamin, "Paris, The Capital of the Nineteenth Century" (1935), trans. Howard Eiland, in *Selected Writings*, ed. Michael W. Jennings, 4 vols. (Cambridge, Mass.: Harvard University Press, 1996–2003), 3: 40.

87. [George William Curtis], "Editor's Easy Chair," *Harper's New Monthly Magazine* 19 (October 1859): 705.

88. Bob Dylan, "Absolutely Sweet Marie," *Lyrics: 1962–1985* (New York: Alfred A. Knopf, 1985), 233.

89. Mirecourt, *Henry Murger*, 76.

90. Frank Wedekind, *Die Tagebücher: Ein erotisches Leben*, ed. Gerhard Hay (Frankfurt am Main: Athenäum, 1986), 103.

91. See Johann Wolfgang von Goethe, *Wilhelm Meisters Lehrjahre* (1795–96), ed. Wilhelm Voßkamp and Herbert Jaumann, *Sämtliche Werke*, ed. Friedmar Apel et al., 27 vols. (Frankfurt am Main: Deutscher Klassiker Verlag, 1992), 9: 571. In terms of the issue of bohemia's politics, it is interesting that George Sand read this work as prefiguring socialism.

92. Calonne, *Voyage au pays de Bohème*, 11. On this stereotype see Helmut Kreuzer, *Die Boheme: Analyse und Dokumentation der Intellektuellen Subkultur vom 19. Jahrhundert bis zur Gegenwart* (Stuttgart: J. B. Metzlersche Verlagsbuchhandlung, 1971), 244–69.

93. The examples are innumerable; but see, e.g., Veuillot's characterization of bohemians as "a tribe of parasites" in *Les odeurs de Paris*, 84; and the way Georges-Marie Mathieu-Dairnvaell reserves the word *bohemian* for the kind of student who has cultural pretensions but who is a shiftless, idle, unemployed leech upon others, in Satan [Mathieu-Dairnvaell, pseud.], *Physiologie des étudiants, des grisettes et des bals de Paris* ([Paris]: G. Dairnvaell, 1849), 20.

94. Ruskin, *The Political Economy of Art* (1857), in *Essays and Belles Lettres*, 93n.

95. Léon Cladel, *Les martyrs ridicules: Roman parisien* (Plan de la Tour: Éditions d'Aujourd'hui, 1979 [orig. 1862]), 300.

96. William Graham Sumner, *What Social Classes Owe to Each Other* (New York: Harper and Brothers, 1883), 29.

97. Ricardo Palma, *La bohemia de mi tiempo* (1887), in *Recuerdos de España* precedidos de *La bohemia de mi tiempo* (Lima: Imprenta La Industria, 1899), 57.

98. William Makepeace Thackeray, *The Paris Sketch Book of Mr M. A. Titmarsh* (1840), in *The Works of William Makepeace Thackeray*, 26 vols. (London: Smith, Elder, 1901), 16: 48.

99. Gabriel Guillemot, *Le bohême* (Paris: Le Chevalier, 1868), 112.

100. Henry Monnier and Jules Renoult, *Peintres et bourgeois* (Paris: Librarie Nouvelle, 1856), 27.

101. Champfleury, *Souvenirs des funambules* (Paris: Michel Lévy Frères, 1859), 300.

102. Fitz-James O'Brien, "The Bohemian" (1855), in *The Diamond Lens and Other Stories*, ed. William Winter (New York: Charles Scribner's Sons, 1885), 145. See also O'Brien's version of the classic bohemian narrative, in which a young man from the country ceases to be industrious once he falls into the bohemian company of his fellow students in Paris, in "A Paper of All Sorts," *Harper's New Monthly Magazine* 16 (March 1858): 507–15. This anonymously published story is identified as O'Brien's in Francis Wolle, *Fitz-James O'Brien: A Literary Bohemian of the Eighteen-Fifties* (Boulder: University of Colorado Studies, 1944), 157.

103. See Peter Hessler, "Letter from Lishui: Chinese Barbizon: Painting the Outside World," *New Yorker* 85 (26 October 2009): 69.

104. Murger, in a letter to a childhood schoolfellow named Mazuel, quoted in Montorgueil, *Henry Murger*, 146, 145.

105. Pyat, "Les artistes," *Nouveau tableau de Paris au XIXme siècle*, 4: 18.

106. On this point, and for other publication information on which I rely here, see Graham Robb, "Histoire du texte," in Murger, *Scènes de la vie de bohème*, 438–41.

107. D.D., "The Bohemian as 'Gentleman,'" *New-York Saturday Press* 3 (30 June 1860): 2.

108. Quoted in Alejandro Sawa, "La fiesta de la juventud" (1897), in *Crónicas de la Bohemia*, ed. Emilio Chavarría (Madrid: Veintisiete Letras, 2008), 92.

109. Quoted in Delvau, *Henry Murger et la bohème*, 126. Delvau, however, was known for touching up the truth when it suited his purposes to do so. Writing much closer in time to Murger's death, Pelloquet (*Henry Murger*, 34) claims his last words were a simple "adieu" to a friend. Montorgueil (*Henry Murger*, 292–93) reports his last words as a delirious flood of speech, apparently about his mother.

110. Lélioux, in Trois Buveurs d'Eau, *Histoire de Mürger*, 71.

111. Lélioux, in Trois Buveurs d'Eau, *Histoire de Mürger*, 73.

112. Lélioux, in Trois Buveurs d'Eau, *Histoire de Mürger*, 74.

113. Delvau, *Henry Murger et la bohème*, 57–58, 100.

114. Alexandre Schanne, *Souvenirs de Schaunard* (Paris: G. Charpentier, 1887), 270–71.

115. Pelloquet, *Henry Murger*, 22.

116. See A[dolphe] Tabarant, *La vie artistique au temps de Baudelaire* ([Paris]: Mercure de France, 1963), 275.

117. On this point see Montorgueil, *Henry Murger*, 59.

118. In his title Cladel may have been alluding to Murger's description, in the "Préface" to his *Scènes*, of one type of bohemian attitude: "the stoicism of the ridiculous." See Murger, *Scènes de la vie de bohème*, 36.

119. W. C. Morrow, *Bohemian Paris of To-Day*, 3rd ed. (Philadelphia: J. B. Lippincott, 1899), 202.

120. Quoted in Firmin Maillard, *La cité des intellectuels: Scènes cruelles et plaisantes de la vie littéraire des gens de lettres au XIXe siècle*, 3rd ed. (Paris: H. Daragon, 1905), 428.

121. See Cletto Arrighi [Carlo Righetti, pseud.], *La scapigliatura: Romanzo sociale contemporaneo*, ed. Giuseppe Farinelli (Milan: Propaganda Libraria, 1978), 147, where he describes one of his characters, Gustavo, who is cast into poverty when his father dismisses him as an idler.

122. Cladel, *Les martyrs ridicules*, 138–39.

123. Guy de Maupassant, *Bel-Ami*, ed. Gérard Delaissement (Paris: Éditions Garnier Frères, 1959 [orig. 1885]), 47.

124. George Moore, *Confessions of a Young Man*, ed. Susan Dick (Montreal: McGill–Queen's University Press, 1972 [orig. 1888]), 71. This passage elaborates on one in Murger's "Préface" to *Scènes de la vie de bohème*, 41–42, in which Murger describes how bohemians "go everywhere," from elegant salons to popular dances.

125. Friedrich Nietzsche, *The Will to Power*, ed. Walter Kaufmann, trans. Walter Kaufmann and R. J. Hollingdale (New York: Vintage Books, 1968 [orig. c. 1883–88]), 398.

126. From a letter to his friend Mazuel, quoted in Montorgueil, *Henry Murger*, 143.

127. Cf. Friedrich Carl Peterssen's comparison of bohemia to communism and primitive Christian fellowship in "Der Zigeuner," *Genrebilder aus dem modernen Babel* (Stuttgart: A. Kröner, 1870), 25.

128. Nadar, in Trois Buveurs d'Eau, *Histoire de Mürger*, 204.

129. See Firmin Maillard, *Les derniers bohèmes: Henri Murger et son temps* (Paris: Librairie Sartorious, 1874),13–34.

130. John Boyle O'Reilly, *In Bohemia* (Boston: Pilot, 1886), 14–15. On the popularity of O'Reilly's poem, see Emily Hahn, *Romantic Rebels: An Informal History of Bohemianism in America* (Boston: Houghton Mifflin, 1967), 73. On O'Reilly's friendship with Whitman, see Anon., "Whitman's Reminiscences" (1890) and Sylvester Baxter, "Walt Whitman in Boston" (1892), in *Whitman in His Own Times*, ed. Joel Myerson, rev. ed. (Iowa City: University of Iowa Press, 2000), 62–65, 76–89; and Horace Traubel, *With Walt Whitman in Camden*, ed. Sculley Bradley, Gertrude Traubel, Jeanne Chapman, and Robert MacIsaac, 9 vols. (New York: Rowman and Littlefield [vols. 1–3] and Carbondale: Southern Illinois University Press [vols. 4–9], 1905–1996), 3: 17.

131. See Anon., "Simplicissimus Spricht," *Simplicissimus* 1 (16 May 1896): 2.

132. Bark, "La santa bohemia," *La santa bohemia y otros artículos*, 23.

133. Erich Mühsam, "Bohême," *Die Fackel* 7 (30 April 1906): 10.

134. See Champfleury, "L'homme aux figures de cire," *Les excentriques*, 318.

135. Nadar, in Trois Buveurs d'Eau, *Histoire de Mürger*, 240–41.

136. Rafael Cansinos-Assens, "La bohemia en la literatura," in *Los proletarios del arte: Introducción a la bohemia* ([Madrid]: Celeste Ediciones, 1998), 148.

137. Georges Rodenbach, "Murger et la bohème" (1895), *Evocations* (Brussels: La Renaissance du Livre, 1924), 284–85.

138. See, for instance, Julius Bab's identification of "unproductivity" as a defining feature of bohemia in *Die Berliner Bohème* (1904), ed. M. M. Schardt (Paderborn: Igel Verlag Literatur, 1994), 77.

139. Rodenbach, "Murger et la bohème," *Evocations*, 284.

140. See Th[éodore] Barrière and H[enry] Murger, *La vie de bohème*, rev. ed. (Paris:

Calmann Lévy, 1896 [orig. 1849]), in which this refrain appears in songs throughout the play.

141. Émile Zola, *L'oeuvre* (1868), in *Les Rougon-Macquart*, ed. D'Armand Lanoux, 5 vols. (Paris: Gallimard, 1966), 4: 362, 363.

CHAPTER 4. UNKNOWING PRIVAT

1. See A[lexandre] Privat d'Anglemont, *Paris inconnu* (Paris: Adolphe Delahays, 1861), 100.

2. Anon., untitled article, *La presse* (21 July 1859): 3.

3. Victor Cochinat, "Alexandre Privat d'Anglemont," *La causerie* (24 July 1859).

4. Privat d'Anglemont, letter "À Monsieur Havin" (13 February 1856), in *Paris inconnu*, 271.

5. Privat d'Anglemont, *La Closerie des Lilas: Quadrille en prose* (Paris: J. Frey, 1848), 42.

6. See Alexandre Schanne, *Souvenirs de Schaunard* (Paris: G. Charpentier, 1887), 136, 201–2.

7. See Anon., "Spaziergänge durch Paris," *Morgenblatt für gebildete Leser* 52 (1859): 1047; and [George William Curtis], "Editor's Easy Chair," *Harper's New Monthly Magazine* 19 (October 1859): 705.

8. Alfred Delvau, "Alexandre Privat d'Anglemont," in *Paris inconnu*, 10.

9. Edmond and Jules de Goncourt, *Manette Salomon* (Paris: Union Générale d'Éditions, 1979), 374.

10. Champfleury, *Souvenirs des funambules* (Paris: Michel Lévy Frères, 1859), 300.

11. See Gabriel Guillemot, *Le bohême* (Paris: A. Le Chevalier, 1868), 7–8, 11.

12. Firmin Maillard, *Les derniers bohêmes: Henri Murger et son temps* (Paris: Librarie Sartorius, 1874), 187. This account of Privat's funeral is based on Maillard's description as well as those of Cochinat, "Fragment d'un article publié par M. Victor Cochinat," in Privat d'Anglemont, *Paris inconnu*, 22; the article from which this extract is drawn, Cochinat, "Alexandre Privat d'Anglemont," *La causerie* (24 July 1859); and Charles Monselet, "Alexandre Privat d'Anglemont," in Privat d'Anglemont, *Paris anecdote*, ed. Charles Monselet (Paris: P. Rouquette, 1885 [orig. 1854]), 10.

13. Honoré de Balzac, "Un prince de la bohème" (1844), ed. Patrick Berthier, *La comédie humaine*, ed. Pierre-Georges Castex, 12 vols. (Paris: Gallimard, 1977), 7: 819. See also the Goncourts' identification of *blague* with bohemia in *Manette Salomon*, 42–43. Delvau once sought to deny Privat's reputation as a *blagueur*, saying that his stories had at least some foundation in truth, but his objection does not really seem serious and appears in an article that itself offers the reader some blague—most notably, the claim that Privat was an adept in reading cuneiform writing. See Delvau, "Privat d'Anglemont," *Rabelais* (8 June 1857): 4–6. In this same article (4) Delvau compares Privat to La Palférine, the protagonist of Balzac's "Un prince de la bohème"; see Graham M. Robb's speculations about the possible basis of this comparison in "Un modèle possible de La Palférine: Privat d'Anglemont," *L'année balzacienne* 8 (1987): 399–404.

14. Auguste Villemot, *La vie à Paris: Chroniques du Figaro* (Paris: Édition Hetzel, 1858), 209.

15. [Antoine] Claude, *Mémoires de Monsieur Claude, Chef de la Police de Sûreté sous le Second Empire*, 10 vols. (Paris: Jules Rouff, 1883), 10: 5. Claude's story has Privat persuading a man fresh from the provinces that, for the price of a dinner, he can write a letter of recommendation on his behalf to the minister of the interior and get him a position—which, ironically, the man does end up receiving. This story, however, is remarkably similar to one conveyed by Fernand Desnoyers, which involves a naval ensign who desires a promotion and which has the same ironically successful ending. (See Anon., "A. Privat d'Anglemont," in *Almanach parisien pour l'année 1860* [Paris: Eugène Pick, 1860], 93–94.) It is conceivable that the similarity testifies to a well-rehearsed ploy of Privat's, but the similar endings in particular suggest that what we are actually dealing with here is a widely circulated legend.

16. Nadar [Gaspard-Félix Tournachon, pseud.], *Charles Baudelaire intime: Le poète vierge* ([Paris]: Obsidiane, 1985 [orig. 1911]), 26, 24, 50.

17. Théodore de Banville, *Mes souvenirs* (Paris: Charpentier, 1882), 64.

18. Banville, *Mes souvenirs*, 71–72. Monselet also tells this story in "Alexandre Privat d'Anglemont," *Paris anecdote*, 3–4. Even though he reiterates this story, Monselet objects (6) that Banville's image of Privat in his memoirs is idealized.

19. See Privat d'Anglemont, "À Monsieur Alexandre Dumas" (4 September 1854), in *Paris inconnu*, 264–66. See also the comments on these conflicting accounts in Jean-Léo, *Paris-bohême: Alexandre Privat d'Anglemont* ([Paris]: Synthèses, 1964), 18–20.

20. See Nadar, *Charles Baudelaire intime*, 50.

21. See Privat d'Anglemont, *Paris anecdote*, 79.

22. According to one account, at the *École de natation*, confused by his towel-wrapped form, even Honoré de Balzac mistook Privat for Dumas. See Jules Renoult, "Bulletin littéraire," in *Revue de Toulouse et du Midi de la France*, ed. M. F. Lacoint (Toulouse: Bureau de la Revue, 1859), 220–21.

23. Cochinat, "Fragment d'un article publié par M. Victor Cochinat," in *Paris inconnu*, 17.

24. Aside from contemporary accounts, the most important source of biographical information about Privat is Jean Ziegler's "Essai biographique," *Études baudelairiennes* 8 (1976): 219–52, which reveals, among other things, that Privat was the illegitimate child of a "free mulatto," Elisabeth Desmararis, who was herself a slave owner. Willy Alante-Lima, in "Alexandre Privat d'Anglemont, ce Guadeloupéen célèbre et méconnu," *Généalogie et histoire de la Caraïbe* 145 (February 2002), 3402–14, has expanded upon this information. I am indebted as well to Pierre Citron, "Privat d'Anglemont ou les vérités d'un menteur," *Revue des sciences humaines* 103 (July– September 1961), 400–416; and to Ziegler, "Sur Privat d'Anglemont," *Bulletin baudelairien* 12 (Summer 1976): 18–28.

25. Banville (*Mes souvenirs*, 65) says Privat received payments of around five thousand francs at irregular intervals. Ziegler ("Essai biographique," 223–24) judges Banville's description of Privat's wild expenditures to be exaggerated and seeks to develop a more accurate accounting of the payments Privat received from his brother.

26. See Privat d'Anglemont, "Quatre lettres à Eugène Sue," ed. Pierre Citron, *Revue des sciences humaines* 103 (July– September 1961): 399.

27. Delvau, "Alexandre Privat d'Anglemont," *Paris inconnu*, 10. For the line from the play, see Th[éodore] Barrière and Murger, *La vie de bohème* (Paris: Calmann Lévy, 1896), 12.

28. See Signor Saltarino [Hermann Waldemar Otto, pseud.], writing of the figure of the bohemian in *Düsseldorfer Bohèmeleben vor vierzig Jahren* (Düsseldorf: Selbstverlag, 1926), 9: "Sein Leben ist ein permanenter Vorshuß."

29. See Heinrich Heine, *Ideen—Das Buch le Grand* (1826), *Heines Werke*, ed. Helmut Holtzhauer, 5 vols. (Berlin: Aufbau-Verlag, 1964), 3: 30.

30. Privat d'Anglemont, *La Closerie des Lilas*, 36.

31. Privat d'Anglemont, *Paris anecdote*, 185.

32. See Citron, "Privat d'Anglemont ou les vérités d'un menteur," 414–16; and Ziegler, "Sur Privat d'Anglemont," 26. For other writings by Privat, see also Claude Pichois, "'La fanfarlo' de Privat d'Anglemont découverte par Willy Alante-Lima," *Bulletin baudelairienne* 28 (December 1993): 47–60; and Peter J. Edwards, "Une collaboration théâtrale inconnue: Théodore de Banville et Alexandre Privat d'Anglemont, avec une pièce inédite, *Entre l'arbre et l'écorce*," *Bulletin d'études parnassiennes et symbolistes* 17 (Spring 1996): 3–49.

33. Privat d'Anglemont, "Les encyclopédists," in Ph[ilibert] Audebrand et al., *Autrefois, ou le bon vieux temps: Types français du dix-huitième siècle* (Paris: Challamel, 1842), 218–19.

34. In the preceding paragraph and throughout this chapter, the information about Privat not otherwise specifically cited is based on the accounts of Monselet, "Alexandre Privat d'Anglemont," *Paris anecdote*, 1–11; Delvau, "Alexandre Privat d'Anglemont," *Paris inconnu*, 3–16; Cochinat, "Fragment d'un article publié par Mr. Victor Cochinat," *Paris inconnu*, 17–22; and Cochinat, "Alexandre Privat d'Anglemont," *La causerie* (24 July 1859).

35. Auguste Vitu, "Notice géographique, historique, politique et littéraire sur la Bohême" (1849), in *Les mille et une nuits du théâtre*, 8th ser. (Paris: Paul Ollendorff, 1891), 16. *La vie interlope: Histoire des sept bohèmes qui n'ont pas de chateaux* was advertised on the back cover of Privat's *Closerie de Lilas*, along with an ad for Murger's *Scènes de la vie de bohème*, among other works. It evidently was meant to bear some relation to Charles Nodier's *Histoire du roi de Bohême et de ses sept châteaux* (1830).

36. The notable exception is Philibert Audebrand, whose recollections of Privat, almost thirty years after his death, are strikingly at odds with other accounts; among other things, Audebrand was determined to discredit Privat as any sort of writer and even as a notable talker. See Audebrand, *Alexandre Dumas à la Maison d'Or* (Paris: Calmann Lévy, 1888), 349–58.

37. See Jerrold Seigel's comments on Privat's sympathetic portrayal of the *métiers inconnus* in *Bohemian Paris: Culture, Politics, and the Boundaries of Bourgeois Life, 1830–1930* (Baltimore: Johns Hopkins University Press, 1986), 141. The whole of his section on Privat in this book (136–49) is of interest in relation to my arguments here.

38. J[oseph] Barbaret, *La bohême du travail* (Paris: J. Hetzel, [1889]), i.

39. Murger, "Préface," *Scènes de la vie de bohème*, ed. Loïc Chotard and Graham Robb (Paris: Gallimard, 1988), 34.

40. Banville, *Mes souvenirs*, 63.

41. Adolphe d'Ennery and [Eugène] Grangé, *Les bohémiens de Paris*, in *Magasin théâtral: Choix des pièces nouvelles jouées sur tous les théâtres de Paris, v. 30* (Paris: Marchant, 1846), 8–9.

42. Schanne, *Souvenirs de Schaunard*, 96; an anonymous contemporary, in the *Revue anecdotique*, quoted by Ziegler, "Essai biographique," 239; Monselet, "Alexandre Privat d'Anglemont," *Paris anecdote*, 6.

43. Maillard, *Les dernières bohêmes*, 186–87. The comparison with Villon occurred to others as well, such as Delvau, in "Alexandre Privat d'Anglemont," *Paris inconnu*, 9, and Alphonse Duchesne, in "Privat d'Anglemont," *Le Figaro* (9 August 1859): 3.

44. Delvau, "Alexandre Privat d'Anglemont," *Paris inconnu*, 11.

45. Duchesne, "Privat d'Anglemont," *Le Figaro* (9 August 1859): 3.

46. Villemot, *La vie à Paris*, 117. For other examples of the kinds of tales told of Privat, see Louis Loire, "Privat d'Anglemont," *Anecdotes de la vie littéraire* (Paris: E. Dentu, 1876), 226–27.

47. In "Privat d'Anglemont," *Le Figaro* (9 August 1859): 3, Duchesne describes a conversation in which Privat, shortly before his death, asked Duchesne to publish something in *Le Figaro* about how hurtful he found the stories journalists told about him, some of them portraying him as a miserable outcast and others as being secretly wealthy.

48. See Banville, *Mes souvenirs*, 63.

49. Duchesne, "Privat d'Anglemont," *Le Figaro* (9 August 1859): 3.

50. See Alante-Lima, "Alexandre Privat d'Anglemont, ce Guadeloupéen célèbre et méconnu," 3411.

51. Privat d'Anglemont, *Paris inconnu*, 51.

52. Privat d'Anglemont, *La Closerie des Lilas*, 50.

53. Duchesne, "Privat d'Anglemont," *Le Figaro* (9 August 1859): 2.

54. On the relation of writers and artists to the popular media in this era, see Petra ten-Doesschate Chu, *The Most Arrogant Man in France: Gustave Courbet and the Nineteenth-Century Media Culture* (Princeton: Princeton University Press, 2007), esp. 5–44.

55. George Sand, "À François Buloz" (4 and 5 February 1834), *Correspondance*, ed. Georges Lubin, 26 vols. [Paris: Garnier Frères, 1964–95], 2: 492.

56. See Alphonse de Calonne, *Voyage au pays de Bohême* (Paris: E. Brière, 1852), 13–14.

57. Henry James, "Preface to *The Tragic Muse*" (1908), *The Art of the Novel: Critical Prefaces* (New York: Charles Scribner's Sons, 1962), 84.

58. Delvau, "Alexandre Privat d'Anglemont," *Paris inconnu*, 10; Nadar, *Charles Baudelaire intime*, 26.

59. Monselet, "Alexandre Privat d'Anglemont," *Paris anecdote*, 3.

60. Monselet, *Petits mémoires littéraires* (Paris: G. Charpentier, 1885), 337.

61. See Banville, *Mes souvenirs*, 76, 69, and Nadar, *Charles Baudelaire intime*, 26.

62. Banville, *Mes souvenirs*, 69. One suspects that the anonymous "phrasemaker" who coined this witticism may have been Banville himself.

63. See Banville, *Mes souvenirs*, 65.

64. Quoted in Carlo Dossi, *Rovaniana*, ed. Giorgio Nicodemi, 2 vols. (Milan: Edizioni

della Libreria Vinciana, 1946), 1: 441. See also Robert B. Brough's comparison of bohemians to Rodolphe (from whom Murger presumably took the name for his character in *Scenes of Bohemian Life*) in his novel *Marston Lynch* (London: Ward and Lock, 1860), 317–18.

65. Fournier, quoted in Cochinat, "Alexandre Privat d'Anglemont," *La causerie* (24 July 1859).

66. Banville, *Mes souvenirs*, 69.

67. Banville, *Mes souvenirs*, 69.

68. Delvau, "Alexandre Privat d'Anglemont," *Paris inconnu*, 10.

69. Charles Coligny, "Henry Murger et la Bohème," *L'artiste*, n.s., 11 (15 February 1861): 75.

70. Fournier, quoted in Cochinat, "Alexandre Privat d'Anglemont," *La causerie* (24 July 1859).

71. Guillemot, *Le bohême*, 20–23, 40.

72. See also, for instance, the passage in the Irish journalist Edward M. Whitty's *The Bohemians of London* (Philadelphia: T. B. Peterson and Brothers, 1864 [orig. 1857]), 45, in which a *bohémienne* is epitomized as follows: "Read Wilhelm Meister [*sic*], and you may guess a great deal of her life"; and the similar reference in Henry James, *The Tragic Muse* (1890), *The Novels and Tales of Henry James*, 24 vols. (New York: Charles Scribner's Sons, 1922), 8: 130. The American bohemian Fitz-James O'Brien specifically refers to Hamlet as a bohemian type in "Dramatic Feuilleton," *New-York Saturday Press* 2 (1 January 1859): 3. Other such examples appear throughout the literature of this era.

73. Frank Wedekind, "An die Mutter" (12 November 1884), *Gesammelte Briefe*, ed. Fritz Strich, 2 vols. (Munich: Georg Müller, 1924), 1: 73.

74. Privat d'Anglemont, *La Closerie des Lilas*, 38–39.

75. August Vitu did once refer to Privat as "a socialist," but in a joking context. See Vitu, "Notice géographique, historique, politique et littéraire sur la Bohème" (1849), *Les mille et une nuits du théâtre*, 16.

76. Privat d'Anglemont, *Voyage à travers Paris, 1: Le Prado* (Paris: Chez Paulier, 1846), 41. Henceforth *Le Prado*.

77. Between 1845 and 1859, he apparently received eight grants, for a total of 1,650 francs. See Ziegler, "Sur Privat d'Anglemont," 18–28.

78. Privat d'Anglemont, "Quatre lettres à Eugène Sue," 395.

79. Privat d'Anglemont, "Quatre lettres à Eugène Sue," 393.

80. Louis Leroy, *Artistes et rapins*, 2nd ed. (Paris: A. Le Chevalier, 1868), 15.

81. Privat d'Anglemont, *La Closerie des Lilas*, 23.

82. It is notable that Nadar's *Chants et chansons de la bohême* (Paris: J. Bry Aîné, 1853) includes a poem by Charles Woinez, "Le mirage," in the voice of an African, and another, "Le chant du nomade," devoted to an Arab wanderer; but, despite its association with gypsies, writers of this era generally did not explicitly conceptualize a connection between bohemia and race.

83. Banville, *Mes souvenirs*, 64–65.

84. Duchesne, "Privat d'Anglemont," *Le Figaro* (9 August 1859): 3.

85. See Privat d'Anglemont, *Paris anecdote*, 142–43.

86. This was the Café de Bruxelles; see Delvau, *Histoire anecdotique des cafés et cabarets de Paris* (Paris: E. Dentu, 1862), 120. Delvau refers in passing (127) to Privat's acquaintance with Melvil-Bloncourt.

87. See Maillard, *Les derniers bohêmes*, 263.

88. David W. H. Pellow, "Alexandre Privat d'Anglemont, 'Les singes de dieu et les hommes du diable,'" *Études baudelairiennes* 8 (1976): 256.

89. Privat d'Anglemont, *Paris inconnu*, 49, 56. Here and elsewhere, Privat uses the term *nègre*, which today generally corresponds to the American word *nigger*, the more polite term being *noir*, black. The correspondence in the nineteenth century, however, is not perfect; although generally pejorative (as in the phrase *travailler come un nègre*) *nègre* could also be a more neutral term, sharing some of the same territory as the contemporary term *Negro*. In Pierre-Jean de Béranger's poem "Les nègres et les marionnettes," for instance, *nègre* and *noir* are used interchangeably. (See P[ierre]-J[ean] de Béranger, "Les nègres et les marionnettes," *Oeuvres*, new ed., 2 vols. [Paris: Garnier Frères, 1876], 2: 184–85.) Because Privat's use of this term is obviously not meant to be pejorative, I have chosen to use *negro* (in the uncapitalized form common in the nineteenth century) in my attempt to capture a bit of its complexity in my translations here. An argument could be made that *nigger*, used by Privat with profound irony, would be the better translation; I have not chosen that path because it seems to me that it would end up being misleading, in relation to contemporary English usage, and also because it seems to me that Privat's style, while often ironic, did not generally employ irony in this way, as concentrated in individual words. But I could be wrong.

90. W. C. Morrow, *Bohemian Paris of To-day*, 3rd ed. (Philadelphia: J. B. Lippincott, 1899), 125, 122.

91. Delvau, "Alexandre Privat d'Anglemont," *Paris inconnu*, 12.

92. Cochinat, "Fragment d'un article publié par Mr. Victor Cochinat," *Paris inconnu*, 20.

93. See Jean-Didier Wagneur's comments on how Privat's work renovated a tradition of representing Paris that goes back to the Ancien Régime: "Alexandre Privat d'Anglemont et Paris underground," in *Paris, sa vie, son oeuvre*, ed. Jean-Jacques Lefrère et Michel Pierssens (Tusson: Du Lérot, 2004), 79–81.

94. Privat d'Anglemont, "Quatre lettres à Eugène Sue," 393.

95. Privat d'Anglemont, *Paris inconnu*, 53.

96. Privat d'Anglemont, *Paris inconnu*, 53.

97. Privat d'Anglemont, *La Closerie des Lilas*, 9–10.

98. Privat d'Anglemont, *Paris inconnu*, 35, 38. The "egg dance" was a traditional game that involved using only one's feet to maneuver an egg out of and then under a bowl, all the while avoiding various obstacles.

99. Privat d'Anglemont, *Paris anecdote*, 45–46.

100. Privat d'Anglemont, *Paris anecdote*, 49–50, 52–53, 104–5.

101. Privat d'Anglemont, *Paris anecdote*, 109.

102. Privat d'Anglemont, *Paris anecdote*, 65–66.

103. Privat d'Anglemont, *Paris anecdote*, 66–69.

104. Privat d'Anglemont, *Paris anecdote*, 91–97.

105. Privat d'Anglemont, *Paris anecdote*, 110.

106. Banville, *Mes souvenirs*, 64.

107. Ziegler points out ("Sur Privat d'Anglemont," 27) that Alexandre Privat adopted the surname d'Anglemont around 1842, his brother Elie-Victor having used it before 1830. Alante-Lima ("Alexandre Privat d'Anglemont, ce Guadeloupéen célèbre et méconnu," 3403) has identified two white families with this surname in Guadeloupe at the time of Privat's birth. In one of his newspaper articles, Privat answered his own question, "Do you know how one becomes a gentleman?" by explaining that one may do so by gradually dignifying an ordinary name, such as Alfred Durand, so that it becomes Alfred Durand (de Savenay), then Alfred Durand de Savenay, and finally Alfred, Count of Savenay. One can only speculate on what this jesting meant to the author who had added "d'Anglemont" to his name only a few years before. See Privat d'Anglemont, "Tout Paris," *Le Corsaire* (9 August 1846).

108. Duchesne, "Privat d'Anglemont," *Le Figaro* (9 August 1859): 3.

109. *Creole* at this time generally signified a person of European ancestry born in one of the colonies.

110. Maillard, *Les derniers bohêmes*, 187.

111. Delvau, "Alexandre Privat d'Anglemont," *Paris inconnu*, 8, 9, 11.

112. Duchesne, "Privat d'Anglemont," *Le Figaro* (9 August 1859): 2.

113. Cochinat, "Fragment d'un article publié par Mr. Victor Cochinat," *Paris inconnu*, 21.

114. Heine, "Unvollkommenheit" (c. 1847–51), *Heines Werke*, 3: 281; Balzac, quoted in Audebrand, *Alexandre Dumas à la Maison d'Or*, 49.

115. See Ziegler, "Sur Privat d'Anglemont," 18–19.

116. Privat d'Anglemont, "Beaux-Arts—Musée National du Louvre—Salle des Antiquités Américains," *Le siècle* (22 August 1850), 1.

117. Privat d'Anglemont, *Paris anecdote*, 15. Levaillant, Cook, and Caillé were all famous explorers. D'Anglemont also used this sort of reverse ethnographical description elsewhere, in "Voyage à travers Paris. 1. Le Parisien de Paris," *Le Corsaire* 2 (February 1847): "Assuredly, a Russian, a Patagonian, and even an Iowa Indian would not be more out of place in the aristocratic salons of the faubourg Saint-Germain than the native of that province known as the Quarter of the Jardin-des-Plantes would be in a circle of the École des Beaux-Arts."

118. Privat d'Anglemont, *Le Prado*, 58.

119. Banville, *Mes souvenirs*, 67.

120. See, for instance, the identification with a bohemian prostitute in "Je n'ai pas pour maîtresse une lionne illustre" (c. 1840–44) in Charles Baudelaire, *Les fleurs du mal, Oeuvres complètes*, ed. Claude Pichois, 2 vols. (Paris: Éditions Gallimard, 1975), 1: 203–4; and the identification of the prostitute as a sort of gypsy on the fringes of modern life in Baudelaire, "Le peintre de la vie moderne," *Oeuvres complètes*, 2: 718–22. Similar use of this common theme of "prostitutes of the soul and of the body," with specific connections to the representation of bohemia, appear in Theodor Mundt, *Paris und Louis Napoleon: Neue*

Skizzen aus dem französischen Kaiserreich, 2 vols. (Paris: Otto Janke, 1858), 1: 147–49, and in Hans R. Fischer, *Berliner Zigeunerleben: Bilder aus der Welt der Schriftsteller, Künstler und des Proletariats* (Berlin: S. Fischer, 1890), 101.

121. See Privat d'Anglemont, *Le Prado*, 32–22.

122. Privat d'Anglemont, "Quatre lettres à Eugène Sue," 393–94.

123. Banville, *Mes souvenirs*. Further quotations from this work are given within the text.

124. Privat d'Anglemont, *Paris inconnu*, 56. It may be relevant to note that, influenced in part by the popularity of the novels of James Fenimore Cooper, comparisons of members of the Parisian underworld to the natives of America were frequent in this time, as in works by authors such as Sue and Dumas. See the comments by Walter Benjamin, "The Paris of the Second Empire in Baudelaire" (1938), trans. Harry Zohn, in *Selected Writings*, ed. Michael W. Jennings, 4 vols. (Cambridge, Mass.: Harvard University Press, 1996–2003), 4: 22–23.

125. Cf. the characterization of Privat as a performer in Citron's thoughtful, sympathetic, and brilliantly imaginative "Privat d'Anglemont ou les vérités d'un menteur," in which he focuses on the uncertainties involved in the attribution of various writings to Privat.

126. See Aristide Marie, *Henry Monnier* (Paris: Librarie Floury, 1931), 14. Such exhibitions were not unusual; Jules Vallès, for instance, remembered a troupe of Caribes exhibited in 1864, in a traveling circus and freak show. See Vallès, "Le bachélier géant," *Les réfractaires* (1865), ed. Lucien Scheler, *Les oeuvres de Jules Vallès*, ed. Lucien Scheler, 8 vols. (Paris: Les Éditeurs Français Réunis, 1950–57), 207–8.

127. See A[ugustin] Jal, "Les comiques de Paris," *Nouveau tableau de Paris au XIXme siècle*, [ed. Henri Martin], 7 vols. (Paris: Madame Charles-Béchet, 1834–35), 2: 328; Nadar, *Charles Baudelaire intime*, 11, 17.

128. Quoted in Felix Moscheles, *Fragments of an Autobiography* (New York: Harper and Brothers, 1899), 297. The earliest publication I have found of a version of this story is in P.-J. Martin, *L'esprit de tout le monde* ([Paris?]: [E. Guyot], 1859). A slightly different version appears in an unsigned and untitled form in the *Revue anecdotique des excentricités contemporains* 12, pt. 1 (1861): 46; and a version close to the one told by Moscheles appears in a journal entry dated 1869 in Julian Charles Young, *A Memoir of Charles Mayne Young* (London: Macmillan, 1871), 444.

129. Satan [Georges-Marie Mathieu-Dairnvaell, pseud.], *Physiologie des étudiants, des grisettes et des bals de Paris* (Paris: Georges Dairnvaell, 1849), 48.

130. Privat d'Anglemont, *Paris anecdote*, 19.

131. Rubén Darío, "En el 'Pais Latino,'" *Parisiana* (Madrid: Editorial Mundo Latino, 1918), 174.

132. Quoted in Ziegler, "Essai biographique," 251.

133. Citron, "Privat d'Anglemont ou les vérités d'un menteur," 408.

134. Privat d'Anglemont, "Les singes de dieu et les hommes du diable," *Paris inconnu*. Further page references are given within the text.

135. Pellow, "Alexandre Privat d'Anglemont, 'Les singes de dieu et les hommes du

diable,'" 266. One wonders if Privat had heard the folklore from Brittany recorded by Eugène Delacroix, *Journal*, ed. Paul Flat and René Piot, 2nd ed., 3 vols. (Paris: Plon, 1893), 1: 232: "The Bretons believe that the monkey is the work of the devil. After having seen man, the creation of God, the devil believed he could, in his turn, create a comparable being, but he produced only a rough-hewn and hideous emblem of his prideful impotence." (This is from an entry for 17 September 1846.)

136. Delvau, "Alexandre Privat d'Anglemont," *Paris inconnu*, 13.

137. François Villon, "Le Testament," *Poésies*, ed. Jean Dufournet, 3rd ed. rev. (Paris: Gallimard, 1973 [orig. 1489]), 76.

CHAPTER 5. AMERICA, THE BIRTHPLACE OF BOHEMIA

1. Jules Barbey d'Aurevilly, "Edgar Poe" (1858), *Les oeuvres et les hommes*, 26 vols. (Paris: Alphonse Lemerre, 1860–90; rep. Geneva: Slatkine Reprints, 1968), v. 12. Page references are given within the text.

2. Emma Lazarus, "The New Colossus," *Selected Poems*, ed. John Hollander (New York: Library of America, 2005), 58.

3. See the description of the "excessive liberty" of America in George Sand, "À l'Abbé Georges Rochet" (September 1842), *Correspondence*, ed. Georges Lubin, 26 vols. (Paris: Garnier Frères, 1964–95), 5: 776.

4. On this topic see Patrick McGuinness's discussion of the "French 'invention' of Poe and Poe's American 'invention' of French literature," as these established "a rich seam of debate in avant-garde American circles of the 1890s." McGuinness, "From Mallarmé to Pound: The Franco-Anglo-American Axis," in *Symbolism, Decadence and the* Fin de Siècle: *French and European Perspectives*, ed. Patrick McGuinness (Exeter: University of Exeter Press, 2000), 268. One might also compare Barbey's argument to the views of others, such as Louis Veuillot, who identified bohemia with reprehensible democratic impulses. See Veuillot, *Les odeurs de Paris*, 2nd ed. (Paris: Palmé, 1867), 87.

5. Walt Whitman, *Leaves of Grass: A Textual Variorum of the Printed Poems*, ed. Sculley Bradley, Harold W. Blodgett, Arthur Golden, and William White, 3 vols., in *The Collected Writings of Walt Whitman*, ed. Gay Wilson Allen and Sculley Bradley (New York: New York University Press, 1980). All references to Whitman's poems are to this edition; volume and page references are given within the text, together with the year of the edition being cited. In the case of the untitled poems in the first (1855) edition, the titles eventually given to these works are provided within brackets.

6. Whitman, "Walt Whitman and His Poems," *United States Review* (September 1855), in *Walt Whitman: The Contemporary Reviews*, ed. Kenneth M. Price (Cambridge: Cambridge University Press, 1996), 9. This review was originally published anonymously.

7. George Sand, *La Comtesse de Rudolstadt*, in *Consuelo/La Comtesse de Rudolstadt*, ed. Léon Cellier and Léon Guichard, 3 vols. (Paris: Garnier Frères, 1959 [orig. 1844]), 3: 112.

8. Whitman, "Preface" (1872) to "As a Strong Bird on Pinions Free," *Prose Works*, ed. Floyd Stovall, 2 vols., in *The Collected Writings of Walt Whitman*, 2: 463.

9. The translation was by Charles Astor Bristed, writing under the pseudonym of Carl Benson, and was published in installments from January 1853 to May 1854.

10. Quoted in Traubel (entry for 5 December 1891), *With Walt Whitman in Camden*, ed. Sculley Bradley, Gertrude Traubel, Jeanne Chapman, and Robert MacIsaac, 9 vols. (New York: Rowman and Littlefield [vols. 1–3] and Carbondale: Southern Illinois University Press [vols. 4–9], 1905–1996), 9: 206. See also Whitman's praise of Sand's *Le compagnon du tour de France* (1841) in Traubel, *With Walt Whitman in Camden*, 5: 350. *Consuelo* was a touchstone for other nineteenth-century bohemians as well; for instance, two characters read it in Enrique Perez Escrich's *El frac azul: Episodios de un jóven flaco* (Madrid: Manini Hermanos, 1864), 291.

11. Traubel, *With Walt Whitman in Camden*, 2: 502. Before he learned to appreciate *Leaves of Grass*, Henry James icily remarked that Whitman was in no way deserving of the compliment of being compared to Béranger; see [Henry James], "Mr. Walt Whitman," *Nation* (16 November 1865), in Price, ed., *Walt Whitman: The Contemporary Reviews*, 116. The comparison to Béranger also occurred to others; see, for instance, the reference made by the anonymous London reviewer of "Walt Whitman's Poems" (1868) in the London *Sun* (17 April 1868) in *Walt Whitman: The Contemporary Reviews*, 156. Justin Kaplan describes the artists with whom Whitman associated in his "Béranger" days in *Walt Whitman: A Life* (New York: Simon and Schuster, 1980), 168.

12. William Douglas O'Connor, "The Good Gray Poet: A Vindication," in Richard Maurice Bucke, *Walt Whitman* (Philadelphia: David McKay, 1883), 116.

13. Guizot's controversial words were widely publicized, but for a good example of a contemporary reaction against them, see Satan [Georges M. M. Dairnvaell, pseud.], *Les scandales du jour: Révélations édifiantes et curieuses sur les hommes et les choses* (Paris: Librarie Populaire, 1847), 5.

14. D[avid] H[erbert] Lawrence, *Studies in Classic American Literature* (Garden City, N.Y.: Doubleday, 1953 [orig. 1923]), 178.

15. See Esther Shephard, *Walt Whitman's Pose* (New York: Harcourt, Brace, 1938).

16. The only exception I have found in his published works to his avoidance of this term is in a brief editorial comment that he published in the *Brooklyn Daily Times* (8 September 1858), in which he entertains a conventional criticism of bohemianism as creating "a restless craving for mental excitement unsuiting [literary men] to breathe the clear and tranquil atmosphere of home enjoyment." See Whitman, *I Sit and Look Out: Editorials from The Brooklyn Daily Times*, ed. Emory Holloway and Vernolian Schwarz (New York: Columbia University Press, 1932), 67.

17. See, for example, Anon., "Walt Whitman, A Kosmos," *Springfield Sunday Republican* (13 November 1881): 4, at http://whitmanarchive.org/criticism/reviews/leaves/1881/anc.00208.html.

18. Daniel Hoffman, "'Hankering, Gross, Mystical, Nude': Whitman's 'Self' and the American Tradition," in *Walt Whitman of Mickle Street*, ed. Geoffrey M. Sill (Knoxville: University of Tennessee Press, 1994), 12.

19. Whitman, "Poetry To-day in America—Shakespeare—The Future" (1881–82), in *Prose Works* 2: 484.

20. In 1910, Hutchins Hapgood was still seeing this attitude as a test of America's willingness or unwillingness to accept the bohemian: "As yet . . . American Bohemians are very few, for when a man is not busy in America, he is generally a 'bum' or a foreigner. The man who desires to loaf intelligently and temperamentally; to do only enough work to express himself, is a rare bird in this country. The genuine Bohemian charm is almost unknown." See Hapgood, *Types from City Streets* (New York: Funk and Wagnalls, 1910), 118.

21. This is not to say that Whitman's connection to bohemianism went unobserved outside of discussions about Pfaff's and the *New-York Saturday Press* crowd. See, for example, the evident allusion to *Leaves of Grass* in the title of the following newspaper article: Anon., "Journalists, Self-Celebrants, and Bohemians," *Brooklyn Daily Eagle* (9 May 1870): 2. By the beginning of the next century, an excerpt from the opening lines of *Leaves of Grass* could be casually quoted, without attribution—by a former mayor of Philadelphia!—as definitive of bohemia. See Charles F. Warwick, "The Realm of True Fellowship," in *Bohemia: Offical Publication of the International League of Press Clubs for the Building and Endowment of the Journalists' Home*, ed. Alexander K. McClure (Philadelphia: International League of Press Clubs, 1904), 12: "It is a place where you can 'loaf and invite your soul.'" (This book is labeled "Volume 1," but it appears that a scheduled second volume never appeared.)

22. Barbey d'Aurevilly, "Edgar Poe" (1858), *Les oeuvres et les hommes*, 12: 398.

23. For Whitman's meeting with Poe, see *Specimen Days* (1882), *Prose Works* 1: 17, 230–32. See also Traubel, *With Walt Whitman in Camden*, 4: 23.

24. William Winter, *Old Friends: Being Literary Recollections of Other Days* (New York: Moffat, Yard, 1909), 64.

25. For a good example of the publicizing of Pfaff's, see T[homas] B[ailey] A[ldrich], "At the Café," *Vanity Fair* 1 (31 December 1859): 12. Aldrich was one of the *Saturday Press* bohemians; the opening line of this four-stanza poem is "We were all very merry at Pfaff's."

26. James, *The Bostonians*, 2 vols. (London: Macmillan, 1921 [orig. 1886]), 1: 22. On this topic see the excellent study of Pfaff's by Joanna Levin in her *Bohemia in America, 1858–1920* (Stanford: Stanford University Press, 2010), 13–69. See also the detailed study by Mark A. Lause, *The Antebellum Crisis and America's First Bohemians* (Kent, Ohio: Kent State University Press, 2009).

27. Traubel, *With Walt Whitman in Camden*, 4: 195. See also the similar comments at 1: 214 and 2: 375.

28. Anon., [Untitled Review], *Southern Field and Fireside* (9 June 1860): 20, at http://whitmanarchive.org/criticism/reviews/leaves1860/anc.00184.html.

29. Anon., [Untitled Review], *The Critic* (1 April 1856), in *Walt Whitman: The Contemporary Reviews*, 44; Anon., "Rough Poetry," rpt. from the *Portland Transcript*, in *New-York Saturday Press* (21 July 1860): 3; Anon., [Untitled Review], *Westminster Review* (1 October 1860), in *Walt Whitman: The Contemporary Reviews*, 107; Anon., [Untitled Review], *San Francisco Bulletin* (18 December 1865): 5, at http://whitmanarchive.org/criticism/reviews/drumtaps/anc.00057.html; Anon., "Walt Whitman's Leaves of Grass," *San Francisco Evening Bulletin* (7 January 1882): 1, at http://whitmanarchive.org/criticism/reviews/leaves1881/anc.00244.html; Clarence Cook, "Some Recent Poetry," *International Review* 11 (February 1882): 224; Anon. [William Dean Howells], "A Hoosier's Opinion of Walt

Whitman," rpt. from *Ashtabula Sentinel* (18 July 1860) in *New-York Saturday Press* (11 August 1860): 1.

30. Quoted in Horace L. Traubel, "Notes from Conversations with George W. Whitman, 1893: Mostly in His Own Words," in *In Re Walt Whitman*, ed. Horace L. Traubel, Richard Maurice Bucke, and Thomas B. Harned (Philadelphia: David McKay, 1893), 34.

31. Anon., "Editor's Table," *Appleton's Journal of Literature, Science and Art* 15 (1 April 1876): 437–38. For Bayne's review, see "Walt Whitman's Poems," *Contemporary Review* (December 1875): 49–69, at http://www.whitmanarchive.org/criticism/reviews/leaves1871/tei/anc.00199.html.

32. See Jerome Loving, *Walt Whitman: The Song of Himself* (Berkeley: University of California Press, 1999), 107. For an extended analysis of how Whitman was promoted by himself and others, see David Haven Blake, *Walt Whitman and the Culture of American Celebrity* (New Haven: Yale University Press, 2006).

33. Walt Whitman, "Leaves of Grass: A Volume of Poems Just Published," *Brooklyn Daily Times* (1855), in *In Re Walt Whitman*, 23. Other reviews of his work that Whitman published anonymously include "Walt Whitman and His Poems," *United States Review* 5 (September 1855): 205–12; "Walt Whitman, A Brooklyn Boy," *Brooklyn Daily Times* (29 September 1855): 2; and "An English and an American Poet," *American Phrenological Journal* 22 (October 1855): 90–91, all reprinted in *Walt Whitman: The Contemporary Reviews*, 8–14, 21–22, 23–26.

34. Whitman, "Walt Whitman and His Poems," in *Walt Whitman: The Contemporary Reviews*, 8, 9.

35. For the early identification of Whitman as the author of his own reviews, see Anon., [Untitled Review], *New York Daily Times* (13 November 1856): 2, rpt. in *Walt Whitman: The Contemporary Reviews*, 60–66.

36. Algernon Charles Swinburne, "Whitmania" (1887), *Studies in Prose and Poetry* (London: Chatto and Windus, 1894), 129–40. Swinburne's scathing criticism of Whitman represented a general movement toward greater conservatism in his own public image as he grew older; it was a turnabout from his championing of Whitman in his book on Blake (1868) and in his poem "To Walt Whitman in America" (1871).

37. Clarence Stedman, "Walt Whitman," *Poets of America* (Boston: Houghton Mifflin, 1894 [orig. 1885]), 357.

38. John Burroughs, *Whitman: A Study* (Boston: Houghton Mifflin, 1924 [orig. 1896]), 94, 96, 94–95.

39. William Roscoe Thayer, "Personal Recollections of Walt Whitman," in *Whitman in His Own Time*, ed. Joel Myerson, rev. ed. (Iowa City: University of Iowa Press, 2000), 304. This article is taken from *Scribner's Magazine* 65 (June 1919): 674–76. See also the analysis of Whitman as an actor, in his life and poetry, in relation to the performance culture of his day in David S. Reynolds, *Walt Whitman's America: A Cultural Biography* (New York: Alfred A. Knopf, 1995), 160–66.

40. See Anon., "General Gossip of Authors and Writers," *Current Literature* 1 (December 1888): 479. A. L. Rawson also mentions the later course of Howland's life in "A Bygone Bohemia," *Frank Leslie's Popular Monthly* 41 (January 1896): n.p.

41. Getty Gay, "The Royal Bohemian Supper," *New-York Saturday Press* (31 September 1859): 2.

42. Henry Murger, "Préface," *Scènes de la vie de bohème*, ed. Loïc Chotard and Graham Robb (Paris: Gallimard, 1988), 34.

43. Anon., "Bohemians," *New-York Saturday Press* (3 March 1860): 2.

44. D.D., "Bohemia," *New-York Saturday Press* (16 June 1860): 2.

45. Anon. [F. B. Ottarson?], "Dramatic Critics in New York," rpt. from the *Round Table* in *Golden Era* (7 February 1864): 4. For the original article, see *Round Table* (2 January 1864): 43–44. See also the follow-up article: Anon., "Bohemianism," *Round Table* (6 February 1864): 124. On bohemia in other regions of America outside of New York during the nineteenth century, see Levin, *Bohemia in America*, 256–75.

46. The Regular Critic [Frank Wood?], "The Siege of Bohemia," *Golden Era* (14 February 1864): 4–5. For the original article, see "A Knight of the 'Round Table': Bardolph Redivivus," *New York Leader* (16 January 1864): 3.

47. See Charles T[abor] Congdon, *Reminiscences of a Journalist* (Boston: James R. Osgood, 1880), 336–37; Edward Everett Hale, *Old and New*, 11 vols. (Boston: Roberts Brothers, 1870–75), 9: 523–24; Charles De Kay, *The Bohemian: A Tragedy of Modern Life* (New York: Charles Scribner's Sons, 1878), esp. 26–27; Clyde Fitch, "The Westington's 'Bohemian Dinner': A Letter," *The Smart Set: Correspondence and Conversations* (Chicago: Herbert S. Stone, 1897), 176; and William Dean Howells, *The Coast of Bohemia* (New York: Harper and Brothers, 1893), esp. 216–17. See also Howells, "First Impressions of Literary New York," in *Literary Friends and Acquaintance: A Personal Retrospective of American Authorship*, ed. David F. Hiatt and Edwin H. Cady (Bloomington: Indiana University Press, 1968 [orig. 1900]), 62.

48. Frederick B. Vaughan to Walt Whitman (4 September 1860) at http://digital.lib .lehigh.edu/pfaffs/works/search/id-1939_start-1-pd2-47/#fulltext. See also, however, Thomas Dunn English, "That Club at Pfaff's [*sic*]," *Literary World* 17 (12 June 1886): 202: "I have heard Fitz James O'Brien, Henry Clapp, Jr., and George Arnold, who used to laughingly class themselves as Bohemians, speak of Pfaff, and his beer; but they spoke of no club."

49. Henry Clapp to Walt Whitman (12 May 1860), quoted in Traubel, *With Walt Whitman in Camden*, 4: 196. Clapp is here referring specifically to the 1860 edition of *Leaves of Grass*.

50. Henry Clapp to Walt Whitman, quoted in Traubel, *Walt Whitman in Camden*, 1: 237. The poem in question was "Bardic Symbols"; it would later be revised and retitled "As I Ebb'd with the Ocean of Life." Traubel gives the date of this letter as 27 March 1860; but since the poem did not appear in the *Atlantic* until April of that year, the date must be in error.

51. Whitman, quoted in Traubel, *Walt Whitman in Camden*, 1: 236.

52. Anon., "From the Albion, May 26, 1860," *New-York Saturday Press* (2 June 1860): 4.

53. Anon., "Walt Whitman and His Critics," *New-York Saturday Press* (28 July 1860): 2.

54. See Christine Stansell, "Whitman at Pfaff's: Commercial Culture, Literary Life and New York Bohemia at Mid-Century," *Walt Whitman Quarterly Review* 10 (Fall 1993): 107–26. Much useful information is provided in Albert Parry's pioneering work on this subject, *Garrets and Pretenders: A History of Bohemianism in America*, rev. ed. (New York:

Dover, 1960 [orig. 1933]), 14–48. Also of interest is Gene Lalor, "Whitman Among the New York Literary Bohemians: 1859–1862," *Walt Whitman Review* 25 (December 1979): 131–45.

55. See, for instance, Anon., "Bohemians," *New-York Saturday Press* (3 March 1860): 2; D.D., "Bohemia," *New-York Saturday Press* (16 June 1860): 2; D.D., "The Bohemian in Literature," *New-York Saturday Press* (23 June 1860): 2; D.D., "The Bohemian in Government," *New-York Saturday Press* (7 July 1860): 2; D.D., "The Bohemian as a Gentleman," *New-York Saturday Press* (30 June 1860): 2.

56. Ralph Waldo Emerson, *Letters and Social Aims* (1875), in *The Complete Works of Ralph Waldo Emerson*, ed. Edward Waldo Emerson, 12 vols. (Boston: Houghton, Mifflin, 1904), 8: 316. See also, for a contrast to my argument, Levin's discussions of the "good bohemian" and her analysis of how New York's bohemians situated themselves in relation to "respectable" Boston, in *Bohemia in America*, 125–28, 57–68.

57. C.C.W., "A Bohemian" (letter to the editor), *New-York Saturday Press* (16 September 1865): 99.

58. Anon. [Moncure Daniel Conway], "Mannahatta," *Fraser's Magazine* 72 (September 1865): 281.

59. See Augustus Maverick, *Henry J. Raymond and the New York Press, for Thirty Years: Progress of American Journalism from 1840 to 1870* (Hartford, Conn.: A. S. Hale, 1870), 330–33.

60. Anon., "Literary News," *Literary World* 3 (1 May 1873): 192.

61. Anon., "Three New York Poets," *Scribner's Monthly* (July 1881): 469.

62. [George William Curtis], "Editor's Easy Chair," *Harper's New Monthly Magazine* 19 (October 1859): 705.

63. H[enry] C[uyler] Bunner, "Urban and Suburban Sketches: The Bowery and Bohemia," *Scribner's Magazine* 15 (April 1894): 454.

64. Carl Benson [Charles Astor Bristed, pseud.], "A New Theory of Bohemians," *Knickerbocker* 57 (March 1861): 312.

65. Junius Henri Browne, *The Great Metropolis: A Mirror of New York* (Hartford, Conn.: American Publishing, 1869), 158.

66. D.D., "Bohemia," *New-York Saturday Press* (16 June 1860): 2.

67. C.C.W., "A Bohemian," *New-York Saturday Press* (16 September 1865): 99.

68. D.D., "The Bohemian in Literature," *New-York Saturday Press* (23 June 1860): 2.

69. D.D., "The Bohemian as a Gentleman," *New-York Saturday Press* (30 June 1860): 2.

70. Ada Clare, "Thoughts and Things," *New-York Saturday Press* (11 February 1860): 2; rpt. as "A Bohemienne," *New-York Saturday Press* (26 August 1865): 60–61.

71. Anon., "Walt Whitman: Leaves of Grass," *New-York Saturday Press* (19 May 1860): 2.

72. Henry P. Leland, "Walt Whitman," *New-York Saturday Press* (23 June 1860): 1.

73. C.C.P., "Walt Whitman's New Poem," *New-York Saturday Press* (23 June 1860): 1.

74. A Woman, "Walt Whitman," *New-York Saturday Press* (23 June 1860): 3.

75. See Anon., "Bohemianism in New York," *New-York Saturday Press* (7 October 1865): 156. Clapp presented this article as being reprinted from "a late English periodical."

76. Edith Wharton, *The Age of Innocence*, in *Novels*, ed. R. W. B. Lewis (New York: Library of America, 1985), 1259, 1141. The character of Carver seems to recall one of Clapp's

and Clare's acquaintances, the abolitionist, language reformer, and Free Love advocate Stephen Pearl Andrews, who publicized himself as the Pantarch of the New Age.

77. O'Connor upheld Whitman's working-class bona fides, describing his "picturesque costume of the common people" and asserting, "I know that in the subterranean life of cities, among the worst roughs, he goes safely," while simultaneously downplaying talk about him as a "rowdy." See O'Connor, "The Good Gray Poet: A Vindication," *Walt Whitman*, 99, 103, 100n.

78. Whitman, "To William D. O'Connor (For Moncure D. Conway)" (10 November 1867?), in Whitman, *The Correspondence*, ed. Edwin Haviland Miller, 6 vols., *The Collected Writings of Walt Whitman* (New York: New York University Press, 1961–77), 1: 348.

79. See Edmond and Jules de Goncourt, *Journal: Mémoires de la vie littéraire*, ed. Robert Ricatte, 22 vols. (Monaco: Les Éditions de l'Imprimerie Nationale de Monaco, 1956), 1: 236. This entry was written in 1856.

80. See Howells, "First Impressions of Literary New York," *Literary Friends and Acquaintance*, 61–79.

81. Jean-Paul Sartre, *Critique de la raison dialectique* (Paris: Gallimard, 1960), 44.

82. Whitman (c. 1888), quoted in Traubel, *With Walt Whitman in Camden*, 2: 283. On Whitman in relation to issues of race and slavery, see especially Martin Klammer, *Whitman, Slavery, and the Emergence of* Leaves of Grass (University Park: Pennsylvania State University Press, 1995), and Betsy Erkkila, *Whitman the Political Poet* (New York: Oxford University Press, 1989), esp. 44–67.

83. Whitman, in an entry for 8 March 1890, quoted in Traubel, *With Walt Whitman in Camden*, 6: 322.

84. Whitman, *Prose Works*, 2: 762. D. D., "Bohemia," *The New-York Saturday Press* 3 (16 June 1860): 2. Another example of how this tellingly casual racism existed among the regulars at Pfaff's can be taken from Clare's writing in one of her newspaper columns of "a mass of ignorant, gibbering, unmannered blacks" in Jamaica. See Clare, "Coming Out," *Golden Era* (20 March 1864): 4.

85. Ada Cable, "The Spirit of Bohemia," *Bohemia*, 181.

86. B. W. Trafford, "The Telephone of the Future," *Bohemia*, 144–45.

87. Anon., "In and About the City: Death of Charles I. Pfaff: Something About the Proprietor of the Once Famous 'Bohemia,'" *New York Times* (26 April 1890): 2.

88. Clare's original surname is spelled variously in different accounts: McIlhinney, McIlhenney, and McElheny.

89. See S. Frederick Starr, *Bamboula! The Life and Times of Louis Moreau Gottschalk* (New York: Oxford University Press, 1995), 250. The inheritance dispute was a result of her family's outrage at Clare's decision to move to New York City and go on the stage.

90. Anon., "Walt Whitman's New Poem," rpt. from the *Cincinnati Commercial*, *New-York Saturday Press* (7 January 1860): 1.

91. Anon., "The Queen of Bohemia" ("From New York Correspondence of The Philadelphia Dispatch"), *New-York Saturday Press* (10 November 1860): 1.

92. See Charles Warren Stoddard, "Ada Clare, Queen of Bohemia," *National Magazine* 22 (September 1905): 639. One wonders if Henry Harland picked up on this detail

from Clare's life, or from Bernhardt's, in his portrayal of an unapologetically unwed "bohemian girl" and her son in his story "The Bohemian Girl," in *Gray Roses* (Boston: Roberts Brothers, 1895), 9–45.

93. Anon., "Henry Clapp," *New York Times* (11 April 1875): 7. The names not attributed here to the *Times* are mentioned in, among other testimonies, Rawson, "A Bygone Bohemia," n.p.

94. According to William Winter, Clare also wrote an earlier novel, entitled *Asphodel*, which was set in print but never appeared due to the failure of the publisher. See Winter, *Brief Chronicles*, 3 vols. (New York: Dunlap Society, 1889), 1: 48–49.

95. Anon., [Untitled Article], *New York Clipper* (14 March 1874): page unknown. A more sober medical account of her death appeared in Anon., "Hydrophobia," *Medical and Surgical Reporter* 30 (21 March 1874): 270.

96. Anon., "Literary Notices," *Boston Review* 6 (July 1866): 463.

97. Stoddard, "Ada Clare, Queen of Bohemia," *National Magazine* 22 (September 1905): 644.

98. See the story John Burroughs reportedly had from Whitman and retold in an 1862 letter, which involves Clare's advice to "a young man from the country" that he should seduce his fiancée, in Clara Barrus, *Whitman and Burroughs: Comrades* (Boston: Houghton Mifflin, 1931), 3.

99. Alastor [Ada Clare, pseud.], "Appreciative Faculty vs. Small Beer," *New York Atlas* (14 December 1856): 1.

100. Whitman, "Democratic Vistas" (1871), *Prose Works*, 2: 396. For Whitman's admiring notice of Clare in the series of articles he wrote in 1856 for *Life Illustrated*, see Whitman, "Street Yarn," *New York Dissected*, ed. Emory Holloway and Ralph Adimari (New York: Rufus Rockwell Wilson, 1936), 131–32. After one of Whitman's poems, "A Child's Reminiscence" (later revised and published under the title "Out of the Cradle Endlessly Rocking") appeared prominently in the *New-York Saturday Press* (24 December 1859): 1, Clare praised it in "Thoughts and Things," *New-York Saturday Press* (14 January 1860): 2. For Whitman's attendance at the Sunday evening gatherings at Clare's home, see Rose Eytinge, *The Memories of Rose Eytinge* (New York: Frederick A. Stokes, 1905), 22.

101. See Emilie Ruck de Schell, "Is Feminine Bohemianism a Failure?" *Arena* 20 (July 1898): 68–75.

102. For Thomas Mann's account of his sister's suicide, see his *Lebensabriß* (Berlin: S. Fischer, 1930), 49–50. For an example of her remarks on being a single mother in bohemia, see Franziska, Gräfin zu Reventlow, *Tagebücher 1897–1910, Gesammelte Werke*, ed. Else Reventlow (Munich: A. Langen, [1925]), 88. This passage is from an entry dated August 22, 1898. For another example of the special costs to women from an involvement in bohemia, see Reventlow's moving account of a woman's return home to her estranged family when her father is dying, "Pater," in *Simplicissimus* 1 (2 May 1896): 6–7. On this general topic see also the section on "New Women and the Borders of Bohemia" in Levin, *Bohemia in America*, 275–81.

103. See Reventlow, "Viragines oder Hetären" (1899), in Reventlow, *Autobiographisches*, ed. Else Reventlow (Munich: Albert Langen, 1980), 468–81.

104. Ada Clare, "Literary Feuilleton," *New York Leader* (25 April 1863): 1.

105. Anon., "Library Table," *Round Table* (19 May 1866): 308.

106. Clare, *Only a Woman's Heart* (New York: M. Doolady, 1866). Page references are given within the text.

107. Browne, *The Great Metropolis*, 154.

108. Clare, "Thoughts and Things," *New-York Saturday Press* (19 May 1860): 3.

109. Clare, "Lines to _____," *New-York Atlas* (28 January 1855): 1. On Gottschalk's visits to Clare and Pfaff's, see Vernon Loggins, *Where the Word Ends: The Life of Louis Moreau Gottschalk* (Baton Rouge: Louisiana State University Press, 1958), 186. One can trace Clare's desperately self-dramatizing attempts to attract Gottschalk in a series of newspaper articles she wrote at the time, under the pseudonym "Alastor": "Model Concerts," *New York Atlas* (16 November 1856): 1; "Brewers of Small Beer," *New York Atlas* (23 November 1856): 1; "The Automaton Pianist," *New York Atlas* (30 November 1856): 1; "Whips and Scorns of Time," *New York Atlas* (7 December 1856): 1; "Appreciative Faculty vs. Small Beer," *New York Atlas* (14 December 1856): 1; "The Pangs of Despised Love," *New York Atlas* (28 December 1856): 1; and "Ada Clare on Suicide," *New York Atlas* (4 January 1857): 1.

110. Clare, "Literary Feuilleton," *New York Leader* (11 July 1863): 1.

111. Clare, "Thoughts and Things," *New-York Saturday Press* (10 March 1860): 2.

112. Clare, "Thoughts and Things," *New-York Saturday Press* (22 October 1859): 2.

113. Clare, "A Miserable," *Golden Era* (10 April 1864): 4.

114. Clare, "Thoughts and Things," *New-York Saturday Press* (7 January 1860): 2.

115. Page had exhibited a now lost painting of Venus in the Boston Atheneum in the spring of 1859, causing such controversy that it was taken down and put into storage. In the wake of this controversy, the painting Clare saw was a different but related one, on the theme of Venus guiding Aeneas, that Page exhibited at the Düsseldorf Gallery in New York City in October 1859. See Joshua C. Taylor, *William Page: The American Titan* (Chicago: University of Chicago Press, 1957), 165.

116. Clare, "Thoughts and Things," *New-York Saturday Press* (29 October 1859): 2.

117. Clare, "Thoughts and Things," *New-York Saturday Press* (17 March 1860): 2.

118. Clare, "Matilda Heron as Camille," *New York Leader* (14 March 1863): 1.

119. Clare, "Literary Feuilleton," *New York Leader* (17 October 1863): 5.

120. Clare, "Some False Proverbs," *New York Leader* (7 March 1863): 1.

121. Clare, "Literary Feuilleton," *New York Leader* (28 March 1863): 4.

122. Clare, "Literary Feuilleton," *New York Leader* (6 June 1863): 5.

123. Clare, "Literary Feuilleton," *New York Leader* (12 December 1863): 5.

124. Clare, "Literary Feuilleton," *New York Leader* (25 April 1863): 1.

125. Clare, "Literary Feuilleton," *New York Leader* (3 January 1863): 1.

126. Clare, "Literary Feuilleton," *New York Leader* (16 May 1863): 5.

127. Clare, "Literary Feuilleton," *New York Leader* (28 March 1863): 4. See also her praise of this work, "A Spasm of Sense," when it was published in a book of Hamilton's essays, in "Literary Feuilleton," *New York Leader* (3 October 1863): 5.

128. Clare, "Literary Feuilleton," *New York Leader* (1 August 1863): 1.

129. Clare, "Literary Feuilleton," *New York Leader* (26 September 1863): 1.

130. Alastor, "Whips and Scorns of Time," *New York Atlas* (7 December 1856): 1.

131. Clare, "Thoughts and Things," *New-York Saturday Press* (21 April 1860): 2.

132. Clare, "On Some False Proverbs," *New York Leader* (14 February 1863): 1.

133. Anon., "Ada Clare," *Golden Era* (20 March 1864): 4.

134. Hale, *Old and New*, 9: 524.

135. On this point see Stoddard, "Ada Clare, Queen of Bohemia," *National Magazine* 22 (September 1905): 644.

136. Clare, "Thoughts and Things," *New-York Saturday Press* (2 June 1860): 2.

137. See Reynolds, *Walt Whitman's America*, 154–93.

138. Clare, "Thoughts and Things," *New-York Saturday Press* (2 June 1860): 2.

139. Charlotte Brontë, *Jane Eyre* (1847), ed. Q. D. Leavis (Harmondsworth: Penguin Books, 1985), 281. For Clare's role in Brougham's *Jane Eyre, or The Orphan of Lowood*, see George C. D. Odell, *Annals of the New York Stage*, 15 vols. (New York: Columbia University Press, 1931), 6: 455.

140. Brontë, *Jane Eyre*, 301.

CHAPTER 6. THE POVERTY OF NATIONS

1. Henry Murger, "Préface," *Scènes de la vie de bohème*, ed. Loïc Chotard and Graham Robb (Paris: Gallimard, 1988 [orig. 1851]), 34. For how Murger's claim was repeated, see, for instance, Max Mordau, "Die Bohème," *Paris: Studien und Bilder aus dem wahren Milliardenlande*, 2 vols. (Leipzig: Duncker & Humblot, 1881), 1: 229.

2. For examples of Italian writers who explicitly reproduced Murger's international conception of bohemia, see Fantasio [Ferdinando Martini], "Viaggio nel paese di bohême" (1874), in *La pubblicistica nel periodo della scapigliatura*, ed. Giuseppe Farinelli (Milan: Istituto Propaganda Libraria, 1984), 283–84 and G [Francesco Giarelli], "Parenthesis" (1880), in *La pubblicistica nel periodo della scapigliatura*, 1107–8.

3. Cletto Arrighi [Carlo Righetti, pseud.], *La Scapigliatura: Romanzo sociale contemporaneo*, ed. Giuseppe Farinelli (Milan: Istituto Propaganda Libraria, 1978 [orig. 1862]), 117. Farinelli adopts the title of the 1880 version of the novel; I quote this passage as it appeared in the introduction to the 1862 edition, which differs slightly from the prologue to the 1880 edition. The ellipses are the author's own.

4. For his use of it in the earlier novel, see Arrighi, *Gli ultimi coriandoli: Romanzo contemporaneo* (Milan: Lampi di stampa, 2004 [orig. 1857]), 113. In 1857 Arrighi also published a version of what became the prologue to *La Scapigliatura e il 6 febbraio* in the *Almanacco del pungolo*; it is reproduced, along with the other versions, in Giuseppe Farinelli, *La Scapigliatura: Profilo storico, protagonisti, documenti* (Rome: Carocci editore, 2003), 209–18.

5. Arrighi, *La Scapigliatura*, 118. The fleeting reference to the scapigliatura in *Gli ultimi coriandoli* had also identified it with France's bohemia, and in 1868 Arrighi noted that the first three chapters of *La Scapigliatura* had been translated in France under the title *Bohème Milanaise*. See C[letto] Arrighi, "Libro grigio" (1868), in *La pubblicistica nel periodo della scapigliatura*, 212.

6. K.X. [Eugenio Camerini], *"La Scapigliatura e il 6 febbraio,"* *La perseveranza* (26 January 1862), in *La pubblicistica nel periodo della scapigliatura*, 886.

7. Gian Vincenzo Bruni's *Scene della vita d'artista* (1859) was this work's first translation into Italian.

8. See Jules Barbey D'Aurevilly, "Edgar Poe" (1858), *Les oeuvres et les hommes*, 26 vols. (Paris: Alphonse Lemerre, 1860–90); rep. Geneva: Slatkine Reprints, 1968), 12: 376–84.

9. Camerini, "Cletto Arrighi," *Nuovi profili letterari*, 4 vols. (Milan: Presso Natale Battezzati, 1875), 2: 126.

10. Igino Ugo Tarchetti, "Conversazioni," in *Convegno nazionale su Igino Ugo Tarchetti e la Scapigliatura*, ed. Giorgio Barberi Squarotti et al. (San Salvatore Monferrato: Comune di San Salvatore Monferrato e della Cassa di Risparmio di Alessandria, [1976]), 309. Note that Tarchetti was baptized "Igino" but later preferred to write his name "Iginio," as I represent it in this book.

11. Arrighi, "Il diavolo a quattro della stampa milanese, II: Al 'Gazzettino Rosa,' " in *La Scapigliatura: Profilo storico, protagonisti, documenti*, 227.

12. Arrighi, *La Scapigliatura*, 118.

13. [Arrighi], "Il diavolo a quattro della stampa milanese" (1868), in *La pubblicistica nel periodo della scapigliatura*, 213; and Achille Bizzoni, "Due parole alla 'Frustra,' " in *La Scapigliatura: Profilo storico, protagonisti, documenti*, 228.

14. Bizzoni, "Chi siamo e perché siamo," in *La Scapigliatura: Profilo storico, protagonisti, documenti*, 232.

15. Bizzoni, "Chi siamo e perché siamo," in *La Scapigliatura: Profilo storico, protagonisti, documenti*, 233.

16. I cannot pin down exactly when this term was coined; for a relatively early use, see, e. g., C.M., "Il barabba," *Milano libera: Panorama politico-sociale* (Milan: Presso l'Amministrazione dal Giornale, 1863), 39.

17. Farfalla [Francesco Giarelli], "La bohème," in *La Scapigliatura: Profilo storico, protagonisti, documenti*, 262, 263. He refers to Giuseppe Rovani, Emilio Praga, Iginio Ugo Tarchetti, Vicenzo Pezza, Giulio Pinchetti, and Teobaldo Cicone; I have not been able to identify the full names of the others he cites.

18. Quoted in Salvatore Farina, *La mia giornata: Care ombre* (Sassari: Editrice Democratica Sarda, 1997 [orig. 1913]), 30.

19. Quoted in Giarelli, *Vent'anni di giornalismo (1868–1888)* (Codogno: A. G. Cairo, 1896), 51.

20. Carlo Dossi, *Rovaniana*, ed. Giorgio Nicodemi, 2 vols. (Milan: Edizioni della Libreria Vinciana, 1946), 1: 399.

21. Dossi, *Note azzure*, ed. Dante Isella (Milan: Adelphi Edizioni, 1964 [orig. 1912]), 431.

22. On this subject see Gaetano Mariani, "La formazione di un mito: Biografia e leggenda di Giuseppe Rovani," *Storia della scapigliatura*, 2nd ed. (Rome: Salvatore Sciascia, 1971), 201–2.

23. Dossi, *Note azzure*, 442–43.

24. Dossi, *Note azzure*, 466; Dossi, *Note azzure*, 471; Roberto Sachetti, "La vita

letteraria a Milano nel 1880" (1880), in *Racconti della Scapigliatura milanese*, ed. Vittorio Spinazzola (Novara: Istituto geografico De Agostini, 1959), 491.

25. Arrighi, *La Scapigliatura*, 117.

26. Giorgio Nicodemi, "Una testimonia anonima per la storia della scapigliatura Milanese," in *Scritti storici e giuridici in memoria di Alessandro Visconti* (Milan: Istituto Editoriale Cisalpino, 1955), 339.

27. Dossi, *Note azzure*, 414.

28. Dossi, *Note azzure*, 543–33.

29. See Mikhail Bakhtin, *Rabelais and His World*, trans. Hélène Iswolsky (Blooming-ton: Indiana University Press, 1984).

30. See I[ginio] U[go] Tarchetti, "Appunti settimanali" (1868), in *La pubblicistica nel periodo della scapigliatura*, 619.

31. Farfalla [Francesco Giarelli], "La bohème" (1876), in *La Scapigliatura: Profilo storico, protagonisti, documenti*, 62. Giarelli's formula, published in *La farfalla*, echoed the words of Cameroni three years earlier in *Il gazzettino rosa*: "Realists in art, republicans in politics, rationalists in philosophy, the *bohèmes* represent the type opposed to conservatism of every shade." Cameroni also emphasized "paradox," a term used among the scapiglia-tura to signify markedly unconventional ideas, just as it had been in France's bohemia; it would seem that this shorthand formulation was in general circulation. See Stoico [Felice Cameroni], "Sì! Siamo la Bohème della stampa" (1873), in *La Scapigliatura: Profilo storico, protagonisti, documenti*, 251.

32. Giarelli, *Vent'anni di giornalismo*, 138–39.

33. In France, too, though to a lesser extent, terms that were basically synonyms for *bohemians* arose over the course of the century—*réfractaires*, as mentioned above, but also *irréguliers* and *déclassés*.

34. Arnaldo Nobis, in a letter to Arcangelo Ghisleri (3 February 1876), in *La scapiglia-tura democratica: Carteggi di Arcangelo Ghisleria: 1875–1890*, ed. Pier Carlo Masini (Milan: Feltrinelli Editore, 1961), 226.

35. C.M., "Gli operai," in *Milano libera*, 39. See also M[ichele] Uda, "Gli spostati" (1859), in *La pubblicistica nel periodo della scapigliatura*, 33–34. This dramatic fragment was prefaced by Leone Fortis's "La spostatura."

36. Leone Fortis, *Conversazioni* (Milan: Fratelli Treves, 1877), 144.

37. B. Clerici, "Passeggiate a vespro," in Aldo Barilli et al., *Il ventre di Milano: Fisiolo-gia della capitale morale*, 2 vols. (Milan: Carlo Aliprandi, 1888), 2: 152.

38. Umberto Silvagni, *Napoleone Bonaparte e i suoi tempi*, 2 vols. (Rome: Forzani, 1895), 1: 741.

39. C[onstantino] Arlía, "La vita boema," *Il borghini: Giornale di filología e di lettere italiane* 4 (15 January 1878): 227.

40. Gerolama Boccardo, *L'economia politica moderna e la sociologia* (Turin: Unione Tipografico-Editrice, 1883), cxxvi.

41. Anon., "La bohème di Parigi," *Gazzetta letteraria* (8–15 June 1878): 182.

42. Blasco [pseud.], "Note milanese" (1876), in *La pubblicistica nel periodo della scapi-gliatura*, 292–93.

43. Anon., "L'esposizione di belle arti in Roma," *Nuova antologia di scienze, lettere ed arti* 37, 2nd. ser. (1883): 534.

44. Quoted in Mariani, *Storia della Scapigliatura*, 613–14. Giarelli (*Vent'anni di giornalismo*, 64–5) claims that this term was coined by Giuseppi Guerzoni, the future biographer of Giuseppi Garibaldi, to designate "the young legion of Garibaldian democracy, the avant-garde of the Fronde of Italian journalism."

45. Stoico [Felice Cameroni], "Sì! Siamo la Bohème della stampa," in *La Scapigliatura: Profilo storico, protagonisti, documenti*, 249.

46. Jules Vallès, *Les réfractaires* (1865), ed. Lucien Scheler, *Les oeuvres de Jules Vallès*, ed. Lucien Scheler, 8 vols. (Paris: Les Éditeurs Français Réunis, 1950–57), 4: 23.

47. Amadeo Roux, "Cronaca letteraria di Francia," *La revista Europea* 4 (November 1872): 594.

48. L'Appendicista [Felice Cameroni], "Le biografie dei vinti" (1872), in *La Scapigliatura: Profilo storico, protagonisti, documenti*, 249.

49. Pessimista [Felice Cameroni], "Viva la Scapigliatura!" (1870), quoted in Arrighi, *La Scapigliatura e le 6 febbraio*, 24n. Cameroni repeated this characterization of Heine and Murger in a later article. See the introduction to excerpts from Vallès's *Les réfractaires* by Un Perduto [Cameroni], "Caro Fortunio" (1871), in *La pubblicistica nel periodo della scapigliatura*, 526.

50. See Cameroni, "I funerali di Rovani" (1874), *Interventi critici: Sulla letteratura italiana* (Naples: Guida Editori, 1974), 31–32.

51. Ferruccio Mosconi, "Le classi sociali al Brasile e loro funzioni," *La riforma sociale* (15 January 1897): 590.

52. Arrighi, *La Scapigliatura*, 117.

53. Orso, "Scapigliatura" (1870), quoted in Arrighi, *La Scapigliatura e il 6 febbraio*, 24n.

54. See Arrighi, *La Scapigliatura*, 117.

55. In *Les Confessions: Souvenirs d'un demi-siècle*, 6 vols. (Paris: E. Dentu, 1885–1891), 1: 294–95, Arsène Houssaye describes the bohemia in which he participated, of which he offers Théophile Gautier as an exemplar, as consciously apolitical. For the crowd at Pfaff's, see my Chapter 5. On the apolitical nature of the scene in Lima, see Ricardo Palma, "La Bohemia de mi tiempo," in *Recuerdos de España precedidos de La Bohemia de mi tiempo* (Lima: La Industria, 1899), 17.

56. See Un Perduto [Cameroni], "Caro Fortunio" (1871), in *La pubblicistica nel periodo della scapigliatura*, 527.

57. Oreste Vaccari, "La Scapigliatura: Divagazioni" (1875), in *La Scapigliatura: Profilo storico, protagonisti, documenti*, 259. See the similar characterization in Girolamo Ragusa Moleti, "I bohèmes" (1878), in *La Scapigliatura: Profilo storico, protagonisti, documenti*, 279.

58. Stoico [Felice Cameroni], "Sì! Siamo la Bohème della stampa," *La Scapigliatura: Profilo storico, protagonisti, documenti*, 252.

59. C.M., "Il barabba," *Milano libera*, 39–40.

60. Antonio Cima, in an 1877 review of Raffaello Barbiera's *Simpatie*, quoted in Mariani, *Storia della scapigliatura*, 877–78n.

61. On Tarchetti's abortive collaboration with Eugenio Torelli Viollier, see "Pagine di romanzo," *Tutte gli opere*, 2: 543–56.

62. Eugenio Torelli Viollier, "La Bohème" (1878), in *La Scapigliatura: Profilo storico, protagonisti, documenti*, 270.

63. See O[reste] Cenacchi, "Il primo Elzevir dello Zanichelli," *Teatro e romanzo: Note e ricerche* (Bologna: Nicola Zanichelli, 1886), 165.

64. Torelli Viollier, "La Bohème," 270.

65. See Cameroni, "La moda letteratura" (1873), *Interventi critici*, 28.

66. Boccardo, *L'economia politica moderna e la sociologia*, cxxv.

67. E[lme-Marie] Caro, "La fin de la bohème," *Revue des deux mondes* 94 (15 July 1871): 251. For other examples of writers across Europe who helped to popularize this kind of formula, see, for instance, its reproduction in Franz Mehring, "Die Pariser Commune 1871," *Preußische Jahrbücher* 43 (1879): 283; F.L. [Frédéric Loliée?], "Bohème," in *Dictionnaire de dictionnaires: Encyclopédie universelle des sciences et des arts*, ed. Paul Guerin, 7 vols. ([Paris]: A. Picard, 1884), 2: 75; Ferdinando Martini, "Tradimenti e traditori," *Cose Affricane: Da Saati ad Abba Carima* (Milan: Fratelli Treves, [1896]), 184–85; and Luis Antón del Olmet, "Los desocupados," *El libro de la vida bohemia* (Madrid: Jaime Ratés, [1909]). For Crozat's pioneering use of the formula later adopted by Caro and these others, see Émile Crozat, *La maladie du siècle, ou les suites funestes du déclassement social*, 4th ed. (Bordeaux: A. R. Chaynes, 1856), which is described on its title page as "A work written under the woeful influences of a *barrister* without a case, a *notary* and a *solicitor* without clients, a *doctor* without a practice, a *merchant* without capital, a *laborer* without work." This formula was already in the air, as a way of describing bohemians, before Caro picked up on it; see Anon. [Taxile Delord, Arnould Frémy, Edmond Texier], *Paris-bohème* (Paris: A. Taride, 1854), 75. On Caro's article and related contemporary analyses, see also Jerrold Seigel, *Bohemian Paris: Culture, Politics, and the Boundaries of Bourgeois Life, 1830–1930* (Baltimore: Johns Hopkins University Press, 1986), 182–85.

68. G.P.A., "Il vero nei libri, negli scrittori ed i suoi effetti," *La rassegna nazionale* 2 (1885): 200.

69. Anon., "Una dolorosa perdita" (1869), in *La pubblicistica nel periodo della scapigliatura*, 451; G.P.A., "Il vero nei libri, negli scrittori ed i suoi effetti," *La rassegna nazionale* 2 (1885): 201.

70. See Otto von Leixner, *1888 bis 1891: Soziale Briefe aus Berlin* (Berlin: Friedrich Pfeilstücker, 1891), 209–13; E[dmond] Lepelletier, "La bohème féminine," *L'echo de Paris* (11 August 1884): 1. This article was approvingly quoted by Édouard Drumont, *La France Juive: Essai d'histoire*, 2 vols., 43rd ed. (Paris: C. Marpon and E. Flammarion, 1886), 445.

71. Ghidetti, *Tarchetti e la scapigliatura lombarda* (Naples: Libreria Scientifica Editrice, 1968), 274–75. In making this comment, Ghidetti perhaps forgot his own earlier description of how the recollections of Tarchetti's contemporaries focused on—which is to say, served to create—what Marino Parenti called "the romance of his life." See Ghidetti, *Tarchetti e la scapigliatura lombarda*, 47.

72. In addition to the contemporary sources cited elsewhere, I am indebted for the biographical information here and below to Mariani, "Nota biobibliographica," *Tutte gli*

opere, 1: 63–65; and to Ghidetti, *Tarchetti e la scapigliatura lombarda*. See also the concise account of Tarchetti's life and works, including a summary of critical responses to his writing and a useful bibliography, in the editor's "Introduction" to Tarchetti, *Fosca*, ed. Luca Della Bianca (Turin: Societá Editrice Internazionale, 1995), 1–16.

73. Farina, *La mia giornata: Care ombre*, 21. Farina also observes that the practice of assuming a new literary name was common in the small "artistic cenacle" in which he met Tarchetti. See *La mia giornata: Dall'alba al meriggio* (Sassari: Editrici Democratica Sarda, 1996 [orig. 1910]), 73–74.

74. See Farina, *La mia giornata: Care ombre*, 34–37.

75. See Farina, *La mia giornata: Dall'alba al meriggio*, 124–25.

76. Tarchetti, "Conversazioni" (1868), in *Convegno nazionale su Igino Ugo Tarchetti e la Scapigliatura*, 339. Nicolas Gilbert and Jacques Louis de Malfilâtre were eighteenth-century poets whom Murger famously listed as bohemian exemplars in the preface to his *Scenes of Bohemian Life*—although he did so in order to inveigh against their idealization as martyrs.

77. For Tarchetti's objections to how he was represented, especially in regard to misanthropy, see the quotations from a letter he sent to the editor of the journal *Il gazzettino* as quoted by an unnamed columnist [Felice Cavallotti?], "Sotto voce" (1867), in *La pubblicistica nel periodo della scapigliatura*, 495.

78. Quoted in Piero Nardi, *Scapigliatura: Da Giuseppe Rovani a Carlo Dossi* (Verona: Arnoldo Mondadori Editore, 1968), 61.

79. Farina, *La mia giornata: Dall'alba al meriggio*, 69.

80. Quoted in Farina, *La mia giornata: Care ombre*, 30.

81. Eddore Socci, *Da Firenze a Digione: Impressioni di un reduce Garibaldino* (Prato: Tipografia Sociale, 1871), 93.

82. Anon., "Il mio album" (1867), in *La pubblicistica nel periodo della scapigliatura*, 495.

83. A[chille] Bizzoni, "Oh! gli amici!" (1868), in *La pubblicistica nel periodo della scapigliatura*, 500.

84. Quoted in Giulio Carnazzi, "L'iride degli scapigliati," in *La Scapigliatura milanese: Note colori versi umori della Compagnia Brusca*, ed. Mario Chiodetti ([Milan]: Fabbrica Arte in collaborazione con Zecchini Editore, 2001), 96.

85. Tarchetti, "Canti del cuore 6," *Disjecta versi* (Bologna: Presso Nicola Zanichelli, 1879), 69.

86. Carlo Catanzaro, "Igino Ugo Tarchetti," *Cari estinti: Bozzetti letterari*, 3rd ed. (Sienna: Giulio Muccì, 1876 [orig. 1873]), 23.

87. P[ompeo] G. Molmenti, "Iginio Ugo Tarchetti," *Impressioni letterarie*, 2nd ed. (Milan: N. Battezzati e B. Saldini, 1875), 49.

88. Sacchetti, "La vita letteraria a Milano nel 1880," *Racconti della Scapigliatura milanese*, 481, 483.

89. Raffaelo Barbiera, *Il salotto dalla Contessa Maffei e la società milanese (1834–1886)* (Milan: Fratelli Treves, 1895), 298.

90. Vittorio Bersezio, *Il regno di Vittorio Emanuele II: Trent-anni di vita italiana*, 8 vols. (Turin: Roux Frassati, 1895), 8: 553.

91. In 1880 the future Nobel Prize winner Giosuè Carducci remarked that, although one could not tell from Tarchetti's narratives whether he had allied himself with the world of those who advocated democracy, "it would require that ambiance, or, better, that lack of oxygen, to proclaim the greatness of the tales of poor Tarchetti." See Carducci, "Dieci anni a dietro" (1880), *Opere di Giosuè Carducci*, 20 vols. (Bologna: Nicola Zanichelli, 1889), 3: 277.

92. Anon., "I. U. Tarchetti," *Rivista contemporanea* 57 (1869): 157.

93. Giarelli, *Vent'anni di giornalismo*, 216, 217.

94. Tarchetti, "Conversazioni" (1868), in *Convegno nazionale su Igino Ugo Tarchetti e la Scapigliatura*, 332.

95. See Gary S. Becker and Julia Jorge Elías, "Introducing Incentives in the Market for Live and Cadaveric Organ Donations" (2003/2006): http://home.uchicago.edu/gbecker/ MarketforLiveandCadavericOrgan Donations_Becker_Elias.pdf.

96. Tarchetti, "Pensieri" (1868), *Convegno nazionale su Igino Ugo Tarchetti e la Scapigliatura*, 326.

97. Tarchetti, "Conversazioni a spizzico" (1867), quoted in Franco Contorbia, "Tarchetti e 'L'emporio pittoresco,'" *Convegno nazionale su Igino Ugo Tarchetti e la Scapigliatura*, 281n. The author of this article was identified only as "T" in *La palestra musicale*, in which it originally appeared, but was apparently Tarchetti, who was the editor of this journal in the first months of 1867.

98. See Tarchetti, "La fame" (1868), in *Convegno nazionale su Igino Ugo Tarchetti e la Scapigliatura*, 297.

99. See Ghidetti's comments on the influence of Proudhon in *Paulina* and *La nobile follia* in "Introduzione," *Tutte gli opere*, 1: 20n, 25n, and in *Tarchetti e la scapigliatura lombarda*, 145–46. For a trace of the influence of Hugo, see the allusion in *Paulina* (1: 326) to Jean Valjean. Richardson's influence, of course, is evident in the tale of the poor heroine's rape.

100. Torelli Viollier, "Corriere di Milano" (1867), in *La pubblicistica nel periodo della scapigliatura*, 617. See also the related comments he published about six months later: Torelli Viollier, "La settimana milana milanese" (1868), in *La pubblicistica nel periodo della scapigliatura*, 441–42.

101. Tarchetti, "La letture popolari" (1868), in *Convegno nazionale su Igino Ugo Tarchetti e la Scapigliatura*, 293.

102. Fantasio [Ferdinando Martini], "Biblioteca di Fanfulla" (1874), in *La pubblicistica nel periodo della scapigliatura*, 286.

103. Anon., "Notizie letterarie," *Rassegna di scienze sociali e politiche* 1 (1893): 319.

104. Enrique Perez Escrich, *El frac azul: Episodios de un jóven flaco* (Madrid: Manini Hermanos, 1864), 102.

105. F[elice] Cavallotti, "Appunti letterari" (1868), in *La pubblicistica nel periodo della scapigliatura*, 444.

106. Tarchetti, "Pensieri" (1868), in *Convegno nazionale su Igino Ugo Tarchetti e la Scapigliatura*, 328.

107. Sébastien-Roch-Nicolas de Chamfort, *Maximes et pensées, Oeuvres complètes de Chamfort*, 5 vols. ([Paris]: Chaumerot Jeune, 1824–25 [orig. 1796]), 1: 413.

108. François, Duc de La Rochefoucauld, *Maximes, Oeuvres complètes de La Rochefoucauld*, ed. A. Chassang, new ed., 2 vols. (Paris: Garnier Frères, 1884 [orig. 1665]), 2: 82.

109. Cf. Roberto Tessari's fine analysis of the relation between the perception of an unaccommodating bourgeois modernity and the representation of sickness, bodily corruption, and death in Tarchetti's work: "L'immagini della morte nell'opere di Tarchetti e nella scapigliatura," *Convegno nazionale su Igino Ugo Tarchetti e la Scapigliatura*, 198–211.

110. Farina, *La mia giornata: Care ombre*, 27.

111. Pessimista [Felice Cameroni], "Divagazioni del Pessimista" (1870), in *La pubblicistica nel periodo della scapigliatura*, 513.

112. Lepidottero, "Chi siamo noi?" (1879), in *La pubblicistica nel periodo della scapigliatura*, 382.

113. Faust [Francesco Giarelli], "I nostri morti" (1878), in *La pubblicistica nel periodo della scapigliatura*, 370.

CHAPTER 7. SHERLOCK HOLMES MEETS DRACULA

1. Bram Stoker, *Dracula*, ed. Nina Auerbach and David J. Skal (New York: W. W. Norton, 1997). Page references are given within the text.

2. On this topic see Stephen Arata, "The *Occidental Tourist*: Dracula and the Anxiety of Reverse Colonization," *Victorian Studies* 33 (1990): 621–45.

3. E[nrique] Gomez Carrillo, *Bohemia sentimental* (1899), in *Tres novelas immorales* (Madrid: Editorial Mundo Latino, [1920]), 106. The logic of linking vampirism to bohemianism lay ready to hand in the cultural environment of this time, in which their critics often assailed bohemians as parasites; see also the use made of this logic in Guy de Charnacé's novel *Le baron vampire* (1885), in Willy Pastor's novel *Der Andere: Aus den Aufzeichnungen eines Dichters* (1896), and in Emilio Carrere's story "El dolor de llegar" (1909).

4. George Gissing, *The Private Papers of Henry Ryecroft* (New York: E. P. Dutton, 1927 [orig. 1903]), 25.

5. Friedrich Carl Peterssen, "Die Zigeuner," *Genrebilder aus dem modernen Babel* (Stuttgart: A. Kröner, 1870), 21.

6. Quoted in Horace Traubel, *With Walt Whitman in Camden*, ed. Sculley Bradley, Gertrude Traubel, Jeanne Chapman, and Robert MacIsaac, 9 vols. (New York: Rowman and Littlefield [vols. 1–3] and Carbondale: Southern Illinois University Press [vols. 4–9], 1905–1996), 2: 145. See also 4: 180–85 for the fan letters the young Bram Stoker sent to Whitman; and for his own account of his relations with the poet, see Stoker, *Personal Reminiscences of Henry Irving*, 2 vols. (New York: Macmillan, 1906), 2: 92–111.

7. See George Sand, *La Comtesse de Rudolstadt*, in *Consuelo/La Comtesse de Rudolstadt*, ed. Léon Cellier and Léon Guichard, 3 vols. (Paris: Garnier Frères, 1959 [orig. 1844]), 3: 245 et passim. The "Invisibles" in this novel are associated with the Freemasons, the

Knights Templar, the Moravian Brethren, the Taborites, the Illuminati, and the Rosicrucians, among others.

8. Félix Pyat, "Les artistes," in *Nouveau tableau de Paris au XIXme siècle*, [ed. Henri Martin], 7 vols. (Paris: Madame Charles-Béchet, 1834–35), 4: 18.

9. Edmond and Jules de Goncourt, *Journal: Mémoires de la vie littéraire*, ed. Robert Ricatte, 22 vols. (Monaco: Les Éditions de l'Imprimerie Nationale de Monaco, 1956), 1: 236. This entry was written in 1856.

10. Jules Barbey d'Aurevilly, "Edgar Poe" (1858), *Les oeuvres et les hommes*, 26 vols. (Paris: Alphonse Lemerre, 1860–90; rep. Geneva: Slatkine Reprints, 1968), 12: 377.

11. Karl Marx, *The Eighteenth Brumaire of Louis Bonaparte* (1852), in Marx and Friedrich Engels, *Collected Works*, trans. Richard Dixon et al. (New York: International Publishers, 1975—), 1: 149.

12. For other representations of bohemians that, like Marx's, associate them with specific types of crime, see, for instance, Adolphe d'Ennery and [Eugène] Grangé, *Les bohémiens de Paris* (1843), in *Magasin théâtral: Choix des pièces nouvelles jouées sur tous les théâtres de Paris* (Paris: Marchant, 1846), 1–43; and Peter Paterson [James Glass Bertram, pseud.], *Glimpses of Real Life as Seen in the Theatrical World and in Bohemia: Being the Confessions of Peter Paterson, a Strolling Comedian* (Edinburgh: W. P. Nimmo, 1864; rep. Hamden, Conn.: Archon Books, 1979).

13. Theodor Mundt, *Paris und Louis Napoleon: Neue Skizzen aus dem französischen Kaiserreich*, 2 vols. (Berlin: Otto Janke, 1858), 1: 168–69.

14. Marx, *The Eighteenth Brumaire of Louis Bonaparte*, *Collected Works*, 1: 157.

15. See Nina Auerbach's argument that Dracula "serves to catalyze homoerotic friendship among the humans who hunt him" and her speculation that "Dracula's primary progenitor is . . . Oscar Wilde in the dock" in *Our Vampires, Ourselves* (Chicago: University of Chicago Press, 1995), 81, 83.

16. Charles Baudelaire, "Mon coeur mis à nu" (c. 1859–1867), *Oeuvres complètes*, ed. Claude Pichois, 3 vols. (Paris: Gallimard, 1975), 1: 701.

17. On the image of vampiric women in this period, see Bram Dijkstra, *Idols of Perversity: Fantasies of Feminine Evil in Fin-de-Siècle Culture* (New York: Oxford University Press, 1987).

18. On this topic, see Eve Kosofsky Sedgwick, *Between Men: English Literature and Male Homosocial Desire* (New York: Columbia University Press, 1985).

19. In the early nineteenth century, at a time when there were only twelve such designated districts in Paris, "a marriage of the thirteenth arrondissement" became the term for the common arrangement in which students and grisettes, or sexually available working-class girls, set up housekeeping together.

20. One consequence of this development was the "Bohemian Brigade" of Civil War reporters. See Louis M. Starr, *Bohemian Brigade: Civil War Newsmen in Action* (New York: Alfred A. Knopf, 1954), and James M. Perry, *A Bohemian Brigade: The Civil War Correspondents—Mostly Rough, Sometimes Ready* (New York: John Wiley and Sons, 2000).

21. See Anon., "A Typical Bohemian," *Brooklyn Daily Eagle* (5 October 1872): 2.

22. G.J.M., "Bohemianism: A Fast Fading Phase of Literary and Artistic Life," *Brooklyn Daily Eagle* (20 April 1884): 4.

23. J. A. Hammerton, ed., *Mr. Punch in Bohemia* (London: Carmelite House, 1898), 5. For an account of London's bohemia in the decades immediately following those with which I am most concerned here, see Peter Brooker, *Bohemia in London: The Social Scene of Early Modernism* (New York: Palgrave Macmillan, 2004).

24. See George Gissing, *New Grub Street* (New York: Modern Library, 1926 [orig. 1891]), 415; and Gissing, *The Odd Women* (New York: Macmillan, 1893), 269.

25. See L.W., "The Bowery Song Writer: A Sketch of a Lower New York Character," *Brooklyn Daily Eagle* (5 April 1885): 10; and Anon., "Bohemians and Bohemians: One Set Counteracting the Movements of Another," *Brooklyn Daily Eagle* (31 January 1889): 5.

26. Edward M. Whitty, *The Bohemians of London* (Philadelphia: T. B. Peterson and Brothers, 1864 [orig. 1857]), title page. This epigraph is attributed to the *London Athenæum*.

27. G.J.M., "Bohemianism: A Fast Fading Phase of Literary and Artistic Life," *Brooklyn Daily Eagle* (20 April 1884): 4.

28. Vernon Lee (Violet Paget, pseud.), *Miss Brown*, 3 vols. in 1 (Edinburgh: William Blackwood and Sons, 1884; rep. New York: Garland, 1978), 3: 3; Florence Brooks Emerson, "Dinner in Bohemia," *Vagaries* (Boston: Small, Maynard, 1900), 32.

29. Eugenio Torelli Viollier, "La bohème," in *La Scapigliatura: Profilo storico, protagonisti, documenti*, ed. Giuseppe Farinelli (Rome: Carocci editore, 2003); Hermann Bahr, "Die Überwindung des Naturalismus," *Zur Kritik der Moderne*, 2 vols. (Dresden: G. Pierson's Verlag, 1891), 2: 222; Rubén Darío, "Este era un rey de Bohemia . . ." (1891), *Obras completas*, 5 vols. (Madrid: Afrodiso Aguado, 1950–55), 2: 134. Bahr was writing in reference to Luis Paris's *Gente nueva* (1888).

30. Bruno Wille, *Philosophie der Befreiung durch das reine Mittel: Beiträge zur Pädagogik des Menschengeschlechts* (Berlin: S. Fischer, 1894), 17; Frank Norris, "Salt and Sincerity," *Essays on Authorship*, in *Blix/Moran of the Lady Letty/Essays on Authorship* (New York: P. F. Collier and Son, 1898), 377.

31. See Henry James, *The Tragic Muse* (1890), *The Novels and Tales of Henry James*, 24 vols. (New York: Charles Scribner's Sons, 1922), 8: 227–28; Franziska Gräfin zu Reventlow, *Ellen Olestjerne* (1903) in *Autobiographisches*, ed. Else Reventlow (Munich: Albert Langen, 1980), 221; Julia Ward Howe, "What and Where Is Bohemia?" in *Bohemia: Offical Publication of the International League of Press Clubs for the Building and Endowment of the Journalists' Home*, ed. Alexander K. McClure (Philadelphia: International League of Press Clubs, 1904), 395; and Anon., "Music: The Week," *Athenaeum* (1 May 1897): 587.

32. Otto von Leixner, *1888 bis 1891: Soziale Briefe aus Berlin* (Berlin: Friedrich Pfeilstücker, 1891), 212; Camille Mauclair, "Le préjugé de la 'Vie de Bohème' et les moeurs de l'artiste actuel," *La revue des revues* 31 (December 1899): 463.

33. Alejandro Sawa, *Declaración de un vencido* (1887), in *Declaración de un vencido y Criadero de curas*, ed. Francisco Guttiérrez Carbajo (Madrid: Ediciones Atlas, 1999). Page numbers are given within the text.

34. Darío, *Autobiografía* (1912), *Obras completas*, 1: 103. Darío's characterization of Sawa joined what was, by the time he wrote it, a well-established tradition that Luis París

had helped to establish when he wrote about Sawa as one of the "gente nueva" of his time. See París, "Alejandro Sawa," *Gente nueva: Crítica inductiva* (Madrid: Imprento Popular, [1888]), 103–17. On Sawa's social and cultural background, see also Allen W. Phillips, *En torno a la bohemia madrileña 1890–1925: Testimonios, personajes y obras* ([Madrid]: Celeste Ediciones, 1999).

35. Paul Heyse, *Abenteuer eines Blaustrümpfchens* (Stuttgart: Carl Krabbe [1897]). Page references are given within the text.

36. See especially Reventlow, "Viragines oder Hetären" (1899), in *Autobiographisches*, 468–81.

37. George Saintsbury, "Henry Murger," *Fortnightly Review* 24 (August 1878): 231.

38. See Félix Pyat, "Les artistes," in *Nouveau tableau de Paris au XIXme siècle*, 4: 9; and Henry Murger, "Préface," *Scènes de la vie de bohème*, ed. Loic Chotard and Graham Robb (Paris: Gallimard, 1988 [orig. 1851]), 29.

39. Morley Roberts, *Immortal Youth* (London: Hutchinson, 1902), 9.

40. Roberts, *Immortal Youth*, 38.

41. See Ernesto Bark, *Modernismo* (Madrid: Biblioteca Germinal, 1901), esp. 70, 77.

42. Émile Zola, "Édouard Manet, étude biographique et critique" (1867), *Écrits sur l'art*, ed. Jean-Pierre Leduc-Adine (Paris: Gallimard, 1991), 145, 143. See also the way that Duranty (Louis Émile Edmond, pseud.), also using the public reputation of Manet as his example, makes much the same point in his story "La simple vie du peintre Louis Martin," in *Les séductions du Chevalier Navoni* (Paris: Librarie de la Société des Gens de Lettres, 1877), 327–62.

43. Pío Baroja, "Bohemia y Seudobohemia," in *Los proletarios del arte: Introducción a la bohemia*, ed. José Esteban and Anthony N. Zahareas ([Madrid]: Celeste Ediciones, 1998), 110.

44. Henry Bacon, *A Parisian Year* (Boston: Roberts Brothers, 1882), 53.

45. G[ustave] L[ouis] M[aurice] Strauss, *Reminiscences of an Old Bohemian*, new ed. (London: Downey, 1895 [orig. 1883]), 263.

46. S. J. Adair Fitzgerald, *Sketches from Bohemia: Stories of the Stage, the Study, and the Studio* (London: Tarstow, Denver, 1890), 9, 157.

47. Morley Roberts, *In Low Relief: A Bohemian Transcript* (New York: D. Appleton, 1890), 18.

48. Hammerton, ed., *Mr. Punch in Bohemia*, 5.

49. W. C. Morrow, *Bohemian Paris of To-Day*, 3rd ed. (Philadelphia: J. B. Lippincott, 1899), 172.

50. Anon., "The Lecture on 'Bohemians,'" *Brooklyn Daily Eagle* (12 April 1876): 3; Anon., "The Bohemians Next Tuesday," *Brooklyn Daily Eagle* (15 April 1876): 6.

51. For his reading of Mark Twain, see Arthur Conan Doyle, "To Mary Doyle" (Birmingham, June 1879), in *Arthur Conan Doyle: A Life in Letters*, ed. Jon Lellenberg, Daniel Stashower, and Charles Foley (New York: Penguin, 2007), 114; and for his recommendation of Strauss's work, "To Mary Doyle" (Southsea, 15 June 1883), *Arthur Conan Doyle*, 203. For the Twain passage to which Conan Doyle was referring, see *The Innocents Abroad, or The New Pilgrim's Progress*, 2 vols. (New York: P. F. Collier and Son, 1911 [orig. 1869]), 1: 147–48.

52. Conan Doyle, *The Stark-Munro Letters* (London: Longmans, Green, 1898 [orig. 1895]), 87, 5.

53. Conan Doyle, *Memories and Adventures* (Oxford: Oxford University Press, 1989 [orig. 1924]), 27.

54. Conan Doyle, "To Mary Doyle" (Lerwick, Scotland, February 1880), in *Arthur Conan Doyle*, 123.

55. For a description of this hoax, see *Arthur Conan Doyle*, 117.

56. Unless otherwise specified, quotations from Conan Doyle's works are taken from A[rthur] Conan Doyle, *The Complete Sherlock Holmes* (Garden City, N.Y.: Garden City Publishing, 1938). Titles and page references are given within the text.

57. Thomas Mann, "Tonio Kröger," *Sämtliche Erzählungen* (Frankfurt: S. Fischer Verlag, 1963), 269, 236.

58. Strauss, *Reminiscences of an Old Bohemian*, 65.

59. See Conan Doyle, *Memories and Adventures*, 79. In his account of the dinner, Conan Doyle describes *Dorian Gray* as "a book which is surely upon a high moral plane." See also the account of this dinner in Andrew Lycett, *The Man Who Created Sherlock Holmes* (New York: Free Press, 2007), 159–61.

60. Paterson, *Glimpses of Real Life as Seen in the Theatrical World and in Bohemia*, 81.

61. Thomas Hardy, *Jude the Obscure*, ed. Norman Page, 2nd ed. (New York: W. W. Norton, 1999 [orig. 1895]), 121.

62. Moore, *Confessions of a Young Man*, 181.

63. Moore, *Confessions of a Young Man*, 124–25.

64. Moore, *Confessions of a Young Man*, 76.

65. Alexandre Privat d'Anglemont, *La Closerie des Lilas: Quadrille en prose* (Paris: J. Frey, 1848), 50.

66. For a charming example of this ongoing reproduction of a traditional conception of bohemia, see Herbert Gold's memoir, *Bohemia: Where Art, Angst, Love, and Strong Coffee Meet* (New York: Simon and Schuster, 1993).

CONCLUSION

1. Anon. [Fitz-James O'Brien], "A Paper of All Sorts," *Harper's New Monthly Magazine* 16 (March 1858): 509. O'Brien is identified as the author of this article in Francis Wolle, *Fitz-James O'Brien: A Literary Bohemian of the Eighteen-Fifties* (Boulder: University of Boulder Studies, 1944), 157.

2. Théophile Gautier, "Fatuité" (1843), *Poésies complètes* (Paris: Charpentier, 1845), 305.

3. On this topic of bohemia's definitional complexity or uncertainty, see Jerrold Seigel, *Bohemian Paris: Culture, Politics, and the Boundaries of Bourgeois Life, 1830–1930* (Baltimore: Johns Hopkins University Press, 1986),12; Neil McWilliam, *Dreams of Happiness: Social Art and the French Left, 1830–1850* (Princeton: Princeton University Press, 1993), 28; and Joanna Levin, *Bohemia in America, 1858–1920* (Stanford: Stanford University Press, 2010), 72.

4. Ernesto Quesada, "Adolfo Mitre: Sus poesías" (1887), *Reseñas críticas* (Buenos Aires: Félix Lajouane, 1893), 267.

5. Hans Wachenhusen, *Schmetterlinge* (Berlin: J. C. Huber, 1857), 86.

6. Adolphe d'Ennery and [Eugène] Grangé, *Les bohémiens de Paris*, in *Magasin théâtral: Choix des pièces nouvelles jouées sur tous les théâtres de Paris*, v. 30 (Paris: Marchant, 1846), 8.

7. Julius Bab, *Die Berliner Bohème*, ed. M. M. Schardt (Paderborn: Igel Verlag Literatur, 1994 [orig. 1904]), 40, 5.

8. Hans Jäger, *Kristiana-Boheme*, trans. Niels Honer (Hamburg: Adolf Harms, 1921 [orig. 1899]), 153.

9. Bab, *Die Berliner Bohème*, 23.

10. Erich Mühsam, *Namen und Menschen: Unpolitische Erinnerungen* (Leipzig: Volk und Buch Verlag, 1949 [orig. 1927–29]), 200.

11. Fritz Kunert, "Aus unserem modernen Kunstleben," *Die neue Zeit* 12 (1893–94): 435.

12. Philibert Audebrand, *Un café de journalistes sous Napoléon III* (Paris: E. Dentu, 1888), 92.

13. Enrique Perez Escrich, *El frac azul: Episodios de un jóven flaco* (Madrid: Manini Hermanos, 1864), 135.

14. Oscar A. H. Schmitz, *Das wilde Leben der Boheme*, in *Tagebücher*, ed. Wolfgang Martynkewicz, 3 vols. (Berlin: Aufbau-Verlag, 2006–7), 1: 88.

15. Gautier, *Histoire du romantisme: Suivi de notices romantiques et d'une étude sur la poésie française, 1830–1868* (Paris: Charpentier, 1874), 83.

16. E[nrique] Gómez Carrillo, *Bohemia sentimental* (1899), in *Tres novelas inmorales* (Madrid: Editorial Mundo Latino, [1920]), 106.

17. Erich Mühsam, "Bohême," *Die Fackel* 7 (30 April 1906): 10, 8, 9.

18. Alphonse Lemonnier, *Les femmes de théâtre* (Paris: Jung-Treuttel, 1865), 65.

19. Ludwig Klages, *Stefan George* (Berlin: George Bondi, 1902), 60.

20. Théodore Muret, "Le quartier Latin," in *Nouveau tableau de Paris au XIXme siècle*, [ed. Henry Martin], 7 vols. (Paris: Madame Charles-Béchat, 1834–35), 206. Murger repeats this almost word for word ("The good times when they were so unhappy") in "Stella" (*Oeuvres complètes*, 12 vols. in 6 [Paris: (Michel Lévy), 1855–61; rep. Geneva: Slatkine Reprints, 1971], 72), but this sentiment, along with variations of this phrase, appears throughout his work. For the original source of the epigraph in "Army of Shadows," see Georges Courteline, "Souvenirs et impressions," in *La vie de caserne* (Paris: Armand Magnier, 1896), 8.

21. Stefan George, "Neulandische Liebesmahle," *Hymnen*, in *Hymnen—Pilgerfahrten—Algabal* (Berlin: George Bondi, 1899), 27.

22. Henry James, *The Ambassadors* (1903), *The Novels and Tales of Henry James*, 26 vols. (New York: Charles Scribner's Sons, 1922), 22: 262.

23. Anon. [Taxile Delord, Arnould Frémy, and Edmond Texier], *Paris-Bohème* (Paris: Librairie d'Alphonse Taride, 1854), 5.

24. Theodor Mundt, *Paris und Louis Napoleon: Neue Skizzen aus den französischen Kaiserreich*, 2 vols. (Berlin: Otto Janke, 1858), 1: 157. This image was already a cliché at the

time Mundt was writing; see, for instance, the similar reference to the bohemian as the first and perhaps only love of the lorette in Wachenhusen, *Schmetterlinge*, 18.

25. Arthur Bartlett Maurice, *The New York of the Novelists* (New York: Dodd, Mead, 1916), 115.

26. Eugenio Torelli Viollier, "La Boheme" (1878), in Giuseppe Farinelli, *La Scapigliatura: Profilo storico, protagonisti, documenti* (Rome: Carocci Editore, 2003), 270; Max Nordau, "Die Bohème," *Aus dem wahren Milliardenlande: Pariser Studien und Bilder*, 2 vols. (Leipzig: Duncker und Humblot, 1878), 1: 234.

27. Rubén Darío, "En el Barrio Latino" (1912), *Obras completas*, 5 vols. (Madrid: Afrodisio Agnado, 1950–55), 2: 654, 653.

28. James L. Ford, *Forty-Odd Years in the Literary Shop* (New York: E. P. Dutton, 1921), 133.

29. See, for instance, Lee Siegel, "Who's Right? Who's Left? Who Cares?" *New York Observer* (11 May 2010) (http://www.observer.com/2010/culture/who's-right-who's-left-who-cares?page=1): "There are no bohemians, period."

30. Alexandre Privat d'Anglemont, quoted in Edmond and Jules de Goncourt, *Manette Salomon* (Paris: Union Générale d'Éditions, 1979 [orig. 1867]), 374.

31. Mühsam, *Namen und Menschen*, 237.

32. Mühsam, *Namen und Menschen*, 61.

33. Roger Shattuck, *The Banquet Years: The Origins of the Avant-Garde in France—1885 to World War I*, rev. ed. (New York: Vintage Books, 1968 [org. 1955]), 39. See also Mary Gluck's argument that "the artists of the 1830s were identified . . . not by what they did, but by how they lived and what they looked like" in *Popular Bohemia: Modernism and Urban Culture in Nineteenth-Century Paris* (Cambridge, Mass.: Harvard University Press, 2005), 27.

34. Gustave Flaubert, "À Madame Tennant" (25 December 1876), *Correspondance*, rev. ed., 9 vols. (Paris: Louis Conard, 1930), 7: 378.

35. John Henry MacKay, "Hans, mein Freund," in *Neuland: Ein Sammelbuch moderner Prosadichtung*, ed. Cäsar Flaischlen (Berlin: Verlag des Vereins der Bücherfreunde, 1894), 379–80.

36. James Joyce, *A Portrait of the Artist as a Young Man* (New York: B. W. Huebsch, 1922), 252.

37. See Roderich Huch, *Alfred Schuler, Ludwig Klages, und Stefan George: Erinnerungen an Kreise und Krisen der Jahrhundertwende in München-Schwabing* (Amsterdam: Castrum Peregrini Press, 1973), 35–37.

38. Huch, *Alfred Schuler, Ludwig Klages, und Stefan George*, 18.

39. See Alexander Schanne, *Souvenirs de Schaunard* (Paris: G. Charpentier, 1887), 222.

40. Marie Herzfeld, "Skandinavische Litteratur," *Die Gesellschaft: Monatschrift für Litteratur und Kunst* (September 1890): 1402.

41. See Marilyn R. Brown's comments about "the linked chain of appropriation" throughout bohemia that "eventually led to sound art investment" in *Gypsies and Other Bohemians: The Myth of the Artist in Nineteenth-Century France* (Ann Arbor: UMI Research Press, 1985), 6; and Colin Campbell's argument connecting bohemianism to consumerism

in *The Romantic Ethic and the Spirit of Modern Consumerism* (Oxford: Basil Blackwell, 1997), 200–201.

42. Seigel, *Bohemian Paris*, 12.

43. Moses Gras, "Karl Kraus," *Die Fackel* 26 (August 1924): 176.

44. Karl Kraus, "Eine Kulturtat," *Die Fackel* 9 (18 November 1907): 5, 4.

45. See Charles Baudelaire, "Anniversaire de la naissance de Shakespeare" (1864), *Oeuvres complètes*, ed. Claude Pichois, 4 vols. (Paris: Gallimard, 1976), 2: 225.

46. Henry Murger, *Scènes de la vie de bohème*, ed. Loïc Chotard and Graham Robb (Paris: Gallimard, 1988 [orig. 1851]), 34.

47. Franziska Gräfin zu Reventlow, *Ellen Olestjerne* (1903) in *Autobiographisches*, ed. Else Reventlow (Munich: Albert Langen, 1980), 220.

48. Seigel's *Bohemian Paris*, the best single book on bohemia in France, offers the most extended, thoughtful, and nuanced version of this argument. For a valuable recent example, see Bruce Robbins, "A Portrait of the Artist as a Social Climber: Upward Mobility in the Novel," in *The Novel*, ed. Franco Moretti, 2 vols. (Princeton: Princeton University Press, 2006), 2: 409–35.

49. Anon., "Paris y Londres: Comparaciones sobre su aspecto moral y social," in *Artículos escogidos*, ed. "Edicion de Monitor Republicano" (Mexico: V. G. Torres, 1862), 586.

INDEX

ACKNOWLEDGMENTS

Among other things, Bohemia was, first and last, a sense of comradeship; and, though I cannot pride myself on being a bohemian, I do know that my work has been supported by a community of sorts. For her generous reading of the entire manuscript, I am indebted to Joanna Levin; and for their helpful reading of portions of this book at various stages of its composition, I would like to acknowledge the generosity of Mary Childers, Michelle Lekas, Tim Murphy, Francesca Sawaya, and Nancy Armstrong. I also appreciate the support and encouragement I have received while working on it from Ron Schleifer, David Mair, Amitava Kumar, Arden Reed, Wendy Martin, Janet Farrell Brodie, and, as always, the one without whom none of this would have been possible, Deborah Brackenbury. I am glad also to be able to acknowledge the support given to this project by my editor, Jerome Singerman, and by production editor Noreen O'Connor-Abel and manuscript editor Otto Bohlmann. In addition, I would like to express my thanks to the editors and publishers of *Novel*, in which an earlier version of Chapter 2 first appeared, and to the editors and publishers of *ELH*, in which a version of Chapter 6 was published. Molly Murphy and Ann Raia, of the University of Oklahoma libraries, have been a continual source of help to me, and for their assistance above and beyond the call of ordinary librarianship, my thanks go as well to Patti Harper and Christine Taylor of the Carleton University Library; to Fredric Woodbridge Wilson, curator of the Harvard Theatre Collection; to Joe Bourneuf, head of reference at Harvard's Widener Library; to Alex Guindon, David Thirlwall, and Wendy Knechtel of Vanier Library at Concordia University; to Elizabeth B. Dunn of the Rare Book, Manuscript, and Special Collections Library of Duke University; to David Carpenter, Bryan T. Kurowsky, and Melinda Brown of the Baudelaire Center at Vanderbilt University; and to Violet Lutz, Special Collections librarian at the Joseph P. Horner Memorial Library of the German Society of Pennsylvania.